The War the Women Lived

THE WAR THE WOMEN LIVED

Female Voices from the

Confederate South

Edited by
WALTER SULLIVAN

with a foreword by George Core

J.S.SANDERS & COMPANY
Nashville

The paperback edition of this book carries the following ISBN:
1-56663-513-6

Library of Congress Cataloging-in-Publication data

The war the women lived : female voices from the Confederate South / edited by
    Walter Sullivan : with a foreword by George Core.
        p. cm.
    Includes bibliographical references and index.
    ISBN 1-879941-30-9 (hardcover : alk. paper)
    1. United States—History—Civil War, 1861–1865—Personal narratives,
Confederate.   2. United States—History—Civil War, 1861–1865—Women.
3. Confederate States of America—History—Sources.   4. Women—Confederate
States of America—History—Sources.   I. Sullivan, Walter, 1924-   .
E605.W275   1995   95-36150
975'.03'0922—dc20   CIP

Designed by Dianne Pinkowitz

Published in the United States by
J.S.Sanders & Company
P.O. Box 50331
Nashville, Tennessee 37205

1995 Printing
First Edition

For Jane, Pam, Molly,
Anne Laurence, and Elizabeth

Contents

Part I. Hope and Glory
1859–1861

Part II. Shot and Shell
1861–1862

Part III. Advance and Retreat
1863

CONTENTS

Part V. Last Things
1865

Foreword

You may be wondering why this book has been published—and what its principals, some twenty southern women, have to tell us at the end of the twentieth century, over 125 years after the American Civil War fitfully ground to a halt and left the South shattered and bleeding. You may be thinking that these lively and plucky witnesses have little or nothing to tell us, even about their own time, that we, in our time, do not know. If so you would be mistaken, for what these writers provide, over the wide divide of the intervening years, is an informal history of the war as it affected southern domestic life during 1861–1865. Such a history exists nowhere else in a single volume.

Most of us, whether general readers or professional specialists, know this war — the first total war of modern times — chiefly through its great battles, such as Chancellorsville and Gettysburg and Cold Harbor, battles that have been studied by everyone from American school boys to the German general staff in World War II. We have read of those battles not only in histories like Douglas Southall Freeman's *Lee's Lieutenants* and Shelby Foote's wonderful trilogy but in William Faulkner, Caroline Gordon, and other novelists. But even in fiction, whether it be *The Unvanquished* or *None Shall Look Back* or another novel, you do not feel the war's gritty impact on everyday life as it is re-created in the writing of the women who endured it — the authors represented here. Often their accounts were written as the experience unfolded or soon thereafter — not at the reach of memory some years or decades later. These accounts have the immediacy, precision, and veracity that were achieved at the terrible cost of living with and through the war as it altered individual lives and the communities in which those lives were lived — plantations, small towns, cities.

These narrative sequences originally appeared in journals and memoirs. But they have the scope and drama of fiction since each selection tells a story; most have a beginning, middle, and end; they incorporate scenes as well as pictures drawn from daily life; and for the most part they embody action that is both dramatic and memorable. As the war goes on, the selections become more gripping as the writers turn wholly away from sentiment and imbue their writing with increasing realism and irony.

The War the Women Lived can be read from beginning to end as a sprawling novel or a fragmentary history that dramatizes domestic life during the Civil War, but the selections can also be read independently — out of sequence — as individual narratives of the war's impact upon a given locale. The book has been made so that it can be read either way — so that its individual parts both stand alone and add up to a satisfying whole. Everything here — title pages, running heads, editorial notes, biographical profiles, the epilogue, and so on — has been shaped with the general reader in mind. The idea is that you can relish this book in the way that you think best — and that you do not have to cut your way through an underbrush of scholarly apparatus to find the words that these remarkable women wrote.

Some of these writers are all but lost to history, for we know little of them aside from what they wrote about this great event in their lives and in the life of the nation; but we do have their words, some of which were published soon after the war and some of which have appeared in print only lately. A glance at the bibliography will show the unfolding record, only recently completed — at least for the time being.

These narratives are drawn from Walter Sullivan's reading of many years, which went from casual and spotty to systematic and comprehensive. But the editor did not wish to be exhaustive (and exhausting): he has avoided the compilation in shaping this lively and engaging book, which constitutes far more than the usual anthology or guidebook or reader. The writers whom Sullivan has chosen are representative, just as the selections reprinted here are representative, in that they embody the best of their makers' work as they reported on the Civil War on the southern domestic front; and they provide an informal narrative history of the war as it occurred. Although the scene is usually domestic, it includes the battle front on more than one occasion.

The War the Women Lived: Female Voices from the Confederate South stands as a unique account of the war's impact on the noncombatants in the South, especially the sweethearts and wives and the mothers and sisters of the soldiers who fought as Confederates. These writers provide an illuminating record of war's vicissitudes. In reading them, we understand anew why wars are made by men and why peace is cherished by women.

— George Core

Introduction

The women whose work is included here were strong and courageous and extraordinarily patriotic. To the best of my knowledge, all of them were against slavery, but they loved the Confederacy as people loved their countries in those days, and they were willing to sacrifice all that they cherished for Confederate independence. Those who were rich gave up their fortunes. Those who were not rich invested what they had. When the war was over, most of them were not only penniless, but bereaved. Even Mary Chesnut, whose husband survived the war and who had no children, grieved for the sons of her friends. "I loved that young soldier," she said of Preston Hampton who had died on the battlefield in his brother's arms.

Phoebe Pember and Kate Cumming, one a childless widow, the other never to marry, worked in hospitals where they became attached to wounded soldiers who died lingering deaths. Mary Ann Gay's brother died in the war. Cornelia McDonald's husband died soon after his release from a Federal prison where he had been weakened by exposure and too little food. Two of Kate Stone's brothers died in Confederate service, as did two of Sarah Morgan's. In Richmond, throughout the war, funeral bells tolled day after day — and, following big battles, almost continuously. Dying soldiers wanted those at home to know the circumstances of their deaths, which, of course, those at home ardently wanted to know, but means of communication, always unreliable in the Confederacy, became increasingly uncertain as the war went on. One of Sarah Morgan's brothers died nine days after the other, but the family heard of the second death first.

Like the women who kept these diaries, most of the men were devout. The messages they sent home were of Christian resignation, of trust in God's providence, and of faith in a life to come. Those at home were comforted by these sentiments, southern society being overwhelmingly a community of believers, parochial differences blurred by hardships shared. Phoebe Pember tells of two Catholic women, strangers to her and to the young man being buried, dropping to their knees in the mud beside the grave while a battle raged outside Richmond, rain fell in the cemetery, and the officiant, recruited at the gates by Mrs. Pember, read the service from the Episcopal Book of Common Prayer. Kate Cumming, a lifelong Episcopalian, was a connoisseur of sermons who attended the church where she thought the preaching would be best.

When bad news came, when bad things happened, these women turned to God, but they were sustained as well by their ability to carry on with their lives. Though frequently wrenched, their hearts were resilient. With Robert E. Lee's approval, the women of Richmond dressed up in their aging clothes, played and danced and sang with furloughed and convalescing soldiers, only now and then feeling pangs of guilt. Kate Stone, whose family had escaped to Texas, compared her and her friends' gaiety to that of the doomed royalty of the French Revolution who spent their last days in prison devising costumes, playing charades. Mary Chesnut and others made the same comparison because they had read the same history books. Though educated in different environments, they had learned the same things.

Mary Chesnut and Sarah Pryor each had a few years of formal schooling, but most of what they knew they had learned at home. Cornelia McDonald educated herself by reading books from her father's library. Céline Frémaux was taught by her mother, a stern taskmaster according to Céline. Constance Cary, who married Burton Harrison after the war, had a French governess and spent several years at boarding school. Kate Stone learned from a tutor hired to school the family children. Eliza Andrews attended a "seminary for girls" and what was then called a "female college." Belle Boyd also went to college. Emma LeConte had some formal education, but principally she was taught by her father who was a professor and a scientist. However they were taught, they learned English literature and European history. Most of them knew Latin, many knew French, some knew German.

Unlike the court of Louis XVI, to which they compared themselves, they were more than social ornaments playing games while they waited for the end. In antebellum times, whether plantation mistress or wife of a small farmer, they had been responsible to see that family and servants were fed, clothed, cared for when sick. In most cases the women arranged for or conducted the education of the children, and although they were not allowed to preach on Sunday, much of the religious training of both family and slaves was left to them. Doubtless the wife of a small farmer endured more drudgery than the plantation wife, whose duties were chiefly executive; but in either case the work continued season after season, year after year.

When the war came, those who could continued to live where they were. Dolly Burge was already a widow when the war started. Mary Jones lost her husband in 1863. Both were still running their plantations when Sherman's soldiers passed through on their march to the sea. Like Kate Cumming and Phoebe Pember, many women who lived in cities, and some like Ada Bacot, who owned a plantation, became nurses. Many others, particularly those who lived in Northern Virginia and Tennessee and Southern Louisiana — areas that fell to the Yankees early in the war — fled from the advancing enemy, the Virginians to Richmond, the others to whatever haven they could find.

The Civil War began when South Carolina troops fired on Fort Sumter, an event Mary Chesnut watched from the roof of the Mills House Hotel in Charleston; but, until the collapse of the Confederacy, the war in the east was focused on Richmond which was the Confederate capital. When Federal troops left Washington in July 1861, their purpose was to capture Richmond. They were stopped by the Confederates at the Battle of First Manassas, but, except for occasional Confederate thrusts north, the war in Virginia continued to follow the same pattern. The Yankees moved against Richmond; the Confederates attempted, successfully until April 1865, to head them off. There were battles in other parts of Virginia. Stonewall Jackson's campaigns in the Shenandoah Valley in 1862 took pressure off Richmond by threatening Washington, but wherever the battle was fought in Virginia, Richmond was the ultimate prize.

In Virginia, after First Manassas the two major armies, neither of which had been ready for combat, paused to rearm and regroup. In the West, the war went on with Confederate defeats at Forts Henry and Donelson on the Tennessee and Cumberland Rivers in February 1862, and the evacuation of Nashville that sent Julia Morgan scurrying to Georgia. In April 1862 New Orleans was captured by the Federals who soon moved up the Mississippi River toward Port Hudson and Baton Rouge. Sarah Morgan, Kate Stone and Céline Frémaux fled before them. Not everyone left. Phoebe Pember's sister, Eugenia Phillips, stayed in New Orleans and was accused by General Benjamin F. Butler — Beast Butler to the Confederates — of laughing when the funeral cortege of a Federal officer passed her house. Her reply to Butler when he sentenced her to imprisonment on Ship Island became famous both in the Confederacy and abroad. "It has one advantage over the city, sir. You will not be there."

In April 1862 the Battle of Shiloh was fought to a draw in Tennessee, but was costly to the Confederates because General Albert Sidney Johnston was killed. Near the end of June of the same year, outside Richmond, the Seven Days began, a week of battles that culminated in the bloody confrontation at Malvern Hill. The Confederates held, but the lives of the women in Richmond, natives and refugees alike, were from now on shaped by the exigencies of war. Both Mary Chesnut and Judith McGuire remembered how, during church services when battles were raging, the sexton would fetch men and women from their pews to go the station where trains were arriving with their sons and husbands, dead or wounded. Once Mr. Minnegerode, rector of St. Paul's, left the altar in midservice. At the church door, his wife told him that their son lay dead at the railroad station. The report was in error. The dead man was someone else, "but somebody's son, all the same," said Mary Chesnut.

Hospitals in Richmond often overflowed; people took the wounded into their homes, but, during times of heavy fighting, casualties had to be left on the street until accommodations could be arranged for them. Women and men who were too old to fight treated the soldiers where they lay, found water with which to bathe their wounds, cloths with which to bind them. It was the same in the West. Julia Morgan, who had escaped from Nashville with some money, had the wounded from Murfreesboro brought into the hotel where she was staying, bought food and clothing for them, and found women to help nurse them. By this time, the autumn of 1863, Kate Cumming had become expert at cadging food and drink and bandages for her soldiers.

Because of the blockade and the impact of the war on the economy, throughout the Confederacy, everything was scarce. Before the war the financial structure of the South had been founded on cotton, which was exported to the North and to Europe. Now cotton languished on southern wharves. The little that could be run through the blockade went to pay for ships and arms and ammunition. Southerners, women in particular, had to survive on what they had. Constance Cary made old hats look different, if not exactly new. Sarah Pryor could discover something useful to make out of a scrap of lace or a piece of braid or the lining of an old coat. All Confederate women, not merely Scarlett O'Hara, knew the trick of refashioning window curtains into dresses.

Getting shoes was a problem Catherine Hopley encountered before she left the Confederacy to return to her native England in 1862. In Jackson, Louisiana, the children in Céline Frémaux's family made their shoes out of cloth tops sewed to soles cut from the leather of cartridge boxes scavenged from battle fields. Céline's coat was made from an old bedspread. Part of the trouble that women had keeping themselves clothed resulted from their generosity. They gave their tablecloths and napkins, their good sheets, and their linen undergarments to be folded into bandages. In rural areas, where fleece was still to be had, they carded wool, spun thread, wove cloth that usually was sent to the soldiers.

Commenting on the shortage of food, Sarah Morgan said if the war went on long enough it would "make gluttons of us all." Now and then in Richmond and other cities, food and wine came through the blockade, how and at what cost remained a secret. Early in the war, chicken, turkey, and ham were available, but at prices that increased daily. Beef went to feed the soldiers. Later, as Yankee raiders penetrated more deeply into the rural South, burning houses and outbuildings, stealing food and contaminating what they could not carry away, any kind of meat became a rarity. Toward the end of war, the diet on many farms and plantations consisted almost solely of field peas. They were prepared in as many ways as resourceful cooks could devise, but, as Eliza Andrews observed, however they were cooked, they were "still field peas."

It would be wrong to say that the spirits of these women were never dampened by hardship and suffering, but they never despaired. The Confederate government made no provision for the widows of soldiers; it even stopped the pay of men who were captured. Many women turned to relatives, parents or siblings, aunts and uncles, even cousins in this time when members of extended families assumed responsibility for one another. Some were reluctant to go to relatives, but for those who had to rent quarters, staying in the cities became increasingly difficult.

In 1864, in Richmond, single rooms rented for more than a civil servant or an officer was paid. Judith McGuire tramped the streets searching for a place for her and her husband to live, but in her anxiety she was sustained by memories of the past, hope for the future.

Near Decatur, Georgia, with the help of a faithful servant, Mary Ann Gay gathered the corn Federal cavalrymen had dropped when they fed their horses, washed it, and ground it into meal. With the help of the same servant, she found an underfed horse with a sore back that had been abandoned by the Yankees. She nursed the horse back to health, while another servant gathered sufficient castoff material to build a cart for the horse to pull, an equipage so outrageous in appearance that Mary Ann Gay did not attempt to describe it. However it looked, it served to transport a starving mother and children to their relatives southeast of Atlanta.

"War is hell," General William T. Sherman is supposed to have said, and whether or not the remark was his, he did all in his power to prove its veracity. After Sherman's troops had captured Atlanta, John Bell Hood, who had replaced Joseph E. Johnston in command of the Confederate Army of Tennessee, took his force north hoping to get behind Sherman and cut his line of supply. This left Sherman free to march unopposed toward Savannah, plundering, burning, and destroying as he went. Sherman had ordered his men not to molest civilians or to enter their houses, but, with no enemy in front of them, his soldiers did as they pleased, and he made scant effort to impede them. Visiting her sister in Albany, Georgia, after Sherman's troops had passed through, Eliza Andrews found herself in a land of death and desolation.

The invading soldiers had tried to leave behind nothing that could be used to sustain life. Houses and outbuildings, including the quarters of the slaves, had been burned. Food that could not be taken away had been ruined. Eliza Andrews saw the bloated carcasses of horses, cows, pigs, even dogs rotting in fields and on the roads, blocking the way and tainting the atmosphere. Animal remains had been piled in the shallow water at fords to prevent passage. Papers and books that had been pillaged from libraries were strewn along the way. A detritus of slashed portraits, smashed dishes, and broken furniture littered a surreal landscape.

And still the Yankees came. Living in Mary Jones' house were three women, one pregnant and expecting daily to go into labor, and five terrified children. The first group of invaders entered the house, broke open the cabinets and chests, took everything that was of value and much that was not, robbed the slaves, and threatened and cursed the women. They took the food they could carry, then ruined what was left. Every day, there was a new group to rifle the already plundered wardrobes, to seize or destroy whatever could be eaten that those who had come before had missed. They demolished the wagons and buggies and carriages. They took the chain from the well to deprive the family of drinking water. While they cursed outside her window, Mary Mallard endured the difficult delivery of her fourth child. The last bit of food on the Jones plantation, a ham belonging to one of the slaves, was seized by a Yankee cavalryman and fed to the dogs. But no one could deprive Mary Jones of her courage. At the end of particularly trying days, she turned to her daughter and her friend Kate King. "Tell me, girls," she would say. "Did I act like a coward?"

And then it was over. "Grief and despair took possession of my heart," Cornelia McDonald wrote. She felt a humiliation that she had not known she could feel, and regretted that she could do nothing to comfort her sorrowing children. Through her window, she saw her seven year old son, who had not wept in her presence, crying and wringing his hands. Emma LeConte articulated what was in every woman's mind: all the suffering, all the loss of life had been for nought. Everywhere there was poverty, everywhere there was bereavement, everywhere there was sorrow. The women were ready for peace. They were weary of death and destruction. They were eager to put together what was left of their country and their lives and to start again.

Brief Chronology
of the War

Virginia, Maryland, Pennsylvania, North Carolina, South Carolina

1861

4/12 Firing on Fort Sumter (South Carolina).
7/21 Battle of First Manassas (Virginia).

1862

5/31 Battle of Seven Pines (Virginia).
6/25 Beginning of the Seven Days fought outside Richmond culminating in the Battle of Malvern Hill (Virginia).
8/9 Battle of Cedar Mountain (Virginia).
8/29 Battle of Second Manassas (Virginia).
9/17 Battle of Antietam (Maryland).
12/13 Battle of Fredericksburg (Virginia).

1863

5/1 Battle of Chancellorsville (Virginia).
7/1 Battle of Gettysburg (Pennsylvania).

1864

5/5 Battle of the Wilderness (Virginia).
6/1 Battle of Cold Harbor (Virginia).
6/15 Siege of Petersburg begins (Virginia).

1865

3/30 Battle of Five Forks (Virginia).
4/3 Fall of Richmond (Virginia).
4/9 General Robert E. Lee surrenders the Army of Northern Virginia at Appomattox (Virginia).

WESTERN THEATER

Kentucky, Tennessee, Georgia, Alabama, Mississippi, Louisiana

1862

2/16 Fall of Fort Donelson (on the Tennessee River north of Nashville).
2/25 Confederate evacuation of Nashville (Tennessee).
4/16 Battle of Shiloh (Tennessee).
4/29 Fall of New Orleans (Louisiana).
10/4 Battle of Corinth (Mississippi).
10/8 Battle of Perryville (Kentucky).
12/31 Battle of Murfreesboro (Tennessee).

1863

7/4 Fall of Vicksburg (Mississippi).
9/19 Battle of Chickamauga (Tennessee).
10/23 Battle of Lookout Mountain (Tennessee).

1864

5/13 Battle of Resaca (Georgia).
5/25 Battle of New Hope Church (Georgia).
6/27 Battle of Kennesaw Mountain (Georgia).
7/22 Battle of Atlanta (Georgia).
11/30 Battle of Franklin (Tennessee).
12/15 Battle of Nashville (Tennessee).

1865

4/26 General Joseph E. Johnston surrenders the Army of Tennessee near Durham Station, North Carolina.
5/14 General Richard Taylor surrenders his Alabama–Louisiana command, including Forrest's cavalry at Citronelle, Alabama.
5/26 General Edmund Kirby Smith surrenders his Trans–Mississippi command at New Orleans, Louisiana.

A Note on the Selections

It would be wrong to say that the women whose work is included here are a cross section of Confederate society. In 1861 illiteracy was common all over America, more common in the rural areas than in the cities, and therefore more common in the South than in the North. Many Confederate women could not write, and among those who could, many were too busy doing their own work and the work of their husbands who had gone to war to consider keeping journals. Many were too poor to buy paper and ink, both of which became increasingly scarce in the South as the war lengthened. But of those who could and did write, these authors are a fair sampling. When the war started, they lived in Virginia, South Carolina, Georgia, Louisiana, Alabama, Tennessee, Maryland, Missouri, and Washington, D.C. Most of them were forced to flee as the Federal armies advanced. Many went to Richmond. Others moved as the battle lines shifted. Some stayed where they were and suffered.

In spite of the women who could not or did not write, there are still many Confederate women's diaries, and whoever would choose among them is faced with an embarrassment of riches. In selecting passages for inclusion here, I wanted to find work that was clearly, if not always elegantly, written; engaging for its own sake; and representative of the experience of women at each stage of the conflict. By using shorter passages, I could have included more women, but I believe that longer passages convey a deeper sense of the quality of Confederate life and the character of the women who lived it. I could have included the work of a greater number of women had I not used the work of any woman more than once. But it seemed to me valuable that readers make friends, rather than acquaintances, with a few of these women. I hope you will like those I have chosen to be your friends.

I have taken liberties with some of these diaries. Some of the writers, as is often the case with diarists, were given to digression. I have silently deleted paragraphs of political commentary and matters of insignificant family history to get on with the story. In some instances I have attempted to speed the narrative along by deleting extraneous modifiers and passages of general description. But I have added nothing. Every word in the excerpts, occasional bracketed insertions aside, was written by one of the women.

Let me also explain that the individual selections are internally consistent — but not subject to the overall consistency of a single style. Each selection therefore follows the original text and the house style that each publisher imposed upon the given author's work. So, as will be obvious, some passages appear with British spelling and punctuation while others follow American usage. Most, of course, were printed in the late nineteenth and early twentieth centuries and so do not reflect the current conventions of spelling and punctuation practiced in Great Britain and the United States. The reader should always assume that the selections follow the original texts, idiosyncratic or not.

I offer these passages in chronological order, with some inevitable overlapping, in time, hoping that the passages will reflect the relation of the lives of the women unfolding against the progress of the war. Fortunes at home were linked to fortunes on the battlefields. In an effort to make it convenient for you to relate the passages to the events of the conflict, I have included a table of the main events and battles of the war.

Having said all this I should emphasize that what is important here is not the war itself or the effect of the war on the lives of the women so much as the responses of the women themselves — their courage, their fidelity, their strength, their generosity, their kindness. They were extraordinary in peace as well as in war as their lives before, during, and after the war demonstrate.

The Women

ELIZA FRANCES ANDREWS was born in 1840 on a plantation near Washington, Georgia, and was educated at Washington Seminary for Girls and at the LaGrange Female College. Though her father was a strong opponent of secession, her three brothers fought for the Confederacy and Eliza and her sister Metta surreptitiously sewed the Confederate flag that was raised in Washington the day Georgia voted to secede from the union. Andrews began her diary when she and Metta set out to visit her older sister in South Carolina in late December, 1864.

BELLE BOYD was born in 1843 in Martinsburg, Virginia, and was educated at Mount Washington College. She was not yet eighteen at the beginning of the war, and barely nineteen when she was arrested on suspicion of being a spy. She was confined for a month in Old Capitol Prison in the cell recently vacated by Rose O'Neal Greenhow. After her second and more lengthy stay in Carroll Prison, she was sent south and sailed for England, where her memoirs were published in 1865.

DOLLY SUMNER LUNT BURGE was a widow with a young daughter whose plantation southwest of Atlanta lay on Sherman's route to the sea. Except for a few late entries, her diary covers only the period when members of the Federal army were invading her home and her property.

MARY BOYKIN MILLER CHESNUT was born March 31, 1823, near Camden, South Carolina. In 1840 she married James Chesnut, who was then twenty–five and the only surviving son of one of the largest landholders in South Carolina. In 1859 and 1860 James Chesnut served in the United States Senate. During the war he was a delegate to the Confederate Provisional Congress, aide to General Beauregard, liaison between Richmond and other parts of the Confederacy. Wherever he went, Mary Chesnut was usually at his side, recording what she saw and heard and thought in her diary.

KATE CUMMING was born in Edinburgh, Scotland, in 1835, and emigrated with her parents first to Montreal, then to Mobile, where her father prospered and where she enjoyed, as she put it, "an easy and rather indolent manner of living" until the beginning of the war. Against the strong opposition of the male members of her family who thought nursing an immodest profession for women, Cumming began her service in Confederate hospitals in Mississippi in April 1862. Early in 1863 she went to Georgia to serve in the hospitals of the Army of Tennessee.

CÉLINE FRÉMAUX was born in Donaldsonville, Louisiana, in 1850 and moved with her family to New Orleans in 1853, to Baton Rouge two years later, and to Port Hudson early in 1862, where her father, an engineer, helped plan and build the Confederate fortifications. Just before the siege of Port Hudson began, Céline's mother took her children to Jackson, Louisiana, where they stayed until the end of the war. Céline attended schools in Baton Rouge and Jackson, but her best and most strictly rendered education came from her mother, for whom the children had daily to recite. Céline's memoir, written in the early 1900s, is based on diaries she kept when she was a child.

MARY ANN HARRIS GAY was a spectator at the convention in Montgomery, Alabama, where the Confederacy was formed and where she witnessed the inauguration of Jefferson Davis. She spent the war years with her mother and two or three remaining slaves in Decatur, Georgia. She hoped that her memoirs would re–create the Confederate South for her nephew whose father was killed at the Battle of Franklin, but the nephew died before she had her manuscript in order.

ROSE O'NEAL GREENHOW was part of a Confederate espionage group operating in Washington. She secured the Federal battle plan for the first battle of Bull Run, thus helping the Confederates to victory. She was born in 1815, probably in Maryland. In 1835 she married Robert Greenhow, a doctor, lawyer, linguist, and politician, whose duties as a representative of the State Department took him and Rose to various locations on the west coast and in Mexico until his accidental death in 1854. Returning to Washington, Rose used the salon she kept as a meeting place for Confederate sympathizers and as a listening post for her work as a spy. On August 23, 1861, a month after Bull Run, Rose was arrested by Allan Pinkerton on her Washington doorstep.

CONSTANCE CARY HARRISON traced her lineage back to Thomas Jefferson on her father's side and on her mother's side to the dukes of Fairfax. She was born in Alexandria, Virginia, in 1843. She was educated at a day school in Cumberland, Maryland, where, for several years, her father edited a newspaper, by a French governess at Vaucluse, her grandmother's plantation near Alexandria, and at a boarding school in Richmond. Forced to flee Vaucluse by the Federal occupation of Northern Virginia, she spent the war years in and around Richmond where she met Burton Harrison, Jefferson Davis's private secretary, whom she would marry after the war.

CATHERINE COOPER HOPLEY, a native of England who returned there in 1862, settled first in the North where she had friends and relatives. She came south to serve as governess in a large Northern Virginia family. The longer she stayed in the South, the fonder she became of southern people. She was often bemused by the slow pace of southern life, and she was offended by the familiarity with which servants conversed with their masters. In her memoir, which was published in England in 1863, she refers to herself as "Miss Jones." According to her passport, a copy of which she included in her book, she was thirty in 1862, four feet, eleven inches tall, red headed, and "robust" of figure.

MARY JONES, whose maiden name was also Jones, was born in Liberty County, Georgia in 1808. Educated at McIntosh Academy at Baisden's Bluff, Georgia, and at Abiel Carter's academy in Savannah, in 1830, she married her cousin, the Rev. Dr. Charles Colcock Jones. Three of her four children lived to maturity, including *MARY JONES MALLARD*, born in Liberty County, Georgia, in 1835, who was educated in Philadelphia and at home. In 1857 she married the Rev. Robert Quarterman Mallard. Georgia Maxwell Mallard, the child born while Sherman's soldiers were on the Jones property, was the fourth of her five children.

EMMA LECONTE was born in 1848 in Augusta, Georgia. She was the oldest child of Caroline Nisbet and Joseph LeConte, a scientist and professor who moved from the University of Georgia to the University of South Carolina at Columbia while Emma was still a child. She attended school in Columbia, but her principal education came from her father who began to teach her the scientific names of plants and animals when she was still an infant. She began her diary on December 31, 1864, after Sherman had turned his army north following his occupation of Savannah.

LUCY NICKOLSON LINDSAY and *MRS. ALEXANDER MAJOR* were among a hundred or more contributors to *Reminiscences of the Civil War in Missouri*, an anthology compiled by members of the St. Louis chapter of the United Daughters of the Confederacy in 1920. No biographical sketches were included in that volume, and I have not been able to learn anything further of them.

CORNELIA PEAKE MCDONALD was born June 14, 1822, in Alexandria, Virginia, daughter of a physician whose imprudent financial dealings forced him to move his family to Missouri in 1835. She was largely self–educated — she read the books in her father's library. In

1847 she married Angus McDonald, twenty–three years older than she and a widower with nine children, and returned with him to Virginia, where she bore nine children of her own. When Angus McDonald died in December 1864, Judith McGuire used three pages of her diary to give an account of his life as frontiersman, lawyer, and man of affairs. Like most other southerners, he had been impoverished by his devotion to the Confederacy. Cornelia kept her diary that her husband might know what happened to her while he was away.

JUDITH WHITE BROKENBROUGH MCGUIRE was born in Richmond in 1813, daughter of a member of the supreme court of Virginia, and was married to the Rev. John P. McGuire, principal of Episcopal High School in Alexandria. She began her "refugee life" early in the war when Federal troops occupied Northern Virginia. With her husband and daughters — her sons were in the army — she went to Richmond, Lynchburg, Charlottesville, then back to Richmond, where she was living when the city fell and when Lee surrendered.

JULIA MORGAN was the wife of a successful Nashville businessman who served the Confederacy as a procurement officer before volunteering for active duty. To avoid the war, Morgan took her children and a few servants to Marietta and, as the fighting progressed, moved to Augusta, Georgia.

SARAH IDA FOWLER MORGAN was nineteen when the war began and almost twenty when she started her diary early in 1862. She was born in New Orleans, the seventh of eight children of Judge Thomas Gibbes Morgan and Sarah Hunt Fowler Morgan. In 1850 she moved with her family to Baton Rouge and was living there when the war began. She had less than a year of formal education, but she was taught well by her mother, and, like Cornelia McDonald, she was widely read. Two of Morgan's brothers served in the Confederate army. One was in the Confederate navy. Her half brother, Philip Hicky Morgan, who is "Brother" in the diary, remained loyal to the Union and spent the war as a civilian in New Orleans.

PHOEBE YATES PEMBER was born August 18, 1823, in Charleston, and she was probably educated at home. Some time before the war, she married Thomas Pember of Boston, who died of tuberculosis in Aiken, South Carolina, on July 9, 1861. After the death of her husband, Phoebe, who had no children, lived briefly with her father and mother in Marietta, Georgia. She was appointed matron of Chimborazo Hospital in Richmond in November, 1862, and was still tending the sick and wounded in the occupied city when Lee surrendered.

SARAH AGNES RICE PRYOR was born February 19, 1830, in Halifax County, Virginia, and raised by an uncle and aunt who moved when Sarah was nine to Charlottesville. She was educated mostly by her aunt, by a German music teacher, and by her friends among the students of the University of Virginia. In 1848 she married Roger Atkinson Pryor, then a twenty year old law student at the university. Pryor was a member of the United States Congress at the beginning of the war.

SARAH KATHERINE (KATE) STONE, who was born in Hinds County, Mississippi, in 1841, moved with her family to a plantation near Delta, Louisiana, when she was twelve or thirteen years old. She was educated at home by tutors who lived with the family and began her diary on May 15, 1861, the day her oldest brother left home to join the Jeff Davis Guards then forming in Vicksburg, Mississippi. The details of her life before the war are found in the passage from her diary that is reprinted here.

LORÉTA JANÉTA VELAZQUEZ was born in 1842 in Havana where her father, a native of Spain, was a government official. She was educated at home by a governess and by her mother, later by an aunt, and finally by the Sisters of Charity in New Orleans. In 1857 she eloped with an officer in the United States Army, lived on an army post in the West, and bore two children, neither of whom survived. Her husband, who resigned his commission to serve the Confederacy, was killed early in the war. Some scholars have considered Velazquez' memoir to be, at least in part, spurious. However, her accounts of her undercover work for the Confederacy ring true, and are typical of those of many southern women who served their country as spies and couriers.

PART I
Hope and Glory
1859–1861

Oh, the beautiful sunny South, the home of my birth, my childhood and of my womanhood, could I leave thee, could I claim another home? Ah, no! Thou art dearer to me than all else earthly. As long as I live, let it be on southern soil, and when I die let my remains be covered by her warm and genial sod. Truly, I am a child of the South. I love her as a fond mother. I couldn't survive in a colder, less genial clime.

— Ada Bacot, 1861

The Days That Are No More

KATE STONE

NEAR TALULLAH, LOUISIANA, 1859

Life at Brokenburn, as described by Kate Stone, was typical of life on plantations throughout the South. The work Kate's mother did was essentially the same as that performed by all mistresses of plantations, and it was much more complex and often more burdensome than the work done by the men. For example, after supervising the making of a season's clothes for all the members of the plantation community, Kate's mother was often weary to the point of exhaustion, but she did not allow herself a great deal of time in which to rest. A large part of the plantation mistress's job was to exercise a benign influence over her establishment. She adjudicated quarrels among servants and used her authority, gently in most cases, to maintain domestic peace.

In looking over the yellowing pages and faded writing of my old diary written in the troubled years from 1861 to 1865, how the old life comes back, the gay, busy life of the plantation at Brokenburn with Mamma, a beautiful brilliant woman of thirty–seven at the head of it all. Having been left a widow six years before with eight children and a heavily involved estate, she had managed so well that she was now the owner of a handsome property on which the crop of 1861 would pay off the last indebtedness. What a large houseful we were! Brother Will, a young man of twenty, had left school two years before, tired of college life and anxious to take charge of the place then just bought. I, fifteen months younger, had graduated at Dr. Elliott's Academy in Nashville and was of course the much indulged young lady of the house. The other children were being fitted for college at home under the care of a tutor to whom they were much devoted. Mr. Newton had been with us for two years, and we imagined would be with us until the last of the five boys was ready for school. Brother Coley and Ashburn Ragan, Mamma's young brother who lived with us — boys about the same age — expected to enter the University of Virginia in the fall and were studying hard to be able to enter the junior class. Living with us also, was Mamma's older brother Bo[hannan] Ragan, the happiest, most carefree young man in three states — gay, rollicking, fond of pleasure, generous to a fault, without a care in the world. On the death of his mother a few years before when the old homestead had been sold, he had come to live with us, putting all his property in Mamma's hands and not allowing any settlement at the close of the year, only asking that his bills be paid. Fortunately, the price of his Negroes brought in plenty for his spending and the giving of many handsome gifts. Never a girl had a more generous, loving uncle than he had been to me. Last of all was Little Sister, a child of nine, the pet and plaything of the house. And coming and going all the time were the friends and relatives, for the people of those times were a sociable folk and the ties of kindness were closely drawn.

There were usually girls visiting me and young men visiting my brothers; and as we lived in a populous neighborhood, for the swamp, there was always something going on — formal dining, informal "spend the days," evening parties, riding frolics — and in the grey of the morning great squads of hunters starting out with their packs of hounds baying, blowing of horns, and stamping and racing of horses.

Brokenburn was a newly opened place when Mamma bought it. There were some cabins but no residence, but a sawmill had soon been built in connection with the gin, lumber sawed, and cabins and house went up in rapid order. The house, a long, eight-room affair with long galleries and two halls, was expected to be only a temporary shelter until the place should be well cleared and in good working order; then would be built in the large grove of native water oak, sweet gum, and sycamore, a house that would be a pride and pleasure to us all.

Looking out from the side gallery across the wide grassy yard through the trees and wild vines that had been spared when the place was cleared for building, one could see the two long rows of cabins facing each other across a broad sweep of thick Bermuda grass, set with an occasional great tree, grey in the winter with long festoons of moss. Leading from each door was a little, crooked white path, ending at the road down the middle of the grass plot, beaten smooth by the march of the many black feet that journeyed over it in the early dawn, the weary, hot noonday, and the welcome dusk. Loath to go out in the sunrise for the weary hours of plowing, hoeing, clearing land, and long days of cotton picking in the lovely fall weather, the Negroes really seemed to like the cotton picking best of all. Nearly every picker would be racing with some other rival or friend, and at the great windup there were generally prizes for those who headed the list — money for the men and gay dresses for the women. It was no uncommon thing for the "boss pickers" to pick five or six hundred pounds each day for maybe a week at a time. (Now, in these times of leisure and ease, two hundred pounds is considered good work.)

Facing the cabins in a grove of trees was the overseer's four-room log house, rough but substantial. Many an occupant for it came and went. Some were too severe on the Negroes; others allowed them to idle away the time, the crop suffering in consequence; some were dishonest and lazy. Altogether it was a difficult position to fill satisfactorily. The men were a coarse, uncultivated class, knowing little more than to read and write; brutified by their employment, they were considered by the South but little better than the Negroes they managed. Neither they nor their families were ever invited to any of the entertainments given by the planters, except some larger function, such as a wedding given at the home of the employer. If they came, they did not expect to be introduced to the guests but were expected to amuse themselves watching the crowd. They visited only among themselves, except an occasional call of the wife and children on the family of the employer. The overseer ranked just above the Negro trader, whose work was considered the very lowest and most degrading a white man could undertake, and the stigma clung for generations, notwithstanding the money the traders usually accumulated.

Of course in case of sickness at the overseer's, the lady at the great house saw that they were not neglected and that they were well waited on. There was always a woman furnished to wait on the overseer's family, and if he had many children, a half-grown girl was furnished to nurse. There were often the kindest relations existing between the two families until the overseer would leave or be discharged; then they would drop entirely out of each other's lives.

I cannot recall an instance when a lady on one place called on the overseer's wife of another planter. Then, it seemed a very natural custom, but looking back it seems an odd state of affairs.

The cookhouse and the stables with the great, roughly-built barns stood in easy reach of the overseer's house, so that, standing on his front gallery, he could see what was going on in the "quarter lot." But he was expected to be most of the day on his horse in the field watching the hands. He was responsible for all that went on: he must see that the two old Mammys in the nursery, a great big room with a fireplace at each end and two rows of cradles, took good care of the little darkies — fed them and kept them decently clean; and he must see that the women at the cookhouse kept it clean and that the food was well cooked and abundant. Sometimes when the hands were in a remote part of the field, the dinner would be sent them at 12 o'clock. As I remember, the Negroes were expected to cook their own suppers and breakfasts, but each plantation was a law unto itself and customs varied. The rations were meat and meal, and there was a large garden to furnish vegetables for the dinner. Most of the Negroes had little gardens back of their houses, and it was a very lazy "cullud pusson" who did not raise chickens and have eggs.

The overseer had to see that the mules were well looked after, curried, fed, and watered; that the milkwoman did her duty by the cows; and that the stockman gave his best care to the hogs, calling them up at night and penning them away from the wolves or other varmints. For on this new place, stretching back into a cypress swamp that extended miles away, the wolves were still at home; and sitting on the back gallery in the late evenings, we would often hear them howling in the canebreak. And there was still an occasional bear to be killed by the hunters. Then there was the gin and sawmill work to be directed; so you will see that the manager earned his salary, varying from $800 to $1,200 as he was efficient or otherwise.

There were about one hundred and fifty Negroes on the place, "big and little," as we used to say, and the feeding and clothing was no light job. They were furnished only two or three suits a year, with a calico or linsey dress, head handkerchiefs, and gingham aprons for Christmas for the women, with presents of some kind for the men, and with tobacco and a drink to each grownup and always beeves, hogs, and material for a big Christmas supper, and a holiday two or three days or a week was granted if the plantation work was not pressing.

The clothes for the men and boys and for many of the women who could not sew, were cut and made by seamstresses on the place under the supervision of the master's, or occasionally of the overseer's, wife. I used to be sorry for Mamma in the spring and fall when the time would come to have everything cut out; a room would be cleared out and the great bolts of white woolen jeans, Osnabergs, with bolt after bolt of red flannel for the little ones, would be rolled in and the women with great shears would commence their work. There were several sets of patterns with individual ones for the very tall and the very fat, but there was not much attention paid to the fit, I fancy.

Usually Mamma would lay a pattern on several layers of the goods, chalk it around, and a woman would cut it out. After a day or so of this work, Mamma would go to bed quite broken down and Aunt Lucy, the colored housekeeper, would finish the superintending.

The style of goods used then must have gone out with slavery. I have not seen any of that white jeans for years and years. It would last years and years and after many washings become as soft as flannel. The Negroes often dyed the white suits tan or grey with willow bark or sweet gum. And those heavy russet shoes that all clumped about in, the old and the young, men and women — whoever sees them now? And a good riddance, for they were oh! so ugly and must have been excessively uncomfortable — about as pliable as wood. After many, many greasings, the poor darkies could at last bend their feet in them.

It required quite a corps of servants to keep us well waited on at Brokenburn, for no one expected to wait on himself. The most important was Aunt Lucy, the housekeeper, a nice-looking, middle-aged griffe woman, who waited on Mamma and superintended the others and was expected to see that all household affairs moved smoothly. Annie, the cook, was thin and dark. Her office was certainly no sinecure, as there were always from thirteen to maybe twenty white people and all the house servants to cook three abundant warm meals for every day with no scant cold tea at night but perhaps the most generous meal of the day. I wonder now how the cooks of those days got through with it all. Nearly every week there was a large dining, and often entertainments in the evening with elaborate suppers. It is true that the mistress or daughter of the house and Aunt Lucy always helped with the desserts and the fancy dishes. Thinking it over by the light of later experience, I know our cook was a hard-worked creature. Then, we never thought about it.

Also, there was the seamstress, only next in importance to the cook, and always with piles of work ahead. In those days there were no ready-made clothes for women or children and not many for men, otherwise than pants, vests, and coats. The handsome dresses were made by city dressmakers and everything else made at home. Sewing machines were just coming in and were easily put out of order, and so few Negro seamstresses could use them. They were good only for the mistress of the house and she was usually too busy to bother with them. Aunt Lucy in her spare time was expected to help the seamstress, and my maid, Frank, "Francesca Carrorra" to give her full name, was also learning to sew. But as Frank was said by all the Negroes to be the "most wofless girl" on the place, she was not making much progress. She certainly was lazy. A bright yellow mulatto, just the color of a pumpkin, with straight black hair and intense black eyes, she was odd to look at and so unreliable at any kind of work that she was a trial to everybody. She had been mine since we were children together (she was two years younger), and I could not bear to have her punished. So she dawdled along, doing as little as she could.

The washwoman, Emma, lived in a house in the corner of the yard with Harriet, and her job, to keep the whole family in clean clothes, necessitated an assistant most of the time. And they were busy all the week. People did not have as many clothes in those days and they must needs be washed oftener.

Webster, a griffe Negro, was the dining room servant and some times the coachman, though if he was very busy Uncle Tom from the quarter would drive. To help Webster was a half-grown little darkie, Charles, to rub the knives, do errands, help clean the boots. There were seven pairs and generally several more belonging to the visitors, and boots were boots, reaching to the knee if for hunting or tramping — not many men wore shoes.

Uncle Hoccles (Hercules? I suppose), a native African, had been brought over after he was full grown and was now quite an old man who looked wonderfully like a gorilla. He was the gardener and a most faithful old fellow — low, heavy built, with long arms, and as black as tar. He spoke a most curious lingo that only those accustomed to him could understand. He had entire charge of the garden and could not bear for the overseer to come in to give him directions. He quite loved for Mamma and the children to come in and admire the splendid vegetables and the beautiful order, but he never troubled to obey Mamma's orders, unless they agreed with his ideas of what was necessary. He gathered the vegetables and there was a standing feud between him and the cook; she would slip in and get something he wished to keep for next day.

The last of the household was a slim, brown child of ten, Sarah, whose province was to stand or sit on a low footstool just behind Mamma's chair, to run errands and carry messages all day long, and to pick up the threads and scraps off the carpet. She never spoke unless spoken to and stood like a bronze statue.

Each of the boys owned a little darkie in the quarter who would eventually become his body servant when the owner should arrive at the dignity of manhood.

There were ponies for the younger children and horses for the big boys. My Brother Will and I each owned a beautiful horse, fast and spirited, and many were the wild, dashing rides we enjoyed in company, little and big, all riding together. Mamma did not like riding on horseback, but she had nice carriage horses and they did not grow fat from idleness. They had to be renewed more frequently than any stock on the place because they would so frequently founder.

Brokenburn, with twelve hundred and sixty acres, about eight hundred cleared and deadened, was a most fertile place, new and productive. The Negroes seemed as much ours as the land they lived on. The crop of 1861 would pay off all indebtedness, leaving a surplus, and hereafter we would have nothing to do but enjoy ourselves. Mamma, My Brother, and I were to make the Northern tour in the summer, leaving Sister with Aunt Laura and the boys at home under Mr. Newton's care. Then the next year we would go sight-seeing in Europe, taking Little Sister and leaving two of the boys at college and the others still in Mr. Newton's charge. Mamma had planned to spend so much of the income of the place every year in making first and second payments on her plantation and Negroes, the places as they were bought being put in the names of her children in order of their seniority. Thus by the time the youngest child was grown, each would have his own plantation.

Life seemed so easy and bright before us when in the winter of 1861 commenced the great events that swept away this joyous future and set our feet in new and rugged paths. And now, forty years from then, we are still walking the same rough path, laden with heavy burdens.

Holbein's Ghost

SARAH RICE PRYOR

WASHINGTON, D.C., WINTER 1860–1861

On the eve of the war, Sarah Pryor, whose husband was a congressman from Virginia, was intimately acquainted with the most influential political figures of her time, including President James Buchanan. Stephen A. Douglas, who was to lose to Lincoln in a four–man race for president in 1860, was despised by most southerners, a feeling that was amply reciprocated by most Yankees, especially Mrs. Douglas.

As painter to Henry VIII, Holbein, to whom Sarah refers, executed the portraits of many members of Henry's court — including several of his wives — before Henry executed them. The poetry the men recite derives from Macbeth.

Our social lines were now strictly drawn between North and South. Names were dropped from visiting lists, occasions avoided on which we might expect to meet members of the party antagonistic to our own. My friend Mrs. Douglas espoused all her husband's quarrels and distinctly "cut" his opponents. There were very few boxes to be had at our little theatre — and the three best were usually secured by Mrs. Douglas, Miss Harriet Lane, and Mrs. John R. Thompson. The feud between the President and Judge Douglas was bitter, and Mrs. Douglas never appeared at Miss Lane's receptions in the winter of 1859–1860. One evening we were all in our theatre boxes, Miss Lane next to us, and I the guest of Mrs. Douglas. Mr. Porcher Miles, member from South Carolina, who had opposed Judge Douglas's nomination, appeared at the door of our box. Instantly Mrs. Douglas turned and said, "Sir, you have made a mistake. Your visit is intended for next door!" "Madam," said Mr. Miles, "I presumed I might be permitted to make my respects to Mrs. Pryor, for whom my call was intended." I had the benefit, of course, of the private opinions of each, and was able to be the friend of each. "This, I suppose, is Southern chivalry," said my fair friend. "It savors, I think, of ill–bred impertinence." "I had supposed her a lady," said Mr.

Miles, "or at least a woman of the world. She behaved like a rustic — an *ingénue*."

I could but receive their confidences in silence, perfectly well knowing that both were in the wrong. Both were betrayed by the mad passions of the hour — passions which caused older heads to misunderstand, mislead, and misbehave! "I am the most unpopular man in the country," said Judge Douglas (one of the presidential candidates); "I could walk from Boston to Chicago by the light of my own burning effigies, — and I guess you all know how much Virginia loves me."

I had the good fortune to retain some of my Northern friends. The family of the Secretary of State was loyal to me to the end. When my husband was once embroiled in a violent quarrel, growing out of sectional feeling, General Cass sent his granddaughter, pretty Lizzie Ledyard (my prime favorite), with his love to bid me "take heart," that "all would turn out right." Mrs. Douglas never abated one jot of her gentle kindness, although she knew we belonged to a party adverse to her husband. Mrs. Horace Clark's little brown ponies stopped as often as ever at my door to secure me for a drive down the avenue and a seat beside her in the House. She had been a Miss Vanderbilt and was now wife of a member from New York. All of them were prompt to congratulate me upon my husband's speech on "the state of the country," and to praise it with generous words as "calm, free from vituperation, eloquent in pleading for peace and forbearance."

The evening after this speech was delivered, we were sitting in the library on the first floor of our home, when there was a ring at the door–bell. The servants were in a distant part of the house, and such was our excited state that I ran to the door and answered the bell myself. It was snowing fast, a carriage stood at the door, and out of it bundled a mass of shawls and woollen scarfs. On entering, a manservant commenced unwinding the bundle, which proved to be the Secretary of State, General Cass! We knew not what to think. He was seventy–seven years old. Every night at nine o'clock it was the custom of his daughter, Mrs. Canfield, to wrap him in flannels and put him to bed. What had brought him out at midnight? As soon as he entered, before sitting down, he exclaimed: "Mr. Pryor, I have been hearing about secession for a long time — and I would not listen. But now I am frightened, sir, I am frightened! Your speech in the House to–day gives me some hope. Mr. Pryor! I crossed the Ohio when I was sixteen years old with but a pittance in my pocket, and this glorious Union has made me what I am. I have risen from my bed, sir, to implore you to do what you can to avert the disasters which threaten our country with ruin."

Never was a spring more delightful than that of 1860. The Marine Band played every Saturday in the President's grounds, and thither the whole world repaired, to walk, or to sit in open carriages and talk of everything except politics. Easy compliments to the ladies fell from the lips of the men who could apply to each other in debate abuse too painful to remember. Sometimes we would be invited for the afternoon to sit on the veranda of the White House — and who could fail to mark the ravages of anxiety and care upon the face of the President [James Buchanan]! All the more because he insistently repeated that he was never better — that he slept finely and enjoyed the best health. Nevertheless, if one chanced to stand silently near him in a quiet corner, he might be heard to mutter, "Not in my time — not in my time." Not in his time let this Union be severed, this dear country be drowned in blood.

On other afternoons we visited Mr. and Mrs. Robert E. Lee at Arlington, or drove out to Georgetown through the fragrant avenue of blossoming crab-apples, or to Mrs. Gale's delightful house for tea, returning in the soft moonlight. Everybody in Washington dined early. Congress usually adjourned at four o'clock, and my little boys were wont to be on the roof of our house, to watch for the falling of the flag over the House of Representatives, the signal that we might soon have dinner. The evening meal was late, usually handed. It was considered not "stylish" to serve it at a table. A servant would enter the drawing-room about eight o'clock with a tray holding plates and little doilies. Another would bring in buttered biscuits and chipped beef or ham, and a third tray held cups of tea and coffee. Some delicate sweet would follow. Little tables of Chinese lacquer were placed between two or more ladies, and lucky was the man who would be invited to share one of them. Otherwise he must improvise a rest for his plate on his trembling knees. "Take care! Your plate will fall," I said to one. "Fall! I wish it would — and *break*! The only thing that worries me is when the blamed thing takes to rolling. Why, I have chased plates all around the room until I thought they were bewitched or held the secret of perpetual motion!" These suppers were very conversational, and one did not mind their being so light. There would be punch and sandwiches at eleven.

Such were the pleasant happenings that filled our days — clouded now by the perils which we could not ignore after the warnings to which we listened at the Capitol. We were conscious of this always in our round of visits, receptions, dinners, and balls, with the light persiflage and compliments still in our ears.

But when late evening came, the golden hour of reunion in the library on the first floor of our home was marked by graver talk. There would assemble R.M.T. Hunter, Muscoe Garnett, Porcher Miles, L.Q.C. Lamar, Boyce, Barksdale of Mississippi, Keitt of South Carolina, with perhaps some visitors from the South. Then Susan would light her fires and show us the kind of oysters that could please her "own white folks," and James would bring in lemons and hot water with some choice brand of old Kentucky.

These were not convivial gatherings. These men held troubled consultations on the state of the country — the real meaning and intent of the North, the half-trusted scheme of Judge Douglas to allow the territories to settle for themselves the vexed question of slavery within their borders, the right of peaceable secession. The dawn would find them again and again with but one conclusion — they would stand together: "Unum et commune periculum una salus!"

But Holbein's spectre was already behind the door, and had marked his men! In a few months the swift bullet for one enthusiast, for another (the least considered of them all), a glorious death on the walls of a hard-won rampart — he the first to raise his colors and the shout of victory; for only one, or two, or three, the doubtful boon of existence after the struggle was all over; for *all* survivors, memories that made the next four years seem to be the sum of life — the only real life — beside which the coming years would be but a troubled dream.

The long session did not close until June, and in the preceding month Abraham Lincoln was chosen candidate by the Republican party for the presidency, and Stephen A. Douglas by the Democrats. The South had also a candidate, and hoping to make things better, the ruffled-shirt gentry — the Old-Line Whigs — had also named their man.

My little boys and I were glad to go home to Virginia. A season of perfect happiness awaited them, with their sisters and the dear old people whom they called grandfather and grandmother. Under the shade of the trees, and in the veranda covered with Lamarque roses, who could dream of war?

We were all in our places in November, setting our houses in order, several weeks before the assembling of Congress. We were warmly welcomed into our pleasant home by Susan, whose authority, now fully established and recognized, kept us in perfect order. Everything promised a season of unusual interest. We now knew everybody — and what is more I, for one, liked everybody. It takes so little to make a woman happy!

In Washington our social life did not begin before New Year's Day. Among our first cards this winter was an invitation to the marriage of Mr. Bouligny, member from Louisiana, and Miss Parker, daughter of a wealthy Washington grocer. Rumors reached us of unusual plans for this wedding. Mr. Parker's large house was to be converted into a conservatory filled with blossoming roses and lilies. Fountains were to be introduced, new effects in lighting. The presents were to be magnificent, the bridal dress gorgeous.

Upon arriving at the house (I think it was an afternoon wedding) I found the President seated in an arm–chair at one end of the drawing–room, and the guests ranging themselves on either side. A crimson velvet curtain was stretched across the other end of the room. Presently the curtain parted, and the bridal tableau appeared in position behind it. After the ceremony the crowd waited until the President went forward to wish the bride and her husband "a great deal of happiness." Everybody remained standing until Mr. Buchanan returned to his seat. I stood behind his chair and observed that he had aged much since the summer.

He had had much to bear. Unable to please either party, he had been accused of cowardice, imbecility, and even insanity, by both parties. "The President is pale with fear," said General Cass. "He divides his time equally between praying and crying. Such an imbecile was never seen before," said another. A double–leaded editorial in the *New York Tribune* of December 17 suggested that he might be insane. On the day of the wedding, December 20, he stoutly denied that he was ill. "I never enjoyed better health nor a more tranquil spirit," said the hard–pressed President. "I have not lost an hour's sleep nor a single meal. I weigh well and prayerfully what course I ought to adopt," he had written on that day.

The crowd in the Parker drawing–room soon thinned as the guests found their way to the rooms in which the presents were displayed. The President kept his seat, and I stood behind him as one and another came forward to greet him. Presently he looked over his shoulder and said, "Madam, do you suppose the house is on fire? I hear an unusual commotion in the hall."

"I will inquire the cause, Mr. President," I said. I went out at the nearest door, and there in the entrance hall I found Mr. Lawrence Keitt, member from South Carolina, leaping in the air, shaking a paper over his head, and exclaiming, "Thank God! Oh, thank God!" I took hold of him and said: "Mr. Keitt, are you crazy? The President hears you, and wants to know what's the matter."

"Oh!" he cried, "South Carolina has seceded! Here's the telegram. I feel like a boy let out from school."

I returned and, bending over Mr. Buchanan's chair, said in a low voice: "It appears, Mr. President, that South Carolina has seceded from the Union. Mr. Keitt has a telegram." He looked at me, stunned for a moment. Falling back and grasping the arms of his chair, he whispered, "Madam, might I beg you to have my carriage called?" I met his secretary and sent him in without explanation, and myself saw that his carriage was at the door before I reentered the room. I then found my husband, who was already cornered with Mr. Keitt, and we called our own carriage and drove to Judge Douglas's. There was no more thought of bride, bridegroom, wedding cake, or wedding breakfast.

This was the tremendous event which was to change all our lives — to give us poverty for riches, mutilation and wounds for strength and health, obscurity and degradation for honor and distinction, exile and loneliness for inherited homes and friends, pain and death for happiness and life.

The news was not known, except in official circles, until the evening. The night was dark. A drizzling rain was falling; the streets were almost impassable from mud.

At the house of a prominent South Carolina gentleman a crowd soon collected. The street was full of carriages, the house brilliantly lighted.

Admiral Porter, then a lieutenant, had heard the startling news, and called at this house to tell it. He found the mistress of the mansion descending in cloak and bonnet, and as soon as she saw him she exclaimed: "Oh, Captain, you are just the man I want. I'm going to the White House to tell the President some good news. The horses are sick and I'm going to walk over."

"It is impossible for you to walk through the rain and mud," said the Lieutenant. "There are ten or twelve hacks at the door, and I will press one into your service." So saying, he called a carriage and helped her to enter it, getting in after her.

"I was under the impression," he said, as they started, "that you were having a party at your house, it was so brilliantly lighted up, and I thought I would venture in uninvited."

"No, indeed," she replied; "but we have received glorious news from the South, and my husband's friends are calling to congratulate him.

South Carolina has seceded, and oh, Captain, we will have a glorious monarchy, and you must join us,"

"And be made Duke of Benedict Arnold?"

"Nonsense!" she exclaimed, "we will make you an admiral."

"Certainly," said Lieutenant Porter, "Admiral of the Blue. For I should feel blue enough to see everything turned upside down, and our boasted liberty and civilization whistled down the wind."

"What would you have?" she inquired. "Would you have us tamely submit to all the indignities the North puts upon us, and place our necks under their feet? Why, this very day my blood boiled while I was in Congress, and I could scarcely contain myself. An old black Republican was berating the Southern people as if they were a pack of naughty children. However, Mr. Rhett took the floor and gave the man such a castigation that he slunk away and was no more heard from."

Just then they reached the White House. "Come in," said the lady, "and hear me tell the President the good news."

Lieutenant Porter preferred returning to her house. There he found a crowd around a generous bowl of punch. When he had an opportunity, he asked the host if he thought it possible the Southern states would secede. "What more do they want?" he inquired. "They have a majority in the Senate and the House, and, with the Supreme Court on their side, they could make laws to suit themselves."

"True," his host replied, "most people would be satisfied with that. 'Better to bear the ills we have than fly to others that we know not of.' But *you* will join us? *You must!* We will have a navy to be proud of, and we'll make you admiral."

"There's one comfort," said an old society dame who now joined the party. "South Carolina is a fickle young thing and may change her mind! She declared herself ready once before to walk out, — you all remember it, — and changed her mind. She took off her things and concluded to stay a little longer."

"She has gone for good and all this time, depend upon it," said the host. "She was only giving warning then! Her time is up now and she is off."

Meanwhile the lady of the house was telling the President news that was no news to him. He was fully prepared to receive it calmly and gravely. I had preceded her by some hours.

Lieutenant Porter little dreamed of the good fortune the secession of South Carolina would bring to him. From a poor lieutenant with anxious cares about a large family, he was speedily raised by Mr. Lincoln to the proud position of rear-admiral of the United States.

His own comment upon the enthusiasm of his Southern friends is amusing. He declared that if the capital and its surroundings had been less stupid, that if those vivacious Southerners could have had a court, theatres, and opera–houses, the catastrophe which overwhelmed North and South might have been prevented. "The Romans understood these things better than we. They omitted nothing to keep the people amused; they even had the street fountains at times run with wine, and the investment was worth the money spent." "But what," said Admiral Porter, "could one expect at a court presided over by an old bachelor whose heart was dead to poetry and love; who sat at dinner with no flowers to grace the festive board, and never had a *boutonnière* on his coat lapel?" which was one way, at least, of accounting for things.

Of course, we all paid our respects to the President on the next New Year's Day, and joined the motley crowd of men and women of every degree who were admitted after the starred and beribboned dignitaries from foreign lands had been received. "Here I am, Mr. President," said one of the witty Southern women, "and my cook will be here in a few minutes! I left her dressing to come."

The day that ushered in the eventful year 1861 was gloomy out of doors, but within the Executive Mansion flowers, music, gay attire, and bright smiles ruled the hour. "I wish you a happy New Year, Mr. President," fell from every lip, but in every heart there was a gloomy foreboding of impending disaster. What would the year bring to the "wayward sister," whose sons had all gone home? How we missed them! — Mr. Porcher Miles, Mr. Boyce, Mr. and Mrs. Keitt, always so delightful a part of our Washington social life. Some of us might expect to return; but this was adieu, not *au revoir*, to our President. This was his last New Year's Day in the White House, not his last day of perplexity and trouble. Very soon more wayward sisters would depart, and the hour he had dreaded would "come in his time."

There is no time at the President's New Year's reception to gather in corners for private talk. We must hurry on our rounds to the houses of the Cabinet and of the foreign Ministers. Sending the gentlemen of our party forward to visit the Senators' wives, we hastened home to our own punch–bowl.

I brewed a mighty bowl that last New Year's Day. Dr. Garnett and Judge Scarborough presided over the mixing, to be sure that the arrack was proportioned rightly, and that there were just as many and no more toasted crab–apples than there should be.

Late in the afternoon my rooms were thronged — with Virginians and

Southerners mainly, but with some Northern friends as well, for Virginia was not yet classed. Like Touchstone, I was "in a parlous state," lest some of my guests who had already honored many punch–bowls should venture on forbidden subjects. More than one came in on the arm of James, but it took a better man than James to conduct him out again and into his carriage. My friend who had distinguished himself at my first President's dinner was in high feather, as were some grave judges I knew.

There was but one thought in every mind, gay or sober. "Is this a meeting of the Girondists?" queried one.

"When shall we three meet again?" quoted another.

"When the hurly–burly's done —
When the battle's lost and won,"

was the prompt answer. "Sh–h–h!" said an old army officer. "It is not lucky to talk of lost battles on New Year's Day, nor of Girondists' feasts on the eve of a revolution."

The season which was always ushered in on New Year's Day resolved itself literally this year into a residence in the galleries of the Senate Chamber and the House of Representatives.

Before the first of February, Mississippi, Florida, Alabama, Georgia, Louisiana, and Texas had dissolved their bonds with the Federal Union. The farewell addresses of the Representatives of the seceded states became the regular order of the day. Jefferson Davis's final farewell closed with these solemn words: "May God have us in his holy keeping, and grant that, before it is too late, peaceful counsels may prevail."

Virginia, had she retained her original colonial bounds, could have dictated to the rest. Now, should she elect to join the Southern Confederacy, the states she had given to the Union — her own children — would be arrayed against her.

Virginia now essayed to arbitrate. Her Peace Commission met in Washington, but without result, except that it was for her a fleeting moment of enthusiasm.

Mr. Kellogg of Illinois said: "She has thrown herself into the breach to turn aside the tide of disunion and revolution, and she says to the nation, 'Be united and be brothers again.' God bless the Old Dominion!" Said Mr. Bigler of Pennsylvania, January 21: "Pennsylvania will *never* become the enemy of Virginia! Pennsylvania will never draw the sword on Virginia."

Apprehension was felt lest the new President's inaugural might be the occasion of rioting, if not of violence. We were advised to send our women and children out of the city. Hastily packing my personal and household belongings to be sent after me, I took my little boys, with their faithful nurse, Eliza Page, on board the steamer to Acquia Creek, and, standing on deck as long as I could see the dome of the Capitol, commenced my journey homeward. My husband remained behind, and kept his seat in Congress until Mr. Lincoln's inauguration. He described that mournful day to me — differing so widely from the happy installation of Mr. Pierce. "O'er all there hung a shadow and a fear." Everyone was oppressed by it, and no one more than the doomed President himself.

We were reunited a few weeks afterward at our father's house in Petersburg; and in a short time my young Congressman had become my young colonel — and Congressman as well, for as soon as Virginia seceded he was elected to the Provisional Congress of the Confederate States of America and was commissioned colonel by Governor Letcher.

I am afraid the evening is at hand, when we must bid adieu to the bright days — the balls, the merry hair-dresser, the round of visits, the levees, the charming "at homes." The setting sun of such a day should pillow itself on golden clouds, bright harbingers of a morning of beauty and happiness. Alas, alas! "whom the gods destroy they first infatuate."

The View from the Mills House

MARY BOYKIN CHESNUT

CHARLESTON, SOUTH CAROLINA, APRIL 1861

The firing on Fort Sumter was preceded by complex, but fruit-less, negotiations between the Confederate and the United States governments in which Mary Chesnut's husband, recently resigned from the United States Senate, was involved. Mary Chesnut was with her husband in Charleston when the first shot was fired. She began this passage in Charleston and finished it at her plantation near Camden.

Governor Manning walked in, bowed gravely, and seated himself by me. Again he bowed low in mock heroic style, and with a grand wave of his hand, said: "Madam, your country is invaded." When I had breath to speak, I asked, "What does he mean?" He meant this: there are six men–of–war outside the bar. Talbot and Chew have come to say that hostilities are to begin. Governor Pickens and Beauregard are holding a council of war. Mr. Chesnut then came in and confirmed the story. Wig-fall next entered in boisterous spirits, and said: "There was a sound of revelry by night." In any stir or confusion my heart is apt to beat so painfully. Now the agony was so stifling I could hardly see or hear. The men went off almost immediately. And I crept silently to my room, where I sat down to a good cry.

Mrs. Wigfall came in and we had it out on the subject of civil war. We solaced ourselves with dwelling on all its known horrors, and then we added what we had a right to expect with Yankees in front and negroes in the rear. "The slave–owners must expect a servile insurrection, of course," said Mrs. Wigfall, to make sure that we were unhappy enough.

Suddenly loud shouting was heard. We ran out. Cannon after cannon roared. We met Mrs. Allen Green in the passageway with blanched cheeks and streaming eyes. Governor Means rushed out of his room in his dressing–gown and begged us to be calm. "Governor Pickens," said he, "has ordered in the plentitude of his wisdom, seven cannon to be fired as a signal to the Seventh Regiment. Anderson will hear as well as the Seventh Regiment. Now you go back and be quiet; fighting in the streets has not begun yet."

So we retired. Dr. Gibbes calls Mrs. Allen Green Dame Placid. There was no placidity to–day, with cannon bursting and Allen on the Island. No sleep for anybody last night. The streets were alive with soldiers, men shouting, marching, singing. Wigfall, the "stormy petrel," is in his glory, the only thoroughly happy person I see. To–day things seem to have settled down a little. One can but hope still. Lincoln, or Seward, has made such silly advances and then far sillier drawings back. There may be a chance for peace after all. Things are happening so fast. My husband has been made an aide–de–camp to General Beauregard.

Three hours ago we were quickly packing to go home. The Convention has adjourned. Now he tells me the attack on Fort Sumter may begin to–night; depends upon Anderson and the fleet outside. The Herald says that this show of war outside of the bar is intended for Texas. John Manning came in with his sword and red sash, pleased as a boy to be on Beauregard's staff, while the row goes on. He has gone with Wigfall to Captain Harstein with instructions. Mr. Chesnut is finishing a report he had to make to the Convention.

Mrs. Hayne called. She had, she said, but one feeling; pity for those who are not here. Jack Preston, Willie Alston, "the take–life–easys," as they are called, with John Green, "the big brave," have gone down to the islands — volunteered as privates. Seven hundred men were sent over. Ammunition wagons were rumbling along the streets all night. Anderson is burning blue lights, signs, and signals for the fleet outside, I suppose.

To–day at dinner there was no allusion to things as they stand in Charleston Harbor. There was an undercurrent of intense excitement. There could not have been a more brilliant circle. In addition to our usual quartette (Judge Withers, Langdon Cheves, and Trescott), our two ex–Governors dined with us, Means and Manning. These men all talked so delightfully. For once in my life I listened. That over, business began in earnest. Governor Means had rummaged a sword and red sash from somewhere and brought it for General Chesnut, who had gone to demand the surrender of Fort Sumter. And now patience — we must wait.

Why did that green goose Anderson go into Fort Sumter? Then everything began to go wrong. Now they have intercepted a letter from him urging them to let him surrender. He paints the horrors likely to ensue if they will not. He ought to have thought of all that before he put his head in the hole.

• • •

April 12th. — Anderson will not capitulate. Yesterday's was the merri-
est, maddest dinner we have had yet. Men were audaciously wise and
witty. We had an unspoken foreboding that it was to be our last pleasant
meeting. Mr. Miles dined with us to–day. Mrs. Henry King rushed in
saying, "The news, I come for the latest news. All the men of the King
family are on the Island," of which fact she seemed proud.

While she was here our peace negotiator, or envoy, came in — that is,
Mr. Chesnut returned. His interview with Colonel Anderson had been
deeply interesting, but Mr. Chesnut was not inclined to be communicative. He wanted his dinner. He felt for Anderson and had telegraphed to
President Davis for instructions — what answer to give Anderson, etc.
He has now gone back to Fort Sumter with additional instructions.
When they were about to leave the wharf A. H. Boykin sprang into the
boat in great excitement. He thought himself ill–used, with a likelihood
of fighting and he to be left behind!

I do not pretend to go to sleep. How can I? If Anderson does not
accept terms at four, the orders are, he shall be fired upon. I count four,
St. Michael's bells chime out and I begin to hope. At half–past four the
heavy booming of a cannon. I sprang out of bed, and on my knees prostrate I prayed as I never prayed before.

There was a sound of stir all over the house, pattering of feet in the
corridors. All seemed hurrying one way. I put on my double–gown and a
shawl and went, too. It was to the housetop. The shells were bursting. In
the dark I heard a man say, "Waste of ammunition." I knew my husband
was rowing about in a boat somewhere in that dark bay, and that the
shells were roofing it over, bursting toward the fort. If Anderson was
obstinate, Colonel Chesnut was to order the fort on one side to open
fire. Certainly fire had begun. The regular roar of the cannon, there it
was. And who could tell what each volley accomplished of death and
destruction?

The women were wild there on the housetop. Prayers came from the
women and imprecations from the men. And then a shell would light up
the scene. To–night they say the forces are to attempt to land. We
watched up there, and everybody wondered that Fort Sumter did not fire
a shot.

To–day Miles and Manning, colonels now, aides to Beauregard, dined
with us. The latter hoped I would keep the peace. I gave him only good
words, for he was to be under fire all day and night, down in the bay carrying orders, etc.

Last night, or this morning truly, up on the housetop I was so weak and weary I sat down on something that looked like a black stool. "Get up, you foolish woman. Your dress is on fire," cried a man. And he put me out. I was on a chimney and the sparks had caught my clothes. Susan Preston and Mr. Venable then came up. But my fire had been extinguished before it burst out into a regular blaze.

Do you know, after all that noise and our tears and prayers, nobody has been hurt; sound and fury signifying nothing — a delusion and a snare.

Louisa Hamilton came here now. This is a sort of news center. Jack Hamilton, her handsome young husband, has all the credit of a famous battery, which is made of railroad iron. Mr. Petigru calls it the boomerang, because it throws the balls back the way they came; so Lou Hamilton tells us. During her first marriage, she had no children; hence the value of this lately achieved baby. To divert Louisa from the glories of "the Battery," of which she raves, we asked if the baby could talk yet. "No, not exactly, but he imitates the big gun when he hears that. He claps his hands and cries 'Boom, boom.'" Her mind is distinctly occupied by three things: Lieutenant Hamilton, whom she calls "Randolph," the baby, and the big gun, and it refuses to hold more.

Pryor, of Virginia, spoke from the piazza of the Charleston hotel. I asked what he said. An irreverent woman replied: "Oh, they all say the same thing, but he made great play with that long hair of his, which he is always tossing aside!"

Somebody came in just now and reported Colonel Chesnut asleep on the sofa in General Beauregard's room. After two such nights he must be so tired as to be able to sleep anywhere.

Just bade farewell to Langdon Cheves. He is forced to go home and leave this interesting place. Says he feels like the man that was not killed at Thermopylae. I think he said that unfortunate had to hang himself when he got home for very shame. Maybe he fell on his sword, which was the strictly classic way of ending matters.

I do not wonder at Louisa Hamilton's baby; we heard nothing, can listen to nothing; boom, boom goes the cannon all the time. The nervous strain is awful, alone in this darkened room. "Richmond and Washington ablaze," say the papers — blazing with excitement. Why not?

To us these last days' events seem frightfully great. We were all women on that iron balcony. Men are only seen at a distance now. Stark Means, marching under the piazza at the head of his regiment, held his cap in his hand all the time he was in sight. Mrs. Means was leaning over the balcony looking with tearful eyes, when an unknown creature asked, "Why did he take his hat off?" Mrs. Means stood straight up and said: "He did that in honor of his mother; he saw me." She is a proud mother, and at the same time most unhappy. Her lovely daughter Emma is dying in there, before her eyes, of consumption. At that moment I am sure Mrs. Means had a spasm of the heart; at least she looked as I feel sometimes. She took my arm and we came in.

April 13th. — Nobody has been hurt after all. How gay we were last night. Reaction after the dread of all the slaughter we thought those dreadful cannon were making. Not even a battery the worse for wear. Fort Sumter has been on fire. Anderson has not yet silenced any of our guns. So the aides, still with swords and red sashes by way of uniform, tell us. But the sound of those guns makes regular meals impossible. None of us go to table. Tea–trays pervade the corridors going every-where. Some of the anxious hearts lie on their beds and moan in solitary misery. Mrs. Wigfall and I solace ourselves with tea in my room. These women have all a satisfying faith. "God is on our side," they say. When we are shut in Mrs. Wigfall and I ask "Why?" "Of course, he hates the Yankees, we are told. You'll think that well of Him."

Not by one word or look can we detect any change in the demeanor of these negro servants. Lawrence sits at our door, sleepy and respectful, and profoundly indifferent. So are they all, but they carry it too far. You could not tell that they even heard the awful roar going on in the bay, though it has been dinning in their ears night and day. People talk before them as if they were chairs and tables. They make no sign. Are they stolidly stupid? or wiser than we are; silent and strong, biding their time?

So tea and toast came; also came Colonel Manning, red sash and sword, to announce that he had been under fire and didn't mind it. He said gaily: "It is one of those things a fellow never knows how he will come out until he has been tried. Now I know I am a worthy descendent of my old Irish hero of an ancestor, who held the British officer before him as a shield in the Revolution, and backed out of danger gracefully." We talked of St. Valentine's eve, or the maid of Perth, and the drop of the white doe's blood that sometimes spoiled all.

The war–steamers are still there, outside the bar. And there are people who thought the Charleston bar "no good" to Charleston. The bar is the silent partner, or sleeping partner, and in this fray it is doing us yeoman service.

• • •

April 15th. — I did not know that one could live such days of excitement. Some one called: "Come out! There is a crowd coming." A mob it was, indeed, but it was headed by Colonels Chesnut and Manning. The crowd was shouting and showing these two as messengers of good news. They were escorted to Beauregard's headquarters. Fort Sumter had surrendered! Those upon the housetops shouted to us "The fort is on fire." That had been the story once or twice before.

When we had calmed down, Colonel Chesnut, who had taken it all quietly enough, if anything more unruffled than usual in his serenity, told us how the surrender came about. Wigfall was with them on Morris Island when they saw the fire in the fort; he jumped in a little boat, and with his handkerchief as a white flag, rowed over. Wigfall went in through a porthole. When Colonel Chesnut arrived shortly after, and was received at the regular entrance, Colonel Anderson told him he had need to pick his way warily, for the place was all mined. As far as I can make out the fort surrendered to Wigfall. But it is all confusion. Our flag is flying there. Fire–engines have been sent for to put out the fire. Everybody tells you half of something and then rushes off to tell something else or to hear the last news.

In the afternoon, Mrs. Preston, Mrs. Joe Heyward, and I drove around the Battery. We were in an open carriage. What a changed scene — the very liveliest crowd I think I ever saw, everybody talking at once. All glasses were still turned on the grim old fort.

Russell, the correspondent of the London Times, was there. They took him everywhere. One man got out Thackeray to converse with him on equal terms. Poor Russell was awfully bored, they say. He only wanted to see the fort and to get news suitable to make up into an interesting article. Thackeray had become stale over the water.

Mrs. Frank Hampton and I went to see the camp of the Richland troops. South Carolina College had volunteered to a boy. Professor Venable (the mathematical) intends to raise a company from among them for the war, a permanent company. This is a grand frolic no more for the students, at least. Even the staid and severe of aspect, Clingman, is here. He says Virginia and North Carolina are arming to come to our rescue, for now the North will swoop down on us. Of that we may be sure. We have burned our ships. We are obliged to go on now. He calls us a poor, little, hot–blooded, headlong, rash, and troublesome sister State. General McQueen is in a rage because we are to send troops to Virginia.

Preston Hampton is in all the flush of his youth and beauty, six feet in stature; and after all only in his teens; he appeared in fine clothes and lemon–colored kid gloves to grace the scene. The camp in a fit of horse–play seized him and rubbed him in the mud. He fought manfully, but took it all naturally as a good joke.

Mrs. Frank Hampton knows already what civil war means. Her brother was in the New York Seventh Regiment, so roughly received in Baltimore. Frank will be in the opposite camp.

Good stories there may be and to spare for Russell, the man of the London Times, who has come over here to find out our weakness and our strength and to tell all the rest of the world about us.

Camden, S.C., April 20, 1861. — Home again at Mulberry. In those last days of my stay in Charleston I did not find time to write a word.

And so we took Fort Sumter, *nous autres*; we — Mrs. Frank Hampton, and others — in the passageway of the Mills House between the reception–room and the drawing–room, for there we held a sofa against all comers. All the agreeable people of the South seemed to have flocked to Charleston at the first gun. That was after we had found out that bombarding did not kill anybody. Before that, we wept and prayed and took our tea in groups in our rooms, away from the haunts of men.

Captain Ingraham and his kind also took Fort Sumter — from the Battery with field–glasses and figures made with their sticks in the sand to show what ought to be done.

Wigfall, Chesnut, Miles, Manning, took it rowing about the harbor in small boats from fort to fort under the enemy's guns, with bombs bursting in air.

And then the boys and men who worked those guns so faithfully at the forts — they took it, too, in their own way.

Old Colonel Beaufort Watts told me this story and many more of the *jeunesse dorée* under fire. They took the fire easily, as they do most things. They had cotton bag bomb–proofs at Fort Moultrie, and when Anderson's shot knocked them about some one called out "Cotton is falling." Then down went the kitchen chimney, loaves of bread flew out, and they cheered gaily, shouting, "Bread–stuffs are rising."

Willie Preston fired the shot which broke Anderson's flag–staff. Mrs. Hampton from Columbia telegraphed him, "Well done, Willie!" She is his grandmother, the wife, or widow, of General Hampton, of the Revolution, and the mildest, sweetest, gentlest of old ladies. This shows how the war spirit is waking us all up.

Colonel Miles (who won his spurs in a boat, so William Gilmore Simms said) gave us this characteristic anecdote. They met a negro out in the bay rowing toward the city with some plantation supplies, etc. "Are you not afraid of Colonel Anderson's cannon?" he was asked. "No, sar, Mars Anderson ain't daresn't hit me; he know Marster wouldn't 'low it."

I have been sitting idly to-day looking out upon this beautiful lawn, wondering if this can be the same world I was in a few days ago. After the smoke and the din of the battle, a calm.

Pistols in the Churchyard

CATHERINE COOPER HOPLEY

NEAR FREDERICKSBURG, VIRGINIA, LATE SPRING 1861

Catherine Hopley, a native of England, had lived in the North where she had relatives. She had had misgivings about living in the South, but she became fond of southern people and was increasingly sympathetic to the Confederacy — not so much so, however, that she lost her English sense of irony or her belief that the war was folly for both sides. She was governess for the Quence family in Virginia in 1861. In her journal, she refers to herself as Miss Jones.

No epidemic ever attacked a population so universally as did this war fever the Americans. No mandate was ever obeyed with such eager willingness as was the voice of Secession, which was then echoing from the mountains and through the valleys of Virginia. It was not statesmen and politicians, not rulers and governors, to whom were yielded the organization of regiments and the control of arming the country; not even, indeed, to *men* alone. If the women did not positively shoulder their muskets and set out for the camp, they nevertheless took no mean share in the common cause, using all their influence and eloquence in urging upon sons and brothers to "resist aggression."

Those same ladies who "graced the harbours of Charleston with their presence," during the taking of Fort Sumter, had been for weeks assembling themselves in societies, to prepare clothing for the soldiers, and make lint, bandages, and whatever might be needed for the wounded. These things were the women of America then doing all over the country, both North and South; the war was theirs, because the cause was theirs; theirs the soldiers, husbands, sons, and brothers; theirs the country, homes, and firesides; their liberty to be fought for, their wrongs to be redressed. So at least they felt, and with an ardour that found the mere making of bandages and clothing too tame and unsatisfying. If they could not fire a musket, they would at least help to load it, by making cartridges and bullets, which they did with astonishing dexterity; and this brought them nearer in imagination to the scene of action. Flags and banners, tents and gun–cases, also were prepared; nothing, in fact, that a woman's hand could accomplish was left undone for those who fought their battles. The same feeling that animated the women of Virginia in the revolutionary war was observable on this occasion; mothers urged upon their sons their responsibility; the honour and independence of their country must be preserved; "death is preferable to dishonour," was the universal word. Heiresses brought their jewels to be disposed of to support the war. Wives of rich planters doffed their finery, and set an example of forbearance and moderation, the more remarkable where fashion and display had been the prevailing foible. Neither were the ladies behind–hand in getting up excitements, and their names into newspapers — an ambition the chivalrous editors were only too happy to gratify. Thus we were continually reading, "The ladies of such a county have presented an elegantly–wrought banner to such a company of militia. There were present on the occasion, etc., etc., and many patriotic speeches did honour to the noble spirit and fidelity of the county." Then the ladies of another county followed the example, and received more compliments, which still further stimulated them and their neighbours. Again, "The young ladies of such a seminary succeeded in raising a splendid Secession flag upon the observatory of the building. Twice the superintendent ordered it down, but the fair Virginians finally prevailed, and it is now gaily floating in the breeze." So far from having to study a homily on the charm of feminine reserve, or being confined to their rooms, which we should think the mildest discipline to these juvenile candidates for notoriety, their "spirit" was extolled in the newspapers, and immediately another society of Virginia's fair daughters resolved to do likewise.

The raising of Secession flags had been one of the most popular amusements in all the Southern States during the past spring. The war was the people's, and the excitement of preparation for it had so much of romance — there was such an opportunity for heroism on a small scale — that as yet it had seemed more like the fitting out for a summer trip, or preparing for an archery party, than any really serious and solemn undertaking. When these light–hearted girls began to lose their lovers and brothers, when lists of killed and wounded were passed around, and we read of the thousands of slain, then the reality of war and all its terrors crowded around them.

Before the confirmed Secession of Virginia from the Northern States' Government, the "Secession flag," as an indication of the prevailing sentiment, was set floating from many public buildings and private dwellings. In the thinly–populated country districts, the county court–house, or a church, as being the only places where gatherings of people were likely to occur, were popular points for flag raisings. Churches in America are appropriated to many purposes besides "preaching." Therefore, at a vast number of churches had Secession flags been raised, and on one of these occasions we were invited to be present. The church for the present demonstration was the one which we attended every third Sunday, and where our Baptist minister preached his political sermons. It was situated on the outskirts of a wood, on a small space of cleared land near Crossroads, where also were the necessary appendages of either a pump, a well, or spring of water, an "upping stock" for the assistance of riders, and plenty of shady trees, under which vehicles, horses, and mules, reposed during the hours of service.

When we arrived on the present occasion, a goodly company had already assembled; a number of carriages and saddle–horses were scattered about beneath the trees. The little church was open; ladies and children were sitting on the steps, or leaning against the door–posts in friendly chat. Other groups were gossiping in the shade, or helping themselves to water from a bucket, into which they dipped the long–handled gourd that answered the purpose of a general drinking–cup. Negro nurses in full finery, and other sable attendants, with their picturesque head–gear and dazzling displays of ivory, varied the scene.

On the shady side of the building about a dozen young ladies were standing in a row, attended by sundry young gentlemen, and I had scarcely time to wonder what engaged their attention before several reports were heard, more or less loud and irregular; wonder was succeeded by astonishment, and almost horror; these fair young girls were positively firing off pistols! With a firm hand and steady eye, vowing to shoot the first "Yankee" who came within sight of their homes, did these quiet and delicate–looking creatures (for such they appeared) continue their practice as fast as their "beaus" could load for them, some despising assistance, and even loading for themselves. Our readers are not to suppose that these young girls entertained the least idea of turning into modern Amazons, and joining the ranks themselves; they were actuated only by the spirit which was on fire throughout the country, feeling that if the worst should come — if, after months and years of fighting, their country should be still invaded — "every man in Virginia shall leave his home to fight, and we will protect ourselves." Such were their sentiments. "There's not a man, woman, or child, who can hold a gun or pull a trigger, who will not fight or die sooner than be any longer under the control of the Yankee."

The ladies used every effort to persuade me to join in the sport, and at length prevailed on me to try a shot. When I summoned courage to take a pistol, an elegant little Colt's revolver, quite light and easy to handle, it seemed like child's play; as did indeed these whole preparations for killing fellow–creatures. Still this first handling of an instrument of death had something terrible in its reality, and it was some moments before my hand could grasp it with sufficient steadiness to aim at the devoted tree, which some of the party were devoutly wishing could be transformed into a "living Yankee."

They picked up a fragment of bark, and pointing to the place where the shot had entered, congratulated me upon my success! Mere chance, not skill from such a trembling hand. And if "prayer is the soul's sincere desire," how earnest was mine that circumstances need never warrant the necessity of such a means of self defence.

And now came the most important part of the ceremony. The flag was introduced to the company, and obtained unlimited admiration from the ladies, and a salute from the gentlemen, about twenty of whom were provided with firearms of various descriptions. Then followed some speeches in honour of the occasion, the pastor, Mr. Quence, taking the lead, and pronouncing himself "ready, not only to *preach* the cause of liberty, but to go himself and join the ranks if need be, as many of his brethren had already done." Other speeches from the members of the church, and some compliments to the ladies, followed, and then six young ladies conveyed the flag to the foot of a tall straight tree, whose upper limbs had been cut away to receive and display the symbol of the "Southern Confederacy." Several young gentlemen, with the aid of a ladder, mounted the stem, and by their united efforts succeeded at last in securing the staff; and behold, the flag was "thrown to the breeze," and the achievement was immediately followed by "repeated salutes;" that is, all whose guns were loaded fired them off, the rest loading and firing as fast as they could, singly or together, as they happened to be ready.

One little after–piece that now took place was not less interesting than any part of the previous performances, and was equally characteristic of young Virginia. The whole collection of guns was handed over to boys of from nine to sixteen years of age, who were then put through a sort of drill by a West Point cadet present.

Johnny (Quence — son of Mr. Q.) was one of the youngest of the boys who were admitted to the ranks, but he took his stand with the rest. This child was, however, a "capital shot," and often supplied our table with the fruits of his sport. These young heroes now shot at a mark, and fired salutes, and acquitted themselves to the entire satisfaction of the assembly. This being over, and the company about to disperse, a lady asked Johnny if he were not "afraid to carry that gun?" The child displayed no less of modesty than of good breeding, though he coloured violently whilst hesitating what to reply. "Afraid, madam!" exclaimed an old gentleman who had overheard the remark; "this boy is one of our best shots; that is his own double–barrelled gun, and many a brace of birds has he shot with it." "I only wish I could meet three Yankees in the woods as I go home," quietly remarked Johnny to his friend; "two, any how," added he, reflectively, as he contemplated the two barrels. By what distinguishing plumage this kind of game might be known, the boy had not considered; but that "Yankees" were to be easily recognized, and unerringly shot down, seemed to admit of no doubt in his own mind. I may here observe, that amongst the majority of negroes and children in the Southern States, a "Yankee" is as much a bugbear as was a Frenchman some years ago to our English nursemaids. Thus do these young Southerners from their earliest years imbibe the wild daring which, by education and surrounding influences, is strengthened into a too impatient eagerness to revenge an insult, or rush to the battlefield.

How unreal, how dreamlike and incredible, did all this farce appear as we rode homewards through the woods and lanes, glorious with floral beauty! How hard to assure ourselves, when surrounded by the sweet influences of Virginia's loveliest season, that we were in a land of war and terror; that the very next mail might bring us tidings that the terrible warfare had begun; that we were even within the sound of the cannon's roar; that aggressions and provocations were daily occurring on the borders, to which thousands of troops were hourly flocking; and that the inevitable result must be the sacrifice of precious lives, human beings, living souls, sent recklessly into the presence of their Maker, to answer for the sins of their leaders.

PART II
Shot and Shell
1861–1862

I know how it feels to die. I have felt it again and again. For instance, some one calls out, "Albert Sydney Johnston is killed." My heart stands still. I feel no more. I am, for so many seconds, so many minutes, I know not how long, utterly without sensation of any kind — dead; and then, there is that great throb, that keen agony of physical pain, and the works are wound up again. The ticking of the clock begins, and I take up the burden of life once more. Some day it will stop too long, or my feeble heart will be too worn out to make that awakening jar, and all will be over. I do not think when the end comes that there will be any difference, except the miracle of the new wind-up throb. And now good news is just as exciting as bad. "Hurray, Stonewall has saved us!" The pleasure is almost pain because of my way of feeling it.

— Mary Chesnut, 1862

In Prison for My Country

ROSE O'NEAL GREENHOW

WASHINGTON, D.C., AUGUST 1861–MAY 1862

Because the war was still in progress in 1863 when Rose Green-how published her memoir in England, she did not disclose how she got the Federal battle plan before First Manassas or how she sent it through the lines to the Confederate generals. Without question, she was a Confederate spy, but the Federal authorities were unable to find sufficient evidence to make a case against her.

On Friday, August 23, 1861, as I was entering my own door, on returning from a promenade, I was arrested by two men, one in citizen's dress, and the other in the fatigue dress of an officer of the United States Army. This latter was called Major Allen, and was the chief of the detective police of the city. They followed close upon my footsteps.

I had stopped to enquire after the sick children of one of my neighbours, on the opposite side of the street. From several persons on the side–walk at the time, *en passant*, I derived some valuable information; amongst other things, it was told me that a guard had been stationed around my house throughout the night, and that I had been followed during my promenade, and had probably been allowed to pursue it unmolested, from the fact that a distinguished member of the diplomatic corps had joined me, and accompanied me to that point. This caused me to observe more closely the two men who had followed, and who walked with an air of conscious authority past my house to the end of the pavement, where they stood surveying me.

I continued my conversation apparently without noticing them, remarking rapidly to one of our humble agents who passed, 'Those men will probably arrest me. Wait at Corcoran's Corner, and see. If I raise my handkerchief to my face, give information of it.' The person to whom this order was given went whistling along. I then put a very important note into my mouth, which I destroyed; and turned, and walked leisurely across the street, and ascended my own steps.

A few moments after, and before I could open the door, the two men above described rapidly ascended also, and asked, with some confusion of manner, 'Is this Mrs. Greenhow?' I answered, 'Yes.' They still hesitated; whereupon I asked, 'Who are you and what do you want?' 'I come to arrest you.' 'By what authority?' The man Allen, or Pinkerton (for he had several aliases), said, 'By sufficient authority.' 'Let me see your warrant.' He mumbled something about verbal authority from the War and State Departments, and then both stationed themselves upon either side of me and followed me into the house. I rapidly glanced my eye to see that my signal had been understood, and remarked quietly, 'I have no power to resist you; but, had I been inside of my house, I would have killed one of you before I had submitted to this illegal process.' They replied, with evident trepidation, 'That would have been wrong, as we only obey orders, and both have families.'

This scene occurred in much less time than is requisite to describe it. I took a rapid survey of the two men, and in that instant decided upon my own line of conduct; for I knew that the fate of some of the best and bravest belonging to our cause hung upon my own coolness and courage.

By this time the house had become filled with men; who also surrounded it outside, like bees from a hive. The calmness of desperation was upon me, for I recognised this as the first step in that system of infamy which was yet to hold up this nation of isms to the scorn of the civilised world. This was the first act of the new copartnership of Seward, M'Clellan, & Co., — the strategic step, on coming into power, of the young general so lauded — an attack upon women and children, and a brilliant earnest of the laurels to be won on his march to Richmond.

I asked, after a few moments' survey of the scene, 'What are you going to do?' 'To search,' Allen replied. 'I will facilitate your labours;' and, going to the mantel, I took from a vase a paper, dated Manassas, July 23, containing these words — 'Lt.–Col. Jordon's compliments to Mrs. R. Greenhow. Well but hard–worked' — the rest of the letter being torn off before it reached me, some ten days before, through the city post–office. I suspected its delicate mission, so kept it, from an instinct of caution, and had shown it to Major Bache, of U.S.A., Captain Richard Cutts, Wilson, of Massachusetts, and several others. I threw it to Allen, saying 'You would like to finish this job, I suppose?' He took it, discarding, however, the city envelope in which I had received it.

My cool and indifferent manner evidently disconcerted the whole party. They had expected that, under the influence of the agitation and excitement of the trying position, I should have been guilty of some womanly indiscretion by which they could profit.

An indiscriminate search now commenced through–out my house. Men rushed with frantic haste into my chamber, into every sanctuary. My beds, drawers, and wardrobes were all upturned; soiled clothes were pounced upon with avidity, and mercilessly exposed; papers that had not seen the light for years were dragged forth. My library was taken posses- sion of, and every scrap of paper, every idle line was seized; even the torn fragments in the grates or other receptacles were carefully gathered together by these latter–day Lincoln resurrectionists.

My library, be it remembered, was *my sanctum*; it was there also that I gave lessons to my children, many of whose unlettered scribblings were tortured into dangerous correspondence with the enemy.

I was a keen observer of their clumsy activity, and resolved to test the truth of the old saying that *'the devil is no match for a clever woman!'* I was fully advised that this extraordinary proceeding might take place, and was not to be caught at a disadvantage.

I had received a note a few days before, stating that one of M'Clellan's aides had informed a lady in George Town that I was to be arrested, also that the name of the Honourable William Preston, U.S. Minister Plenipotentiary to Spain, who was at that time in Washington, stood in the proscribed list. He was warned by me in time to effect his escape.

Meanwhile I was a prisoner in one of my own parlours, not allowed to move, with stern eyes fixed upon my face, to read certainly what they did not find; for, although agonising anxieties filled my soul, I was apparently careless and sarcastic, and, I know, tantalising in the extreme. My servants were subjected to the same surveillance, and were not allowed to approach me.

Every effort was made to keep my arrest a secret. My house externally was quiet as usual; three sides of it, being surrounded by a high wall, screened the guard from observation. It was considered the headquarters of the Secessionists, and I being regarded as the head of the conspirators at Washington, a rich haul was anticipated. They reckoned without their host this time.

In despite of all their wisely taken precautions, the news of my arrest rapidly spread. At eleven o'clock I was taken prisoner — at about three o'clock my young friend Miss Mackall, and her sister, came to make enquiries; she had heard it in the city. As she entered she was rudely seized by the detective, who stood concealed behind the door, and pushed forward, as was also her sister. They were terrified at the sight of the rude lawless men who were in possession of my once peaceful quiet home. The dear, brave–hearted girl put her head on my shoulder and wept, for she said, 'I did not know what they had done with you.' I whispered, 'Oh, be courageous, for we must outwit these fiends.'

But before I had succeeded in completely reassuring her, the detective called Captain Dennis approached, and in a loud authoritative voice demanded her name and residence, as well as that of her sister. We were all, after this, ordered to return to the back parlour, under escort of this Captain Dennis, whose duty for the time was to watch me.

The work of examining my papers had already commenced. It was indeed a hard struggle to remain a quiet spectator of this proceeding, but I nevertheless nerved myself to the task, as my object was to throw the detectives off their guard. I had no fear of consequences from the papers which had as yet fallen into their hands. I had a right to my own political opinions, and to discuss the question at issue, and never shrank from the avowal of my sentiments. I am a Southern woman, born with revolutionary blood in my veins, and my first crude ideas on State and Federal matters received consistency and shape from the best and wisest man of this century, John C. Calhoun. These ideas have been strengthened and matured by reading and observation. Freedom of speech and of thought were my birthrights, guaranteed by our charter of liberty, the Constitution of the United States, and signed and sealed by the blood of our fathers.

The search still went on. I desired to go to my chamber, and was told that a woman was sent for to accompany me. It did not even then flash upon my mind that my person was to be searched. I was, however, all the more anxious to be free from the sight of my captors for a few minutes; so, feigning the pretext of change of dress, &c., as the day was intensely hot, after great difficulty, and thanks to the slow movements of these agents of evil, I was allowed to go to my chamber, and then resolved to accomplish the destruction of some important papers which I had in my pocket, even at the expense of life. (The papers were my cipher, with which I corresponded with my friends at Manassas, and others of equal importance.) Happily I succeeded without such a fearful sacrifice.

The detective Dennis little dreamed that a few paces only stood between him and eternity. He rapped at my door, calling 'Madam! madam!' and afterwards opened it, but seeing me apparently legitimately employed, he withdrew. Had he advanced one step, I should have killed him, as I raised my revolver with that intent; and so steady were my nerves, that I could have balanced a glass of water on my finger without spilling a drop.

Shortly after the female detective arrived. I blush that the name and character of woman should be so prostituted. But she was certainly not above her honourable calling. As is usual with females employed in this way, she was decently arrayed, as if to impress me with her respectability. Her face reminded me of one of those india–rubber dolls, whose expression is made by squeezing it, with weak grey eyes which had a faculty of weeping. Like all detectives, she had only a Christian name, Ellen. I began to think that the whole foundling hospital had been let loose for my benefit.

Well, I was ushered into my chamber, a detective standing on guard outside of the door to receive the important documents believed to be secreted on my person — nothing less, I suppose, than a commission of Brigadier–General from President Davis, upon the principle that, whereas President Lincoln had conferred that distinguished grade upon many who deserved to be old women, President Davis had, with characteristic acuteness, discovered qualities in a woman equally entitled to reward.

I was allowed the poor privilege of unfastening my own garments, which, one by one, were received by this pseudo–woman and carefully examined, until I stood in my linen. After this, I was permitted to resume them, with the detectress as my tire–woman.

During all this time, I was cool and self-possessed. I had resolved to go through the trying ordeal with as little triumph to my persecutors as possible. I had already taken the resolution to fire the house from garret to cellar, if I did not succeed in destroying certain papers in the course of the approaching night; for I had no hope that they would escape a second day's search. My manner was therefore assumed to cover my intentions. I was also sustained by the conscious rectitude of my purpose, and the high and holy cause to which I had devoted my life. I felt that a people struggling to maintain their rights and to transmit unimpaired to their children the glorious heritage of revolutionary fathers, was under the protection of that Divine overruling Providence, which could carry me unscathed across the burning plough–shares spread for my destruction. With this conviction in my soul, I resigned myself to the law of the strongest, for I knew not what further trials were in store for me.

The orders were to entrap everybody who called at my house. Miss Mackall and her sister were already in durance. Mrs. Mackall, who came in pursuit of her children, was seized and detained, as also several other casual visitors. I know not, in fact, how many were taken into custody, for, as the evening advanced, I was ordered upstairs, accompanied by my friends, a heavy guard of detectives being stationed in the rooms with us.

A little later I had reason to regard it as a signal act of Divine mercy that those friends were sent me. As I have said, it was believed that all the Secessionists in the city were in communication with me, so everyone who called, black or white, was viewed as an emissary; a former man–servant of mine, and his sister, in passing the house, were made prisoners. The man was confined below stairs, and the young girl taken into the parlour, with only those brutal men as her companions. I was not aware of her being in the house until startled by a smothered scream. My first idea was that some insult had been offered to my maid, but, being satisfied on that point, I tried to believe that my sense of hearing had deceived me. Still, I could not divest myself of the horrible fear, and after a while succeeded in sending some one down. The girl was found in a state of great alarm, from the rudeness to which she had been exposed, and was sent below to her brother; and I began fully to realise the dark and gloomy perils which environed me.

The chiefs of detectives having gone out, several of the subordinates left in charge now possessed themselves of rum and brandy, which aided in developing their brutal instincts; and they even boasted, in my hearing, of the 'nice times' they expected to have with the female prisoners.

As every evil is said to be checkmated by some corresponding good, I was enabled by this means to destroy every paper of consequence. I had placed them where they could be found by me at any hour of the day or night, and was not slow to avail myself of the state of inebriation in which the guards were plunged. Stealing noiselessly to the library in the dark, I mounted up to the topmost shelf, took from the leaves of a dusty folio papers of immense value to me at that moment, concealing them in the folds of my dress, and returned to my position on the bed without my gaolers having missed me. The papers were much more numerous than I imagined, and the difficulty was how to dispose of them. The chance of my friends being searched on going out (as they were assured they should do) at three o'clock made me hesitate as to that method. I remembered, however, that, in the search of my person in the morning, my boots and stockings had not been removed; so Miss Mackall concealed the papers in her stockings and boots. This proceeding of course occupied some time, but it was noiselessly accomplished in the presence of the guard. It was agreed between Miss Mackall and myself, that if, after leaving my room, she learned that her person would be searched, she should be seized with compunction at leaving me, and return to share the honours of the conflagration.

It is proper here to state that the mother of Miss Mackall was not cognisant of this, or any other circumstance calculated to have involved her in the difficulties surrounding me.

The guard, meanwhile, all unconsciously continued their conversation, which, under the influence of the ardent spirits they had imbibed, became heated and angry. I exerted myself to promote the discussion, and arrayed their different nationalities one against the other — they were English, German, Irish, and Yankee.

I reasoned that so unusual a circumstance as men wrangling in my house would warn my friends of the existence of an extraordinary state of things. It was a clear moonlight night, and fear, like death, had hushed every sound in that section of the city. It was a judicious conclusion, as I subsequently learned.

I must here record a circumstance which will go far to prove that a certain *gentleman in black* does not always take care of his own. The chief detective, Allen, having gone out on some other errand of mischief, on returning about nine o'clock encountered a gentleman who was at that time Provost-Marshal of the city, and who was about to call to make a visit at my house. Allen, being ignorant of or disregarding his official position, attempted to arrest him. He ran, pursued by Allen, until he reached the Provost's quarters, when, ordering out his guard, he arrested Allen, and held him in close confinement until the next morning, regardless of his oaths, or his prayers to be allowed to send a message to Lincoln, or Seward, or M'Clellan. By these indirect means Providence seems to have watched over and averted destruction from me.

Between the hours of three and four, on the morning of the 24th, my friends were permitted to depart, under escort of a detective guard, who were stationed around their houses for the following day.

After this I was allowed to snatch a few hours of repose, much needed after the mental and bodily fatigue of that most trying day. But I must also state that the two doors leading into my chamber were kept open, with a guard stationed inside of each.

On the morning of the 24th at about eleven o'clock, my friend Miss Mackall, much to the surprise of the Yankee detective police, returned, and for several weeks shared my imprisonment.

For seven days my house remained in charge of the detective police, the search continuing throughout all that time, as also the examination of my papers and correspondence. The books in the library were all taken down and examined leaf by leaf. There would have been some wisdom in this the first day. Several large boxes, containing books, china, and glass, which had been packed for several months, were subjected to the like ordeal. Finally, portions of the furniture were taken apart, and even the pictures on the walls received their share of attention also. My beds even were upturned many times, as some new idea would seize them.

I now watched their clumsy proceedings free from anxiety, as I had, under their own eyes, sent off or destroyed all my papers of value. Seemingly I was treated with deference. Once only were violent hands put upon my person — the detective, Captain Dennis, having rudely seized me to prevent my giving warning to a lady and gentleman, on the first evening of my arrest (which I, however, succeeded in doing), and as the birds escaped his snare, his rage grew beyond bounds, and he seized me with the spring of a tiger, and crushed my poor arm, which long bore the marks of the brutal outrage. The story of the hapless Queen of Scots was most feelingly called to my recollection. A strong effort was afterwards made to drive this from my mind, as if aught but the life's blood of the dastard could efface it.

My orders were asked for my meals, which I humoured as one of the necessities of my situation. But Lily [Mackall] and I were like the siamese twins, inseparable. My pistol had been taken from me, and I had no means of defence, and for the first time in my life I was exposed to the dread of personal violence.

I had, however, the satisfaction, after a few days, of perceiving that even my lawless captors were rebuked into more quiet and reserve before me, although they still presumed to seat themselves at table with me, with unwashed hands, and shirt–sleeves.

The tactics of my gaolers changed many times. Occasionally, it seemed that my confinement was only nominal; all this, of course, was to throw me off my guard. The subordinates threw themselves in my way, as if disgusted with the task assigned to them, and, with hearts overflowing with kindness, and hands ready to be bribed, discoursed most fluently upon the outrage committed in my arrest.

Two deserve especial notice. One was a burly Irishman, with smooth tongue, professing the religion of my ancestors, that of the holy Catholic faith. He marvelled that so noble a lady should have been treated as a common malefactor; and, by the way of still further showing his sympathy, he set himself to the task of making love to my maid, hoping by this means to possess himself of the important State secrets of which he believed her to be the repository. Sentimental walks, and treats at confectionaries at Uncle Sam's expense, were a part of the programme. She, Lizzy Fitzgerald, a quick–witted Irish girl, warmly attached to me as a kind mistress, and knowing nothing which the severest scrutiny could elicit to my disadvantage, entered keenly into the sport, and, to use her own expressive words, '*led Pat a dance*,' and, under these new auspices, performed some very important missions for me.

The other, a canny Scotchman, whom they called Robert, expatiated, with tears in his eyes, upon '*the sublime fortitude*' I had exhibited on this my moral gridiron; and, seeking still further to commemorate the meek and lowly grace with which I had borne myself, asked me to present him with M'Clellan's report on the Crimea, with my autograph, for, he said, 'Madam,' choked with emotion, '*there is no telling what may happen*; and I would like to look at your name, and know that you had forgiven me.' His manner was touchingly pathetic, and very like what I should suppose Jack Ketch's to be, on asking for the *black cap after all was over*. These two men offered to take letters for me.

I learned, incidentally, that the Provost–Marshal's office was kept on the *qui vive* by the daily report of these proceedings, from which important results were expected to be derived.

During all this time I was never alone for a moment.

On Friday morning, the 30th of August, I was informed that other prisoners were to be brought in, and that my house was to be converted into a prison, and that Miss Mackall and myself, and little girl and servant, were to be confined in one room. After considerable difficulty and consultation with the Secretary of War, another small room was allowed for my child and maid, with the restriction, however, that I should not go into it, as it was a front room, with a window on the street. Subsequently my library was also allotted to me.

My parlours were stripped of their furniture, which was conveyed into the chamber for the use of the prisoners. By this time I had become perfectly callous. Everything showed signs of contamination. Those unkempt, unwashed wretches — the detective police — had rolled themselves in my fine linen; their mark was visible upon every chair and sofa. Even the chamber in which one of my children had died only a few months before, and the bed on which she lay in her winding–sheet, had been desecrated by these emissaries of Lincoln, and the various articles of *bijouterie*, which lay on her toilet as she had left them, were borne off as rightful spoils.

Soon armed men filled the house, the clank of whose muskets

resounded through it like the voice of doom. I was confined to my chamber, at the door of which two soldiers stood, musket in hand.

Other prisoners were arriving. They were the Philips family — Mrs. Philips, and her two oldest daughters, and her sister Miss Levi. A silent greeting, *en passant*, was all we were allowed to exchange. These ladies had been arrested the day after I was, and were subjected to the like, if not greater indignities, from which the presence of the husband and the father could not protect them; and now they were dragged from their own homes, the mother from her little children, several of whom were infants of tender age; her house ransacked, her papers overhauled, without finding anything to base even a suspicion upon — the only circumstance against her really being, that she was a Southern woman, and a lady, scorning association with the '*mudsills*' whom the upheaving of the revolution had brought to the surface of society.

Another prisoner was to be confined in the room adjoining mine. A heavy bar of wood had been nailed across the door between, so as to prevent all communication. She was brought in late at night; her deep and convulsed sobs broke on the stillness of the hour. I sat by the door, and heard the officer in charge call her name. It was Mrs. Hasler, of whom I had some previous knowledge; but, had she been a stranger, her hapless lot would have established a claim to my sympathy.

I had sent to this person's house, the night of my arrest, to warn her, but found her house already in charge of soldiers, and my messenger barely escaped arrest. I was, of course, intensely anxious to let her know that she was in my house, and to communicate with her. She had been accredited to me as a reliable messenger by Colonel Jordon; had successfully served in that capacity several times; and it was through her means (most innocently, however) that my despatches had been betrayed into the hands of the Government. Special care was taken to prevent this prisoner and myself from communicating, as they hoped through her to establish direct evidence against me. The morning after her arrival I diverted the attention of the guard, whilst Miss Mackall slipped into her room, and warned her to deny all knowledge of me — which was, however, limited to the fact of her having been an agent of communication.

Poor woman! She had been most infamously used — dragged from her own lodgings to a station–house, where she had been kept for a whole week, lying on a dirty straw–bed, without sheets or pillow, amidst the lowest and most disgusting class of the community; and her nervous system had been completely shattered by it.

My house, which had been transformed into a Government prison, now became a sort of Mecca. Strangers visiting Washington thronged to see the residence of so 'noted a rebel,' and the newspapers pandered to the greedy curiosity to know something of my habits and tastes. The apartments of the unfortunate Marie Antoinette were not more thoroughly scrutinised, or her occupations for the weary hours given with more minute details, than were mine.

The house was called Fort Greenhow. Photographs of it appeared in several of their illustrated papers, and their mimic 'Punch,' 'Vanity Fair,' devoted a number to me, wherein, with very heavy wit, it proved that I, a simple woman, had outwitted Seward, and discomposed the whole Yankee nation.

Coarse abuse was ofttimes levelled against me, which they took care should reach my ear. These cowardly vituperations passed harmlessly by, as I had a proud consciousness of superiority, and regarded them as testimonials in favour of my devotion to the cause of my country's freedom.

Other prisoners were from time to time brought in, and generally of the lowest class, with the exception of Mrs. Eleanor Lowe, an English lady, whose son was in the Confederate service, and the Posey family of Maryland, who were most estimable people. These were, however, only detained for a few days, under suspicion of giving signals to the Confederate army across the Potomac.

On the 30th of December, a woman named Baxley was confined as a prisoner. She was arrested on the Truce boat, by reason of her garrulous boasting of having gone to Richmond to obtain a commission for her lover, one Dr. Septimus Brown, of having nuts from President Davis's table, and of instructions to open communication with my prison; being also, as she said, the bearer of a letter to me. All this, I need scarcely say, was the result of a disordered imagination, although it afforded a pretext for what was to follow. The conduct of this woman on arriving at the prison confirmed the impression entertained at the time of her arrest, of her being *non compos mentis*. She raved from early morn till late at night, in language more vehement than delicate. I was an involuntary listener to her cries and imprecations, and pity and disgust were often strangely commingled. My chief care was to prevent my child from hearing much that was unfit for her ear. But I felt the horrors of my position hourly increasing.

Occasional excitement was now produced in the prison by the real or affected faints of Miss Poole and this Mrs. Baxley — the premonitory symptoms being a loud cry, and heavy fall upon the floor of one or other, followed by the call of the sentinel on duty, of 'Corporal of the guard,

No. 3!' This individual usually rushed to the rescue, accompanied by two or three of the stoutest sentinels, bayonet in hand — the officer of the guard bringing up the rear, with the judicial gravity of Sancho Panza, conspicuously flourishing a brandy bottle, that being the masculine panacea for all the ills of life.

At about four o'clock on January 18, 1862, I turned my back upon what had once been a happy home; and, what was to me an additional grief, parted from my faithful maid, who had thus far stayed with me through all my trials, and served me with a fidelity and devotion not often equalled in the higher walks of life. My child wept bitterly on parting from her, and I confess that the pathetic appeals of the faithful creature, to be allowed to follow my gloomy fortunes, quite unnerved me.

The majority of the guard were drawn up in front of the house to witness my departure. Several of them had been very kind, and, on taking leave, I said, 'I trust that your next duty will be a more honourable one than that of guarding helpless women and children.'

I cast my eye up, and saw that the windows were all crowded with men, amongst whom I recognised several correspondents of the New York and Philadelphia press eagerly watching my words and looks.

I reached the Old Capitol Prison just at dark; but, whether in anticipation of some demonstration on the part of my friends I know not, but the whole guard were under arms to receive me; a general commotion was visible in all directions, and it was evident that a great deal of interest and curiosity was felt as to the destination of 'so noted a rebel.' The receiving–room or office was crowded with officers and others, all peering at me. It was with a strange feeling of indifference that I found myself in this prison. I had already gone through so many trials, that this crowning act of villany could only elicit a smile of scorn.

After the lapse of some half–hour I was taken up to the room which had been selected for me by General Porter. It was situated in the back building of the prison, on the north–west side, the only view being that of the prison–yard, and was chosen purposely so as to exclude the chance of my seeing a friendly face. It is about ten feet by twelve, and furnished in the rudest manner — a straw bed, with a pair of newly–made unwashed cotton sheets — a small feather pillow, dingy and dirty enough to have formed part of the furniture of the Mayflower — a few wooden chairs, a wooden table, and a glass, six by eight inches, completed its adornment. The second day of my sojourn in this dismal hole a carpenter came to put up bars to the windows.

• • •

EXTRACTS FROM NOTES KEPT IN THE OLD CAPITOL: —

January 25 — I have been one week in my new prison. My letters now all go through the detective police, who subject them to a chemical process to extract the treason. In one of the newspaper accounts, prepared under the direction of the secret police, I am supposed to use sympathetic ink. I purposely left a preparation very conspicuously placed, in order to divert attention from my real means of communication, and they have swallowed the bait and fancy my friends are at their mercy.

How I shrink from the notoriety which these dastards force upon me: for five months I have had a daily paragraph. One would think that curiosity would have been satiated; but not so. And I have the uneasy consciousness that every word I utter will appear with exaggeration in the newspapers. Even my child of eight years is deemed of importance enough to have her childish speeches recorded. Well! I bide my time, confident in the retributive justice of Heaven. Rose is subject to the same rigorous restrictions as myself. I was fearful at first that she would pine, and said, 'My little darling, you must show yourself superior to these Yankees, and not pine.' She replied quickly, 'O mamma, never fear; I hate them too much. I intend to dance and sing "Jeff. Davis is coming," just to scare them!'

January 28 — This day, as I raised my barred windows, and stood before one of them to get out of the smoke and dust &c. the guard rudely called, 'Go away from that window!' and raised his musket and levelled it at me. I maintained my position without condescending to notice him, whereupon he called for the corporal of the guard. I called also for the officer of the guard, who informed me that I 'must not go to the window.' I quietly told him that, at whatever peril, I should avail myself of the largest liberty of the four walls of my prison. He told me that his guard would have orders to fire upon me. I had no idea that such monstrous regulations existed. To–day the dinner for myself and child consists of a bowl of beans swimming in grease, two slices of fat junk, and two slices of bread. Still, my consolation is, 'Every dog has his day.'

January 30 — I wonder what will happen next. My child has been ill for several days, brought on by close confinement and want of proper food. Just now I went to the door and rapped, that being the prescribed manner of making known my wants. The guard came, 'What do you want?'

'Call the corporal of the guard,' I said. 'What do you want with him?' 'That is no business of yours; call him?' 'I won't call him.' 'You shall' (rap, rap, rap). The guard — 'G—d d—n you, if you do that again I will shoot you through the door.' 'Call the corporal of the guard!' Here horrid imprecations followed. I thereupon raised the window and called, 'Corporal of the guard.' The ruffian called also, finding that I was not to be terrified by his threats. But, when the corporal came and opened the door, I was seized with laughter, for there stood the Abolitionist blubbering like a child, that *he had 'not orders to shoot the d—d Secesh woman, who was not afraid of the devil himself.'*

The rules with regard to my child were barbarously rigid. The act of commitment ran thus: — 'Miss Rose Greenhow, although not a prisoner, is subject to the same rules and regulations prescribed for a prisoner.' She was in fact as much a prisoner as I was. I had never been consulted on the subject. And when occasionally, from very shame, she was allowed to go down in the yard, the child often came up crying, from the effects of the brutality and indecency to which she was exposed. The superintendent was disposed to be kind, but there was a constant struggle going on between him and the military authorities for supremacy, by which the comfort of the prisoner was sacrificed, and his liberty abridged. It would seem to have been purposely arranged that these respective jealousies, should result in stricter vigilance over the helpless victims.

I can conceive no more horrible destiny than that which was now my lot. At nine o'clock the lights were put out, the roll was called every night and morning, and a man peered in to see that a prisoner had not escaped through the keyhole. The walls of my room swarmed with vermin and I was obliged to employ a portion of the precious hours of candlelight in burning them on the wall, in order that myself and child should not be devoured by them in the course of the night. The bed was so hard that I was obliged to fold up my clothing and place them under my child; in spite of this she would often cry out in the night, 'Oh, mamma, the bed hurts me so much.'

The tedium of my prison life at this time was greater than I can depict, and I now also began to realise the fact that my physical health was being gradually undermined by want of exercise and want of proper food. A feeling of lassitude was stealing over me, and a nervous excitability which prevented me from sleeping. My child's health was failing alarmingly also.

All her buoyancy was gone, and she would now lie for hours upon my lap with — 'Mamma, tell me a story;' and, with a heavy heart, I have often beguiled her with wild and improbable legends, until she would fall into feverish slumbers in my arms. Finally I resolved to make another appeal in behalf of my family physician being permitted to visit her, and wrote to General Wordsworth on the subject, stating her condition, &c. General Wordsworth, upon the receipt of my note, and the endorsement by the superintendent of the alarming condition of the child, gave orders that Dr. Miller (who was himself under surveillance) should have a special order to visit me.

Dr. Miller, upon visiting me, found the condition of the child critical, and represented to the General the necessity of her having more nutritious food, also air and exercise; and henceforward she was taken out very generally for a short time each day by one or other of the officers. Captain Higgins, Lieutenant Miller, and Lieutenant Holmes, were each very kind to Rose; they seemed to be ashamed of the persecution which could go so far as to threaten the life of a little child of eight years.

Saturday, May 10 — Altogether this has been a dark day in the prison. It may perhaps be well to say that my notes are principally in cipher. Captain Bryan and Harry Stewart are going to escape to–night — the attempt to be made when the guard whom they have bribed comes on at midnight. I long for the morrow, and the 'All's well!' A presentiment of evil weighs me down. I have a raging nervous headache. I have just bidden them both good–bye, and given Bryan my pistol. This continued anxiety is killing me.

Sunday Morning, May 11 — I was aroused at a little after five by the report of a rifle, and a cry enough to startle the dead: Harry Stewart had been shot by the guard whom he had bribed. Being disappointed in the attempt at night, Bryan had given it up. But poor impetuous confiding Harry Stewart was induced by the guard, when he came on again at five, to renew the attempt. Dr. Cox and the other Yankee officers confined in the room above heard the plot between the guards to murder him; the man who was in his pay saying to the other, 'When he gets fairly out of the window I will cry "Halt!" and fire at the same time; you hold your fire until he is down, and then give it to him.' The agreement by Stewart had been to give the man fifty dollars after he got down. The supposition was that they thought to rob him as they carried him round to the prison entrance. His friends, however, defeated this by drawing him up into his room. His leg was dreadfully shattered, making amputation necessary; but he was so much prostrated by loss of blood previous to the operation that he could not rally from the effects of the chloroform, but died between three and four o'clock.

On the evening of the 12th an examination took place in the prison, ostensibly for the purpose of establishing the fact of the bribery, and Dr. Cox and the other Yankee officers made the statement above; and it is inexplicable why the victim had not been warned by them of the murderous plot.

My own evidence was taken, having been cognisant of the whole affair, and hearing the agreement with the guard. I was asked if I would aid a prisoner in an attempt, &c. I answered 'Yes.' I considered it a point of honour to render any aid in money or otherwise. The woman calling herself Morris certified that I had furnished the means, through my sister, Mrs. Leonard, for the escape, &c., thereby causing the arrest and detention of my sister for several days. She demanded to be brought before the Secretary of War, when the Assistant-Secretary Watson informed her that the charge had been made against her by this woman; at the same time he released her from custody. I saw my sister but once afterwards, when she left the city as no longer a safe place for her.

My child is so nervous from a repetition of these dreadful scenes that she starts and cries out in her sleep. Horrors like this will shatter the nerves of the strongest.

13th — The murderer has been released from custody, promoted to a corporal, and put again on duty on this post. I sent for the officer of the guard, and remonstrated against it as an outrage and insult to every prisoner, and that, if allowed to remain, he would probably be killed before the day was over. He was in consequence sent away.

Saturday, May 31 — At two o'clock to-day Wood came in with the announcement that I was to start at three o'clock for Baltimore. It being impossible to be ready at that hour, the time was extended to five o'clock. There was a terrible scene between Wood and the woman Baxley last night; she raved and screamed throughout the night. I could not sleep, so have a dreadful nervous headache with which to begin my journey. I do not pretend to understand the merits of the case. In justice I must state how very kind Captain Higgins, Lieutenant Miller, and Mr. Wood have been to-day. Captain Higgins carried me throughout the prison, to say 'Good-bye' to my companions in captivity. I exhorted them all to bear up bravely under their misfortune — not that they needed it, for all burned to be free, to share in the glorious struggle now going on. God grant that they were, for many a stout arm would strike a blow for freedom!

After taking leave of these kind friends, Captain Higgins introduced Lieutenant ——— , who was, by order of the War Department, to be the chief of my escort. He had six men detailed to accompany him, making quite a military display, dressed in full uniform, with sword and carbine in hand. Outside of the prison the whole guard were drawn up under arms, besides a mounted guard of twelve men, also with swords and carbines. Before entering the carriage I turned to the officer and said, 'Sir, ere I advance further, I ask you, not as Lincoln's officer, but as a man of honour and a gentleman, are your orders from Baltimore to conduct me to a Northern prison, or to some point in the Confederacy?' He replied, with politeness and promptness, 'On my honour, madam, to conduct you to Fortress Monroe, and thence to the Southern Confederacy, in proof of which I show you my order for transportation, &c.' Satisfied on this head, I entered the carriage.

A Cold Way Home

LUCY NICKOLSON LINDSAY

JEFFERSON CITY, MISSOURI, WINTER 1861–1862

In May 1861 there was fighting in the streets of St. Louis between Union soldiers and civilians sympathetic to the South, an event that foreshadowed the bitter ruthlessness with which the war would be pursued in Missouri. By 1862 the Union was in control of most of the state, but bushwhacking, sabotage, and guerrilla warfare continued throughout the war. Atrocities were committed by both sides.

At the beginning of the Civil War we had an underground road of communication in Missouri, and by that means people that were southerners would go from one point to another, then were finally directed to Price's army in Springfield — from Jefferson City on down to Springfield. They would come from Doctor Lewis' to our house. We would then direct them on out to Versailles to Doctor James'.

One day during the time of this underground system some one knocked at our door. The ladies generally went to the door, for they were in the habit of shooting down the men (I don't know the number of men who were shot down in our own immediate neighborhood during those times). In response to the knock I went to the door. Two men were standing there. One asked me if I was Miss Lucy Nickolson. I replied that I was Miss Nickolson. He then said they wished to see me privately. I knew from the manner of their speaking they were southern men. They gave me messages from Mr. Harper and Mr. Thornton, and also from General Price. They reported that they were out of quinine and morphine, and they were very much in need of clothing. They wanted to know if the ladies could do something for them. I told them I would do all I could to help them. I said nothing at all to my mother of this interview.

The following day I got in our carriage and went over to Doctor Ellis'. Mrs. Jim Ellis and her sister were there. After relating the conversation I had had with the two southern gentlemen I finally said, "Well, I will go after these things if you (Mrs. Ellis and her sister) will go with me."

Mrs. Ellis asked, "What can you do to obtain the quinine and morphine?"

I replied, "I'll get it all right."

I did not return home but went on to Boonville. I went into Mr. Harper's store (his brother kept the general store, also a drug store, there). I knew he was a southern man; so I called him aside, telling him what his brother George had said. I then said, "Now you will have to supply me with quinine and morphine."

"I can't do it," he said, "it would be the ruination of me; but here it is, I am compelled to go down town."

I took the hint, and when he had gone I closed the door and just helped myself. I got nearly all the quinine and morphine in the store. That was the only drug store in the town. I suppose the people would have blessed whoever took it. I then went to a dry goods store. I knew the owner quite well. I told him I wanted some gray flannel and some black velvet. I bought two pieces of gray flannel. I said, "I am not going to pay for this now."

He asked, "When are you going to pay for them?"

I replied, "O, some of these days."

He wrapped the flannel and velvet up for me, and I went out of the store.

Mrs. Ellis and I cut the flannel into shirt lengths and made a skirt out of the whole two pieces. In those days skirts were made very full and plaited to the belt. It sounds almost incredible, but I put twenty–two pair of home–knit socks in that skirt. It was then the fashion to wear velvet rolls on the head; so I made two immense rolls of the velvet and filled one with quinine and the other with morphine. I put one 'round the coil of my hair and the other 'round the crown of my head. When I put the skirt on my dress wouldn't touch the ground, of course, and I looked like "Mother Bunch." Mrs. Ellis was very tall, so she gave me one of her loose wrappers; I put that on and a white apron. My brother brought out our carriage and Mrs. Ellis let us have her horses. Dressed in this way I rode out of Boonville. Mrs. Ellis went with us.

We had gone almost to Versailles when we met a company of Federals. Brother turned 'round to me and said "Now, what are you going to do? They will search the carriage?"

I said, "If you will hold your tongue and not speak a word, whether I tell a lie or not, I can get through all right."

Mrs. Ellis commenced crying.

I said, "Now, that isn't any way to do; if you are going to cry I will just give up."

The soldiers came up to where we were and halted. One asked where we were going. I replied, "I have an aunt out here about twenty-five miles who is very ill; I want to get to see her before she dies. If you want to search the carriage, you may — there is my valise."

They picked up the valise, saw it was very light — there was nothing in it — and put it down. The spokesman finally said, "You say your aunt is ill?"

I said, "Yes, sir; she is quite ill."

So they let us pass.

We got through the lines and went on out to Springfield, where we stayed three weeks and made up the flannel skirt into shirts.

On our way home we stopped in Versailles again. While there it turned bitter cold. I had just gone to bed one night when Doctor James (we were staying at his house) came in and said, "Miss Nickolson, you will have to get up. There are three thousand Federals and the home guards not five miles from here."

So brother got out the horses and carriage and off we rode. When we reached the creek it was just booming, and so bitter cold that we could scarcely breathe. Brother stopped right at the creek's edge and said, "Now, which will you do, go through the creek — 'look at it,'" he says, "or fall into the hands of the Federals or the home guards?"

I replied, "Go through the creek" and we went. The horses had to swim, the carriage rolled back and the water came up to my waist. We were dripping wet, of course, and we rode three or four miles in that condition, and my brother's beard was a sheet of ice. We rode on until we came to the house of Mr. Garrett. My brother called him out and said, "We are just from the southern army and had to come through the creek, and my sister is nearly frozen" (one whole side of my face I could not move).

They took me in and put me in a large tub of water and I remained there one entire day and night. I was nigh frozen. My big toe nails came out.

After a few days at Mr. Garrett's we started home. I was sick and excited, of course, and we had no more than reached home before Judge Baker, who was a Union man, came to our house and said to mother, "You send Miss Lucy away, for Epstine, provost marshal, knows that she has gotten home and he is going to arrest her."

We found out later that some one at Springfield, instead of keeping my visit to themselves, had written of it to their friends. So we made all arrangements to leave; but that very evening Epstine sent a party of men out and arrested me and took me to Boonville. There I was called up before him — he made a great many ugly remarks, and I expect I did, too. However, while I was there Colonel Crittenden, in the Union army, came through with his regiment. Of course he could do as he pleased, so when he heard I was there he came to see me. He expressed a great many regrets that "that Dutchman," Epstine, had had me arrested. He said, "If there is anything I can do to atone for this I will do it, for this is an outrage. I am not out to make war on women and children."

I told him, "They have my brother out at the fair grounds, a prisoner likewise; he has just returned from California and has had nothing in the world to do with this affair."

So he sent out and had him brought in and turned us both loose.

Then I went out home again. I had not been home very long before they set out to arrest me again for something — I never knew what. But I got off this time and went to Boone county, where I taught school the entire winter.

I had a good many Confederate visitors — at least would–be Confederates — as they were trying to get away. One day a note was handed me in the schoolhouse. It was from Colonel Jackman. I said, "very well, very well," and tore the note into small pieces. I met Colonel Jackman that evening and had a talk with him. The next Sunday I went to church at Rocheport.

As we came from church Colonel Connell said to me, "Why, there is a party of Federal troops! What can they be doing out there? They have an ambulance."

I said jokingly, "They are after you; they know what a rascal you are."

We went on home and had not been there long before the troops came up. Colonel Connell went out and they asked him if Miss Nickolson was there. There was a Lieutenant Wood commanding. He asked if I could be seen immediately.

I went out at once and said, "I am Miss Nickolson, what do you want?"

He replied, "I have an order here from General Guitar to arrest you."

"What! arrest me? What for?"

He said, "I cannot tell you what for, Miss Nickolson, but I have an ambulance here, and I would be glad if you would get in it and go with us without any fuss."

I replied, "Well, you don't expect me to fight, do you?"

He was very polite — I will do the man justice. I finally told Lieutenant Wood I would have to get my bonnet and wrap.

He said, "You will not try to escape?"

I said, "How can I escape? No; I am not going to escape; I will not get any one into trouble." I just took time to write a note to Mrs. Lintz, the lady whom I was boarding with, and told her to get my trunk and burn every paper and everything she could find. Then I went out and got in the ambulance and drove twenty–five miles to Columbia, where I was left at the hotel for the night. There were two soldiers detailed to walk beside me everywhere I went. When I went up to my room to go to bed they went up and stood at my door. When I went down to breakfast next morning they stood at the back of my chair. I attracted a great deal of attention.

From there we went to Centralia. They sent an escort of one hundred men with me. I said to Lieutenant Wood, "What are you sending so many men for? Are you afraid I am going to try to escape? Well, now, you had better be careful, for Colonel Jackman is in this vicinity, and you will hear from him." At this he was much alarmed.

From there they sent me to St. Louis, where I was taken before Provost Marshal Dicks. They plied me with questions; they tried to get me to tell if I had taken the quinine and morphine. I never opened my mouth. They then sent me to Gratiot Street prison. There were never but two women put in that prison — Mrs. Lowden was the other. Lieutenant Wood told Marshal Dicks to make me tell about the quinine and morphine, but I would not answer his questions. It would have gotten so many people into trouble. The drug store and everything would have been burned down, so of course I was not going to tell.

At this Gratiot Street prison there was a man by the name of Masterson, who was the keeper. Oh, he was a horrid man! When I was escorted into his presence, he said: "Huh! southern aristocrat, dressed in silk! Wonder how she'll like prisoner fare?"

When I was taken to my room this Masterson led the way; when he opened the door he said, "I hope you are not afraid of ghosts — this is Doctor McDowell's dissecting room, and the floor and table are covered with blood."

I said, "Well, I much prefer ghosts to Federals."

Mrs. Lowden, whom I have mentioned before, was in this room. When I entered she commenced screaming and said, "Oh, they haven't brought you here, have they?"

I said, "Why, this is a very good place."

She cried and cried, saying "It is bad enough to bring me, a married woman, here, but to bring a young girl here!"

Mr. Masterson then went out, closing and locking the door, and took the key with him.

Mrs. Lowden was almost dead with consumption. They had put her in this prison because she would not tell where her husband was. He was a southern courier. They had taken her away from her children, one a six–months–old baby. She told me all about it after she got quiet and composed.

Just above us was the hospital. Every time they brought our meals they would take that time to wash up the hospital, and down would come the water on us. We would have starved if it had not been for the Sisters of Charity. Mrs. Lowden was a Catholic, so the sisters would come in with their baskets every day. They always brought plenty and the meals were good, but somehow or other that water didn't taste good.

We had a straw pallet on the floor. One night Mrs. Lowden said, "O, there is something in this straw!"

We ripped the tick and found there were mice in the straw — just two. Mrs. Lowden was very frightened and began coughing and had a hemorrhage.

I went to the door and pounded on it, crying, "There is a lady in here who has a hemorrhage, and I want a doctor."

"Damn her, let her die!" was the reply. So we did not get a doctor, but we lived through it.

We were there quite awhile, I think three weeks. One day one of the officers came in and said to Mrs. Lowden, "Can you stand trouble?"

She sprang to her feet, thinking only of her children. "O," she said, "one of my children is dead."

"Yes; your baby died last night of croup," was the reply.

She commenced screaming and had another coughing fit.

I said to the officer, "There is not one word of truth in that; you know you are lying." I gave him a good tongue lashing.

He laughed and said, "I just wanted to see how much grit she had."

I said, "Well, you knew before you came in that she is sick and has no grit." He then turned and walked out.

They tried me the same way. Masterson came in and brought one of those yellow envelopes, saying, "Miss Nickolson, I have bad news for you."

"I don't suppose you have," I replied.

"Yes, I have; your brother was shot by Colonel Epstine day before yesterday."

I said, "Well, I know that isn't so. Colonel Epstine had no right to shoot him; he would have been killed before night; my brother is not shot."

"Well," he said, "you seem to know." With that remark he turned and walked out. My brother was not shot.

At the end of three weeks we were taken to the Chestnut Street prison. We stayed there two weeks.

Colonel Dicks then said all the women who had been in prison for disloyalty must be banished. They were Mrs. Frost, Mrs. Dr. Pallan, Mrs. McClure, Mrs. Clark, Mrs. Haines, Mrs. Sappington, Mrs. Smizer and others. They all had children and were obliged to leave them behind. That was the worst part of it. When we were ready to start south the children were all brought to say good-bye. You never heard such screaming — two of the ladies fainted. O, it was dreadful, one of the worst scenes I have ever seen.

Then we were all put into ambulances and carried down to the boat. I have forgotten the name of the boat. Major McKinney had charge of the ladies, and we all went down as far as Memphis. Then we got in the ambulances and were sent into Mississippi — I have forgotten the name of the town — but I do remember very well that after we got into Mississippi they sent all the provisions back and said, "Now, you are in your own country; you will have to depend upon it for something to eat and something to drink."

Mrs. Frost, Mrs. McClure, Mrs. Clark, Mrs. Smizer and myself were all in the same ambulance. We didn't have a thing to eat from Sunday night until Wednesday night. One of the Federals who was with our company came up to me with a cup of coffee and some of his hard tack, and asked me if I wouldn't eat it. He said, "It is dreadful; I have children of my own and I know what it is."

I drank the coffee, and that night we got into a farmhouse and they gave us a meal; that is to say, they gave it to our ambulance. I do not know what the others did for something to eat.

Then we went to Columbus, Miss., and there we stayed awhile. General Frost, hearing we were there, sent Colonel Smizer for us, and we went to Arkansas.

While in Arkansas Major Lindsay and I were married at General Frost's headquarters. General Price's division was there also.

The evening before our wedding a lady in Pine Bluff sent a large box with a note: "To the young lady who is to be married tomorrow eve." Upon opening the box I found it contained a most elegant white satin dress, white slippers and white kid gloves, also a lovely bridal veil. I said to Mrs. Frost, "It would be the heighth of folly for anybody to wear such beautiful garments at this distressing time when we are all nearly starving." I returned the box with a note thanking the lady for her kindness, but told her under the circumstances I would much prefer being married in what I had. However, she sent back the white kid gloves, insisting I wear them at least, so I did.

We were married in the year 1862. All the officers of the brigade were present at the wedding.

After we left Pine Bluff we were tossed from pillar to post, first one place, then another. We would pack our trunk nearly every week and move; it would be only a short while till the Federals would be on us again.

While going through Arkansas we came upon two women who were digging with spades along the side of the road. Upon making inquiry we found they were digging a grave for a child. Major Lindsay got out of the ambulance, took the spade, finished digging the grave, buried the child and said a prayer.

I was in Columbus the night after that terrible battle when 800 of our soldiers lay dead upon the field. There was scarcely a family in that large city that did not have some loved one dead or dying. All night long we could hear the screams of the women.

I was in Arkansas after one of the battles. We were traveling and stopped for the night at a farmhouse. The lady at this house had just received word that her son had been killed that day, and her husband and another son had been killed the day before. Think of it! Now they say "forget;" but we can't forget, no, nor can we forgive. I can go so far as to wish them no harm.

The Sleep of the Living

PHOEBE YATES PEMBER

RICHMOND, VIRGINIA, MAY 1862

As matron of Chimborazo Hospital, Phoebe Pember's official responsibilities were administrative. She ordered and distributed supplies, supervised the cooking and serving of food, and had charge of the whiskey. As the war progressed, she increasingly spent her time caring for the wounded.

About this time, an attack on Drewry's Bluff, which guarded Richmond on the James River side, was expected, and it was made before the hospital was in readiness to receive the wounded. The cannonading could be heard distinctly in the city, and dense smoke descried rising from the battlefield. The Richmond people had been too often, if not through the wars at least within sight and hearing of its terrors, to feel any great alarm.

The inhabitants lying in groups, crowded the eastern brow of the hill above Rockets and the James River; overlooking the scene, and discussing the probable results of the struggle; while the change from the dull, full boom of the cannon to the sharp rattle of musketry could be easily distinguished. The sun was setting amidst stormy, purple clouds; and when low upon the horizon sent long slanting rays of yellow light from beneath them, athwart the battle scene, throwing it in strong relief. The shells burst in the air above the fortifications at intervals, and with the aid of glasses dark blue masses of uniforms could be discerned. About eight o'clock the slightly wounded began to straggle in with a bleeding hand, or contused arm or head, bound up in any convenient rag.

Their accounts were meagre, for men in the ranks never know anything about general results — they almost always have the same answer ready, "We druv 'em nowhere."

In another half–hour, vehicles of all kinds crowded in, from a wheelbarrow to a stretcher, and yet no orders had been sent me to prepare for the wounded. Few surgeons had remained in the hospital; the proximity to the field tempting them to join the ambulance committee, or ride to the scene of action; and the officer of the day, left in charge, naturally objected to my receiving a large body of suffering men with no arrangements made for their comfort, and but few in attendance.

I was preparing to leave for my home at the Secretary of the Navy, where I returned every night, when the pitiful sight of the wounded in ambulances, furniture, wagons, carts, carriages, and every kind of vehicle that could be impressed detained me. To keep them unattended to, while being driven from one full hospital to another, entailed unnecessary suffering, and the agonized outcry of a desperately wounded man to "take him in, for God's sake, or kill him," decided me to countermand the order of the surgeon in charge that "they must be taken elsewhere, as we had no accommodations prepared." I sent for him, however.

He was a kind–hearted, indolent man, but efficient in his profession, and a gentleman; and seeing my extreme agitation, tried to reason with me, saying our wards were full, except a few vacant and unused ones, which our requisitions had failed to furnish with proper bedding and blankets. Besides, a large number of the surgeons were absent, and the few left would not be able to attend to all the wounds at that late hour of the night. I proposed in reply that the convalescent men should be placed on the floor on blankets, or bed–sacks filled with straw, and the wounded take their place, and, purposely construing his silence into consent, gave the necessary orders, early offering my services to dress simple wounds, and extolling the strengths of my nerves.

He let me have my way (may *his* ways be of pleasantness and his paths of peace), and so, giving Miss G. orders to make an unlimited supply of coffee, tea, and stimulants, armed with lint, bandages, castile soap, and a basin of warm water, I made my first essays in the surgical line. I had been spectator often enough to be skillful. The first object that needed my care was an Irishman. He was seated upon a bed with his hands crossed, wounded in both arms by the same bullet. The blood was soon washed away, wet lint applied, and no bones being broken, the bandages easily arranged.

"I hope that I have not hurt you much," I said with some trepidation. "These are the first wounds that I ever dressed."

"Sure they be the most illegant pair of hands that ever touched me, and the lightest," he gallantly answered. "And I am all right now."

From bed to bed till long past midnight, the work continued. Fractured limbs were bathed, washed free of blood and left to the surgeon to set. The men were so exhausted by forced marches, lying in entrenchments and loss of sleep that few even awoke during the operations. If aroused to take nourishment or stimulant they received it with closed eyes, and a speedy relapse into unconsciousness. The next morning, but few had any recollection of the events of the night previous.

There were not as many desperate wounds among the soldiers brought in that night as usual. Strange to say, the ghastliness of wounds varied much in the different battles, perhaps from the nearness or distance of contending parties. One man was an exception and enlisted my earnest sympathy. He was a Marylander although serving in a Virginia company. There was such strength of resignation in his calm blue eye.

"Can you give me a moment?" he said.

"What shall I do for you?"

"Give me some drink to revive me, that I do not die before the surgeon can attend to me."

His pulse was strong but irregular, and telling him that a stimulant might induce fever, and ought only to be administered with a doctor's prescription, I inquired where was he wounded.

Right through the body. Alas!

The doctor's dictum was, "No hope: give him anything he asks for;" but five days and nights I struggled against this decree, fed my patient with my own hands, using freely from the small store of brandy in my pantry and cheering him by words and smiles. The sixth morning on my entrance he turned an anxious eye on my face, and hope had died out of his, for the cold sweat stood in beads there, useless to dry, so constantly were they renewed.

What comfort could I give? Only silently open the Bible, and read to him without comment the ever–living promises of his Maker. Glimpses too of that abode where the "weary are at rest." Tears stole down his cheek, but he was not comforted.

"I am an only son," he said, "and my mother is a widow. Go to her, if you ever get to Baltimore and tell her that I died in what I consider the defense of civil rights and liberties. I may be wrong. God alone knows. Say how kindly I was nursed, and that I had all I needed. I cannot thank you, for I have no breath, but we will meet up there." He pointed upward and closed his eyes, that never opened again upon this world.

{}

We Run for Our Lives

SARAH MORGAN

NEAR BATON ROUGE, LOUISIANA, AUGUST 1862

Sarah, her mother, and her sister, Miriam, left their home in Baton Rouge to escape the fighting and went to the plantation of Dr. John T. Nolan across the river from Baton Rouge. Linwood, to which they retreated to get further away from the war, was the plantation of General Albert G. Carter, whose daughter, Lydia, was married to Sarah's brother, Gibbes. Sarah's mother and Miriam visited Lilly, another of Sarah's sisters, who was living in Clinton, Louisiana, before returning to the Carter plantation.

August 10th. Sunday — Is this really Sunday? Never felt less pious, or less seriously disposed! Listen to my story, and though I will, of course, fall far short of the actual terror that reigned, yet it will show it in a luke warm light, that can at least recall the excitement to me. To begin, then, last evening, about six o'clock, as we sat reading, sewing, and making lint in the parlor, we heard a tremendous shell whizzing past, which those who watched, said passed not five feet above the house. Of course there was a slight stir among the unsophisticated; though we who had passed through bombardments, sieges, & alarms of all kinds, coolly remarked "a shell," and kept quiet. (The latter class was not very numerous.) It was from one of the three Yankee boats that lay in the river close by (the Essex and two gunboats) which were sweeping teams, provisions, and negroes from all plantations they stopped at from B.R. up. The negroes, it is stated, are to be armed against us as in town, where all those who manned the cannon on Tuesday, were, for the most part, killed, and served them right!

Another shell was fired at a carriage containing Mrs. Durald and several children, under pretense of discovering if she was a guerilla, doubtless. Fortunately she was not hurt, however. By the time the little émeute [disturbance] had subsided, determined to have a frolic, Miss Walters, Ginnie and I got on our horses, and rode off down the Arkansas lane, to have a gallop and a peep at the gunboats from the levee. But mother's entreaties prevented us from going that near, as she cried that it was well known they fired at every horse or vehicle they saw in the road, seeing a thousand guerillas in every puff of dust, and we were sure to be killed, murdered, and all sorts of bloody deaths awaited us; so to satisfy her, we took the road about a mile from the river, in full view, however.

We had not gone very far before we met a Mr. Watson, a plain farmer of the neighborhood, who begged us to go back. "You'll be fired on, ladies, sure! you don't know the danger! Take my advice and go home as quick as possible before they shell you! They shoot buggies and carriages, and of course they wont mind *horses* with women! Please go home!" But Ginnie, who had taken a fancy to go on, acted as spokeswoman, and determined to go on in spite of his advice, so, nothing loth to follow her example, we thanked him, and rode on. Another met us; looked doubtful, said it was not so dangerous if the Yankees did not see the dust; but if they did, we would be pretty apt to see a shell soon after. Here was frolic! so we rode on some mile or two beyond, but failing to see anything startling, turned back again.

About two miles from here, we met Mr. Watson coming at full speed. The ladies he said, had sent him after us in all haste; there was a report that the whole coast was to be shelled; a lady had passed flying with her children; the carriage was ordered out; they were only waiting for us, to run too. We did not believe a word of it, and were indignant at their credulity, as well as determined to persuade them to remain where they were, if possible. When told their plan was to run to the house formerly used as a guerilla camp, we laughed heartily. Suppose the Yankees fired a shell in it to discover its inhabitants? The idea of choosing a spot so well known! And what fun in running to a miserable hole, when we might sleep comfortably here? I am afraid rebellion was in the air. Indeed, an impudent little negro who threw open the gate for us, interrupted Ginnie in the midst of a tirade with a sly "Here's the beginning of a little fuss!"

We found them all crazy with fear. I did not say much; I was too provoked to trust myself to argue with so many frightened women. I only said I saw no necessity. Ginnie resisted, but finally succumbed. Mr. Watson, whom we had enlisted on our side also, said it was by no means necessary, but if we were determined, we might go to his house about four miles away, and stay there. It was very small, but we were welcome. We had in the mean time thrown off our riding skirts, and stood just in our plain dresses, though the others were freshly dressed for an Exodus. Before the man left, the carriage came, though by that time we had drawn half the party on our side; we said we would take supper, and decide after, so he went off.

In a few moments, a rocket went up from one of the boats, which attracted our attention. Five minutes after, we saw a flash directly before us. "See it? Lightning, I expect," said Phillie. The others all agreed; but I kept quiet, knowing that some, at least, knew what it was as well as I, and determined not to give the alarm — for I was beginning to feel foolish. Before half a minute more came a tearing, hissing sound, a sky rocket whose music I had heard before. Instantly I remembered my running bag, and flew up stairs to get it, escaping just in time from the scene which followed on the gallery which was afterwards most humorously described to me. But I was out of hearing of the screams of each (and yet I must have heard them), neither saw Miss Walters tumble against the wall, or mother turn over her chair, or the general mêlée that followed, in which Mrs. Walters, trying to scale the carriage, was pulled out by uncle Will who shouted to his plunging horses first, then to the other unreasoning creatures "Whoa, there! 'taint safe! take to the fields! take to the woods! run to the sugar house! take to your heels!" in a frenzy of excitement.

I escaped all that, and was putting on my hoops and hastily catching up any article that presented itself to me in my speed, when the shell burst over the roof, and went rattling down on the gallery, according to the account of those then below. Two went far over the house, out of sight. All three were seen by Mr. Watson, who came galloping up in a few moments, crying "Ladies, for God's sake leave the house!" Then I heard mother calling "Sarah! You will be killed! leave your clothes and run!" and a hundred ejaculations that came too fast for me to answer except by an occasional "Coming, if you will send me a candle." Candle was the same as though I had demanded a hand grenade, in mother's opinion, for she was sure it would be the signal for a bombardment of my exposed room; so I tossed down my bundles, swept comb and hair-pins in my bosom (all points up), and ravished a candle from some one. How quickly I got on, then! I saved the most useless of articles with the greatest zeal, and probably left the most serviceable ones. One single dress did my running bag contain — a white linen cambric with a tiny pink flower — the one I wore when I told Hal good bye for the last time. The others I left. When I got down with my knapsack, mother, Phillie and Mrs. Walters were. . .

At Randallson's Landing. August 11th — I don't mean those ladies were, but that I am at present. I'll account for it after I have disposed of the stampede. Imagine no interruption and continue — in the carriage urging uncle Will to hurry on, and I had barely time to thrust my sack under their feet before they were off. Lilly [Nolan] and Miss Walters were already in the buggy, leaving Ginnie and me to follow on horseback. I ran up after my riding skirt, which I was surprised to find behind a trunk, and rolled up in it, was my running bag, with all my treasures! I was very much provoked at my carelessness; indeed I cannot imagine how it got there, for it was the first thing I thought of. When I got back, there was no one to be seen except Ginnie and two negroes who held our horses, and who disappeared the instant we were mounted; so with the exception of two women who were running to the woods, we were the only ones on the lot, until Mr. Watson galloped up to urge us on.

Again I had to notice this peculiarity about women — that the married ones are invariably the first to fly, in time of danger, and always leave the young ones to take care of themselves. Here were our three matrons, prophesying that the house would be burnt, the Yankees upon us, and all murdered in ten minutes, flying down the guerilla lane, and leaving us to encounter the horrors they foretold, alone.

It was a splendid gallop in the bright moonlight, over the fields, only it was made uncomfortable by the jerking of my running bag, until I happily thought of turning it before. A hard ride of four miles in about twenty minutes brought us to the house of the man who so kindly offered his hospitality. It was a little hut, about as large as our parlor, and already crowded to overflowing, as he was entertaining three families from B.R. Cant imagine where he put them, either. But it seems to me the poorer the man, the smaller the house, the greater the hospitality you meet with. There was [sic] so many of us, that there was not room on the balcony to turn. The man wanted to prepare supper, but we declined, as Phillie had sent back for ours which we had missed.

I saw another instance of the pleasure the vulgar take in the horrible. A Mr. Hill, speaking of Dr. Nolan, told Phillie he had no doubt he had been sent to New Orleans on the Whiteman, that carried Genl. Williams' body; and that every soul had gone down on her. Fortunately, just then the overseer brought a letter from him saying he had gone on another boat, or the man's relish of the distressing, might have been gratified.

It was so crowded there, that we soon suggested going a short distance beyond to Mr. Lobdell's, and staying there for the night as all strenuously objected to our returning home, as there was danger from prowling Yankees. So we mounted again, and after a short ride, we reached the house, where all were evidently asleep. But necessity knows no rules; and the driver soon aroused an old gentleman who came out and invited us in. A middle aged lady met us, and made us perfectly at home by leaving us to take care of ourselves; most people would have thought it indifference; but I knew it was manqué de savoir faire, merely, and preferred doing as I pleased. If she had been officious, I would have been embarrassed.

So we walked in the moonlight, Ginnie and I, while the rest sat in the shade, and all discussed the fun of the evening, those who had been most alarmed laughing loudest. The old gentleman insisted that we girls had been the cause of it all; that our white bodices (I wore a russian shirt) and black skirts could easily have caused us to be mistaken for men. That at all events, three or four people on horseback would be a sufficient pretext for firing a shell or two. "In short, young ladies," he said, "there is no doubt in my mind that you were mistaken for guerillas, and that they only waited to give you time to reach the woods where they hear they have a camp, before shooting at you. In short, take my advice, and never mount a horse again when there is a Yankee in sight."

We were highly gratified at being mistaken for them, and pretended to believe it was true. I hardly think he was right, though, it is too preposterous. Pourtant, Sunday morning the Yankees told a negro they did not mean to touch the house, but were shooting at some guerillas at a camp just beyond. We know the last guerilla left the parish five days ago.

Our host insisted on giving us supper, though Phillie represented that ours was on the road; and by eleven o'clock, tired alike of moonlight and fasting, we gladly accepted, and rapidly made the preserves and batter cakes fly. Ours was a garret room, well finished, abounding in odd closets and corners, with curious dormer windows that were reached by long little corridors. I should have slept well; but I lay awake all night. Mother and I occupied a narrow single bed, with a bar of the thickest, heaviest material imaginable. Suffocation awaited me inside, gnats and mosquitoes out. In order to be strictly impartial, I lay awake to divide my time equally between the two attractions, and think I succeeded pretty well. So I spent the night on the extreme edge of the bed, never turning over, but fanning mother constantly.

I was not sorry when day break appeared, but dressed and ascended the observatory to get a breath of air. Below me, I beheld four wagons loaded with the young Mrs. Lobdell's baggage. The Yankees had visited them in the evening, swept off every thing they could lay their hands on, and with a sick child she was obliged to leave her house in the night, and fly to her father in law. I wondered at their allowing her four wagons of trunks and bundles; it was very kind. If I was a Federal, I think it would kill me to hear the whisper of "Hide the silver" where ever I came. Their having frequently relieved families of such trifles, along with negroes, teams, etc., has put others on their guard.

As I sat in the parlor in the early morning, Mrs. Walters en blouse volante and all échevelée, came in to tell me of Mr. Lobdell's misfortunes. "They took his negroes; (right hand up) his teams; (left hand up) his preserves; (both hands clutching her hair); they swept off everything, except four old women who could not walk! they told him if he didn't come report himself, they'd come fetch him in three days! they beggared him!" (both eyes rolling like a ship in a storm). I could not help laughing. Mr. Bird sat on the gallery, and had been served in the same way, with the addition of a pair of handcuffs for a little while. It was not a laughing matter; but the old lady made it comical by her gestures.

When we suggested returning [to the Nolan home], there was another difficulty. All said it was madness; that the Yankees would sack the house and burn it over our heads, we would be insulted, etc. I said no one yet had ever said an impudent thing to me, and Yankees certainly would not attempt it; but the old gentleman told me I did not know what I was talking about; so I hushed, but determined to return, Ginnie and I sat an hour on horseback waiting for the others to settle what they would do, and after having half roasted ourselves in the sun, they finally agreed to go too, and we set off in a gallop which we never broke until we reached the house which to our great delight we found standing, and not infested with Yankees.

Linwood. Aug. 12th — Another resting place! Out of reach of shells for the first time since last April! For how long, I wonder? for where ever we go, we bring shells and Yankees. Would not be surprised at a visit from them out here, now!

Let me take up the thread of that never ending story, and account for my present position. It all seems tame now; but it was very exciting at the time. As soon as I threw down bonnet and gloves, I commenced writing; but before I had halfway finished, mother who had been holding a consultation down stairs, ran up to say the overseer had advised us all to leave, as the place was not safe; and that I must pack up instantly, as unless we got off before the Essex came up, it would be impossible to leave at all. All was commotion; every one flew to pack up. Phillie determined to go to her friends at Grosse Tête, and insisted on carrying us off with her. But I determined to reach Miriam and Lilly if possible, rather than put the Federal army between us.

All en déshabillé I commenced to pack our trunk, but had scarcely put an article in, when they cried the Essex was rounding the point, and our last opportunity passing away. Then I flew; and by the time the boat got opposite to us, the trunk was locked, and I sat on it completely dressed waiting for the wagon. We had then to wait for the boat to get out of sight, to avoid a broadside; so it was half past ten before we set off, fortified by several glasses of buttermilk apiece. All went in the carriage except Ginnie, Lilly [Nolan], and me, and we perched on the baggage in the wagon.

Such stifling heat! The wagon jarred dreadfully, and seated at the extreme end, on a wooden trunk traversed by narrow slats, Ginnie and I were jolted until we lost our breath, all down Arkansas lane, when we changed for the front part. I shall never forget the heat of that day. Four miles beyond, the carriage stopped at some house, and still determined to get over the river, I stepped in the little cart that held our trunk, drove up to the side of it, and insisted on mother's getting in, rather than going the other way with Phillie. I had a slight discussion, and overcame mother's reluctance and Phillie's objections with some difficulty; but finally prevailed on the former to get in the cart, and jolted off amid a shower of reproaches, regrets, and good byes. I knew I was right though; and the idea reconciled me to the heat, dust, jarring, and gunboat that was coming up behind us.

Six miles more brought us to Mr. Cain's, where we arrived at two o'clock, tired, dirty, and almost unrecognizable. We were received with the greatest cordiality in spite of that. Mother knew both him and his wife, but though I had never seen either, the latter kissed me as affectionately as though we had known each other. It was impossible to cross when the gunboat was in sight, so they made us stay with them until the next morning. A bath, and clean clothes soon made me quite presentable, and I really enjoyed the kindness we met with, in spite of a "tearing" headache, and a distended feeling about the eyes as though I never meant to close them again — the consequence of my vigil, I presume. O those dear, kind people! I shall not soon forget them. Mr. Cain told mother he believed he would keep me; at all events, he would make an exchange, and give her his only son in my place. I told him I was willing, as mother thought much more of her sons than of her daughters.

I forgot to say that we met Genl. Allen's partner a mile or two from Dr. Nolan's, who told us it was a wise move; that he had intended recommending it. All he owned had been carried off, his plantation stripped. He said he had no doubt that all the coast would be ravaged, and they had promised to burn his, and many other houses, and Dr. Nolan's though it might *possibly* be spared in consideration of his being a prisoner, and his daughters being unprotected, would most probably suffer with the rest, but even if spared, it was no place for women. He offered to take charge of all, and send the furniture in the interior before the Yankees should land, which Phillie gladly accepted.

What a splendid rest I had at Mrs. Cain's! I was not conscious of being alive, until awaked abruptly in the early morning, with a confused sense of having dreamed something very pleasant. The first dream in a strange house comes true; but I tried in vain to recall it. Sometimes it was all before me, but the same instant it was gone. I only remembered writing a letter to Howell, in which I wished to tell him something that I did not wish to be seen by someone else who must first read it, and that Mr. Talbot's name stood out in most extraordinary relief on the page; but what connection it had with the rest, I could not remember.

Mr. Cain accompanied us to the ferry some miles above, riding by the buggy, and leaving us under care of Mr. Randallson, after seeing us in the large flat, took his leave. After an hour spent at the hotel after landing on this side, we procured a conveyance and came on to Mr. Elder's, where we astonished Lilly by our unexpected appearance very much. Miriam had gone over to spend the day with her, so we were all together, and talked over our adventures with the greatest glee. After dinner Miriam and I came over here to see them all, leaving the others to follow later. I was very glad to see Helen Carter once more. If I was not, I hope I may live in Yankee land! — and I cant invoke a more dreadful punishment than that.

Well! here we are, and heaven only knows our next move. Mother stays with Lilly, Miriam and I here. But we must settle on some spot, which seems impossible in the present state of affairs, when no lodgings are to be found. I feel like a homeless beggar. Will P. told them here, that he doubted if our house were still standing, as the fight occurred just back of it, and every volley directed towards it. He says he thought of it every time the cannon was fired, knowing where the shot would go. O my lost home! Wonder if Tiche left my poor little bird there? I'll never get over it if she did. Poor Jimmy! What an extraordinary waste of paper, in recording all the trifles that led to our forsaking our former haven! But if I had had the power to describe it fully (for absurd as it may seem, it is very much abridged) it would really be an undertaking.

The Pain of Remembering

CORNELIA PEAKE MCDONALD

WINCHESTER, VIRGINIA, SEPTEMBER 1862

Wood and Anne were children of Angus McDonald by his first wife. Wood was killed in the Seven Days fighting outside Richmond in the summer of 1862. Cornelia's daughter, Bessie, whom she calls Angus's "pretty baby girl," was born in October 1861 and died in August 1862.

The merry sound of voices in the parlour recalls the old happy time when we were at peace, and when none of our circle was silent forever. I can never forget the tones of Wood's rich, sweet voice singing as he generally was when in the house, or walking about the yard. Sitting alone, I can almost think I hear him singing among the trees, and expect to see him lolling on a bench with his books, or playing with the children on the grass, when at home during his vacation.

I had never understood him well till he became a man. When a boy he was wayward, as all boys are, had his sharp angles. Only when he was grown did I understand him fully, and know what a noble affectionate character he was, and what a good warm heart he had. The boy's roughness had all gone and given place to a manly grace, and a tender gallantry that became him so well.

That last summer when he was at home from the University none of the family were here but he and me and the children.

I enjoyed so much the sweet summer nights sitting on the porch with him, talking in the dim starlight of all the beautiful things we had read or seen in poetry or in nature.

I repeated one night an old fragment of a poem I had seen somewhere long ago, not remembering where or by whom it was written.

> We parted in silence, we parted by night
> On the banks of that lovely river,
> Where the fragrant limes their boughs unite
> We met, and we parted forever!

The nightbird sang, and the stars above
　　Told many a touching story
Of friends long gone to the kingdom of love
　　Where the soul wears its mantle of glory.

We parted in silence — Our cheeks were wet
　　With the tears that were past controlling
And we vowed we would never, no never forget,
　　And those vows at the time were consoling.
But the lips that echoed that vow of mine
　　Are cold as that lovely river,
And the eye, the beautiful spirit's shrine,
　　Has shrouded its fires forever!

And now on the midnight sky I look
　　And my heart grows full to weeping,
Each star is to me a sealed book,
　　Some tale of the loved one keeping.
We parted in silence — We parted in tears
　　On the banks of that lovely river,
But the colour and bloom of those bygone years
　　Shall hang on its waters forever!

He admired it very much and seemed much moved by it. I remarked that it was possible its beauty consisted more of the melody of the verse, the peculiar rhythm of the measure, than in the poetry itself. He said no, that it was poetry, beautiful and touching, and asked me to repeat it again. How little I thought that the verses that had no associations for me, then would be from that time freighted with memories of him. I never think of them, or look upon "the midnight sky" without seeing his image as he then was before my mind.

He was so sad when he went away from home the last time. He looked back at the house often as he went till he was out of sight.

I could not help recalling how dejected he was, and how silent he sat as I made the preparations for his departure. His wistful glance around at everything as he was leaving.

He often went to see his sisters at Charlottesville while the army was in that neighborhood, and the last evening he spent with them he proposed singing some hymns and began himself to sing —

　　"My days are gliding swiftly by."

Anne followed him down to the gate. He said good bye, and looked long and earnestly in her face; went some distance and returned to where she stood in the moonlight, and kissed her again.

In three days from that time he was lying a corpse on the battlefield.

The many voices in the parlour, the laughter and chat of the young people make me remember all I have lost. I miss the sweet blue eyes that sparkled with joy to see me; the outstretched arms and lovely smile. The white baby face hid in the coffin and the smell of those fading roses I can never forget. That odour seems always to linger near.

A bitter grief it was to my husband to lose at the same time his young soldier and his pretty baby girl, who, he had said, was to be his old age's darling.

I remember a sojourn in the Alleghanies once in my early married life, and it is a part of my experience that I never could forget. I went on horseback with my husband, Angus, and Anne to a mountain where he owned some land and was then surveying it. We took up our quarters at a country house, a poor one as far as external appearance went, but abounding in all the most delightful and precious things of life. Cool delicious air, fragrant with the breath of the pines and hemlocks, and the fresh earth that plow had never touched, and within, the warmest welcome I ever remember to have received, for the host was a tall old mountaineer whose heart my husband had won when employed as Commonwealth's Attorney, he prosecuted a man who had killed the son of the old man — Mr. Dixon. His manner of conducting the case, and the speeches he made so won the old man that he was ever after his willing slave, he and his six other sons, all nearly seven feet high.

When we sat down to our meals we were waited on by the host, his wife, and some of his sons; they never sat down with us. And oh, the delicate, rich food! Cold milk, thick with cream, from a dairy on the side of the mountain, fresh venison steaks, the whitest bread, and tenderest broiled chicken revelling in the sweetest butter. No king ever fared better than that; and then every day the rides through the mountains, the views from first one point and then another; the deep glens we visited, the dark hemlock groves we peered into, but could not penetrate except with our eyes. The heights we climbed to see spread out before us billows of mountain tops below us and far away from us, green lanes through the thick trees, and above all we had the joy of youth and love to make every scene lovely. One day in those mountains I can never forget. We got off our horses at midday by a trout stream in which we, the ladies, were to fish, and on the banks of which we were to dine. The bank of the stream was very steep and leaning over it and looking down we could see down in the deep water, six or eight feet deep and clear as crystal, the brightly speckled trout darting about, the red, green, gold, and blue spots glittering in the sun as it shone down over our heads. On the sides of the stream the pink laurel bloomed in such profusion that the reflection in the clear water made it a vivid pink, and all up the high mountain sides, and all around us the flowers hung; the lovely pink bell–like flowers with the delicate specks of black inside, and the glossy, deep green leaves.

We fished for trout and when the gentlemen joined us we dined, and that dinner, nothing on this earth of food was ever so sweet. The midday sun was not hot as it shone directly down on us, and the leaves waved up and down over our heads in the gentle air, and we all enjoyed so intensely, that after a time we had nothing to say.

Presently the gentlemen dozed on the soft grass, and Anne and I went off some distance down the stream where was a waterfall of about five feet high. We took off our dresses, put on wrappers and went in and sat on the rocks under the fall. It poured its clear cold water over us and we were young and strong and had never a rheumatism or any ill consequence. We rode back in the shadow of the mountains and sat down to our trout for supper; sat out late after listening to the sighing of the night wind through the tall trees, and the lovely notes of some nightbird. Went to bed and slept sweetly.

That was a day of days. Well, on this November day we kept on our winding way along the shelving road till we came out on the bank of the Shenandoah. I looked long at the smooth peaceful water, at the shadows of the trees and clouds reflected on its shining surface.

When a child I spent a few years in the neighborhood of the Shenandoah, and nothing ever so fascinated me as it did, either afar when its glassy bosom mirrored the blue sky with its garments of white clouds, the fringe of thick trees on its brink, and the large wild birds sailing serenely over it, or when near enough to look down into the clear green water. I used to spend hours gazing on it and fancying, as I often did when suffering from a childish trouble or disappointment, or from that heartsickness that only children feel, that weariness and disgust for the sordid things of life; that down there in those blue depths was a world of sweet repose, a blissful, fanciful world peopled with beings different from, and more delightful, than any that I knew.

A little story of an Indian maiden and her brother, Hawkseye, had I suppose, given the fancy, for I remember well that for days after I read of her plunge into the still waters of the lake of Canandagua I wept and grieved at her fate; and that of her brother, turning sadly away from her watery grave, and the bones of his fathers to pursue his lonely journey towards the setting sun, whither his people had already gone. Two years after we left the neighborhood I met some children in traveling who belonged to a family living in the town of Canandagua and near the lake.

I remember the deep interest with which I regarded the favored children who had dwelt by that enchanted lake, and my asking one of them if she had ever seen the place where the maiden had sprung from the rock into the lake, and if she had known Hawkseye.

PART III

Advance and Retreat
1863

Gathered like a knot within and without the window, we six women up here watched in the faint star light the flashes from the guns, and silently wondered which of our friends were lying stiff and dead, and then shuddering at the thought, betook our selves to silent prayer. I think we know what it is to "wrestle with God in prayer"; we had but one thought. Yet for women, we took it almost too coolly. No tears, no cries, no fear, though for the first five minutes every body's teeth chattered violently. Mrs. Carter had her husband in Fenner's battery, the hottest place if they are attacked by the land force, and yet to my unspeakable relief she betrayed no more emotion than we who had only friends there.

— Sarah Morgan, 1863

An Invasion of Graybacks

JULIA MORGAN

MARIETTA, GEORGIA, JANUARY 1863

The Battle of Murfreesboro was fought December 31, 1862. By the time Julia Morgan saw the wounded soldiers at Marietta, several days had passed since they had been wounded, and they had traveled several hundred miles.

Nancy [Morgan's nurse] was my courier, always on the alert to get startling news. After the battle of Murfreesboro she came up early one morning and told me the house was filled with wounded soldiers. Their destiny was Atlanta, as they had hospitals there and none at Marietta at that time. The poor fellows had heard that a great many Nashville refugees were there, and as the train stopped they slipped off in the dark and came to the hotel and sent word to us that they wanted to see the Nashville ladies; but just at the time most of them had left. I got up though, and as soon as I dressed I went down to see them. I went from room to room, and found twenty–seven poor fellows — some terribly wounded — shot in the legs and arms, and one had his eye put out. Different parts of the brave boys' bodies felt the effects of the Yankee bullets. I went in one room, and found Dr. Lowe, from Shelby County, shot through the eye, the ball coming out of the back of his neck, and it was strange that it did not kill him. His hair was very long, all bloody, and dried to his face, and all caked with blood around his eye, or the socket, as the eye was gone. I felt sick at heart, but went to work with my nurse to assist me. I had warm water brought, and with a soft cloth bathed the bloody hair until I could remove it from the wounded part, got a pair of scissors, and soon made the poor fellow more comfortable by cutting off his long, matted hair, and a more grateful man I never saw. He was in a fearful condition, but as I looked at the poor, sightless eye and pleased face I felt repaid for my efforts; and he told me he felt more comfortable and so thankful to me. I did not take time to hunt help, but went from room to room. The wounded men were all dirty, hungry, and bloody. My heart would give a big bound as I looked eagerly into each face, thinking maybe some of our Nashville boys were among them. I found Capt. Jackson, from the Hermitage, Capt. Lynn and Mr. Herran, from near Memphis, and others, whose names, after the lapse of so many years, I have forgotten, but all in the same condition: dirty, bloody, and hungry. As fare was high at the hotel, and most of the poor fellows were without money, I sent Nancy out, bought light bread, butter, and eggs, and had strong coffee made in my room, and we went to work cooking, and in a little while had enough prepared for them to eat to satiety. The next thing to be done was to get them some clothes. I started and hunted up all the Nashville ladies at the other hotel, and those boarding in town, and also called on the ladies of Marietta to help us. I had a hundred yards of pressed flannel my husband had bought to use in case of an emergency, as goods were getting very scarce; but when such scenes of distress were brought to me, my first impulse was to help relieve, so I got the ladies together and we cut out and made up as long as the cloth held out, and what I lacked others furnished. Hurrying and sewing for several days, we got all supplied with flannel shirts, drawers, and undershirts, and as "cleanliness is next to godliness," they felt nearer to heaven in clean beds, and new underclothes, and good women around them ministering to their wants, than they had in some time before. In the meantime we sent for Drs. Stewart and Setz, and they did all they could for their comfort. Mr. White, the proprietor, came to me and said: "I am a poor man and am not able to feed them, but will let them stay until places can be provided for them." I told them I would see to their being fed, and I did; and had them well fed, too. I put on my bonnet and started out to hunt homes in private families for them, and I had good success. Mrs. Gen. Hansel took four; Mrs. Col. Atkinson, four; Mrs. Brumby, three; Mrs. Dennead, three; and so on until all had comfortable homes provided, and I felt happy to know that they would be so well cared for. Most of the ladies sent their carriages for them, and they went with thankful hearts. As they were the first wounded soldiers who had stopped in Marietta, they all fared sumptuously, and Dr. Setz and dear old Dr. Stewart visited them regularly and did all in their power to alleviate their sufferings. Some of the boys were extremely ill from their wounds, as erysipelas set in. I got a home for two country boys who were badly wounded, with an old lady and gentleman who had no children. Two days after, the old lady sent for me to come to see her on important business. I hurried down, called for her, and she said: "You must move those boys from my house, I can't stand them." I asked what on earth was the matter. She told me her place and all she had was about to walk off with, as the soldiers called them, "graybacks." The neat housekeeper was in despair. Allusion to these pests is not very delicate, but they were common in the army, where so many were crowded together they could not help getting them on their clothing. It made no difference how neat and cleanly they were, they were all in the same category, liable to the "pests." I said: "Please don't move them; one has high fever now and is delirious, and the other is too sick to be disturbed." I got some one to help her clean her house; then sent for a negro barber and told him I would pay him well if he would help me. He asked me what I wanted done, and I told him to get a large kettle, heat water, then get a big tub, soap, and towel. He got every thing in readiness and attempted to take one of the soldier's clothes off, and I was waiting to hear the result. The negro came out puffing and blowing, and said: "I can't do anything with him. He fit me and scratched, and tried to bite me." I told him that was a small matter, not to give up, but to go and hire a strong man to help him, for I told him it must be done. He went off for assistance, and in a little while was back with help. After waiting quite a time, and hearing a big fuss in the room, he came out and said: "Missus, I done soap him and scrub him good, and now he is done dress up nice." I thanked him and told him to go through the same process with the other one. He did so, and had no trouble with him. He came and told me he had finished them both, and I then directed him to cut their hair. This was accomplished, and he sent for me to come in and see how well he had done his work. Strange to say, the delirium was relieved, fever cooled, and they began to improve from that bath. The next thing was to look after their clothing. They each had a suit of Confederate gray, and as clothes were scarce and hard to get, I could not think of throwing them away. I had them all taken out in the yard and told the barber to go right off and get an old darky to come and wash them. He soon brought an old woman, and, for a stipulated price, she undertook the job. She looked at the clothes, and said: "Missus, dem's powerful 'ceitful t'ings, dey hides in ebery seam and crack. You has to bile dem all day and all night, and den dey ain't dead." I told her to "bile 'em all day and all night," just so she got them clean. "But missus, dat ain't all; you has to get the hottest flatiron, and iron in all de seams." I told her I would leave it with her, just so she got them all right, and she worked over them faithfully until they were clean and nice, and hung up for future use.

I went down the next day, and the boys looked like new men, and the old lady was bright and cheerful, and I felt happy at my success. Some of the women of the present day may think it would have been more suitable for men to attend to these things. But where were our men? Most of them were tramping through mud and dirt, rain and cold fighting battles, many lying on the cold ground wounded, and others passed to "that bourn whence no traveler returns." No, when duty led the Southern women, we did not stop to consider if the thing necessary to be done was elegant or delicate, but could we do ought to alleviate suffering, and cool a parching brow, or make a bed softer to the maimed and shattered limbs of our dear ones. Many of them had loving kindred thinking and praying for darling husbands, brothers, and sons. I thought I had my country charges all settled and happy, but in a few days I was sent for to come as quickly as I could: they wanted to see me. I went down and was received at the door by the old lady. She was very kind, and told me her boys were doing finely, but were somewhat nervous. I walked in and asked if they wished to see me about anything important. They said "Yes," in a low, confidential way, and continued, "I believe the old lady wants to kill us, as she has a loom in the next room, right against the partition at the head of our bed, and she has been weaving for two days, and late last night, and says she has a good deal more to do before she finishes her cloth." I told them I would make it all right; I knew the old lady was good and kind, and I knew too she didn't mean to annoy them. They said: "Yes, she is good to us; gives us plenty that is nice to eat, and talks kindly to us, but that rattle, rattle, rattle (said in a wail) will kill us; we can't stand it." I had a talk with the old lady, and she promised to postpone the weaving, and seemed sorry that she had annoyed them. They stayed with her until they were well enough to join their regiments. Two days before they left the servant came in and announced two soldiers in the parlor; said they wanted to see me, and I immediately went in. They looked neat, fresh, and cheerful in their suits of gray that the old negress had "biled all day and all night," and to my astonishment, each one had a fiddle under his arm. They said they were going away and thought they would play some for the children and myself; said they were considered "powerful good players" at home. I thanked them for their thoughtfulness, called the children in, then they tuned and tuned, and finally started off on some jigs, and they played all the country breakdowns you ever heard. The more and louder they played, the more numerous became their audience. The children and servants in the hotel came in numbers, until they had a crowd of attentive listeners. As the excitement increased, the louder they played, until they seemed in perfect ecstasy. After they had played all they knew, we all thanked them, bade them good–bye, and it was the last I ever saw or heard of them. On shaking their hands in farewell I felt touched, for the poor fellows had paid what they conceived to be the greatest compliment in life: given me the benefit of what they imagined fine music.

Fleeing from Our Servants

KATE STONE

NEAR TALULLAH, LOUISIANA, MARCH 1863

With southern Louisiana under Federal control, Kate Stone and her mother felt threatened both by Union soldiers and freed slaves. They decided to flee to Texas.

Jane, Aunt Laura's cook, and Aunt Lucy [another slave] had a terrible row Tuesday night. Jane cut a great gash in Lucy's face with a blow from a chair and hurt her severely. Mamma had Jane called up to interview her on the subject, and she came with a big carving knife in her hand and fire in her eyes. She scared me. She is nearly six feet tall and powerful in proportion, as black as night and with a fearful temper. She is a splendid cook and that is why Dr. Buckner has kept her so long. Aunt Laura always was afraid of her, and I always thought Dr. Buckner stood in wholesome dread of her. He would never scold her, but he would not sell her, though Aunt Laura often begged him to get rid of her. Aunt Laura had a long, lingering illness lasting several months, and she always thought Jane kept her poisoned. Jane showed a very surly, aggressive temper while Mamma was talking to her, and so Mamma did not say much. Jane went to her room and that night took her two children, a girl and a boy about half–grown, and in company with one of Mr. Hardison's men started for the [Federal] camp at DeSoto. I think we are all glad she has gone. We felt her a constant menace. She must have had a bad trip. They were out in that blinding rain Wednesday and Wednesday night with only two blankets as protection and not much to eat. Mr. Graves saw them yesterday sitting on the levee at Mr. Utz's in company with fifty others, waiting to be ferried across at the break there in a dugout, and so there are crowds waiting all the time. Col. Graves went down there yesterday to try to reclaim three of his who had escaped. Three had just been drowned, trying to get over, and he thought from the description they were his.

Poor creatures, I am sorry for them. How horrible it all is. We had a scene of terror the night Jane left: The quarreling and screaming, the blood streaming down Lucy's face, Jane's fiery looks and speeches, Johnny and Uncle Bob's pursuit of her as she rushed away, the discovery that the children were gone, and then just as we had all quieted down, the cry of fire. The loom room had caught from some hot ashes, but we at once thought Jane was wreaking vengeance on us all by trying to burn us out. We would not have been surprised to have her slip up and stick any of us in the back. Johnny was our only protector as Jimmy was away. I went around bravely in appearance with a five-shooter in my hand. Found out afterwards it was only dangerous to look at as it was not loaded.

Mamma spoke of sending next day for Jane, but Aunt Laura implored her not to. She was only too thankful to get rid of her. She had been a terror to her for years. I think everybody on the place was thankful to get rid of her. The Negroes dreaded her as much as the white folks. They thought her a hoodoo woman.

Johnny who has been out scouting reports the Yankees at Rescue, the adjoining place, yesterday hunting horses and Negroes, and today they are scattered all through the lower neighborhood on the same quest. This band is said to be Kansas Jayhawkers, the very off scourings of the Northern Army. They say they will take by force all Negroes, whether they wish to go or not. A great number of Negroes have gone to the Yankees from this section. Mr. Watson and his father-in-law, Mr. Scott, living, I think, on Eagle Lake near Richmond, got up one morning and found every Negro gone, about seventy-five, only three little girls left. The ladies actually had to get up and get breakfast. They said it was funny to see their first attempt at milking. Mr. Matt Johnson has lost every Negro off one place and a number from the other places. Keene Richards has lost 160 from Transylvania and fifty of them are reported dead. The Negroes at work on the canal have what they call black measles, and it is very fatal to them.

March 5: Mr. Valentine came over last evening in very low spirits indeed. He says his Negroes will not even pretend to work and are very impudent, and he thinks they will all go off in a body, the next time the Yankees come on his place.

He brought the welcome news of the departure of that body of Jayhawkers that was on Mrs. Evans' place. They have completely ruined Mr. Catlin's, Mrs. Evans', and Mrs. Stevens' places, taking all the Negroes and all kinds of stock. The Negro women marched off in their mistresses' dresses.

Jimmy has been for some time with the Negroes at the salt works. We are in a helpless situation, three ladies and two little girls and not a white man or even a gun on the place, not even a boy until Johnny gets back. And the scouts may take him. We can find rest only in the thought that we are in God's hands.

There are only twenty Negroes left on Mrs. Tibbetts' five places, and Dr. Tibbetts has only one left, a superannuated woman helpless to do anything. The ladies are cooking, washing, etc., while Hiram Tibbetts is wood chopper.

The Yankees have five thousand Negroes camped at Lake Providence, all they have taken from the places up the river. They had an army of 30,000 men camped there, but they find the canal through to the Macon not feasible. They have moved up to Ashton to try a new canal there, if they can close the break at that point.

[Near Trenton, La.] April 25: On Thursday, March 26, hearing that Mr. Hardison had returned from Monroe, Sister and I walked up in the afternoon to hear what news he had brought. As we approached the house, it struck me that something was wrong. As we were going through the garden George Richards came out and told us a party of Yankees and armed Negroes had just left, carrying with them every Negro on the place, most of Mrs. Hardison's and the children's clothes, and all the provisions they could manage. They were led by Charles, Mr. Hardison's most trusted servant, and they were all vowing vengeance against Mr. Hardison. They said they would shoot him on sight for moving two of his Negroes a few days before. Mr. Hardison had fortunately seen them coming, and, knowing he would be arrested or perhaps killed as a conscript officer, had escaped to the woods.

We walked in and found Mrs. Hardison and the children all much excited and very angry, with flaming cheeks and flashing eyes. The Negroes had been very impertinent. The first armed Negroes they had ever seen. Just as we were seated someone called out the Yankees were coming again. It was too late to run. All we could do was to shut ourselves up together in one room, hoping they would not come in. George Richards was on the gallery. In a minute we heard the gate open and shut, rough hoarse voices, a volley of oaths, and then a cry, "Shoot him, curse him! Shoot him! Get out of the way so I can get him." Looking out of the window, we saw three fiendish–looking, black Negroes standing around George Richards, two with their guns leveled and almost touching his breast. He was deathly pale but did not move. We thought he would be killed instantly, and I shut my eyes that I might not see it. But after a few words from George, which we could not hear, and another volley of curses, they lowered their guns and rushed into the house "to look for guns" they said, but only to rob and terrorize us. The Negroes were completely armed and there was no white man with them. We heard them ranging all through the house, cursing and laughing, and breaking things open.

Directly one came bursting into our room, a big black wretch, with the most insolent swagger, talking all the time in a most insulting manner. He went through all the drawers and wardrobe taking anything he fancied, all the time with a cocked pistol in his hand. Cursing and making the most awful threats against Mr. Hardison if they ever caught him, he lounged up to the bed where the baby was sleeping. Raising the bar, he started to take the child, saying as he waved the pistol, "I ought to kill him. He may grow up to be a jarilla. Kill him." Mrs. Hardison sprang to his side, snatched the baby up, and shrieked, "Don't kill my baby. Don't kill him." The Negro turned away with a laugh and came over where I was sitting with Little Sister crouched close to me holding my hand. He came right up to us standing on the hem of my dress while he looked me slowly over, gesticulating and snapping his pistol. He stood there about a minute, I suppose. It seemed to me an age. I felt like I would die should he touch me. I did not look up or move, and Little Sister was as still as if petrified. In an instant more he turned away with a most diabolical laugh, gathered up his plunder, and went out. I was never so frightened in my life. Mrs. Hardison said we were both as white as marble, and she was sure I would faint. What a wave of thankfulness swept over us when he went out and slammed the door. In the meanwhile, the other Negroes were rummaging the house, ransacking it from top to bottom, destroying all the provisions they could not carry away, and sprinkling a white powder into the cisterns and over everything they left. We never knew whether it was poison or not.

The Negroes called and stormed and cursed through the house, calling each other "Captain" and "Lieutenant" until it nearly froze the blood in our veins, and every minute we expected them to break into our room again. I was completely unnerved. I did not think I could feel so frightened.

Mrs. Alexander went into her room hoping to prevent their robbing her bed, when one of them pointed his pistol at her and said, "I told you once before, old woman, to keep out of here and stop your jaw." Mr. McPherson and George were all the time on the gallery with Negroes guarding them with leveled guns.

After carrying on this way about two hours they lit matches, stuck them about the hall, and then leisurely took themselves off, loaded down with booty. We rushed around, put out all the matches, gathered up the few little articles left, and started at once for home. Since the Negroes declared as they moved off that they were coming back in a little while and burn every house on the place, I took the baby and Mrs. Hardison, Mrs. Alexander, and the children with George and Mr. McPherson gathered up everything of any value left, and we hurried home, reaching there spent with excitement. Mrs. Hardison was almost crazy.

As we passed through our quarters, there were numbers of strange Negro men standing around. They had gathered from neighboring places. They did not say anything, but they looked at us and grinned and that terrified us more and more. It held such a promise of evil. Jimmy went out at once to where Mr. Hardison was in hiding to tell him his family were with us. Jimmy just escaped being shot by Mr. Hardison, who, in the dusk, took him for a Yankee. Mr. and Mrs. Hardison and the small children went off as soon as possible, not thinking it safe to remain so near home. During the night a party came to the yard looking for them, but on the house servants' assuring them that the Hardisons were gone, they did not come to the house.

We made preparations that night to move at daybreak, but something deterred us. Mamma thought she would go out and get letters of protection but later abandoned the idea. It was then too late for us to get off, and we spent a night and day of terror. The next evening the Negroes from all the inhabited places around commenced flocking to Mr. Hardison's, and they completely sacked the place in broad daylight, passing our gate loaded down with plunder until twelve at night. That more than anything else frightened Mamma and determined her to leave, though at the sacrifice of everything we owned.

We made arrangements to get Dr. Carson's skiffs and sent Webster around collecting saddles and bridles. On account of the water we could go only on horseback to take the skiffs. With much difficulty we got everything ready for the start at midnight. Aunt Laura was the only one who did not want to go. She begged Mamma to let her and Beverly stay, saying that she would get old Mr. Valentine to stay with her, but of course Mamma could not allow that. The boys brought in everything we had buried out, except Aunt Laura's silver. That had to be left packed in a barrel and buried in the yard. The boys had done it one very dark night, when they hoped all the Negroes were in their cabins as it was raining. All the servants behaved well enough except Webster, but you could see it was only because they knew we would soon be gone. We were only on sufferance.

Two days longer and we think they would all have gone to the Yankees, most probably robbing and insulting us before they left. About eleven the boys went off with their guns to have the horses saddled and brought up. After a good deal of trouble, they came. The boys carried their guns all the time. Without them I think we would never have gotten off. Webster tried every artifice to get hold of one of them, but the boys never relaxed their watch. The night was cloudy and dark with occasional claps of thunder, but we had to go then or never. We knew the news would be carried to camp, and the Yankees had forbidden citizens to leave their places. Aunt Laura, protesting all the time she could not ride, was at last after much coaxing and fixing mounted on poor Little Jack Fisher, the family pony, old and gentle, with Annie perched behind her. I took Beverly in my lap. All the others mounted, and with the baggage cart with Uncle Bob driving and Jimmy guarding it in the extreme rear, the procession moved off.

It was too dark to see the road but Johnny led off, and each one followed the shadow in front. At first Aunt Laura was loud in exclamation and complaint, until someone suggested that she would bring the Negroes down on us. That acted as a quietus, and thereafter she groaned only in spirit. Several times as the clouds lifted and it grew something lighter, I saw her pony struggling in a mud hole and Aunt Laura reeling in the saddle, but not a scream disturbed the stillness of the night. As we opened gates and rode through place after place in perfect silence, not a light was visible anywhere. After passing Out Post, the road was so bad and it was so dark that we were forced to wait for daylight. We dismounted in the middle of the road, and to Aunt Laura's surprise and amazement Mamma lay her head down in Johnny's lap and went sound asleep. Riding in the dark made her sick, and she was worn out with excitement and loss of sleep.

As soon as it was light enough to see, the sleepers were awakened, and we mounted and went on over the very worst road it was possible for ladies to travel — just a long bog from one end to the other. The morning air was pleasantly cool, and as the red light crept up the sky we heard all kinds of wildwoods sounds — squirrels chattering in the trees, birds waking with a song, the calls of the wild ducks and turkeys, and three or four deer bounding into the woods just before us.

When we reached within a mile of our place of debarkation, the road became impassable, and we struck off into the woods. The cart had to be left there and the baggage carried on by mules. After much trouble, getting lost and riding through water up to our saddle skirts — I actually swam a bayou with Beverly in my arms — we succeeded in getting all of our party and a little of our baggage to the landing place below Mrs. Stevens'. We sent Webster back to the cart for the baggage, and no sooner was he out of sight than he mounted a horse and set off for home. He told Charles that he knew he was not going to Bayou Macon with Miss Manda and that Charles had better come on with him. Thus by his treachery we lost almost everything we brought away with us, for when we heard it, it was already too late to send back for the things. We knew the Yankees would certainly be where we were by 8 o'clock, and it was nearly that hour. We knew that we must get off at once if at all, for when the Yankees came they would turn us back. They never allow anyone to leave if they can help it.

Returning to Brother

SARAH MORGAN

NEAR NEW ORLEANS, LOUISIANA, APRIL 1863

Sarah, Miriam, and their mother had left the Carter plantation and joined Lilly in Clinton, Louisiana. At the urging of Brother, Sarah's older half–brother who had remained loyal to the Union, Sarah, Miriam, and their mother set out for New Orleans where Brother could take care of them. Lilly remained in Clinton where she would be closer to her soldier husband. This passage begins after the Morgans have left Clinton. Sarah was recovering from a back injury that she had suffered in a riding accident.

Sunday April 19th — Friday morning we arose at daylight and prepared to resume our journey for Bonfoucard, twenty three miles away. The man walked in very unceremoniously to get corn from the armoir as we got up, throwing open the windows and performing sundry little offices usually reserved for femmes de chambres, but with that exception every thing went on very well. Breakfast being a luxury not to be procured, we got in the carriages before sunrise, and left this romantic abode of dogs and contentment. Again our road lay through Piney Woods, so much like that from Hammond to Ponchatoula, that involuntarily I found myself looking through the window to see if Mr. Halsey was there. It lacked only his presence to make the scene all in all the same. But alas! this time the driver picked me wild flowers, and brought me haws. Mr. Halsey, in blissful ignorance of our departure, was many, and many a mile away. The drive was not half as amusing. The horse would not suffer any one except Miriam to drive, and at last refused to move until the driver got down and ran along by the carriage. Every time the poor boy attempted to occupy his seat, the obstinate animal would come to a dead stop and refuse to go until he dismounted again. I am sure that he walked nineteen miles out of the twenty three, out of complaisance to the ungrateful brute.

All equally fatigued and warm, we reached this place about twelve o'clock. Mrs. Bull had arrived before us; and as the carriage stopped, her girl Delia came to the gate the personification of despair crying "You cant get out, ladies. They say we cant stop here; we must go right back." The panic which ensued is indescribable. Go back when we were almost at our journey's end, after all the money we had spent, the fatigue we had undergone, to be turned back all the way to Clinton, perhaps! "With my sick babies!" cried Mrs. Ivy. "With my sick child!" cried mother. "Never! you may turn us out of your house, but we will die in the woods first! To go back is to kill my daughter and these babies!" This was to the overseer who came to the carriage. "Madam, I have orders to allow no one to pass who has not written permission. Lieut. Worthington sent the order two days ago; and I am liable to imprisonment if I harbor those who have no passport," the man explained. "But we have Gen. Gardener's order," I expostulated. "Then you shall certainly pass; but these ladies cannot. I cant turn you away though; you shall all come in and stay until something can be determined on."

This much granted was an unlooked for blessing. He showed us the way to a large unfurnished house, one room of which contained a bed with one naked matress, which was to be our apartment. Mrs. Bull sat down in a calm, dignified state of despair; little Mrs. Ivy dissolved in tears; we all felt equally disconsolate; the prospect of getting off was not so pleasant when we thought we should be obliged to leave them behind. Our common misfortunes had endeared us to each other, strangers as we were a week ago. So we all lamented together, a perfect Jérémiade of despair.

The overseer is very tender hearted; he condoled, comforted, and finally determined that if there was any way of getting them off, they should go. A glimpse of sunshine returned to our lowering sky, and cheerfulness reigned once more, to be violently dethroned some hours later. Three of the Madisonville pickets were announced approaching the house. Of course they were coming after us! O that vile Mr. Worthington! We always *did* hate him! There was always such a sneaky look about him! Hypocrite! we always felt we should hate him! O the wretch! "I wont go back!" cried mother. "I shall not" said quiet Mrs. Bull. "He shall pay my expenses if he insists on taking me back!" exclaimed Mrs. Ivy. "Spent all my money! Mrs. Bull, you have none to lend me, remember, and Mrs. Morgan you *shan't*! O that Worthington! let's make him pay for all!" We smothered our laughter to sit trembling within as the pickets stepped on the gallery. I believe we commenced praying.

Just think! Thus far, our journey has cost mother two hundred and twenty dollars. It would cost the same to get back to blessed Clinton, and fancy our spending that sum to settle there again! Besides, we gave away all our clothes to our suffering friends; and what would we do there now?

After half an hour of painful suspense, we discovered that it would have been as well to spare poor Mr. Worthington; for the pickets were not after us, but had come to escort Mrs. Ryan, a woman who was taking the body of her son who was killed at Murfreesboro, to the city for interment. Poor woman! She rode all this distance sitting on her child's coffin. Her husband was one of those who with Breedlove stole that large sum of money from father which came so near ruining him. She speaks of her husband as of a departed saint. I dare say she believes him innocent of the theft in spite of his public confession. The grave has wiped out even the disgrace of the penitentiary where he expiated his offence. Low, vulgar, unrefined, she has lived in affluence. Father was made an old man before his time by the wicked deed, and spent many years in my early life, bowed down by poverty. When I told Tiche who the woman was, she clasped her hands, saying "The Lord is good! Years and years master suffered while she grew rich, and now *her* time comes! The Lord dont forget!" I cant feel that way. It is well for the narrow minded to look for God's judgement on us for our sins; but mine is a more liberal faith. God afflicted her for some wise purpose; but if I thought it was to avenge father, I should be afraid of her. As it is, I can be sorry, oh *so* sorry for her!

As usual I find myself taken care of at the expense of the others. There are but two [mosquito] bars on the place; one, the overseer said, should be for me, the other for the children. Sheets were scarce, covers scarcer still. Tired of being spoiled in this way, I insisted on being allowed to sleep on a mattress on the floor, after a vigorous skirmish with mother and Miriam, in which I came off victorious. For a bar, I impressed Miriam's grenadine dress, which she fastened to the door knob and let fall over me à la Victorian tester arrangement. To my share fell a double blanket, which, as Tiche had no cover, I unfolded, and as she used the foot of my bed for a pillow, gave her the other end of it, thus, (tell it not in Yankee land, for it will never be credited) actually sleeping under the same bed clothes with our black, shiny negro nurse!

We are grateful though even for these discomforts; it might have been so much worse! Indeed I fear that our fellow travellers do not fare as well. Those who have sheets have no bars, those who have blankets have no sheets, and one woman who has recently joined us has nothing except a matress which is to do the duty of all three. But then, we got bread! Real, pure, wheat bread! And coffee! None of your potato, burnt sugar, and parched corn abomination, but the unadulterated berry! I cant enjoy it fully though; every mouthful is cloyed with the recollection that Lilly and her children have none.

As usual, as Mrs. Greyson says, the flowers follow us; yesterday I received three bouquets, and Miriam got one too. In this out of the way place such offerings are unexpected; and these were doubly gratifying coming from people one is not accustomed to receiving them from. For instance, the first was from the overseer, the second from a servant, and the third from a poor boy for whom we have subscribed to pay his passage to the city.

Wednesday April 22d New Orleans — Yesterday we arrived; I thought we should never get here. Monday we had almost given up in despair, believing the schooner would never return. But in the evening when all were gathered in our room discussing our hopes and fears, a sail was perceived at the mouth of the bayou, where upon every one rushed out to see the boat land. I believe I have not mentioned that this Bonfouca is on a bayou of the same name, that runs within a few yards of this house. It is an Indian name signifying Winding river, which struck us as very appropriate when we watched the schooner sailing now to the left, now to the right, apparently through the green fields; for the high grass hid the course of the stream so that the faintest line was not perceptible, except just in front of the house. All was now bustle and confusion, packing, dressing, and writing last words to our friends at home, until half past eleven when we embarked.

This is my first experience of schooners, and I dont care if I never again behold another. The cabin where Mr. Kenedy immediately carried me, was just the size of my bed at home (in the days I had a home) and just high enough to stand in. On each side of the short ladder, there was a mattress two feet wide. One of them Mrs. Ryan had possession of already, the other was reserved for me. I gave the lower part of mine to Minna and Jennie who spent the rest of the night fighting each other and kicking me. Just before twelve we "weighed anchor" and I went on deck to take a last look at Dixie with the rest of the party. Every heart was full. Each left brothers, sisters, husband, children, or dear friends behind. We sang Farewell dear land with a slight quaver in our voices, looked at the beautiful starlight shining on the last boundary of our glorious land, and fervently and silently praying, passed out of sight.

God bless you, all you dear ones we have left in our beloved country! God bless and prosper you, and grant you the victory in the name of Jesus Christ.

I returned to my mattress, and this is the way we spent the night; Mrs. Ryan, rocking and moaning as she sat up in bed, whined out her various bodily ills with a minute description of each, only ceasing the recital to talk of her son's body which lay on deck. (Yesterday morning she was sitting crying on his coffin while a strange woman sat on its head eating her bread and cheese.) Mrs. Bull, one of the most intelligent and refined ladies I have yet met, who is perfectly devoted to me, sat by me, laughing and talking, trying her best to make every one comfortable and happy in her unobtrusive way. Mother talked to Mrs. Ryan and cried at the thought of leaving her children fighting & suffering.

The space between the two beds was occupied by three Irish women, and Mrs. Ivy's two babies. The babies had commenced screaming as they were brought into the pen, at which I was not surprised. Having pitched their voices on the proper key, they never ceased shrieking, kicking, crying, throwing up, and going through the whole list of baby performances. The nurses scolded with shrill voices above the bedlam that had hushed even Mrs. Ryan's complaints, Jennie and Minna quarrelled, kicked and cried, and as an aggravation to the previous discomforts, a broad shouldered, perspiring Irishwoman sat just by my head, bracing herself against my pillows in the most unpleasant style. I endured it without flinching until about half past three, when the condensed odor of a dozen different people and children became unendurable, and I staggered upon deck where Miriam and Mrs. Ivy had been wise enough to remain, without venturing below. They laid me on a bench in the stern, rolled me up in shawls, to keep off the heavy dew, and there I remained until day light with them, as wide awake as ever.

At daylight there was a universal smoothing of heads, and straightening of dresses, besides arrangements made for the inspection of baggage. Being unwilling for any Christian to see such a book as this, I passed a piece of tape through the centre leaves, and made Miriam tie it under her hoops. At sunrise we were in sight of the houses at the lake end. It seemed as though we would never reach land.

I forgot to speak of our alarm as we got in the lake. No sooner had we fairly left the bayou, than the sky suddenly became threatening. The captain shook his head and spoke of a very ugly night for the lake, which sent everybody's heart to their throats, and alarmed us immeasurably.

We got [to] talking of the sailor's superstition of crossing the water with a corpse, until we persuaded ourselves that it was more than probable we would founder in the coming storm. But the severest storm we met was the one in the cabin; and all night the only wind was a head–breeze, and the spicy gale from below.

When we at last entered the canal, I beheld the animal now so long unseen, the Yankee. In their dark blue uniforms they stood around, but I thought of the dear grey coats, and even the pickets of Madisonville seemed nobler and greater men than these. Immediately a guard was placed on board, we whispering before he came "Our dear Confederates, God bless them." We had agreed among ourselves, that come what would, we would preserve our dignity and self respect, and do anything rather than create a scene among such people. It is well that we agreed. So we whispered quietly among ourselves, exhorting each other to pay no attention to the remarks the Yankees made about us as we passed, and acting the martyr to perfection, until we came to Hickock's Landing.

Here there was a group of twenty Yankees. Two officers came up and asked us for papers; we said we had none. In five minutes one came back, and asked if we had taken the oath. No; we had never taken *any*. He then took down our names. Mother was alone in the coop. He asked if there was not another. The schooner had fifteen passengers, and we had given only fourteen names. Mother then came up and gave her name, going back soon after. From that moment I knew she was preparing for a scene. While one went after our passes, others came to examine our baggage. I could not but smile as an unfortunate young man got on his knees before our trunk and respectfully handled our dirty petticoats and stockings. "You have gone through it before," he said. "Of course the Confederates searched it." "Indeed they did not touch it!" I exclaimed. "They never think of doing such work." "Miss, it is more mortifying to me than it can be to you," he answered. And I saw he was actually blushing.

He did his work as delicately as possible, and when he returned the keys, asked if we had letters. I opened my box and put them in his hand. One came near getting me in serious trouble. It was sent by some one I never saw, with the assurance that it contained nothing objectionable. I gave it sealed to the man, who opened it, when it proved to be rather disagreeable I judged from his language. He told me his captain must see it before he could let me have it, and carried it off. Presently he came back and told me it could not be returned. I told him to burn it then, as I neither knew the writer, the contents, nor those it was written to. "I may save you some difficulty if I destroy it" he remarked, whereupon he tore it up and flung it in the canal. I have since found I had cause to be grateful; for just after came an officer to see the young lady who brought that letter. I showed the pieces in the water, saying the young man had torn it up, which seemed to annoy him; it was to be sent to headquarters, he said.

Then came a bundle of paper on board carried by another, who standing in front of us cried in a startling way "Sarah Morgan!" "Here." (*very* quietly) "Stand up!" "I cannot." (firmly) "Why not?" "Unable." (decisively) After this brief dialogue, he went on with the others until all were standing except myself, when he delivered to each a strip of paper and informed the people that Miss, or Mrs. So and So had taken and subscribed the oath as Citizen of the U.S. I thought that was all, and rejoiced at our escape. But after another pause he uncovered his head and told us to hold up our right hands. Half crying I covered my face with mine and prayed breathlessly for the boys and the Confederacy, so that I heard not a word he was saying until the question "So help you God?" struck my ear. I shuddered and prayed harder. There came an awful pause in which not a lip was moved. Each felt as though in a nightmare until throwing down his blank book, the officer pronounced it "All right!" Strange to say, I experienced no change. I prayed as hard as ever for the boys and our country, and felt no nasty or disagreeable feeling which would have announced the process of turning Yankee.

Then it was that mother commenced. He turned to the mouth of the diminutive cave, and asked if she was ready to take the oath. "I suppose I *have* to, since I belong to you" she replied. "No madam, you are not obliged; we force no one. Can you state your objections?" "Yes. I have three sons fighting against you, and you have robbed me, beggared me!" she exclaimed, launching into a speech in which Heaven knows *what* she did not say; there was little she left out, from her despoiled house to her sore hand, both of which she attributed to the at first amiable man, who was rapidly losing all patience. Miriam endeavored in vain to stop her, Mrs. Bull expostulated, Mrs. Ivy entreated. But mother had been preparing herself for just such a scene, and faint with hunger, dizzy with sleeplessness, she had wrought on her own feelings until her nerves were beyond control. She was determined to carry it out, and crying and sobbing went through with it.

I neither spoke nor moved, knowing that at such moments mother is not to be controlled by any one on earth except father or Brother, and that neither could come to her. The officer walked off angrily and sent for a guard to have mother taken before Gen. Bowens. Once through her speech, mother yielded to the entreaties of the ladies and professed herself ready to take the oath, since she was obliged to. "Madam, I did not invite you to come" said the polite officer, who refused to administer the oath, and putting several soldiers on board, ordered them to keep all on board until one could report to Gen. Bowens. Mother retired to the cabin crying still, and thinking every one against her, while we still kept our seats above.

O that monotonous, never ending canal! We thought it would go on for ever. At last we came to the basin in the centre of the city. Here was a position for ladies! Sitting like Irish emigrants on their earthly possessions, and coming in a schooner to New Orleans, which a year ago would have filled us with horror.

Again the landing was reached, and again we were boarded by officers. I dont know how they knew of the difficulty mother had made, but they certainly did, and ordered that none should leave until the General's will was made known. Mrs. Bull and Mrs. Ivy, after a long delay and many representations, at last prepared to leave. I was sitting in the spot I had occupied ever since before daylight, with nothing to support me above my hips. All of us had fasted since an early and light supper the night before, none had slept. I was growing so weak from these three causes, and the burning sun (for it was now twelve), that I could hardly speak when they came to tell me good bye.

Alarmed by my appearance, Mrs. Bull entreated the officer to allow me to leave the boat. No, he said; it was impossible; we should remain on board until Gen. Bowens could come. We may get an answer in half an hour, or we may not get it for some time; but there we must stay until it came. "But this young lady has been ill for months; she is perfectly exhausted, and will faint if she is not removed immediately" pleaded Mrs. Bull. She did not know my powers of self control. Faint! I would have expired silently first! The officer said those were his orders; I could not leave. "Do you think you are performing your duty as a gentleman and a Christian? This young lady has obtained her pass already, without the slightest difficulty" she persisted. Still he said he was acting according to orders. Not to be baffled, she begged that she might be allowed to take me to Brother, telling him who he was, while our trunk, Miriam, Tiche, and mother would remain as hostages. Then he gave a reluctant consent on condition I left my number, so he could go after me when I was wanted.

I dont know what good came of the consent, for there I was to remain until something, I dont know what, happened. I only know I was growing deathly sick and faint, and could hardly hold myself up, when some time after Mrs. Bull and Mrs. Ivy left (under the impression that I was to go immediately) a gentleman in citizen's clothes came to me and said he had obtained permission for me to wait Gen. Bowens' orders in his office a few steps from the schooner. Thankful for that much, I accepted his arm, and slowly dragged myself along to the first shelter I had seen that day. By some wonderful condescension Miriam and mother (the sole offender) were allowed to follow; and with the guard at the door, we waited there for a half hour more until our sentence could be received.

Miriam had written a line to Brother as soon as possible, telling him of the situation mother had placed us in by her rash conduct, and while we were waiting in this office, I half dead with fatigue, a carriage dashed up to the door, and out of it stepped Brother. I felt that all our troubles were over then. He looked so glad to see us, that it seemed a pity to tell the disagreeable story that yet remained to be told. But once heard, he made all go right in a few moments. He got in the carriage with mother to take her to Gen. Bowens, while we got in another to come to the house. I saw no more of the guard or officer.

When we arrived Sister was too astonished to speak. She did not believe we would come when it was ordered that all should take the oath on entering. If we had only realized it I dont think we would, either. In half an hour mother got back. Supported by Brother's presence she had managed to hold up her right hand and say "Yes" to the oath, which was more than any of us had done. If she had done it at first, she would have spared us a most painful scene, and saved me from fatigue that threatened to annihilate me for some time. I thought Miriam would have a brain fever. Brother found an officer at the door who had been ordered (before he took mother to the General) to arrest her and confine her in the Customhouse. I suppose Miriam and I would have shared the imprisonment with her. But Brother has a way of making all these things right; and the man was sent back without accomplishing his mission.

My Yard Is a Battlefield

CORNELIA PEAKE MCDONALD

WINCHESTER, VIRGINIA, JUNE 1863

Winchester, Virginia, changed hands several times during the war. Ultimately Cornelia McDonald, acting on her husband's advice, fled to Lexington. On the day she describes here, the Confederates arrived in time to save her — temporarily, at least — from having her house confiscated by the Yankees.

June 14th — Victory! thanks to our Father in Heaven; our enemies are at last powerless to harm us. Musketry and cannon firing began early in the morning, but not very near us. Mrs. Dailey came over to stay with me as her house was so unprotected, and was within range of the shells. We sat together in the dining room before the windows looking at the west; and it seemed so strange to sit quietly in a rocking chair and watch the progress of a battle. We were yet on the outskirts, and could see the troops deploying, skirmish lines thrown forward and mounted men galloping from one point to another, batteries wheeling into position, and every now and then the thunder of cannon and the shriek of shell. Still they were at a distance, and there we sat, all that sweet June morning, and watched and listened, and occasionally shrank a little when a shell from a battery on the same hill opposite to the house, that one year ago our troops stormed and took, and sent its defenders panic–stricken down the hillside or rolled them in the dust; when a shell came crashing through the trees near the house, and reminded us that we were in danger. Thick and fast they presently came, one after another. A Confederate battery has possession of the hill, and the answering shots are from the fort. We are just in their path. Our battery is south of us, and the fort slightly east of north. So they go, whizzing, screaming, and coming down with a dreadful thud or crash and then burst. We hold our breath and cover our eyes till they pass. I gather all the children in till the firing ceases.

About noon there is a comparative quiet, and Mrs. Daily goes home with her children. I begin to feel that the effort has failed and the Confederates are retiring; but it is only the lull before another greater storm.

About three o'clock I went out into the front porch to see what was going on. The children were playing in the yard. High on the hill opposite the same battery spouted flame and smoke, and the fort slowly responded. Men were passing and repassing, and many looking pale and anxious. Some wearily dropped down and went to sleep under the trees. The two little boys, Donald and Roy, seemed to forget the shells and were playing in the yard, running and catching the men as they passed, saying, "I take you prisoner." Though there was a cessation of the firing in a great measure, the faces of the passing groups of men, or stragglers, as they were, did not look less anxious. I heard one officer telling another that Mulligan was coming from Cumberland to relieve them. Then I felt comfortable to know that they need relief.

I was, up to that time, ignorant of the state of affairs, and of all except what was to be seen from my own point of observation. At five o'clock I again went and stood on the porch, dejectedly fancying that the attempt had failed, and we were again left to our fate. Two officers stood within hearing leaning against a tree, a linden tree that grew close to the house door, and filled the air with its perfume. They were pale and looked disturbed as they talked to each other in a low tone. Suddenly a blaze of fire from those western hills from which Mulligan was to issue for their relief. "That is Mulligan," said one; "Mulligan has come," echoed all around. But the shout was suddenly silenced when they saw the direction in which the balls were sent. Straight into their works they plunged, and soon a dusky line was seen making its way toward their outer works. Crashing of cannon and rattling of musketry till those were taken, and then the guns were turned on the fort. Then it seemed as if shells and cannon balls poured from every direction at once. One battery from the hill opposite our house rushed down and through our yard, their horses wounded and bleeding, and men wounded also, and pale with fright. More artillery and more horses and pale flying men rushed by where I stood. Hurrying groups of stragglers, and officers without swords, and some bareheaded. They were all hastening up to the fort which they had imagined was a place of safety. Gen. Milroy with a few of his body guard galloped by; I saw his pale agitated face as he passed within ten feet of me, and felt sorry for him; so following my impulse of being kind I bowed to him; from pure sympathy; for I really did at the time feel for his misfortunes, though I would not have averted them. He may have thought it a piece of mock respect, but whatever he thought or felt, he bowed low, till his plume almost touched the horse's mane. The fort all the time was sending its huge shot and shell over and through the town to where our troops were, and from the west proceeded a blaze of fire and a cloud of smoke that carried death into their stronghold into which they were crowding by hundreds.

Until now they seemed to be flying to the fort for safety, and it was pitiable to see them as they were hurrying by, turn their eyes to the west, pause and look bewildered, then look around for a place of safety, and finally avail themselves of the only spot the shells did not reach, the angle of our house. I had retreated there with my children when the shots and shells began to fly so fast, and burst all around the house; and then as I sat on the porch bench, men came crowding in. Now a surgeon bringing a wounded man; he, the surgeon, looks so humbled and frightened that I did not at first recognize in him the same one who had behaved so insultingly last winter when he demanded my house. He goes away, but soon comes back more frightened and agitated than ever. They talk openly of being surrounded. The soldiers say they will stay and be captured.

I tried to comfort the wounded man who sat on the bench by me, but he was past comfort; a ball was lodged in his throat and he sat with his poor wretched face distorted with pain through all those weary hours; close to me he was and the hard breathing as he struggled to keep the blood from choking him was dreadful to hear. Crowd after crowd of men continued to pour into the porch till it was packed full; then they crowded as close as they could get, to be sheltered by the angle of the house. Ambulances were backed up to let out their loads of wounded, and horses reared frantic with pain from their bleeding wounds. Some were streaming with blood, and looking wild, with their poor eyes stretched wide with pain and fright. All made an effort to crowd in there and the close atmosphere was almost suffocating. I could not move, or hide the dreadful sights from my eyes.

All the while the batteries thundered, and booming of cannon, the screaming of shells (who that has ever heard that scream can ever forget it?), and the balls of light go shooting over our heads, followed by that fearful explosion. All the weary while the children were leaning on my lap; I was holding my poor little Hunter. Roy and Nelly were perfectly composed, looking up at the shells as they flew over and came crashing down.

Donald, poor little four year old baby, hid his face on my knee and sobbed. Old Aunt Winnie sat not far off, crying and wringing her hands. "Oh Miss Cornelia," she said, "you will all be killed." I did not know whether we would be or not; it really seemed impossible that we could come out of that chaos alive. One object my eyes were so fascinated with that I could scarcely withdraw them; it was the face of Tuss; a more abject looking wretch it would be difficult to conceive of. The expression of woe on his ugly old face was ludicrous; his eyes were fixed on me with a beseeching look as if I could help him if I would. He remembered, no doubt, his past misconduct and that might have given an additional sting to his distress; he was the impersonation of grief and fright.

At last the sun goes down, and the firing is less constant; soon it ceases altogether. Some of the men get up and make a move as if to go away, but only saunter off a few steps, and stop in the yard. Some get to laughing and talking, the reaction from anxiety and dread. These same men had been fighting for two days. Some looked really happy, and I doubt not felt greatly relieved. I got up and went to the kitchen and had some milk boiled for the wounded man that sat near me. He tried to take it but could not. I had him taken in and laid on the hall lounge; others followed, and before I knew it there were at least fifty men in the house. They asked permission to come in, it is true, but it was useless I knew, to withhold it, as they were many and I was one; and I did not then know the result of the contest. After dark I left the children with Aunt Winnie and walked out in the back yard to see what was going on. Most of the men and all the officers had dispersed, and gone I do not know where. Some of the ambulances with wounded, and all of the horses had gone. I met Mr. Wood and Mr. Steel near the house.

They say our forces have captured nearly all of Milroy's command. While that lull was taking place in the middle of the day Early was silently making his way around to the rear of the enemy, and suddenly burst on them with his batteries from the hills at the west, in the manner I have described. When I went into the house the floors were all covered with men, some asleep and others preparing for it by stacking their muskets in a corner and stretching themselves on the floor. It was vain to try to get anything to eat for myself and children, so I took the little ones and preceded by Harry and Allan who had arrived a few minutes before, with Kenneth who had followed them, all full of news, I came up stairs and sent the children to bed without even shutting a house door.

What is the use, have I not a strong guard down stairs? I do not feel the least fear, but will quietly lie down and take my rest.

15th — I did not lock my chamber door and went to bed and slept as soundly as I ever did in my life. The scenes of the day floated through my brain all night, the maneuvering troops scudding over the hills, shells flying, men rushing back and forth, artillery, infantry and ambulances confusedly hurrying by, and amidst it all my little ones playing in the yard in the bright summer sunshine, as happy and unconcerned as if all was peace around them. Poor little things, they have long been used to scenes of strife and confusion, and I suppose it now seems to them the natural course of things.

I was wakened at dawn by cannon, dressed and went down; the floor was still covered with sleeping men. Their sleep was deep for they were very weary I suppose. At any rate I had to push one with my foot to arouse him and told him to awake the others. I waited for them to go, and invited them to depart, but still they lingered. The cannon had ceased. I went to the front door and there filing into the yard was a column of grey coats! I could not help it, but waved my handkerchief high over my head. They came up and halted before the door. I told an officer the Yankees were in the house; he asked me to send them out. I told them to go, and each one laid his musket down and marched sadly out.

They marched them off, and I ran through the wet grass up to the top of the hill where the fort was. I went to it. The United States flag was waving in the morning breeze, but not a soldier was to be seen. They had all gone and destroyed nothing. I stood looking with amazement at the immense work they had constructed so near me and I had never seen it before; never dared to go in that direction. Some one came galloping up the hill. It was Capt. Richardson. He told me of Early's flank movement; he was with him. The Louisiana brigade charged the first outwork and took it, then turned the guns on the fort. That was the time when the firing was heaviest, and the terror so great. General Gordon and his staff soon came riding up, and I turn and go down the hill.

Went in town this afternoon; the girls told me that in the early morning, long before light, many ladies expecting our men to come in had assembled in the streets to greet them; and as the marching column drew near they with one accord burst into singing "The Bonnie Blue Flag." The bands all stopped, and the troops stood still till they had finished, and then their shouts rent the air, caps were waved, and hurrahs resounded. Some Yankee prisoners were standing on the Hotel porch, and one was heard to say the men could fight when they knew such a welcome awaited them.

Lieut. Richardson came to tea; he gave me a description of their approach to the town. Milroy evacuated the fort during the night and stole away leaving the flag flying. All his force was captured about seven miles from town. We captured all their baggage, even their officers' trunks and mess chests. Milroy escaped alone by a byroad. Our men threaten to hang him if they can catch him on account of his treatment of the people of the town. Today I saw forty–five hundred prisoners marched by. Many faces I recognized as those I have had to look at all the winter.

16th — This afternoon a squad of Confederates marched up to the door with a woe begone looking surgeon in the midst of them. When they got him to the door they sent for me to ask if he was the one who behaved so badly to me last winter. I recognized in him the one who had been kind and serviceable in helping me to take care of Aunt Winnie when she was ill, and was glad to testify in his favour. He had asked them to bring him to me that I might convince them that he had not been offensive in his behavior. Every surgeon they had taken was ironed and sent to Richmond to the Libby prison. Dr. Patton was my man, and I think they got him, but for fear of missing him they took all.

17th — Went to town to help make a Confederate flag out of two captured ones. Made it by the new pattern. White flag with the blue flag for the union. We had to work hard, for Gen. Ewell waited to see it float before he left for Pennsylvania. I stood on Mrs. Hopkins' porch holding it up to see how it looked, when Mr. Williams passed. Men were going by, Yankees and all. "It is imprudent," said Mr. Williams, "to let them see you with it." I laughed at his fears, feeling so triumphant, and so secure that our army was there for good.

Guidance for Stonewall

BELLE BOYD

NORTHERN VIRGINIA AND WASHINGTON, MAY 1862–DECEMBER 1863

As this passage opens, Belle Boyd is travelling from her home in Martinsburg in what is now West Virginia, south through Winchester, to her aunt's house at Front Royal, Virginia. Like Rose Greenhow she does not reveal her sources of information other than the hole in the bedroom floor.

Upon arriving at Winchester, we had much difficulty in getting permission to proceed; for General Shields had just occupied Front Royal, and had prohibited all intercourse between that place and Winchester. However, Lieutenant–Colonel Fillebrowne, of the Tenth Maine Regiment, who was acting as Provost–Marshal, at length relented, and allowed us to go on our way.

It was almost twilight when we arrived at the Shenandoah River. We found that the bridges had been destroyed, and no means of transport left but a ferry–boat, which the Yankees monopolized for their own exclusive purposes.

Here we should have been subjected to much inconvenience and delay, had it not been for the courtesy and kindness of Captain Everhart, through whose intervention we were enabled to cross at once.

It was quite dark when we reached the village, and, to our great surprise, we found the family domiciled in a little cottage in the court–yard, the residence having been appropriated by General Shields and his staff.

However, we were glad enough to find ourselves at our journey's end, and to sit down to a comfortable dinner, for which fatigue and a long fast had sharpened our appetite. As soon as we had satisfied our hunger, I sent in my card to General Shields, who promptly returned my missive in person. He was an Irishman, and endowed with all those graces of manner for which the better class of his countrymen are justly famous; nor was he devoid of the humor for which they are no less notorious.

To my application for leave to pass *instanter* through his lines, *en route* for Richmond, he replied, that old Jackson's army was so demoralized that he dared not trust me to their tender mercies; but that they would be annihilated within a few days, and, after such a desirable consummation, I might wander whither I would.

This, of course, was mere badinage on his part; but I am convinced he felt confident of immediate and complete success or he would not have allowed some expressions to escape him which I turned to account. In short, he was completely off his guard, and forgot that a woman can sometimes listen and remember.

General Shields introduced me to the officers of his staff, two of whom were young Irishmen; and to one of these, Captain K., I am indebted for some very remarkable effusions, some withered flowers, and last, not least, for a great deal of very important information, which was carefully transmitted to my countrymen. I must avow the flowers and the poetry were comparatively valueless in my eyes; but let Captain K. be consoled: these were days of war, not of love, and there are still other ladies in the world besides the "rebel spy."

The night before the departure of General Shields, who was about, as he informed us, to "whip" Jackson, a council of war was held in what had formerly been my aunt's drawing–room. Immediately above this was a bed–chamber, containing a closet, through the floor of which I observed a hole had been bored, whether with a view to espionage or not I have never been able to ascertain. It occurred to me, however, that I might turn the discovery to account; and as soon as the council of war had assembled, I stole softly up stairs, and lying down on the floor of the closet, applied my ear to the hole, and found, to my great joy, I could distinctly hear the conversation that was passing below.

I remained motionless and silent until the proceedings were brought to a conclusion, at one o'clock in the morning. As soon as the coast was clear I crossed the court–yard, and made the best of my way to my own room, and took down in cipher everything I had heard which seemed to me of any importance.

I felt convinced that to rouse a servant, or make any disturbance at that hour, would excite the suspicions of the Federals by whom I was surrounded; accordingly I went straight to the stables myself, saddled my horse, and galloped away in the direction of the mountains.

Fortunately I had about me some passes which I had from time to time procured for Confederate soldiers returning south, and which, owing to various circumstances, had never been put in requisition. They now, however, proved invaluable; for I was twice brought to a stand–still by the challenge of the Federal sentries, and who would inevitably have put a period to my adventurous career had they not been beguiled by my false passport. Once clear of the chain of sentries, I dashed on unquestioned across fields and along roads, through fens and marshes, until, after a scamper of about fifteen miles, I found myself at the door of Mr. M.'s house. All was still and quiet: not a light was to be seen. I did not lose a moment in springing from my horse; and, running up the steps, I knocked at the door with such vehemence that the house re–echoed with the sound.

It was not until I had repeated my summons, at intervals of a few seconds, for some time, that I heard the response, "Who is there?" given in a sharp voice from a window above.

"It is I."

"But who are you? What is your name?"

"Belle Boyd. I have important intelligence to communicate to Colonel Ashby: is he here?"

"No; but wait a minute: I will come down."

The door was opened, and Mrs. M. drew me in, and exclaimed in a tone of astonishment —

"My dear, where did you come from? And how on earth did you get here?"

"Oh, I forced the sentries," I replied, "and here I am; but I have no time to tell you the how, and the why, and the wherefore. I must see Colonel Ashby without the loss of a minute: tell me where he is to be found."

Upon hearing that his party was a quarter of a mile farther up the wood, I turned to depart in search of them, and was in the very act of remounting when a door on my right was thrown open, and revealed Colonel Ashby himself, who could not conceal his surprise at seeing me standing before him.

"Good God! Miss Belle, is this you? Where did you come from? Have you dropped from the clouds? Or am I dreaming?"

I first convinced him he was wide awake, and that my presence was substantial and of the earth — not a visionary emanation from the world of spirits — then, without further circumlocution, I proceeded to narrate all I had overheard in the closet, of which I have before made mention. I gave him the cipher, and started on my return.

I arrived safely at my aunt's house, after a two hours' ride, in the course of which I "ran the blockade" of a sleeping sentry, who awoke to the sound of my horse's hoofs just in time to see me disappear round an abrupt turning, which shielded me from the bullet he was about to send after me. Upon getting home, I unsaddled my horse and "turned in" just as the day began to break.

A few days afterwards General Shields marched south, laying a trap, as he supposed, to catch "poor old Jackson and his demoralized army," leaving behind him, to occupy Front Royal, one squadron of cavalry, one field battery, and the 1st Maryland Regiment of Infantry, under command of Colonel Kenly; Major Tyndale, of Philadelphia, being appointed Provost–Marshal.

My mother returned home, and it was arranged that I should remain with my grandmother until an opportunity of travelling south in safety should present itself. Within a few days after my mother's departure, my Cousin Alice and I applied to Major Tyndale for a pass to Winchester. He at first declined to comply with our request, but afterwards relented, and promised to let us have the necessary passport on the following day. Accordingly, next morning, May 21st, my cousin, one of the servants, and myself were up betimes, and equipped for the journey, the carriage was at the door, but no passes made their appearance; and when we sent to inquire for the Major, we were informed he had gone "out on a scout," and would probably not be back until late at night. We were, of course, in great perplexity, when, to our relief, Lieutenant H., belonging to the squadron of cavalry stationed in the village, made his appearance and asked what was the matter.

I explained our case, and said —

"Now, Lieutenant H., I know you have permission to go to Winchester, and you profess to be a great friend of mine: prove it by assisting me out of this dilemma, and pass us through the pickets."

This I knew he could easily manage, as they were furnished from his own troop.

After a few moments' hesitation, Lieutenant H. consented, little thinking of the consequences that were to ensue. He mounted the box, my cousin, myself, and the servant got inside, and off we set. Shortly before we got to Winchester, Lieutenant H. got down from his seat with the intention of walking the rest of the way, as he had some business at the camp, which was close to the town.

Finding we could not return the same day, we agreed to remain all night with some friends.

Early the next morning a gentleman of high social position came to the house at which we were staying, and handed me two packages of letters, with these words: —

"Miss Boyd, will you take these letters and send them through the lines to the Confederate army? This package," he added, pointing to one of them, "is of great importance: the other is trifling in comparison. This also," he went on to say, pointing to what appeared to be a little note, "is a very important paper: try to send it carefully and safely to Jackson, or some other responsible Confederate officer. Do you understand?"

"I do, and will obey your orders promptly and implicitly," I replied.

As soon as the gentleman had left me I concealed the most important documents about the person of my negro servant, as I knew that "intelligent contrabands" — *i.e.*, ladies and gentlemen of color — were "non–suspects," and had *carte blanche* to do what they pleased, and to go where they liked, without hindrance or molestation on the part of the Yankee authorities. The less important package I placed in a little basket, and unguardedly wrote upon the back of it the words, "Kindness of Lieutenant H."

The small note upon which so much stress had been laid I resolved to carry with my own hands; and, knowing Colonel Fillebrowne was never displeased by a little flattery and a few delicate attentions, I went to the florist and chose a very handsome bouquet, which I sent to him with my compliments, and with a request that he would be so kind as to permit me to return to Front Royal.

The Colonel's answer was in accordance with the politeness of his nature. He thanked the "dear lady for so sweet a compliment," and enclosed the much–coveted pass. Lieutenant H., having finished his business at the camp, rejoined our party, and we all set out on our return. Nothing happened until we reached the picket–lines, when two repulsive–looking fellows, who proved to be detectives, rode up, one on each side of the carriage.

"We have orders to arrest you," said one of them, looking in at the window, and addressing himself to me.

"For what?" I asked.

"Upon suspicion of having letters," he replied; and then turning to the coachman, he ordered him to drive back forthwith to Colonel Beale's headquarters. Upon arriving there we were desired to get out and walk into the office.

My cousin trembled like a poor bird caught in a snare; and, to tell the truth, I felt very much discomposed myself, although I did not for a moment lose my presence of mind, upon the preservation of which I well knew our only hopes rested. The negress, almost paralyzed by fear, followed my cousin and myself, and it was in this order we were ushered into the awful presence of our inquisitor and judge.

The first question asked was, had I any letters. I knew that if I said No, our persons would be immediately searched, and my falsehood detected: I therefore drew out from the bottom of the basket the package I had placed there, and which, it will be remembered, was of minor importance, and handed it, with a bow, to the Colonel.

"What!" exclaimed he, in an angry tone — "what is this? 'Kindness of Lieutenant H.!' What does this mean? Is this all you have?"

"Look for yourself," I replied, turning the basket upside down, and emptying its contents upon the floor.

"As to this scribbling on the letter," I continued, "it means nothing; it was a thoughtless act of mine. I assure you Lieutenant H. knew nothing about the letter, or that it was in my possession."

The Lieutenant turning very pale, for it suddenly occurred to him that he had in his pocket a little package which I had asked him to carry for me.

He immediately drew it out and threw it upon the table, when, to his consternation, and to the surprise of the Colonel, it was found to be inscribed with the very identical words — "Kindness of Lieutenant H." — which had already excited the suspicions of the Federal commander.

This made matters worse; and when the package, upon being opened, disclosed a copy of that decidedly rebel newspaper, *The Maryland News–sheet*, the Colonel entertained no further doubt of Lieutenant H.'s complicity and guilt.

It was in vain I asserted his innocence, and repeated again and again that it was impossible he could know that a folded packet contained an obnoxious journal, and that it was highly improbable, to say the least of it, he could be an accomplice in my possession of the letter.

"What is that you have in your hand?" was the only reply to my remonstrances and expostulations on behalf of the unfortunate officer I had so unintentionally betrayed.

"What — this little scrap of paper? You can have it if you wish: it is nothing. Here it is;" and I approached nearer to him, with the seeming intention of placing it in his hand; but I had taken the resolution of following the example set by Harvey Birch, in Cooper's well–known novel of "The Spy," in the event of my being positively commanded to "stand and deliver."

Fortunately, however, for me, the Colonel's wrath was diverted from the guilty to the guiltless: he was so incensed with Lieutenant H., that he forgot the very existence of Belle Boyd, and the precious note was left in my possession.

We were then and there dismissed, Colonel Beale contenting himself with giving a hurried order to the effect that I was to be closely watched. He then proceeded to the investigation of Lieutenant H.'s case. Bare suspicion was the worst that could be urged against him, yet, upon this doubtful evidence, or rather in the absence of any thing like evidence, a court–martial, composed of officers of the Federal army, dismissed him from the service.

Some time after the adventure I have just related the secret of our arrest transpired.

A servant had observed the gentleman to whom I have alluded give me the letter in my friend's house at Winchester. He gave information, and the result was, a telegram was sent to Major Tyndale, who was already incensed against me for having slipped through the pickets and got to Winchester without his pass. He communicated at once with Colonel Beale, and our arrest followed as I have described.

Had it not been for the curious manner in which Lieutenant H. was involved in the affair, and in which that unoffending officer was so unjustly treated, very much to my regret, I should not have escaped so easily.

Among the Federals who then occupied Front Royal was one Mr. Clark, a reporter to the *New York Herald*, and, although an Irishman, by no means a gentleman.

He was domiciled at head–quarters, which were established, as I have before mentioned, at my aunt's residence; and thus it was that I saw him daily, for we could not possibly get into the street without crossing the court–yard and passing through the hall–way.

This Mr. Clark endeavored upon several occasions to intrude his society upon me; and, although I told him plainly his advances were extremely distasteful, he persevered so far that I was forced more than once to bolt the door of the room in which my cousin and myself were seated, in his face.

These rebuffs he never forgave, and from an intrusive friend he became an inveterate enemy. It is to him I am indebted for the first violent, undisguised abuse with which my name was coupled in any Federal journal; but I must do the editors of the Yankee newspapers the justice to admit they were not slow to follow the example set them by Mr. Clark. They seemed to think that to insult an innocent young girl was to prove their manhood and evince their patriotism. I think my English readers will neither admire their taste nor applaud their spirit.

On the evening of the 23rd May I was sitting at the window of our room, reading to my grandmother and cousin, when one of the servants rushed in, and shouted, or rather shrieked —

"Oh, Miss Belle, I t'inks de revels am a'comin', for de Yankees are a–makin orful fuss in de street."

I immediately sprang from my seat and went to the door, and I then found that the servant's report was true. The streets were thronged with Yankee soldiers, hurrying about in every direction in the greatest confusion.

I asked a Federal officer, who just then happened to be passing by, what was the matter. He answered that the Confederates were approaching the town in force, under Generals Jackson and Ewell, that they had surprised and captured the outside pickets, and had actually advanced within a mile of the town without the attack being even suspected.

"Now," he added, "we are endeavoring to get the ordnance and the quartermaster's stores out of their reach."

"But what will you do," I asked, "with the stores in the large dépôt?"

"Burn them, of course!"

"But suppose the rebels come upon you too quickly?"

"Then we will fight as long as we can by any possibility show a front, and in the event of defeat make good our retreat upon Winchester, burning the bridges as soon as we cross them, and finally effect a junction with General Banks' force."

I parted with the Federal officer, and returning to the house, I began to walk quietly up–stairs, when suddenly I heard the report of a rifle, and almost at the same moment I encountered Mr. Clark, who, in his rapid descent from his room, very nearly knocked me down.

"Great heavens! what is the matter?" he ejaculated, as soon as he had regained his breath, which the concussion and fright had deprived him of.

"Nothing to speak of," said I; "only the rebels are coming, and you had best prepare yourself for a visit to Libby Prison."

He answered not a word, but rushed back to his room and commenced compressing into as small a compass as possible all the manuscripts upon which he so much plumed himself, and upon which he relied for fame and credit with the illustrious journal to which he was contributor. It was his intention to collect and secure these inestimable treasures, and then to skedaddle.

I immediately went for my opera–glasses, and, on my way to the balcony in front of the house, from which position I intended to reconnoitre, I was obliged to pass Mr. Clark's door. It was open, but the key was on the outside. The temptation of making a Yankee prisoner was too strong to be resisted, and, yielding to the impulse, I quietly locked in the "Special Correspondent" of the *New York Herald*.

After this feat I hurried to the balcony, and, by the aid of my glasses, descried the advance–guard of the Confederates at the distance of about three–quarters of a mile, marching rapidly upon the town.

To add to my anxiety, my father, who was at that time upon General Garnett's staff, was with them. My heart beat alternately with hope and fear. I was not ignorant of the trap the Yankees had set for my friends. I was in possession of much important information, which, if I could only contrive to convey to General Jackson, I knew our victory would be secure. Without it I had every reason to anticipate defeat and disaster.

The intelligence I was in possession of instructed me that General Banks was at Strasbourg with four thousand men, that the small force at Winchester could be readily re–enforced by General White, who was at Harper's Ferry, and that General Shields and Geary were a short distance below Front Royal, while Fremont was beyond the Valley; further, and this was the vital point, that it had been decided all these separate divisions should co–operate against General Jackson.

I again went down to the door, and this time I observed standing about in groups, several men who had always professed attachment to the cause of the South. I demanded if there was one among them who would venture to carry to General Jackson the information I possessed. They all with one accord said, "No, no. You go."

I did not stop to reflect. My heart, though beating fast, was not appalled. I put on a white sun–bonnet, and started at a run down the street, which was thronged with Federal officers and men. I soon cleared the town and gained the open fields, which I traversed with unabated speed, hoping to escape observation until such time as I could make good my way to the Confederate line, which was still rapidly advancing.

I had on a dark–blue dress, with a little fancy white apron over it; and this contrast of colors, being visible at a great distance, made me far more conspicuous than was just then agreeable. The skirmishing between the outposts was sharp. The main forces of the opposing armies were disposed as follows: —

The Federals had placed their artillery on a lofty eminence, which commanded the road by which the Confederates were advancing. Their infantry occupied in force the hospital buildings, which were of great size, and sheltered, by which they kept up an incessant fire.

The Confederates were in line, directly in front of the hospital, into which their artillerymen were throwing shells with deadly precision; for the Yankees had taken this as a shelter, and were firing upon the Confederate troops from the windows.

At this moment, the Federal pickets, who were rapidly falling back, perceived me still running as fast as I was able, and immediately fired upon me.

My escape was most providential; for, although I was not hit, the rifle–balls flew thick and fast about me, and more than one struck the ground so near my feet as to throw the dust in my eyes. Nor was this all: the Federals in the hospital, seeing in what direction the shots of their pickets were aimed, followed the example and also opened fire upon me.

Upon this occasion my life was spared by what seemed to me then, and seems still, little short of a miracle; for, besides the numerous bullets that whistled by my ears, several actually pierced different parts of my clothing, but not one reached my body. Besides all this, I was exposed to a cross–fire from the Federal and Confederate artillery, whose shot and shell flew whistling and hissing over my head.

At length a Federal shell struck the ground within twenty yards of my feet; and the explosion, of course, sent the fragments flying in every direction around me. I had, however, just time to throw myself flat upon the ground before the deadly engine burst; and again Providence spared my life.

Springing up when the danger was passed, I pursued my career, still under a heavy fire. I shall never run again as I ran on that, to me, memorable day. Hope, fear, the love of life, and the determination to serve my country to the last, conspired to fill my heart with more than feminine courage, and to lend preternatural strength and swiftness to my limbs. I often marvel, and even shudder, when I reflect how I cleared the fields and bounded over the fences with the agility of a deer.

As I neared our line I waved my bonnet to our soldiers, to intimate that they should press forward, upon which one regiment, the First Maryland "rebel" Infantry, and Hay's Louisiana Brigade, gave me a loud cheer, and, without waiting for further orders dashed upon the town at a rapid pace.

They did not then know who I was, and they were naturally surprised to see a woman on the battle–field, and on a spot, too, where the fire was so hot. Their shouts of approbation and triumph rang in my ears for many a day afterwards, and I still hear them not unfrequently in my dreams.

At this juncture the main body of the Confederates was hidden from my view by a slight elevation which intervened between me and them. My heart almost ceased to beat within me; for the dreadful thought arose in my mind, that our force must be too weak to be any match for the Federals, and that the gallant men who had just been applauding me were rushing upon a certain and fruitless death. I accused myself of having urged them to their fate; and now, quite overcome by fatigue, and by the feelings which tormented me, I sank upon my knees and offered a short but earnest prayer to God.

Then I felt as if my supplication was answered, and that I was inspired with fresh spirits and a new life. Not only despair, but fear also forsook me; and I had again no thought but how to fulfil the mission I had already pursued so far.

I arose from my kneeling posture, and had proceeded but a short distance, when, to my unspeakable, indescribable joy, I caught sight of the main body fast approaching; and soon an old friend and connection of mine, Major Harry Douglas, rode up, and, recognizing me, cried out, while he seized my hand —

"Good God, Belle, you here! What is it?"

"Oh, Harry," I gasped out, "give me time to recover my breath."

For some seconds I could say no more; but, as soon as I had sufficiently recovered myself, I produced the "little note," and told him all, urging him to hurry on the cavalry, with orders to them to seize the bridges before the retreating Federals should have time to destroy them.

He instantly galloped off to report to General Jackson, who immediately rode forward, and asked me if I would have an escort and a horse wherewith to return to the village. I thanked him, and said, "No; I would go as I came;" and then, acting upon the information I had been spared to convey, the Confederates gained a most complete victory.

Though the dépôt building had been fired, and was burning, our cavalry reached the bridges barely in time to save them from destruction: the retreating Federals had just crossed, and were actually upon the point of lighting the slow match which, communicating with the bursting charge, would have riven the arches in pieces. So hasty was their retreat that they left all their killed and wounded in our hands.

Although we lost many of our best and bravest — among others the gallant Captain Sheetes, of Ashby's cavalry, who fell leading a brilliant and successful charge upon the Federal infantry — the day was ours; and I had the heartfelt satisfaction to know that it was in consequence of the information I had conveyed at such risk to myself General Jackson made the flank movement which led to such fortunate results.

The Confederates, following up their victory, crossed the river by the still standing bridges, and pushed on by the road which led to Winchester.

General Banks was startled from his lair at Strasbourg, and leaving everything but his own head and a handful of cavalry behind him, with the victorious Confederates in hot pursuit, rushed through Winchester and Martinsburg, and finally crossed the river at Williamsport, Maryland.

During this hasty flight General Banks halted for a few minutes to take breath in the main street of Martinsburg. Upon the sidewalk were standing many children and young girls, among whom was my little sister.

One of these girls, recognizing General Banks' aide–de–camp, walked up to him and said —

"Captain, how long are you going to stay here?"

"Until Gabriel blows his horn," replied he.

To this mistimed vaunt my sister quietly rejoined, looking full in his face as she spoke —

"Ah, Captain, if you were to hear Jackson's horn just outside the town, you would not wait for Gabriel's."

Nor did they wait; for the echo of the Confederate General's bugles had little less terror for them than the sound of the archangel's trump.

When I first returned from the battle–field, tired, or, to say the truth, utterly enervated and exhausted, the Confederates were filing through the town, and the enthusiastic hurrahs with which they greeted me did more than any thing else could have done to revive my drooping spirits and restore my failing powers. The dead and wounded were now being brought in, and our house soon became a hospital.

Notwithstanding my fatigue, I contrived to render some assistance in dressing the wounds and alleviating the sufferings of our poor soldiers, who consoled themselves in their agonies with the reflection that they had done their duty nobly, and that their pangs were not imbittered by the sting and remorse with which defeat always torments a true soldier.

Among the dead who were brought next day to our house for interment were Captains Sheetes, Baxter, and Thaxter, all of Ashby's cavalry, and Major Davis, of Louisiana.

To my great joy my father came safe out of the battle, with but a very slight wound in the leg.

All the Federals left in Front Royal were captured; among them my particular friend, Mr. Clark, who, upon endeavoring to leave his room unseen during the confusion, found himself locked in.

I afterwards heard an amusing account of the manner in which he extricated himself, by letting himself down from the window; this, however, was unfortunately a work of time, and the delay was the cause of his capture. He was being escorted a prisoner down the street when, catching sight of me as I stood upon the doorstep, he shouted out —

"I'll make you rue this: it's your doing that I'm a prisoner here."

During the battle, and while Colonel Fillebrowne was preparing to remove his effects from Winchester, a gentleman of high social position and Southern proclivities stepped into his office and said, "Colonel, how on earth did you get into such a trap? Did you know nothing of the advance of the Confederates?" Colonel Fillebrowne turned, and, pointing to the bouquet I had sent him only a day or two before, he said, "That bouquet did all the mischief: the donor of that gift is responsible *for all* this misfortune."

I could not but be aware that I had been of some service to my country; and I had the further satisfaction of feeling that neither a desire of fame nor notoriety had been my motive for enacting the *rôle* I did in this sad drama. I was not prepared, however, for that recognition of my services which was received on the very day they were rendered and which I here transcribe: —

May 23d, 1862.

Miss Belle Boyd,

> I thank you, for myself and for the army, for the
> immense services that you have rendered your country
> to–day.

Hastily, I am your friend,

T. J. Jackson, C.S.A.

This short note, which was written at Mr. Richard's house, very near Front Royal, was brought to me by a courier, and I am free to confess, I value it far beyond any thing I possess in the world.

The object General Jackson had in view was too important to admit of his leaving behind him an adequate force for the protection of Front Royal; one regiment, the Twelfth Georgia Infantry, was all that could be spared; and thus Front Royal was retaken by the Federals, just one week after its brilliant capture by our troops.

During our short possession of the town, there was, among the prisoners taken in the pursuit beyond beyond the river and sent back into our custody, a woman who represented herself to be the wife of a soldier belonging to the Michigan cavalry. She was handed over to me, and I furnished her with clothing, and did all that lay in my power to make her comfortable and happy.

Upon the arrival of the Federals under General Geary, most of the Twelfth Georgia were taken prisoners, together with all the sick and wounded.

The woman of whom I have just spoken was of course liberated; and the first use she made of her freedom was to report me to General Kimball as a most dangerous rebel, and a malignant enemy to the Federal Government.

The General immediately placed me under arrest, and surrounded our house with sentries, so that to escape was actually impossible. Within a few hours, however, after my incarceration, General Shields arrived; and, being senior in the service to General Kimball, naturally superseded him in the command of the army. He at once released me, and I thank him for his urbanity and kindness.

Rumors soon reached us to the effect that the Confederate army was retreating up the Valley, and once more all this portion of the country fell into the hands of the Yankees.

The Northern journals vied with one another in publishing the most extravagant and improbable accounts of my exploits, as they were pleased to term them, on the battle–field of the 23rd May. One ascribed to "Belle Boyd" the honor of having directed the fire of the Confederate artillery throughout the action; another represented her as having, by the force of her genius, sustained the wavering counsels of the Southern generals; while a third described her as having, sword in hand, led on the whole of the attacking line to the capture of Front Royal; but as I believe that the veracity of the Yankee press is pretty well known and appreciated, I shall give no more extracts from their eloquent pages.

I mentioned that General Shields released me from the arrest under which General Kimball had placed me, upon the report of the ungrateful *ci–devant* prisoner; and, after a short time, finding no further persecution was resorted to, I thought the opportunity favorable for making an attempt to get south.

Meanwhile, General Banks had returned, and encamped close to the town, making my aunt's house his head–quarters.

It was to him, therefore, I applied for permission to depart.

"Where do you wish to go?" he asked.

"To Louisiana, where my aunt resides."

"But what will Virginia do without you?"

"What do you mean, General?"

"We always miss our bravest and most illustrious, and how can your native State do without you?"

I laughingly thanked him for the compliment, and he conversed with the utmost good–nature and pleasantry upon the part that I had taken in his recent defeat. Though a rabid Abolitionist, the General was certainly one of the most affable gentleman I have ever met.

Several weeks passed by in peace and quiet, unmarked by any incident worthy of record, and at the expiration of this period, Front Royal was again evacuated by the Federal troops, with the exception of the Third Delaware Infantry, which corps was left in garrison. Their colonel was a very large, coarse man, with the manners and appearance of a butcher rather than of an officer.

On the other hand, Major McEnnis and Lieutenant Preston, who officiated severally as Provost and Assistant Provost–Marshal, were upon all occasions not only courteous, but kind, the natural consequence of which behavior was, that they were both highly respected and esteemed by us "rebels."

In the court–yard of the General's headquarters, and at a few yards only from our cottage, they had pitched a flag–tent, which served the purposes of their office, and here it was that all passes for the South were granted or refused, as the case might be. How many of these were procured upon false pretenses and transferred to recruits on their way to join the Southern army, or by whom this ingenious *ruse* was practiced, *I* shall not here say.

I was one morning sitting in the drawing–room, when I noticed two men, dressed as Confederate soldiers, standing near the Provost–Marshal's tent. At my request, my grandmother sent for the Major, who obeyed her summons without loss of time.

We asked him who the men were. He told us they were paroled Confederate soldiers procuring passes to go south. We then asked if they might be permitted to dine with us, and received a ready assent. In the mean time they had disappeared; but one of them shortly reappearing, I accosted him thus: —

"Won't you dine with us? The Major says you may."

"With pleasure, if you dine shortly; I have only two or three hours allowed me to get beyond the pickets."

"Poor fellow!" said I; "but I am glad that you will soon be free. Won't you take a letter from me to General Jackson?"

Upon his assenting to this request, I went off towards my own room to write my dispatch; but, as I was passing by the kitchen-door, one of the servants stopped me suddenly, and exclaimed: —

"Miss Belle! who's dat man yose-a-talkin' to?"

"I know no more about him than that he is a paroled rebel soldier, going south."

"Miss Belle, dat man ain't no rebel; I seen him 'mong de Yankees in de street. If he has got secesh clothes on, he ain't no secesh. Can't fool Betsy dat way. Dat man's a spy — dat man's a spy. Please God, he am.

I, however, entertained a different opinion from that of the negro woman, so I persevered in my intention, and wrote a long friendly letter to General Jackson. At the same time, I introduced a great deal of valuable information concerning the Yankees, the state of their army, their movements and doings, and matters of a like nature.

Disregarding the warning voice of my sable Cassandra, I fancied the man was true and might be safely trusted; so as soon as dinner was finished, I called him aside and confided the letter to him with these words: —

"Will you promise me faithfully, upon the honor of a soldier, to take the utmost care of this, and deliver it safe to General Jackson? They tell me you are a spy, but I do not believe it."

He, of course, denied the soft impeachment, and swore, by all the host of heaven, to execute my commission with fidelity and dispatch.

Reader, conceive my feelings when, shortly after this man's departure, one of the officers came in and informed me that he was a spy, and was on his way to the Confederate lines at Harrisburg.

I immediately set about to rectify my unfortunate error, and, after some reflection, I decided upon the following expedient: —

I sat down and wrote Major Harry Gilmore, of the Confederate cavalry, a few lines, giving an accurate account of the man's personal appearance, and explaining the motive and circumstances of his journey south, and by what means I had been entrapped into trusting him with a letter for General Jackson. This note I dispatched by a conveyance, to which we rebels had given the name of "the underground railway."

The locomotive on this railway was an old negro, and the mail-car was an enormous silver watch from which the works had been extracted. I sent off my train, with orders that if, in passing the pickets, any one should inquire the time of day, the answer must be that the imposing-looking time-piece was out of order, and had ceased to mark the hours and minutes.

Our friend the spy, however, went neither to Harrisburg nor to General Jackson, but made his way straight to the Federal General Sigel and gave him my letter. The General, in his turn, forwarded it to Stanton, the Secretary–of–War, who, I make no doubt, still retains it in his possession.

Shortly after this adventure an officer came and told me that further misconduct on my part might bring down upon me the severest punishment, and hinted that the Yankees, once thoroughly incensed, would not hesitate at the perpetration of any atrocity.

Entertaining these views, he recommended my immediate departure; and this kind advice meeting with the approval of my grandmother, I gave my consent, and immediately my maid had orders to prepare for a journey to Richmond. It was on a Tuesday that the officer promised to get a pass, and we were to be sent through the lines on the next ensuring Thursday. But fate had ordained otherwise.

Rather than being allowed to return to her home, Belle was sent to Washington and confined in Carroll Prison, where she immediately resumed her efforts on behalf of the Confederacy. She established communication with southern sympathizers outside the prison by means of a bow and arrow and a rubber ball. An outside agent would attach notes to an arrow which he shot through Belle's window. Belle replied by sewing her letters inside a rubber ball which she threw out of her window upon hearing a prearranged signal.

It was agreed that I should leave for Fortress Monroe on the 1st day of December, 1863. My father was still in Washington, residing with his niece; but he was so ill that he could not visit me previous to my departure.

One evening, whilst I was looking out of my room–door, a significant cough attracted my attention, and, glancing in the direction whence it proceeded — the sentry's back being turned — I perceived a note, tightly rolled up, thrown towards me. I picked it up quickly, and, reading it, found that it was from Mr. K., of Virginia begging me to aid himself and two friends to escape, and also asking for money to advance their object. I wrote, in reply, that I would do all that lay in my power, and, unobserved, I handed him forty dollars. By means of my india–rubber ball I arranged every thing, and the night when the attempt should be made was fixed.

Above Mr. K.'s room was a garret occupied by his two friends, who intended to escape with him; and it was so contrived that he should get into the garret with the others whilst returning from supper.

At one time I was afraid that this attempt would be frustrated, for the sentry, observing Mr. K. upon the garret staircase, commanded him to "Halt!" adding, "You don't belong there; so come down." Standing in the doorway of my chamber at the time, I quickly retorted, "Sentry, have you been so long here and don't know where the prisoners are quartered? Let him pass on to his room." Taking the hint, Mr. K. declared that he "knew what he was about," which it was very evident he did; and the sentinel, thinking that he had made a mistake, allowed him to proceed upstairs.

This part of the scheme being satisfactorily carried out, I wrote a note to the superintendent, informing him that I was desirous of seeing him for a few minutes. He accordingly came, and I managed to detain him by conversing upon various topics. Suddenly, from round the corner of the prison that faced on the street, arose a startling cry of "Murder! murder!" I know that my heart beat violently, but I kept the composure of my face as well as I was able; for this sudden cry was the commencement of a *ruse de guerre* which, if it should succeed, would liberate my friends from thraldom.

Mr. Wood had, at the first cry of "Murder!" rushed to one of the windows and flung it open to see what was the matter; and some soldiers, who were lounging outside, waiting for their turn of sentry duty, ran hurriedly to the spot from which the cries proceeded. Meanwhile, those in the room above were not idle. Removing in haste a portion of the roof, they scrambled out upon the eaves, descended by means of a light-ning–conductor into the street below, and made off, sheltered by the darkness.

Of course, the next morning, when the roll was called, and the prisoners were mustered, Mr. K. and his companions were found to be missing. It was strongly suspected that I had connived at their escape, and knew more than I pretended about the affair; but as they could not prove any thing against me, I was not punished. I subsequently heard, to my great joy, that the fugitives had arrived safely in Richmond.

A Spy in Woman's Clothing

LORÉTA JANÉTA VELAZQUEZ

MOBILE, ALABAMA, TO MEMPHIS, TENNESSEE, AUTUMN 1863

Loréta Janéta Velazquez had come to Mobile from New Orleans, where she had been rightly suspected of spying and was briefly incarcerated by General Butler. Memphis had been occupied since early in the war. General Nathan Bedford Forrest was raiding and harassing Yankee installations and supply lines in North Mississippi and West Tennessee.

Lieutenant Shorter, beyond saying that I was to go through the lines, and endeavoring to impress upon me the great importance of the enterprise, had given me no hint of where I was to go, or what the exact nature of my errand would be, and I consequently had to depend upon myself in making such preparations as were necessary. Having considered the subject as well as I was able, I concluded to procure a very plain suit of woman's clothing, and to make up a small bundle of such few extra articles besides those upon my back, as I thought I would require. My arrangements having been all made, I started for Meridian the next day, and on my arrival at that place found Lieutenant Shorter waiting for me at the depot. Under his escort I went to the hotel kept by a Mr. Jones, and was received with great cordiality by him and by his wife. The lady especially was most attentive to me, and did everything in her power to make me comfortable.

I appreciated her kind attentions the more highly as I was far from being well, and felt that I was scarcely doing either myself or the others interested justice in undertaking such an enterprise, under a strong liability that I might be taken seriously sick before concluding it. I had a great deal of confidence, however, in my power of will, and having promised Lieutenant Shorter that I would go, I was determined to do so, especially as he represented the business as being most urgent.

Having obtained a room where we could converse privately, the lieutenant proceeded to explain what he wanted me to do, and to give me directions for proceeding. He said that he had captured a spy belonging to the Federal General Hurlbut's command, and had taken from him a paper containing quite accurate accounts of the forces of [Confederate generals] Chalmers, Forrest, Richardson, and Ferguson, and their movements. This he had changed so that it would throw the enemy on the wrong scent, and I was to take it to Memphis and deliver it to the Federal General Washburn, telling him such a story as would induce him to believe that I had obtained it from the spy. He also had a despatch for Forrest, which he wanted me to carry to the Confederate secret agent in Memphis, telling me where to find him, describing him so that I would know him, and giving me the password which would enable me to communicate with him without difficulty.

"Now," said Shorter, when he had finished all his explanations, "you see that you will have to keep your wits about you, for if you let the Feds get their fingers on these papers it will be all up with you. When you reach Memphis, deliver this bogus account of the movement of our troops to General Washburn immediately, and get him and his people well impressed with the idea that you are on their side; then, at the earliest possible moment, give this despatch for Forrest to óur agent. I will know by the success of the movement that Forrest is to make whether you are successful or not."

After some further conversation about the best plan of proceeding, and further explanations about what I should do, Lieutenant Shorter suggested some changes in my dress, his idea being, that I should personate a poor countrywoman, who had lost her husband at the outbreak of the war, and who was flying into the Federal lines for protection. He also gave me letters to the different Confederate commanders whom I would meet on my road, directing them to assist me, and put in my hand the sum of one hundred and thirty-six dollars in greenbacks which had been taken from the captured spy. This, he thought, would see me through, but in case it should not prove sufficient, he said, that if I made my wants known, any commanding officer I met would supply me with funds, and that after I reached Memphis I would find plenty of friends of the Confederacy upon whom I could call for assistance.

Everything being in readiness for my journey, the next morning I took the train for Okolona, where procuring a pass from Captain Mariotta, the provost marshal, I hired a conveyance, and drove to the headquarters of General Ferguson. On showing my order for assistance to the general, he received me with the greatest politeness, and invited me into his quarters, where he gave me some information and additional instructions, and reiterated Lieutenant Shorter's cautions to be vigilant and careful, as I was on a mission of great importance.

The general then handed me ninety dollars, and presented me with a pistol, which he said was one of a pair he had carried through the war. The money he was sure I would need, and the pistol might be a handy thing to have in case I should be compelled to defend myself, for my journey would take me through a rough country, and I might chance to meet with stragglers who would give me trouble. He advised me, however, not to use the weapon except in case of absolute necessity, and especially not to carry it with me into the Federal lines, for if it was discovered that I had it about me, it might excite suspicions that I was a spy, when such a thing would not otherwise be thought of.

A fine horse having been provided for me, I said adieu to General Ferguson, who wished me good luck, and started off with an escort who was to conduct me to a point somewhere to the north–east of Holly Springs, from whence I would have to make my way alone, getting into the Federal lines as best I could.

In spite of the fact that I was quite sick, and sometimes felt that I could scarcely sit upon my horse, I rode all that night and nearly all the next day, through lonesome woods, past desolate clearings, — occupied, if at all, by poor negroes, or even poorer whites, all of whom had a half–terrified look, as if they were expecting every moment to have a rapacious soldiery come tramping through their little patches of ground, and appropriating whatever was eatable or worth taking — through gullies and ravines, and over the roughest kind of roads, or sometimes no roads at all. At length we reached a negro's cabin, which, although it was but a poor shelter, was better than nothing at all, and feeling too ill to proceed any farther without rest and refreshments, I resolved to stop there all night.

The inhabitants of the cabin were not very much inclined to be over communicative, and apparently did not want me for a lodger, and their abode was not one that I would have cared to make a prolonged sojourn in. I was too much of a veteran campaigner, however, to be over fastidious about my accommodations for a single night, and was too sick not to find any shelter welcome. From what I could learn from these people, I was not very many miles from the Federal lines, and I secured their good will, to a reasonable degree, by promising to pay well for my night's lodging, and what was given me to eat, and finally succeeded in inducing them to bestir themselves to make me as comfortable as circumstances would permit. I also struck up a bargain with an old man who appeared to be the head of the household, such as it was, to act as a guide for me in the morning, and to conduct me to the neighborhood of the Federal pickets.

I wished my escort now to return to General Ferguson's headquarters, but, as he suggested that the negroes might prove treacherous, we both concluded that it would be best for him to remain until I was fairly started in the morning on my way to the Federal lines. A supper which, under some circumstances I would scarcely have found eatable, was prepared for us, and I partook of it with a certain degree of relish, despite the coarse quality of the food, being too tired and hungry to be critical or squeamish. Then, completely used up by my long and toilsome ride, I retired to the miserable bed that was assigned me, and ere long was in happy obliviousness of the cares and trials of this world.

About three o'clock in the morning I was up and ready to start, after having made a hasty toilet, and after a breakfast which served to satisfy my hunger, but which certainly did not tempt my palate. My escort now bade me good–by, and was soon out of sight, on his way back to camp, while I, mounted on a little pony, and with the old negro to lead the way, faced in the opposite direction.

Not having the most implicit confidence in my guide, I took care to keep him in front of me all the time, and had my hand constantly upon the pistol which General Ferguson had given me, and which I was resolved to use upon my colored companion in case he should be inclined to act treacherously. Fortunately there was no occasion for any violence, and our journey continued without interruption, except such as was caused by the rough nature of the ground, until, at length, I spied through the trees a little church. It was now broad daylight, although the sun was not yet up, and the surroundings of this building, as it was seen through the fog–laden atmosphere, were dismal enough. I surmised, from what my guide had told me before we started out, that the Federal pickets must be somewhere near, and I concluded that it was time for me to get rid of the darkey; so I said to him, "Isn't that the church where you said you saw the Yankee soldiers?"

"Yes, miss, dat's de place; dey's jes' beyond dat church a bit, or dey was las' week."

"Well, I want to find them; but I guess, if you don't want them to catch you, you'd better get back as quick as you can."

Watching the old negro until he was out of sight, I rode up to the church, and dismounting, entered the building. My first care now was to get rid of my pistol. Raising a plank in the flooring, I put the pistol under it, and covered it well with dirt. Having disposed of the pistol, I sat down for a few minutes to think over the situation, and to decide upon the best method of procedure with the first Federal soldier I met. Experience had taught me, however, that no settled plan, in a matter of this kind, amounts to much, so far as the details are concerned, and that it is necessary to be governed by circumstances. I resolved, therefore, to regulate my conduct and conversation according to the character and behavior of those I chanced to meet; and so, having first ascertained that my papers were all right, I mounted my pony again, and started in the direction where I supposed I would find the Federal camp.

Letting my pony take his own gait — and he was not inclined to make his pace any more rapid than there was necessity for — I travelled for a couple of miles before I saw any one. At length a picket, who had evidently been watching me for some time, stepped out of the woods into the road, and when I came up to him, he halted me, and asked where I was from and where I was going.

"Good morning, sir," I said, in an innocent, unsophisticated sort of way. "Are you commanding this outpost?"

"No," he replied; "what do you want?"

"Well, sir, I wish you would tell the captain I want to see him."

"What do you want with the captain?"

"I have got a message to give the captain, but I can't give it to any one else."

"He is over there in the woods."

"Well, you just tell him that I want to see him quick, about something very important."

The soldier then called to his officer, and in a few moments up stepped a good–looking young lieutenant, whose blouse was badly out at the elbows, and whose clothing generally bore marks of very hard service. Although his attire was not of the most elegant description, he was a gentleman, and, as he approached me, he tipped his hat, and said, with a pleasant smile, "Good morning, madam; what is it you wish?"

"Are you the captain?" I queried.

"I am in command of this picket guard," he replied.

"Well, captain," said I, "I want to go to Memphis, to see General Washburn. I have some papers here for him."

This made him start a little, and he began to suspect that he had a matter of serious business on hand, and, evidently with a different interest in me from what he had felt before, he inquired, with a rather severe and serious air, "Where are you from, madam?"

"I am from Holly Springs. A man there gave me these papers, and told me that if I would get them through he would pay me a hundred dollars."

"What kind of looking man was he, and where did he go after he left you?"

"I mustn't tell you that, sir; the man said not to tell anything about him, except to the one these papers are for, and he would understand all about it."

"Well, madam, you will have to go with me to headquarters. When we get there I will see what can be done for you."

His relief came, not a great while after, and off we started for headquarters. As I had informed my new–made friend that I was hungry, having ridden for a considerable distance since very early in the morning, he stopped with me at a white house near the road, and sending the guard on, went in with me, and asked the woman, who appeared to be mistress of the establishment, to give me some breakfast. Quite a comfortable meal was soon in readiness, and while I was eating, the lieutenant busied himself in trying to ascertain something about the number and position of the Confederate troops. I told him that there seemed to be a large force of them near Holly Springs, but beyond that statement, — which was, I believe, far from being the truth, — I am afraid he did not find me a very satisfactory witness. I am sure that such information as I did give him was not likely to be of very great use.

After I had finished my breakfast, the lieutenant took me to Moscow, on the Memphis and Charleston Railroad, and here, for the first time, I was subjected to very serious annoyance, and first began to appreciate the fact that I was engaged in a particularly risky undertaking. The soldiers, seeing me coming into the town mounted on a ragged little pony, and under the escort of an officer, jumped at the conclusion that I was a spy, and commenced to gather round me in crowds.

"Who is she?" some one asked.

"O, she's a spy that the Illinois picket captured."

"You're gone up!" yelled some fellow in the crowd.

"Why don't they hang her?" was the pleasant inquiry of another.

These and other cheering comments greeted me on all sides, and some of the brutal fellows pushed against me, and struck my pony, and otherwise made my progress through the streets exceedingly unpleasant, notwithstanding the efforts of the lieutenant to protect me.

Finally we reached the building occupied by the colonel in command,

and I was ushered by that official into a private room, in the rear of the one used as an office. The lieutenant accompanied me, and related the manner of my coming to the picket station, and the story which I had told him.

The colonel then proceeded to cross-question me, being apparently desirous of finding out whether I was possessed of any information worth his knowing, as well as whether I was exactly what I professed to be. I flattered myself that I played my part tolerably well. I knew very little about the movements of the Confederates, or their number, but, under the process of rigid cross-questioning to which I was subjected, I said just enough to stimulate curiosity, pretending that what I was telling was what I had picked up merely incidentally, and that, as I took no interest in the fighting that was going on, except to desire to get as far away from it as possible, I really knew scarcely anything, except from rumor.

As for myself, I stuck close to one simple story. I was a poor widow woman, whose husband had died about the time of the breaking out of the war; I was for the Union, and had been badly treated by the rebels, who had robbed me of nearly everything, and I had been anxious to get away for some time with a little money I had collected, and had finally got tired of waiting for the Federal troops to come down my way, and had resolved to try and get through the lines; that a man had promised I should be paid a hundred dollars if I would carry a despatch to General Washburn, at Memphis, and had assisted me to get off; that I was to deliver the papers to General Washburn only, and was to tell him alone certain things that the man had told me; I had some friends in Ohio, to whom I was anxious to go, and I hoped that General Washburn, after I had given the despatch to him, would pay me the hundred dollars, and furnish me with a pass to go North.

The colonel tried to make me vary this story, and he several times pretended that I had contradicted myself. He was tolerably smart at a cross-examination, but not by any means smart enough for the subject he had to deal with on this occasion. I had the most innocent air in the world about me, and pretended, half the time, that I was so stupid that I could not understand what his interrogatories meant, and, instead of answering them, would go off into a long story about my troubles, and the hardships I had suffered, and the bad treatment I had received. The colonel then tried to induce me to give him the despatch, saying that he would pay me the hundred dollars, and would forward it to General Washburn. This I refused to do, as I had promised not to let anybody but the general have it, if I could help it. Neither would I tell who it was that had intrusted me with the despatch, or give any clue to the message for the general he had intrusted me to delivery by word of mouth.

In fine, the colonel was practically no wiser when he had finished than when he commenced, and so, finding that no information worth talking about was to be obtained from me, he said, "Where will you go, if I give you a pass?" at the same time winking at the lieutenant.

"I want to go to Memphis, sir, to give this paper to General Washburn, and I hope that the general will be kind enough to send me on to Ohio."

"Have you any money?"

"Yes, sir; I have about one hundred and fifty dollars."

"Confederate money, isn't it?"

"No, sir; it's greenbacks. I wouldn't have that rebel trash; it isn't worth anything."

"Well, madam," then said the colonel, "you will remain here until the train is ready to start, and I will see, in the mean time, what I can do for you."

The colonel then went out; but the lieutenant remained, and engaged in a general sort of a conversation with me for some time. About noon, he suggested that perhaps I was hungry, and went and procured me something to eat. The train came in at one o'clock, and I proceeded to the depot under the escort of the two officers; the colonel, in response to my request that the soldiers should not annoy me as they had done in the morning, assuring me that he regretted anything of the kind had happened, and promising that he would see that I was protected from insult. Whether the presence of the colonel was the sole cause of the difference in their behavior or not, I cannot say, but the soldiers kept their distance as we were going to the depot, and only stared at me. When we reached the depot, the colonel procured me a ticket, and gave me five dollars, and I overheard him say, in an undertone, to the lieutenant, "You get in the rear car, and keep an eye on her movements. I think that she is all right, but it would be just as well to watch her."

The lieutenant said, "O, there's no doubt in my mind but she is all right."

This little conversation made me smile to myself, and served to convince me that I would have no trouble in getting along nicely with my friend the lieutenant.

The colonel moved off, and the lieutenant and I stepped aboard the train, a half dozen soldiers who were near making such comments as,

"She's gone up." "I guess she'll hang." "Hanging's too good for a spy." I took no notice of them, however, but seated myself on the opposite side of the car from where they were standing. The lieutenant was overwhelmingly polite, and after having got me fixed comfortably in my seat, he said, in a low tone, "I may go up with you as far as my camp, if I can get any one to hold my horse."

I thought that this would be a good chance to improve my acquaintance with him; and perhaps do something for the furtherance of my plans; so I said, "O, I would be so glad if you would. I would so much like to have company." And I smiled on him as sweetly as I was able, to impress him with the idea that I profoundly appreciated his courtesy. The young fellow was evidently more than half convinced that he had made a conquest, while I was quite sure that I had. If he had known what my real feelings were, and with what entire willingness I would have made a prisoner of him, could I have got him into the Confederate lines, perhaps he would not have been quite so eager for my society.

When the lieutenant left, the soldiers began to crowd about the windows of the car, for the purpose of staring at me, and using towards me the same kind of abusive language as that which I have already quoted. I came to the conclusion that there must be rather lax discipline when a woman situated as I was, who was especially under the protection of the officers of the command, and whom the colonel had given orders should not be insulted in any way, could be subjected to such continued ill usage as this. I was the more indignant, as there were several officers standing by, who took no notice of the behavior of the men, and made no effort whatever to prevent them from indulging in what, under any circumstances, was a mean and cowardly pastime. At length, provoked beyond measure, I called to an officer near, who wore a major's uniform, and said to him, "I would thank you, sir, to do something to stop the men from insulting me. I am travelling under a pass from the colonel, and he promised that I should not be annoyed in this manner."

The major very promptly came forward, and pushing some of the soldiers away from the windows, said, "Men, keep quiet, and do not insult this lady. She is on our side; she is Union." And then, turning to me, he remarked, "O, you mustn't mind them. You see, they have got it into their heads that you are a spy. They won't trouble you any more."

It struck me, as the major was making this little speech, that the soldiers were wiser than some of their officers, although I did not feel any more amiable towards them on that account. I, however, thanked the major for his promptness in coming to my protection, and we passed a few words, the idea entering my head that if I could fall into a conversation with him I might be able to beguile him into giving me some points of information worth having. Before, however, we had an opportunity to do more than exchange the ordinary civilities of the day, the train began to move, and I was unable to improve my acquaintance with him.

I was just thinking that my lieutenant had deserted me, or that he was in another car for the purpose of keeping an eye on me unobserved, when he appeared beside me, having jumped on the rear end of the car as it was starting.

He said, "You have no objections to my occupying the same seat with you, have you, madam?"

"O, no, sir!" I replied; "I shall be exceedingly glad to have the pleasure of your society, as far as you are going."

"Well, I only intend going up to my camp now, but I have half a mind to run on as far as Memphis — that is, if my company will not be disagreeable to you."

"I will be very greatly pleased if you will go through with me. It has been a long time since I have met any agreeable gentlemen, and I particularly admire officers."

As I said this I gave him a killing glance, and then dropped my eyes as if half ashamed of having made such a bold advance to him. The bait took, however, as I expected it would; and the lieutenant, giving his mustache a twist, and running his hand through his hair, settled himself down in the seat with a most self-satisfied air, evidently supposing that the conquest of my heart was more than half completed, and began to make himself as agreeable as he knew how. *Finesse* was certainly not this youth's most marked characteristic, and he went about making himself agreeable, and endeavoring to discover who I was, where I came from, and all about me, in such an awkward, lubberly manner, that it was mere play for me to impose upon him.

He had not been seated more than a minute or two before he blurted out, "I guess you're married — ain't you?"

"No, sir; I'm a widow."

"Is that so? Well, now, about how long has the old man been dead?"

"My husband died shortly after the breaking out of the war. I have been a widow nearly three years."

"Well, that's a pretty good while to be a widow; but I reckon men are scarce down your way. Got any children?"

"No, sir; unfortunately I have no children."

"Well, that's lucky, anyhow."

I did not exactly understand whether he meant that it was lucky for me, or for him, in case he made up his mind to marry me. I, however, thought it a good occasion for a little sentiment, and so, giving a sigh, said, "Children are a great comfort, sometimes."

"Yes, I suppose so," said he; "especially when they are your own. I don't care much for other people's children, though."

"Are you married, sir?" I suggested, in a rather timid tone, and giving him another killing glance.

"Not much," he replied, with considerable force; "but I wouldn't mind being, if I could find a real nice woman who would have me." And with this he gave me a tender look that was very touching.

"O, there ought to be plenty of women who would gladly have a fine, handsome officer like you."

"Do you think so, now, really? Well, I'll have to look round. By the way, where do you come from? Do you belong down South?"

"No, sir," I replied; "I am a foreigner by birth, but my husband was an American, and lived in Ohio until shortly before the war."

"Is that so, now? You're English — ain't you?"

"No, sir; my parents were French and Spanish."

"I guess you must speak those languages, then?"

"Yes, sir; much better than English."

"Well, said he, "I'm mighty glad I met you."

"Thank you, sir. I may say the same to you."

He then remarked, "I don't believe you'll have any difficulty in getting through to Memphis, or any trouble after you reach there. I will be glad to assist you any way I can."

I thanked him for his kind intentions; and he then, in a hesitating sort of a way, said, "I hope you won't feel offended if I inquire how your finances are."

"O, no, sir; no offense at all. I am sorry to say that my funds are rather low."

"Well, I'll see you fixed all right until you can hear from your friends. How long do you expect to remain in Memphis?"

"No longer than I can possibly help; for I want to get back to Europe, where I have friends who will take care of me, at the earliest opportunity."

"I'm mighty sorry you are going to make such a short stay. I was hoping that we might become better acquainted. It isn't often that we meet with real ladies in these parts."

He then proceeded to inquire who my relatives in Europe were, where they lived, whether they were wealthy or not, — he seemed to be especially anxious on this point, — how old I was, whether I had ever thought much about getting married again, and so forth. I answered his queries as promptly as he could have wished, and perhaps more to his satisfaction than if I had told him the exact truth in every instance.

At length the whistle blew, and the train stopped at his camp. He jumped up, and rushed out, without even saying good–by; and while I was wondering where he had left his politeness, I saw him running as fast as he could go, and presently dodge into a tent. In a moment or two more out he came in his shirt sleeves, and ran for the train, with his coat in his hand, and jumped on board just as we were starting. I turned around, and watched him as he got into the car behind me, and saw him put on a rather better looking uniform coat than the out–at–the–elbows blouse he had been wearing, and a paper collar and black necktie. These last I considered as particularly delicate attentions to myself.

When he had completed his toilet, he came forward, and, seating himself beside me, said, "I will allow myself the pleasure going through to Memphis with you."

I assured him that I was pleased beyond measure, and came to the conclusion that it would be my fault if long before we reached Memphis I did not stand so well in his good graces that I would be able to make a most useful ally of him in carrying out my plans for the benefit of the Confederacy.

"Do you see that field over there?" said he, pointing to a good sized clearing. "That's where our boys had a fight with Forrest."

"Did you run fast?" I asked, rather maliciously.

"We had to run," said he; "they were too many for us."

"O, what a pity," said I; "you ought to have whipped them;" and thought, at the same time, that there would be some more hard running done if I ever succeeded in getting to Forrest the despatch I had for him.

"We'll whip them yet," said the lieutenant. "We've had some big successes lately in Virginia, Missouri, and Arkansas, and we'd treat them worse than we do here if we only had a few more men."

"Why," said I, "there seems to be a great many of you."

"O, there's not half enough to do anything. They've got us scattered along this railroad in such a way that it's almost as much as we can do to hold our own, when any kind of a crowd of rebs puts in an appearance."

This was interesting; but I did not think it prudent just then to question him any closer on such a delicate subject, trusting that before we parted he would let out, of his own accord, some other facts worth knowing; so I merely said, "O, this war is a terrible thing. It makes me sick to think of so many being killed and wounded."

"That's so," he replied. "It is bad, but now we've begun it, I guess we'll have to fight it out."

"What do you think they will do with that miserable fellow, Davis, if they catch him?" said I.

"Well, I'm for hanging Jeff, and all his cabinet. We'll just string up the leaders, and let the little people go, if they will promise to behave themselves."

This made my blood boil; but I controlled my feelings, and remarked, "O, I don't believe they will hang him. They've got to catch him first, you know; and then the government at Washington is disposed to be lenient, isn't it?"

"Yes, that's just what's the matter. Between the milk–and–water policy of the government, and the speculators who have been allowed to do pretty much as they please, it has been hard work carrying on the war at all. We western men have done nearly all the hardest fighting, and we've got the least credit for it. So far as I am concerned, if I had known that it was the niggers we were going to fight for, I never would have raised my sword."

"O, you don't believe in slavery, do you?" said I, with the view of increasing his confidence in me.

"No," said he; "but the niggers are better off where they are, and are not worth fighting for, anyhow."

I tried to draw him out on this subject, but for some reason he did not seem inclined to talk about it any more; and he branched off into anecdotes of army life, the fights he had been engaged in, and a variety of matters that were entertaining enough, but do not merit being placed on record. This conversation amused me, and gave me a good number of points worth knowing in the particular business in which I was engaged, until at length the train reached Memphis, and my escort assisting me to alight, requested me to wait on the platform for him while he engaged a carriage.

In a few moments he returned with a close–bodied carriage, and when I was seated in it he ordered the driver to go to the Hardwick House.

"O, no," said I; "I must go to General Washburn's headquarters first, and deliver my despatch and message."

"Just as you like," said he; "but I thought you might prefer to arrange your toilet before seeing the general."

"No," I replied; "I must see him immediately, as I was told that this was a matter of great importance. The general won't mind my looks."

The driver was accordingly directed to take us to headquarters, and before many more minutes I was ushered into the presence of the provost marshal, to whom I stated my errand. The fact of the lieutenant being with me undoubtedly prevented a great many questions being asked, some of which it might not have been agreeable, or even possible, for me to answer, and I accordingly was more than ever impressed with the value of having him for an acquaintance, especially as he put in a word now and then which had the effect of establishing me on a satisfactory footing with the provost marshal. That official, when he had heard my story, said, "Madam, I am sorry, but the general is very much indisposed, and cannot see you. I will be glad to receive anything you may have for him, and to give him any message from you."

"O, sir I must see him. It is impossible for me to communicate what I have to say to any one else."

"Did the person who confided the paper to you give you any private instructions?"

"Yes, sir, and he was very particular in telling me to communicate with the general in person, and with no one else."

"Well, madam, I am sorry for you; but, as I said before, the general is unable to see you, and you will either have to leave the paper and your message with me, or else call again."

This struck me as being a decidedly odd way of doing business. Here I was professing to be a despatch–bearer, with a confidential message from a spy within the enemy's lines, and the probabilities all in favor of my business being of extreme importance; and yet, the officer who assumed to represent the general placidly requesting me to call again, just as if I was some one who had stepped in to ask a favor of him. I concluded that if matters were managed in this kind of style at headquarters, Memphis would not be a very difficult place for me to operate in, or for the Confederates to operate against, if they thought it worth their while. I knit my brows, looked vexed and perplexed, tapped the ground with my foot, and pretended to be thinking deeply about what course I had better pursue. After a few moments' consideration, I concluded that the best thing I could do was to get the bogus despatch off my hands, and thus be free to attend to other business of more importance; so I said, "That is too bad, for I promised to see the general himself, as the man was so particular that I should; but if he won't see me, I suppose I will have to write him."

The provost marshal accordingly furnished me with a sheet of paper, and I sat down at his desk and scribbled off a brief note to the general, telling him enough about the source from which I had obtained the despatch to induce him to believe in its genuineness, and intimated that if he wanted to know more he could send for me. This note and the despatch I enclosed in the same envelope, and handed it to the provost marshal, with a request that it might be given to the general immediately. I fully expected that when General Washburn received these enclosures he would have me brought before him for the purpose of interrogations, and was much surprised when he did nothing of the kind.

The provost marshal took the envelope back into his private office, and on his return he asked me where I was going to stop. I replied that I did not know yet; whereupon he suggested that there was a nice private boarding–house near the Catholic church. I objected to going there, however, and said that I would prefer to locate myself at the Hardwick House for the present. To the hotel I accordingly went, under the escort of my friend, the lieutenant, and registered myself as Mrs. Fowler, not at all grieved at not having seen the general, and quite satisfied not to see him in the future if he did not wish to see me, for I considered the material part of my errand now practically accomplished.

The lieutenant, when he saw me fairly established in comfortable quarters, asked me to excuse him, saying that, as I seemed to be short of funds, he would see if he could not obtain some for me. I thanked him very much, made all manner of apologies for giving him so much trouble, and as a broad hint that I did not want to see any more of him that day, asked him to call in the morning, as I was feeling quite sick, was tired out with my journey, and would retire to rest after getting some supper. He was not a fool, and understood that I did not desire his company; so, taking his leave, he said that he would give orders for something to eat to be brought up to my room, and would come to see me again in the morning if I would permit him.

He had not been gone a great while before a servant appeared with a very nice supper. This I ate with immense relish, for I was desperately hungry, at the same time making certain inquiries of the servant for the purpose of enabling me to judge whether it would be safe or prudent to attempt to communicate that night with the spy for whom I had the despatch which was to be forwarded to Forrest. It was now nearly dark, and I decided that no better time for meeting the spy could be found. I accordingly asked the servant to try and borrow for me some rather more presentable articles of attire than those I had on, as I desired to go out for the purpose of making a few purchases, and was really ashamed to go into the streets dressed as I was. My real reason was that I was afraid the lieutenant, or the provost marshal, or some one who had seen me, should happen to meet me while I was out, and as, dressed in the rather outlandish fashion in which I had appeared at the picket station, they would not fail to recognize me, suspicions might be excited which would result in spoiling all my plans.

The servant, whose zeal in my behalf was stimulated by a five–dollar greenback, was not long in appearing with a reasonably decent–looking dress, bonnet, and shawl. I then attired myself with as much speed as I could command, and after having the dust and dirt brushed off my shoes, was ready to start.

It is scarcely necessary to say that I was well acquainted with Memphis, and consequently knew exactly how to go and where to go in search of my man. Fortunately for me, the place was not a very great way from the hotel, and persuading the accommodating servant to show me out the back door, under the plea that, meanly attired as I was, I was ashamed to be seen by the officers who were standing about the front of the building, I was not long in reaching it.

I knocked at the door, and the very man I was looking for came to let me in. I had never seen him before, but I knew him immediately by the description I had of him. Giving him the password I was admitted, and he eagerly inquired what I had for him. I handed him the despatch which he was to convey to Forrest, and gave him the verbal instructions which Lieutenant Shorter had ordered me to convey to him, and urged the necessity for his making haste in reaching Forrest at the earliest practicable moment. He, however, said that he thought that a movement of the Federal troops was in contemplation, and that he would like to find out exactly what it was before starting, and as I seemed to be on good terms at headquarters, he urged that I should endeavor to obtain the information for him. I consented to try what I could do, while he promised not to delay his departure longer than two days, at the farthest.

Before parting, I represented the danger to both if we should be seen in conference, and said that I would prefer not meeting him again if some means of communicating with him without a personal interview could be devised. He, therefore, suggested that if I obtained the desired information I should write him a note and deposit it in a certain place which he designated. I consented to this and took my departure, wishing him good luck. On my way back to the hotel, the prudence of my change of dress was sufficiently demonstrated, for on turning a corner I nearly ran against my friend the lieutenant and another officer, who were walking slowly along the street. My heart leaped into my mouth when I saw who it was, but as there was no retreat, I trusted to the darkness and my change of costume, and glided by them as swiftly and quietly as I could, and fortunately was able to gain my room without discovery.

My errand was now accomplished, and in as satisfactory a manner as could be desired, and the only apprehension I had was lest the spy to whom I had given the despatch for Forrest might not succeed in getting off in safety. If he should be arrested and the document found on him, the finger of suspicion would not unlikely point to me as the original bearer of it. I thought, however, that he was probably well able to take care of himself and being too much of a veteran to allow myself to be worried about possibilities that might never come to pass, I went to bed feeling that the responsibility of the business was well off my shoulders, and was soon in happy obliviousness of cares of every kind.

What Modesty Requires

KATE CUMMING

NEWNAN and ATLANTA, GEORGIA, NOVEMBER 1863–JULY 1864

Unlike Phoebe Pember's Chimborazo in Richmond, the hospital in which Kate Cumming worked was forced to move ahead of a retreating army. She had begun her nursing in the deep South, but soon moved to a hospital in North Georgia. This passage begins when she and her hospital are located in Newnan, Georgia, south of Atlanta.

November 3 — A very warm day, and our patients are suffering very much. If the weather was cool it would be better for them. One of the wards, called the carriage ward (as it had been a carriage house), has about fifty patients, and it is heart–breaking to hear them groan. I think it is even worse than Corinth, as the men here seem to suffer much more. There they either died or were taken to another hospital. Fresh wounds are scarcely ever as painful as old ones.

This ward is a large, low–roofed, white–washed room, roughly boarded, so that there are not a few openings where the daylight peeps through.

On entering, the first man to the right is Mr. Robbins, about fifty years of age. The doctors say he is one of the worst wounded men we have. His appearance is weak and languid, and there is very little hope of his recovery. Near him is Mr. McVay, an Irishman, much emaciated. One of his legs has been amputated above the knee, and the bone is protruding about an inch, which is very painful.

To the left is Mr. Groover, wounded in both knees. While marching, a cannon–ball took off the cap of one, and the under part of the other, and his back is one solid bed–sore. We have tried to relieve his suffering in every way. The very sight of his face is distressing, and makes me feel as if I would sacrifice almost any thing to palliate his pain. The effluvia from his wounds is sickening.

Further on are a dozen or so badly wounded: one without a leg; another without an arm, and some with wounds which are awful to look at, but their faces denote all they need is plenty to eat. I passed on, telling them that they are *beneath* my notice.

At the end of this group is Mr. Conda, an Irishman, with his leg in a sling. His wound, though not a bad looking one, is very painful, and he sleeps but little day or night. The clammy sweat constantly on his forehead tells how acutely he suffers; so that there is no need of asking him how he is.

Opposite him is Mr. Horton, another great sufferer. Just beyond is a man who has about two inches of his shin–bone cut out, and it is growing up.

Along side of him is Mr. Sparks, who came here with apparently a slight wound in the leg. It is now so painful that he not only groans day and night, but many a time his plaint can be heard in the street. His nose is pinched, and all his features have the appearance of a great sufferer. A little ways from him is Mr. Robinson, a lad of about seventeen. The calf of his leg is a solid sore. He wails most dolefully, and we find it impossible to assuage his pain.

He and many of the others might have their limbs amputated, but the doctors say that their systems are not in a fit state, and that they would not stand the shock. There are many other badly wounded men in the ward, but they do not seem to suffer so acutely.

In looking over letters received from a friend in Mobile, I was a little astonished at an assertion in one about the planters. It seems they will not sell produce unless at an exorbitant price, and many will take nothing in return but gold and silver. If this is really the case, which I have no reason to doubt, I am at a loss to understand how they can be so blinded. Are they not aware that we are blockaded, and can only procure food from them; and do they not also know, if the enemy succeed — which they assuredly will, if the planters and others act as they are now doing — that they will be ruined, as well as every body else? Heaven help the country! I am getting sick at heart with seeing men from whom we expected so much acting as they are now doing. I wonder if they expect men to fight for them and their property, if they leave their wives and children to starve? The men will be more than mortal if they do it.

It is too bad that President Davis can not devise some way of making these Esaus, who would not only sell their own birth right, but ours, for a mess of pottage, give up their stores. They are ours by right. God did not shower His blessing on the land, as he has done this summer, for them alone.

It is said the planters were to blame for the fall of Vicksburg, and that after its fall the enemy came and took all their cotton, corn, and every thing else they had. If this report be true, it is a just judgment on them. And will they not all suffer the same?

When I think of these wretches, and of the men who are lying here, having suffered so much to save them and their wealth, I can scarcely keep from crying out on them. What is every bushel of corn and acre of land these planters have compared with the sacrifice these men have made? A mere cipher. Why, such comparisons are odious!

December 8 — Miss Womack received a letter from a cousin, a surgeon in the army, entreating her to leave the hospital, saying that it is no place for a refined, modest young lady. I have perhaps made a mistake as regards the meaning of the word modesty. As far as my judgment goes, a lady who feels that her modesty would be compromised by going into a hospital, and ministering to the wants of her suffering countrymen, who have braved all in her defense, would not rightly lay claim to a very large share of that excellent virtue — modesty — which the wise tell us is ever the companion of sense. . . .

I am thoroughly disgusted with this kind of talk. When will our people cease to look on the surface of things? At this rate, never! If the scenes we are daily witnessing will not serve to cure this miserable weakness, nothing will.

There is scarcely a day passes that I do not hear some derogatory remarks about the ladies who are in the hospitals, until I think, if there is any credit due them at all, it is for the moral courage they have in braving public opinion.

A very nice lady, a member of the Methodist Church, told me that she would go into the hospital if she had in it a brother, a surgeon. I wonder if the Sisters of Charity have brothers, surgeons, in the hospitals where they go? It seems strange that they can do with honor what is wrong for other Christian women to do.

Well, I can not but pity those people who have such false notions of propriety.

After getting tired of hearing what is said, I told a lady friend that she would oblige me by telling the good people of Newnan, that when I first went into the hospitals I was not aware of there being such a place in the world as Newnan, and they must excuse me for not asking their advice on the subject; and since without it I had taken the step I had, I could not say I had any thing to regret in the matter; far from that, I can truly say, that there is no position in the world that a woman can occupy, no matter how high or exalted it may be, for which I would exchange the one I have. And no happiness which any thing earthly could give, could compare with the pleasure I have experienced in receiving the blessings of the suffering and dying.

As for no "refined or modest" lady staying in them, from my own experience, and that of every surgeon whom I have heard speak on the subject, I have come to the conclusion that, in truth, none but the "refined and modest" have any business in hospitals. Our post surgeon called on me the other day, and told me he had determined to permit none but such to enter any of his hospitals; and he earnestly warned me to be careful whom I took to stay with me.

But I feel confident we shall always have the approval of the truly good. I have not asked Miss Womack to remain; her own sense of right has determined her to do so.

Mrs. Byrom and I took a walk to the graveyard last Sunday. We saw two of our men buried; one was named S. Brazelton, a member of the fiftieth Alabama Regiment; the name of the other I did not learn; he came from some of the other hospitals. All the men of our hospital are now buried by the chaplain, Mr. Moore.

The graves have head–boards, on which is the occupant's name and regiment.

We had a man by the name of Vaughn die very suddenly on the 3d.

Sunday, December 13 — A gloomy, rainy day. We had service in the carriage ward. Rev. Mr. Ransom, a chaplain from Tennessee, preached an excellent sermon. He told us that the Lord was dealing with us as a surgeon would with sick and wounded men; that we were morally sick, and the Lord was giving us bitter medicines.

I looked about the ward, which is very large, and there were the halt, the lame, and the blind, all eagerly drinking in the words of comfort. Miss J. Lowe, a lady of the place, Miss Womack, Mrs. Williamson, and myself were there. We always make a rule of attending service when it is held in the wards, as we think it gives encouragement to the men.

The reason we have service there is because there are always numbers of wounded men anxious to hear the word of God, and are not able to leave their beds.

December 16 — A very disagreeable day; it is cold, windy, and rainy. I have managed to get round the wards once; nearly all are doing well.

I have spent a good portion of the day with one of our patients, who died to–night at 9 o'clock. Miss Womack and myself were with him when he breathed his last.

He was a young Texan, by the name of Thomas Watson, a member of the Fourth Texas Regiment — one of General Hood's men — and came here with some members of his company, who were wounded, to nurse them. A few days ago he was taken with double pneumonia and sore throat. Dr. Wellford attended him, and did all that mortal could do, but in vain. It was God's will he should go.

He was a handsome lad, in his eighteenth year, and was a general favorite. He often told Miss Womack and myself about his mother, and how she had buckled on his armor, and told him to go and battle for his country.

When he was informed that all hope was over, he sent for me, and told me what he wished done. He wanted the money due him collected and sent to his mother. This I tried to have done, but there was no paymaster here, and we have been told that it will be impossible. He then asked me to write, and tell her he was dying happy, and hoped to meet her in heaven.

Toward night he became delirious, and raved about the battles in which he had participated. He spoke a good deal about some ladies in the place who had been very kind to him; and, more than any thing else, he raved about this mother — spoke to her as he had no doubt done when a child. Toward the last he grew calm, and recognized Miss Womack and myself, who were standing by, and thanked us for past kindness. I wiped the clammy sweat from his forehead, and brushed back the brown curls clustering on it. He muttered a prayer, and while it was on his lips his spirit took its flight to God, who gave it. Mr. Moore has attended him closely since he was first taken. He and another chaplain, Mr. Daniel, were with him this evening.

After our return, Miss Womack told me that she had experienced more real pleasure to–night than she had at all the places of amusement which she had ever attended. I observed the night as we came back, and I never saw such a sky in my life; it was dark in the extreme. . . .

December 17 — Miss Womack, Mrs. M., and myself went to Mr. Watson's grave. We got there in time to see the coffin lowered, and the sod cover his remains. I trust his spirit has gone "where the wicked cease from troubling, and the weary are at rest." He was laid with the true and the brave. No one could wish "couch more magnificent."

• • •

Sunday, December 20 — A very cold day. The patients are all doing pretty well.

Yesterday we lost another of our nurses, named Crittenden. He was about the same age as Mr. Watson. He was a member of the Fifth South Carolina Regiment. He was ill but for a few days, and died from the effects of a sore throat. He was a sincere Christian, and leaves no relatives to mourn for him.

On the 15th, Mr. Robertson died from the effects of a wound in the calf of one of his legs. Gangrene had set in, which destroyed the muscles and integuments extensively. He suffered severely, and nothing could be done to relieve him. Some ladies of the place took great interest in him and were very kind. He was a member of the Sixtieth North Carolina Regiment. His mother lives in Cherokee County, North Carolina, on the borders of Tennessee.

Another man died the same day, named Wm. Kirwin, a member of the Eighth Arkansas Regiment, who has a sister living in Issart County, Arkansas. He suffered a long time from consumption.

In a Mobile paper of the 14th inst. is a letter from Richmond, signed "Gamma." The writer says he knows of four commissaries and quartermasters there who have made fortunes since the war. One, when he entered the service, was not worth a dollar, but after being in office a year and a half bought a farm for fifty thousand dollars, and has now retired with as much more on which to live. The other three, are if anything, worse.

Is the president powerless to remove this moral leprosy which is eating the very vitals of the Confederacy? I really think that honest men who wink at those things are nearly as bad as the culprits. I am acquainted with one instance where we all knew there was as plain a case of robbery as any could be, but nothing was done to the miscreant.

It was reported that one of General Bragg's quartermasters was making thousands off the government.

General Bragg, on making inquiry, had proof enough against him to have him tried. He sent word to the president some two or three times before he could get him to have any thing done in the matter. At last this quartermaster underwent a trial. Fraud after fraud was proved on him; but as some of our most influential men had become his security to a large amount, they managed to get him off with the *penalty* of his losing his commission. I consider the bitterest foe we are fighting openly better than such a man.

• • •

Christmas–day, December 25 — We have had a pleasant one. Miss Womack and myself were up hours before daylight making eggnog. We wished to give some to all in the hospital, but could not procure eggs enough; so we gave it to the wounded who are convalescent, the cooks, and the nurses.

Just at the peep of dawn the little gallery in front of our house was crowded with the wounded. The scene was worthy of a picture; many of them without a leg or an arm, and they were as cheerful and contented as if no harm had ever happened them. I constantly hear the unmarried ones wondering if the girls will marry them now. Dr. Hughes did his best to have a nice dinner for the convalescents and nurses. Turkeys, chickens, vegetables, and pies. I only wish the men in the army could have fared as well.

In the afternoon we had a call from all of our surgeons, and from one or two from the other hospitals. I had hard work to get Mrs. Williamson to spare a few hours from working for "her dear boys," and have a kind of holiday for once, as nearly all of our wounded are doing well. Mr. Deal is still suffering very much, but his surgeon, Dr. Wellford, thinks he will save his leg.

We have only lost one or two from gangrene. I am confident that nothing but the care and watchfulness bestowed on them by the surgeons has been the means of saving the lives of many. They recovery has taken me by surprise, as I could not see how it was possible for such bad wounds to heal.

Many of the wounded are still in tents, with chimneys which smoke badly, and the whole tent has rather an uncomfortable appearance; still I like tents for wounded, as they seem to improve much more rapidly in them than in rooms.

The nurses, on windy nights, are compelled to sit up and hold on to the tent–poles to prevent their being blown down.

Drs. Divine, Reese, Wellford, and Burks are our assistant surgeons. Dr. Divine is one of the best of his profession; he is from Mississippi. Dr. Reese is an odd kind of a man; seems to be an excellent doctor, but I think is rather rough with the wounded, though he is very kind and attentive. He is from Alabama. Dr. Wellford is a perfect Virginia gentleman. He is one of the gentlest and most attentive surgeons that I have ever met. I think we owe the recovery of many of the wounded mainly to his great care. I have known him many a time work from daylight till dark attending to the wounds. Dr. Burks of Kentucky has been here but a short time; so I can say little about him. The men all like him very much, and they are generally good judges. He has taken Dr. Glenn's place, the latter having been transferred to some other post.

Dr. Wellford has a nurse from Arkansas. He came here with the wounded after the battle of Chickamauga. We called him "rough diamond," as he is so rough–looking, and seems to have such a kind heart. He thinks nothing a trouble which he has to do for the wounded.

Another is Mr. Harper. The wounded men have told me that it annoyed them to see him work as much as he does.

We are using a great deal of charcoal on the wounds, and the nurses have it to pulverize, which gives them constant work, besides the dirt which it causes in the wards.

I see by Mobile papers that Captain Hazard, of the Twenty–fourth Alabama Regiment, was captured at Missionary Ridge. Mr. C. Larbuzan is badly wounded, and also a prisoner. Mobile has suffered not a little in this respect.

General Bragg has resigned. For his own sake and ours, I am heartily glad.

Sunday, December 27 — Mr. Moore had service in one of the wards, and preached a very good sermon. He is a great favorite with the men.

We had one man die yesterday; another is dying to–day. It is bitter cold, and pouring down rain.

December 30 — I have spent the whole day trying to get milk for the sick, and I think I have succeeded in securing a little. We have two cows, but the milk they give is but a mite, compared to what we need. Many of the convalescent soldiers go round to the citizens begging for milk, who think they can not make better use of it than giving it to them. I do not doubt but these soldiers are in want of it; still we have others to whom it is a necessity.

Lincoln has again refused to exchange prisoners. I do think this is the cruelest act of which he has been guilty, not only to us, but his own men. He is fully aware that we can scarcely get enough of the necessaries of life to feed our own men; and how can he expect us to feed his. Human lives are nothing to him; all the prisoners we have might die of starvation, and I do not expect they would cost him a thought, as all he has to do is issue a call for so many more thousands to be offered up on his altars of sacrifice. How long will the people of the North submit to this Moloch. He knows that every one of our men is of value to us, for we have not the dregs of the earth to draw from; but our every man is a patriot, battling for all that is dear to him.

December 31 — One of the stormiest and bleakest nights I have ever witnessed. I looked out and the darkness was fearful. The sky appeared as if God had shut out the light of his countenance from us forever. The elements are warring like our poor selves.

I never look on such a night without thinking of the soldier who may be at that moment doing sentinel duty. How dreary must be his walk as he paces along.

Another sun has run its yearly course, and to all appearances we are no nearer the goal of liberty than we were this day last year. No gleam of light comes to tell us that reason has returned to the darkened minds of our ruthless foe. We have to listen to tales of wrong committed on our people, enough to rouse the blood in the coldest heart, and make us in despair cry aloud for vengeance. . . .

In the past year we have suffered disaster after disaster, but nothing is worth having which does not cost a struggle; and, then, as our beloved president tells us, it is only for a little while. The enemy has brought army after army against Richmond, and have as often had to retire in dismay and confusion before the invincible Lee and his veteran army.

The enemy have the Mississippi River only in name. Louisiana is almost as free from them as it has been since the fall of New Orleans. Texas is ours. Mississippi is guarded by that king of cavalrymen, Forrest. Charleston,

"Through coming years its name
A talisman shall be."

Shell after shell has been hurled against its sacred walls. Column after column of the invader round it have found graves.

Ah! would I could say as much about Tennessee. How my heart sickens at the desecration of her sacred vales and mountains! Our dead are not permitted to lie in their resting–places; houses are fired, and their inmates cast out into the ruthless storm. . . .

On the water we have the gallant Captains Semmes and Maffitt, bringing dismay to the grasping Yankee, by destroying what to him is dearer than life.

We have many true and determined men yet, who will never yield as long as the life–blood streams through their veins. I have no fear for our cause; our martyrs have not offered up their lives in vain. . . .

May 17 — There has been fighting near Dalton for some days. Our army has left that place, and is moving down, drawing the enemy with it. We are told that the enemy are suffering severe losses.

I went to Atlanta on the 15th instant, in company with some ladies and gentlemen of this place. We intended going to the scene of conflict, but, as the army is on the move, had to come back. We reached Atlanta on the morning of the 16th, about daylight. Mrs. Harris and myself went to the Gate City Hospital. It is the distributing one. There I met an old friend in Mr. Tucker, the head nurse. The hospital was filled with wounded, who had come in that morning from the front. Mr. Tucker told me that he had dressed the wounds of four hundred men since 4 o'clock the previous day. He had been up all that night at his work.

Mrs. Harrison was told that her son was wounded, and that he had been sent to Newnan.

That morning was one of the gloomiest I ever passed. It was damp and cheerless; and, look which way I would, the prospect was dreary. Hundreds of wounded men, dirty, bloody, and weary, were all around us. And when I thought of the many more which were expected, I was filled with despair, and felt like humbling myself in the dust, and praying more earnestly than ever before, that God would send us peace. . . .

We remained nearly all day in an old car, expecting to get on to the front. There was a relief committee, from Lagrange, in the same car with us. I observed that several such committees were in Atlanta, from every part of Georgia. The good people of Newnan had supplied us with quantities of every thing. In the afternoon, Mrs. Harris, Mrs. Barnes, Mrs. Auld and myself went to the cars, on their arrival from the front; and O, what a sight we there beheld! No less than three long trains filled, outside and in, with wounded. Nearly all seemed to be wounded in the head, face, and hands. I asked some one near me why this was. They replied, because our men had fought behind breastworks.

There were ladies at the depot with baskets filled with edibles of all kinds, and buckets of milk, coffee, and lemonade; and I noticed many had wines. I observed a number of old gentlemen assisting — the only manner in which they could serve their country. I noticed one in particular, an aristocratic-looking gentleman, who wore a white linen apron.

The ladies in Atlanta have been doing this work ever since the commencement of the war. They have had tables set at the depot for the benefit of the soldiers. Our party went to the distributing hospital; there we found plenty of work. A number of the Atlanta ladies were there before us, dressing wounds. I commenced to dress one man's hand, which was badly wounded. (Strange as it may seem, this was the first wound I had ever dressed. I had always had plenty of other work to do.) Just as I had got through, Dr. Jackson, who had gone with us from Newnan, requested me to come and assist him. We were in an immense hall, crowded with wounded; some walking about, others sitting on the floor — all waiting to have their wounds dressed. As soon as that was done, they were sent off to make room for others. Surgeons, ladies, nurses were scattered all about, so intently employed that they did not seem to notice each other. I brought the patients to Dr. Jackson and unbound the stiff bandages from their wounds, making them ready for him to dress. These men were called by the surgeons slightly wounded. One poor fellow from Alabama had both hands disabled. From one he had lost all his fingers excepting the fourth and thumb; and on the other he was shot through the wrist. This man was perfectly helpless. There were many just such *slight* wounds. One or two had lost an eye. Dr. Wellford was near where we were, as busy as he could possibly be, one of the ladies assisting him as I was Dr. Jackson. After getting through, I went into the rooms which were filled with badly wounded men in bed. I noticed many ladies bathing the men's faces and attending to their wants in other ways.

While in one of the rooms, a young man called me by my name, and told me he had seen my brother the night before, and that he was well. This young man was named Laramar, from Mobile, a member of the Fortieth Alabama Regiment. There was another with him; his name, I think, was Reese, a member of the same regiment. There was also a Mr. Cox of Mobile, whom I knew, waiting on them. He is in the ordnance department in Atlanta.

Mr. Laramar informed me that the Seventeenth and Twenty–ninth Alabama regiments had suffered severely, and that Captain Hailey of the Twenty–ninth was killed, and many of the others in that regiment.

It was a bright, moonlight night, and there were some folks who came into the hospital with provisions for the men. Dr. Wellford and a number of us took them and went all over, to see if we could find any in want, but nearly all had been supplied.

The men were lying all over the platform of the depot, preferring to remain there, so as to be ready for the train which would take them to other places.

I was informed that there were about seven or eight hundred wounded who had come in that evening.

Dr. Pursley is surgeon of the receiving hospital, and seemed to be doing all in his power for the sufferers. Every one in it looked wearied and worn out with the constant work which they had to do. The matron was very ill.

Dr. Bemiss, who is assistant medical director, was at the hospital, and going around in his usual kind manner, seeing that the men were attended to. About 10 o'clock he took Mrs. Harris and myself to Mrs. Lowenthall's, where he boarded, who received us very kindly.

There was a young man visiting her, who was dressed in the extreme of fashion, with the addition of a few diamonds. I could not help contrasting him with the men I had just seen, who had been fighting for every thing truly noble — wounded, covered with dust, and many of them in rags.

Foppish dress is bad taste in a man at any time; but if there is one time more than another when it is out of place, it is the present. And I can not see why men think of such things just now, as no woman whose opinion is of any value has respect for those who do.

I have heard soldiers (I mean the fighting kind) say, that nothing disheartens them so much as to see men so over–dressed.

I had promised Dr. Bemiss that I would remain to breakfast the next morning, forgetting I had promised Mr. Tucker to be at the hospital by daylight, as he expected hundreds of wounded.

I kept my first promise, and as Mrs. Harris did not feel very well, I went to the hospital by myself. While crossing at the depot I met my friend, Mr. Gribble, and he accompanied me to it. On arriving there I found that no more wounded had come, but there are many there already, for whom I made toddies.

The scene which presented itself to me in the large room where we had been the night before was sickening.

There was pile after pile of rags, just as they had been taken from the wounds, covered with blood and the water used in bathing them. All of the attendants were too much exhausted to clean up.

There are things to which we have to shut our eyes, if we wish to do any good, as they can not be avoided.

I met Dr. Calvert of the Thirty–eighth Alabama Regiment, who requested me to get some rags for him, which I did, and assisted him as much as I could. He had some badly wounded men from his regiment.

Dr. Calvert told me he had not eaten any thing for some time. I gave him some coffee, bread, and meat; and when I recollect now the place in which he ate it, I think we can get used to any thing. It was in the room or hall which I have just described.

We have concluded to return to Newnan, and as the cars did not start till 9 a.m., I visited one of the other hospitals, Dr. Calvert going with me; I think the name of it was the Medical College. The building is a very handsome one, and had just been fitted up. Every thing about it was in perfect order. It is one of the nicest hospitals in which I have ever been. It was filled with badly wounded men, as I am told is the case with every hospital in Atlanta. I found men there from every state in the Confederacy.

We left Atlanta on the passenger–car, and when half–way down had to get out, as the freight train that had left some hours before had met with an accident, and blocked up the road.

We got into a freight–car in front; in it there was a very large man, who had been in the car on which the accident happened; he had got mashed between two beams; his collar–bone was broken and his chest very much bruised, so that it was with difficulty he could breathe. His face was so much bruised that his eyes were almost closed. There were a number of surgeons on the cars, who were very kind to him. He is in our hospital, under Dr. Wellford's care.

Major Davis of the Twentieth Alabama Regiment is at the Buckner Hospital, wounded in the head. On hearing he was from Mobile, I went to see him. He gave me a great deal of encouragement regarding this retreat of the army. Many can not understand why it is. He spoke very highly of General Johnston as a commander, and said he believed that in all his retreating he had not left as much as an old wheel for the enemy, and he never fought them unless he was certain of a victory. He also said that the men were better fed and better clad than they had ever been.

There is much talk at present about one of our cavalry officers, who is said to have killed six prisoners that he expected would be recaptured. It is reported that many of the men of the army have petitioned Gen. Johnston to send this officer to the enemy, and let them do what they please with him.

Major Davis approved of what the men had done, and regretted that their petition had not been granted, as no punishment could be too severe for any man guilty of such barbarity. He also told me the enemy had shot six of our innocent men in retaliation.

When will men cease to do what is unjustifiable in the eyes of both God and man?

Major Davis spoke highly of Ben Lane Posey; says he is one of the bravest men we have, although a little eccentric.

May 20 — I went up to Atlanta again, but as the army is still retreating I came right back. While there, I met Doctor and Mrs. Hopping, just from Kingston. They came away in a great hurry, leaving a large portion of the hospital stores behind. They did not receive orders to move until our army had entered Kingston. The enemy was expected in Rome, so Johnston has had to fall back.

Mrs. Hopping represented the scene among the inhabitants at Kingston as harrowing, at the prospect of having the enemy come among them, as they carry ruin and desolation in their path.

While in search of Mrs. Harris I went into the Trout House, in the hall of which I saw a young man lying wounded. I learned he was from Mobile. His name is Leslie, and he is a member of the Seventeenth Alabama Regiment. His wound was not a bad one. He told me that his colonel was in the hotel severely wounded. I paid the latter a visit to see if I could be of any service to him, but found him doing much better than I had expected; his wife was with him.

The Seventeenth Regiment was in Mobile when I was there last; since then it has suffered very much.

I again visited the Gate City Hospital. There were not quite as many wounded as when I was last there. While standing on the gallery I heard a young man just come from a hospital in Cassville, grumbling very much at some doctor who had made him leave there in such a hurry that he had not time to get his clothes. He was giving it to officers in general, and spoke as if he was fighting to please them.

I listened awhile, and then asked him what he was fighting for. He replied, for his country. I then told him how he had been talking. He said he knew that it was wrong, but really the men had a great deal to endure from their officers.

I have heard many complaints of this kind; I think that often the men are to blame; they treat their officers with too much contempt.

Our officers should be the best of our men, and their rank respected if they are not.

Let the privates do their part, and if they have got petty officers over them who abuse the "little brief authority" with which they are clothed, take no notice of it, remembering that there are crosses which must be borne for the good of the cause, and that to "bear is to conquer."

I know that our men have a good deal to contend with in that respect, as our officers are elected as our civilians are, and whoever is the best electioneerer gets the office, and often not from any personal merit. I am fearful that this same evil will be the means of doing much harm to our cause, if one half of the tales are true which we are constantly listening to, of the drunkenness and evil of all kinds of which these petty officers are guilty. I know of one instance, the truth of which I can vouch for.

The captain of a battery at one time was inebriated while the company was being drilled. He imagined that one of the men had treated him with contempt; so ordered him to be tied to one of the gun–carriages, and dragged behind for twenty miles. This was done by order of a man who, I am told, was never sober enough at the time of any of the battles to lead his men.

The man who had been thus badly treated was so indignant at the insult, that he immediately applied for an exchange into a company of sharp–shooters — many thought for the purpose of shooting the captain.

I asked a gentleman who had been telling me about some of these misdemeanors, why the culprits were not brought to justice, as drunkenness was a thing which our commanding generals seem very strict about. He answered, that there was a compact between the petty officers to defend each other at all hazards, so it was impossible for a private to have justice.

But we must expect the evil as well as the good. On the other hand, I know of officers so much beloved that their men would lay down their lives in their defense. And the terrible slaughter of our officers shows that there is no lack of bravery among them. It is said that in every battle we lose many more of them, in proportion, than we do privates.

I have seen enough of our men to know that they will do much better by good treatment than bad.

On the cars, coming back, I met Captain O'Rearin of the Twenty-ninth Alabama Regiment; he was wounded slightly. He told me that he did not believe Captain Hailey was killed.

July 15 — We have had an anxious time within the last few days. On the 13th instant a scout brought word that the Federal cavalry had captured a number of men guarding Moore's Bridge, some twelve miles distant, and that in large force they were advancing on the town.

The post commandant, Colonel Griffin, telegraphed to General Johnston, requesting him to send troops here. He then collected all the men from the hospitals who were able for duty, and sent them, under the command of a Kentucky captain, to meet the foe.

We all went to work to prepare for the enemy's reception. The first thing done was to send into the woods the negroes, poultry, cattle, convalescents, and all of the nurses, excepting those actually needed to take care of the sick.

A wagon was loaded with all the valuables and sent to parts unknown. We had valises packed with a few clothes, and baskets filled with provisions, in case we should be compelled to take to the woods.

We have been told that the enemy burn every hospital building, and we had no idea that they would show us any mercy. We packed our trunks, and concluded to remain in the hospital, thinking it might be as safe a place as any.

We had a large quantity of whiskey, which we were afraid to keep, for fear if the enemy should get it they would act worse than without it, so it was sent to the woods.

All the surgeons left except Dr. Hughes, who remained at his post. The excitement in town was very great. I do not suppose there was an eye closed all night. On looking out we could see lights all over the place, the people moving every thing that was movable.

About 12 at midnight, Miss Womack concluded to go down to her aunt's, living near West Point. The train was expected from Atlanta at 2 a.m. She got ready, and some of the men carried her baggage to the depot. I started with her; on our way down we met a gentleman, who informed us that the train would not be down, as the conductor was fearful of its being captured. We sat up all night long, and it was a night of dread. Every now and again someone came into town telling us that the enemy were but a few miles off. Every little noise we heard, we made sure they had come. A man came in and told us that they were on the outskirts of the town, waiting for daylight.

Next morning — the 14th — we waited in vain for the enemy; I thought I never had heard of cavalry taking so long to come a few miles. Our head cook did not leave; saying he was tired of running. We had to have something to eat; so, having no cooks, we all went to work and got breakfast ready, fully expecting the Yankees to eat it instead of our men.

After breakfast there was still no tidings of the foe. We went to work and prepared dinner; Miss Womack peeling potatoes and shelling peas, etc., all the time wondering if the Yankees would like their dinner, as we knew that they would not be backward in helping themselves; but by dinner–time the joyful tidings arrived that General Johnston had sent cavalry and driven them back.

We breathe free again, but only for a little while, as I do not see what is to prevent them coming in at any time. The men are coming back very much exhausted. The negro women are nearly all sick, and vowing they will never run again. One old woman, who, I am certain, the enemy could not be paid to take, is nearly dead. The women carried all their clothes with them, as they hear the Federals rob black as well as white. Many an amusing story is related about the hiding.

It is a blessing we can laugh, for this great anxiety is enough to kill any one. I can not help wishing that our *kind* northern *friends*, who *love* us so dearly that they will have us unite with them, whether we will or no, only had a little of it.

Sunday, July 17 — I went down to the train to see Miss Womack off. After she left we were informed that there was a raid near West Point, and that Miss Womack will reach there in time to meet it. It is useless to think of going any place and getting rid of the enemy, as they seem to have it in their power to overrun the whole country.

Miss Womack and I have agreed that, if either should lose our clothes, the one spared would share with the other. The enemy have a particular liking for ladies' wardrobes. I presume they send them to their *lady-loves* in the North. I wonder how they feel in their stolen finery!

I do not suppose that the men would rob us as they do if they were not incited by the importunities of their women. Many letters, taken from dead Federals on the battle-fields, contain petitions from the women to send them valuables from the South. One says she wants a silk dress; another a watch; and one writer told her husband that now was the time to get a piano, as they could not afford to buy one.

"O shame, where is thy blush!" What a commentary on the society of "the best government the world ever saw!" Would we had the pen of a Thackeray to delineate the angelic and super eminent virtues of this *great* people!

On my return I met a friend from Mobile, Dr. Henderson, the surgeon of a hospital in that place. He brought me a letter from home, which was gladly received. He has been visiting the army, and intends remaining here till the expected great battle comes off. He is an Englishman, and came out from England last fall. On his arrival he received a commission in our army.

This afternoon we went to a funeral in the Methodist Church. Dr. Adams officiated, as the deceased was an Episcopalian — young Colston of Louisville. He was the color-bearer of a Kentucky regiment, and a gallant soldier. He was buried with the full honors of war. The day was very lovely. We walked round that sacred spot, the soldiers' graveyard, and I saw many a familiar name on the head-boards of the graves — the occupants now calmly sleeping, heedless of the cannon's roar, and the peal of musketry. . . .

Though no towering monument is there to mark their last resting place, it matters little, Nature shall adorn them with her choicest sweets. . . .

• • •

July 25 — Heavy fighting is reported at the front. Drs. Henderson, Divine, and Reese are on their way there. Dr. Henderson has spent the week at the Gamble Hospital with Dr. Wildman. Dr. Wildman is an Englishman. Last Monday our surgeons made up their minds that Dr. Henderson had been sent here by Dr. Foard to "spy out the nakedness of the land." It is in vain I protested that I believed such was not the case. In going into the wards I found the nurses all busy, getting ready for the great inspector, as they called him. I did not try to undeceive them, as I knew the wards could not be injured by a little extra cleanliness. The next day the nurses were sadly disappointed, as no inspector had been round to see how nicely they had put on their comforts and set their little bottles in military array.

July 27 — We had heavy fighting on the 22d. Lieutenant John Lyons, whom I visited in Corinth, was killed. His death will be a sad blow to his poor mother and wife. He had a brother wounded at the battle of Spottsylvania Court–house. He lived a short time after the battle, and his devoted mother was with him when he breathed his last.

A day or two ago we received a lot of badly wounded; some of them are shot near the spine, which paralyzes them so they can neither use hands or feet. There is one very large man, named Brown, who is as helpless as an infant. Another, Captain Curran, is almost as bad. A fine–looking young man from Kentucky has lost a leg and arm; there is but little hope of his recovery. Mr. Pullet, a Georgian, is wounded through the lungs; the least movement causes the blood to run in streams from his wound; the doctors have little hope of saving him. Mr. Thomas is wounded through the head; his brain is oozing out, and at times he is delirious. Mr. Orr is injured in the spine, and is perfectly helpless. Mr. Summers of Mississippi is wounded in the right hand and can not feed himself. Mr. Harper is badly wounded, and can scarcely eat any thing. Mr. Latta, his friend, has had his leg amputated. I have written to the chaplain of their regiments, the Twelfth and Forty–seventh Tennessee, informing him of their condition. Mr. Henderson from Tennessee is severely wounded. We have so many poor, helpless fellows, that it is heart–breaking to look at them. I went down to the train when they arrived, and they were a sad sight to behold. A handsome Texan died as soon as he was brought up to the hospital. A particular friend and one of his officers were with him. There were about fifty brought to our hospital. A number were sent to the Gamble.

The first thing we did was to get them something to eat. We had buttermilk, which they relished.

Mrs. Captain Nutt, a lady from Louisiana, brought us some nice rags, an article which we were entirely out of; and she also gave us her aid. Mr. Moore also assisted. At a time like this the nurses are all kept busy attending to the wants of the surgeons. We washed the men's hands and faces, and fed them.

Among these martyrs is a young man who, the surgeons are certain, shot himself intentionally. We have a case of that kind now and then. Some time ago, a man, rather than be returned to duty, cut three of his fingers off with an ax, and a bad job he made of it.

As Miss Womack is gone, Mrs. Williamson takes her place; so we have many more duties now than we had. Many of the men are unable to feed themselves. I go over at mealtime and assist the nurses.

Mr. Rabbit, a member of Garrity's battery, is here badly wounded. He has suffered awfully from having gangrene in his wound. Dr. Wellford, his surgeon, thought at one time he would lose his leg.

There is an old lady here taking care of her sick son; she lives across the river, about fifteen miles distant. She says she has the *felicity* of having the Federal cavalry surrounding her place. They go into houses, and what they do not carry away they destroy. They have a dreadful antipathy to crockery, and break all the poor people's dishes.

I met a Mr. Miller visiting Mr. Dougherty's, who told me that these vandals had called on him, and after robbing him of every thing worth taking, took some dressed leather that he prized very highly, and before his eyes cut it into pieces. It seems to me that they are bent on creating a market for their own wares.

Sunday, July 31 — A most exciting day. The town is filled with troops. Last Thursday, the 28th, about dark, scouts brought in word that the enemy was crossing the river in large force. There was little heed paid to the report, as we had heard so many lately. About 9 o'clock the whole sky was illuminated by a glare of light, in the direction of Palmetto, a small town on the railroad. We knew then what we had to expect, and got ready as usual; whiskey, and every thing of any consequence, was sent off; the men who were able taking to the woods.

Some of the negro women refused to go this time, as they had such a hard time of it before; but off they went, "truck" and all. The old women who had suffered so much before we could not prevail upon to remain behind the others.

On the 29th scouts came in, and reported that the enemy had gone in the direction of Jonesboro, on the Macon road. We had respite again.

Yesterday morning, while I was in the yard of the court–house, attending to the patients, I saw a man ride in haste to town and a crowd collect around him. We were informed he was a courier, and had brought news that the enemy were within six miles of the place.

He was not through talking when the locomotive gave a most unearthly whistle, and immediately we heard the firing of musketry. I asked Captain Curran, to whom I was talking what that meant. He answered — fighting.

I never saw men run as all did. The crowd who had been around the courier dispersed in double–quick time. I hurried across the street to secure some money and little trinkets that the men had given me to take care of, thinking they would be more secure with me than themselves. On crossing, two or three shots whizzed past me, so I have been under fire for once.

After securing my valuables I went to look at the fighting. I had just got out when we heard cheering, and shouting that "the Yankees were running!" A lady and myself were looking at them, when a gentleman told us to hurry away, as the enemy was planting cannon on a hill near, intending to shell the town.

It seems that the night before General Roddy and his command were passing on their way to Atlanta. They were detained here all night; I do not know why. The engineer on the train saw a reconnoitering party of the enemy coming, and blew the whistle as an alarm. All the men near flew to arms. The enemy, not knowing there were any troops there, thought the train was running off, so rode up to demand a surrender, and received a volley of musketry — a thing they were not expecting. They retreated as speedily as possible.

General Roddy got his men into order (they were cavalry, but had no horses), and awaited the advance of the enemy. I saw General Roddy riding about in haste, without coat or saddle. A lady and myself tried to procure him a saddle, but were unsuccessful; the lady got him a blanket.

It was rumored that the enemy had surrounded the town and would likely fire upon it. We all suffered much from suspense, as we had many wounded; and if there was a battle in town, they would fare worse than any others. How I did hate to think about all the poor fellows lying so helpless, momentarily expecting a shell to be thrown in their midst.

We had them all moved into the strongest buildings; the court–house was crowded, although every one said a cannon–ball could easily penetrate its walls.

Roddy's men were drawn up in line of battle on one side of our hospital. The citizens sent baskets of provisions to the soldiers who were in battle array, and we sent them what we could.

At 12 a.m., Wheeler's cavalry was seen approaching the town. O, how joyfully we hailed them! They came galloping in by two different roads; the enemy, in the mean time hearing of their approach, were retreating. They were hotly pursued, and when four miles from town our men came up with them, where they made a stand, and had quite a battle.

We heard the booming of cannon, it seemed to me, about two hours. We eagerly listened to hear if it came nearer, as then we would know whether we were successful or not; but it did not seem to move from one spot. We had no idea in what force the enemy were, so did not know what to expect.

About 4 p.m. word was brought that we had killed and captured the whole command. Then the wounded from both sides were brought in. I do not know how many there were in all, but not over nine or ten were brought to our hospital.

Hundreds of well prisoners marched in in a different manner from what they had expected.

Captain———, a patient in one of the hospitals, went to the battle as a spectator; he took charge of a prisoner, promising to bring him to town. Instead of doing so, he took him into the woods and shot him. A gentleman who was with him did not see the deed, but heard the shot.

A friend has told me that when our soldiers were informed of the circumstance they were very indignant, and vowed, if they could lay hands on the captain, they would hang him.

Such men ought not to be permitted to bring dishonor on a brave people, and deserve punishment. I have never been an advocate of the black flag, but I think it would be mercy to an act of this kind. For then the enemy would know what they had to expect, and would fight valiantly before giving themselves up. This unfortunate man had surrendered in the faith that he would be treated as a prisoner of war.

There might be some excuse for a man in the heat of battle refusing to take prisoners, when he saw his comrades slain around him, but this captain had no such excuse. He has been guilty of murder, and of the most cowardly kind.

I have earnestly prayed that, when the history of this war is written, all the dark pages may be on the side of the enemy; but alas! for poor frail humanity, such is not to be the case.

When this captain was asked by a friend why he had committed the deed, he gave as a justification the barbarous treatment of his mother and sister by Federal soldiers.

It is much to be regretted that a young man who had won enviable laurels on many a battle–field, and is now suffering from his third wound, should have tarnished his former good name by such an act.

Dr. Hughes and other surgeons were for hours on the battle–field, attending to the wounded. Dr. Hughes says he never worked harder in his life.

Four fifths of the wounded were Federals, who appeared very grateful for what he did for them.

At commencement of the battle, Dr. Hughes and others had sent word around to the citizens, telling them to prepare food for our soldiers by the time they would return.

Mrs. Williamson and myself were kept busy all the afternoon receiving the food. All — rich and poor — sent something. One crowd of very poor–looking women brought some corn–bread and beans, which, I am certain, they could ill afford. They said they would gladly do without themselves, so our brave defenders had them.

When the men came in, some of the nurses helped us to serve out the food, as we found it impossible to do so by ourselves.

We were very busy till about 10 o'clock, p.m., when an officer proposed that some of the commissary officers should take the things and divide them.

The men had remained in the yard while we handed them the food. They put me in mind of a lot of hungry wolves. Poor fellows! many of them had not eaten any thing in a long time. They were mainly Wheeler's men; Roddy's men had been fed by the citizens.

I heard many complaints against General Wheeler; the men say, if he had acted differently, not one of the raiders would have escaped. As it is, many hundreds have escaped, and their general, McCook, with them.

It seems that General Roddy had his men all ready to make a charge, and General Wheeler would not give the word of command. Many of the prisoners say, had the charge been made, all would have surrendered, as they were prepared for it. Our men speak very highly of the manner in which the people of Newnan have treated them.

To–day the town has been one scene of military display, as nearly all of the cavalry are here. I have seen many handsome flags — trophies. I sent and asked for a piece of one, which was given me.

The wounded prisoners have been taken to the Buckner Hospital. The cannon that we expected would shell Newnan is here. The firing we heard did not do any damage. It is said that there was so much consternation among the enemy that they did not know where they were firing.

Some of the negro men from the Gamble Hospital have been telling us that there was quite an exciting scene there yesterday morning when the raiders came in. All were at breakfast, and knew nothing of the enemy's approach till they commenced firing. They fired right into the hospital, at the same time shouting and yelling at a terrific rate. The negro men ran and got out of their way as quickly as they could. A number of the citizens were shot at and some captured; all are now released.

One of our patients, Mr. Black, a Kentuckian, who was stopping at a farm–house, was roused from his bed and made a prisoner. He was with them when they heard Wheeler and Roddy were after them, and says he never saw men so badly frightened. They treated him well, as they knew the tables would soon be turned.

Many of them told him, and indeed I have heard it from others, that when they came here they felt confident that they would be captured. Their time would be out in a week; they would then be of no service to the United States government. By sending them on this raid they would draw cavalry from our army.

My wonder is, that the enemy fight as they do, when they are treated with such inhumanity by their own people.

Dr. Henderson has come back from the army, and has started for Mobile. I expect he will have a hard time in getting there, as the road between Opelika, and Montgomery is reported to be torn up by the late raiders.

PART IV

Days of Courage
1864

I did not think two months ago I would ever dance or care to talk nonsense again. But one grows callous to suffering and death. We can live only in the present, only from day to day. We cannot bear to think of the past and so dread the future. The refugees remind me of the description of the life the nobility of France lived during the days of the French Revolution — thrusting all the cares and tragedies of life aside and drinking deep of life's joys while it lasted.

— Kate Stone, 1864

The Soldiers Stare with Open Eyes

MARY BOYKIN CHESNUT

RICHMOND, VIRGINIA, JANUARY 1864

Mary Chesnut was in Richmond with her husband, who in 1864 was an official of the Confederate government. This passage was written in January when the weather and the condition of the roads were too bad for either side to undertake a major offensive.

January 4th — Mrs. Ives wants us to translate a French play. A genuine French captain came in from his ship on the James River and gave us good advice as to how to make the selection. General Hampton sent another basket of partridges, and all goes merry as a marriage bell.

My husband came in and nearly killed us. He brought this piece of news: "North Carolina wants to offer terms of peace!" We needed only a break of that kind to finish us. I really shivered nervously, as one does when the first handful of earth comes rattling down on the coffin in the grave of one we cared for more than all who are left.

January 5th — At Mrs. Preston's, met the Light Brigade in battle array, ready to sally forth, conquering and to conquer. They would stand no nonsense from me about staying at home to translate a French play. Indeed, the plays that have been sent us are so indecent I scarcely know where a play is to be found that would do at all.

While at dinner the President's carriage drove up with only General Hood. He sent up to ask in Maggie Howell's name would I go with them? I tied up two partridges between plates with a serviette, for Buck, who is ill, and then went down. We picked up Mary Preston. It was Maggie's drive; as the soldiers say, I was only on "escort duty." At the Prestons', Major Venable met us at the door and took in the partridges to Buck. As we drove off Maggie said: "Major Venable is a Carolinian, I see." "No; Virginian to the core." "But, then, he was a professor in South Carolina College before the war." Mary Preston said: "She is taking a fling at your weakness for all South Carolina."

Came home and found my husband in a bitter mood. It has all gone wrong with our world. The loss of our private fortune the smallest part. He intimates, "with so much human misery filling the air, we might stay at home and think." "And go mad?" said I. "Catch me at it! A yawning grave, with piles of red earth thrown on one side; that is the only future I ever see. You remember Emma Stockton? She and I were as blithe as birds that day at Mulberry. I came here the next day, and when I arrived a telegram said: 'Emma Stockton found dead in her bed.' It is awfully near, that thought. No, no. I will not stop and think of death always."

January 8th — Snow of the deepest. Nobody can come to–day, I thought. But they did! My girls first; then Constance Cary tripped in — the clever Conny. Hetty is the beauty, so called, though she is clever enough, too; but Constance is actually clever and has a classically perfect outline. Next came the four Kentuckians and Preston Hampton. He is as tall as the Kentuckians and ever so much better looking. Then we had egg–nog.

I was to take Miss Cary to the Semmes's. My husband inquired the price of a carriage. It was twenty–five dollars an hour! He cursed by all his gods at such extravagance. The play was not worth the candle, or carriage, in this instance. In Confederate money it sounds so much worse than it is. I did not dream of asking him to go with me after that lively overture. "I did intend to go with you," he said, "but you do not ask me." "And I have been asking you for twenty years to go with me, in vain. Think of that!" I said, tragically. We could not wait for him to dress, so I sent the twenty–five–dollar–an–hour carriage back for him. We were behind time, as it was. When he came, the beautiful Hetty Cary and her friend, Captain Tucker, were with him. Major von Borcke and Preston Hampton were at the Carys', in the drawing–room when we called for Constance, who was dressing. I challenge the world to produce finer specimens of humanity than these three: the Prussian von Borcke, Preston Hampton, and Hetty Cary.

We spoke to the Prussian about the vote of thanks passed by Congress yesterday — "thanks of the country to Major von Borcke." The poor man was as modest as a girl — in spite of his huge proportions. "That is a compliment, indeed!" said Hetty. "Yes. I saw it. And the happiest, the proudest day of my life as I read it. It was at the hotel breakfast–table. I try to hide my face with the newspaper, I feel it grow so red. But my friend he has his newspaper, too, and he sees the same thing. So he looks my way — he says, pointing to me — 'Why does he grow so red? He has got something there!' and he laughs. Then I try to read aloud the so kind compliments of the Congress — but — he — you — I can not — " He puts his hand to his throat. His broken English and the difficulty of his enunciation with that wound in his windpipe makes it all very touching — and very hard to understand.

The Semmes charade party was a perfect success. The play was charming. Sweet little Mrs. Lawson Clay had a seat for me banked up among women. The female part of the congregation, strictly segregated from the male, were placed all together in rows. They formed a gay parterre, edged by the men in their black coats and gray uniforms. Toward the back part of the room, the mass of black and gray was solid. Captain Tucker bewailed his fate. He was stranded out there with those forlorn men, but could see us laughing, and fancied what we were saying was worth a thousand charades. He preferred talking to a clever woman to any known way of passing a pleasant hour. "So do I," somebody said.

On a sofa or state in front of all sat the President and Mrs. Davis. Little Maggie Davis was one of the child actresses. Her parents had a right to be proud of her; with her flashing black eyes, she was a marked figure on the stage. She is a handsome creature and she acted her part admirably. The shrine was beautiful beyond words. The Semmes and Ives families are Roman Catholics, and understand getting up that sort of thing. First came the "Palmers Gray," then Mrs. Ives, a solitary figure, the loveliest of penitent women. The Eastern pilgrims were delightfully costumed; we could not understand how so much Christian piety could come clothed in such odalisque robes. Mrs. Ould, as a queen, was as handsome and regal as heart could wish for. She was accompanied by a very satisfactory king, whose name, if I ever knew, I have forgotten. There was a resplendent knight of St. John, and then an American Indian. After their orisons they all knelt and laid something on the altar as a votive gift.

Burton Harrison, the President's handsome young secretary, was gotten up as a big brave in a dress presented to Mr. Davis by Indians for some kindness he showed them years ago. It was a complete warrior's outfit, scant as that is. The feathers stuck in the back of Mr. Harrison's head had a charmingly comic effect. He had to shave himself as clean as a baby or he could not act the beardless chief, Spotted Tail, Billy Bowlegs, Big Thunder, or whatever his character was. So he folded up his loved and lost mustache, the Christianized red Indian, and laid it on the altar, the most sacred treasure of his life, the witness of his most heroic sacrifice, on the shrine.

Senator Hill, of Georgia, took me in to supper, where were ices, chicken salad, oysters, and champagne. The President came in alone, I suppose, for while we were talking after supper and your humble servant was standing between Mrs. Randolph and Mrs. Stanard, he approached, offered me his arm and we walked off, oblivious of Mr. Senator Hill. Remember this, ladies, and forgive me for recording it, but Mrs. Stanard and Mrs. Randolph are the handsomest women in Richmond; I am no older than they are, or younger, either, sad to say. Now, the President walked with me slowly up and down that long room, and our conversation was of the saddest. Nobody knows so well as he the difficulties which beset this hard–driven Confederacy. He has a voice which is perfectly modulated, a comfort in this loud and rough soldier world. I think there is a melancholy cadence in his voice at times, of which he is unconscious when he talks of things as they are now.

My husband was so intensely charmed with Hetty Cary that he declined at the first call to accompany his wife home in the twenty–five–dollar–an–hour carriage. He ordered it to return. When it came, his wife (a good manager) packed the Carys and him in with herself, leaving the other two men who came with the party, when it was divided into "trips," to make their way home in the cold. At our door, near daylight of that bitter cold morning, I had the pleasure to see my husband, like a man, stand and pay for that carriage! To–day he is pleased with himself, with me, and with all the world; says if there was no such word as "fascinating" you would have to invent one to describe Hetty Cary.

January 9th — Met Mrs. Wigfall. She wants me to take Halsey to Mrs. Randolph's theatricals. I am to get him up as Sir Walter Raleigh. Now, General Breckinridge has come. I like him better than any of them. Morgan also is here. These huge Kentuckians fill the town. Isabella says, "They hold Morgan accountable for the loss of Chattanooga." The follies of the wise, the weaknesses of the great! She shakes her head significantly when I begin to tell why I like him so well. Last night General Buckner came for her to go with him and rehearse at the Carys' for Mrs. Randolph's charades.

The President's man, Jim, that he believed in as all believe in our own servants, "our own people," as we call them, and Betsy, Mrs. Davis's maid, decamped last night. It is miraculous that they had the fortitude to resist the temptation so long. At Mrs. Davis's the hired servants all have been birds of passage. First they were seen with gold galore, and then they would fly to the Yankees, and I am sure they had nothing to tell. It is Yankee money wasted. I do not think it had ever crossed Mrs. Davis's brain that these two could leave her. She knew, however, that Betsy had eighty dollars in gold and two thousand four hundred dollars in Confederate notes.

Everybody who comes in brings a little bad news — not much, in itself, but by cumulative process the effect is depressing, indeed.

January 12th — To-night there will be a great gathering of Kentuckians. Morgan gives them a dinner. The city of Richmond entertains John Morgan. He is at free quarters. The girls dined here. Conny Cary came back for more white feathers. Isabella had appropriated two sets and obstinately refused Constance Cary a single feather from her pile. She said, sternly: "I have never been on the stage before, and I have a presentiment when my father hears of this, I will never go again. I am to appear before the footlights as an English dowager duchess, and I mean to rustle in every feather, to wear all the lace and diamonds these two houses can compass" — (mine and Mrs. Preston's). She was jolly but firm, and Constance departed without any additional plumage for her Lady Teazle.

January 15th — What a day the Kentuckians have had! Mrs. Webb gave them a breakfast; from there they proceeded *en masse* to General Lawton's dinner, and then came straight here, all of which seems equal to one of Stonewall's forced marches. General Lawton took me into supper. In spite of his dinner he had misgivings. "My heart is heavy," said he, "even here. All seems too light, too careless, for such terrible times. It seems out of place here in battle-scarred Richmond." "I have heard something of that kind at home," I replied. "Hope and fear are both gone, and it is distraction or death with us. I do not see how sadness and despondency would help us. If it would do any good, we would be sad enough."

We laughed at General Hood. General Lawton thought him better fitted for gallantry on the battle-field than playing a lute in my lady's chamber. When Miss Giles was electrifying the audience as the Fair Penitent, some one said: "Oh, that is so pretty!" Hood cried out with stern reproachfulness: "That is not pretty; it is elegant."

Not only had my house been rifled for theatrical properties, but as the play went on they came for my black velvet cloak. When it was over, I thought I should never get away, my cloak was so hard to find. But it gave me an opportunity to witness many things behind the scenes — that cloak hunt did. Behind the scenes! I know a little what that means now.

General Jeb Stuart was at Mrs. Randolph's in his cavalry jacket and high boots. He was devoted to Hetty Cary. Constance Cary said to me, pointing to his stars, "Hetty likes them that way, you know — gilt–edged and with stars."

January 16th — A visit from the President's handsome and accomplished secretary, Burton Harrison. I lent him Country Clergyman in Town and Elective Affinities. He is to bring me Mrs. Norton's Lost and Saved.

At Mrs. Randolph's, my husband complimented one of the ladies, who had amply earned his praise by her splendid acting. She pointed to a young man, saying, "You see that wretch; he has not said one word to me!" My husband asked innocently, "Why should he? And why is he a wretch?" "Oh, you know!" Going home I explained this riddle to him; he is always a year behindhand in gossip. "They said those two were engaged last winter, and now there seems to be a screw loose; but that sort of thing always comes right." The Carys prefer James Chesnut to his wife. I don't mind. Indeed, I like it. I do, too.

Every Sunday Mr. Minnegerode cried aloud in anguish his litany, "from pestilence and famine, battle, murder, and sudden death," and we wailed on our knees, "Good Lord deliver us," and on Monday, and all the week long, we go on as before, hearing of nothing, but battle, mur-der, and sudden death, which are daily events. Now I have a new book; that is the unlooked–for thing, a pleasing incident in this life of monoto-nous misery. We live in a huge barrack. We are shut in, guarded from light without.

February 1st — Mrs. Davis gave her "Luncheon to Ladies Only" on Sat-urday. Many more persons there than at any of these luncheons which we have gone to before. Gumbo, ducks and olives, chickens in jelly, oys-ters, lettuce salad, chocolate cream, jelly cake, claret, champagne, etc., were the good things set before us.

To–day, for a pair of forlorn shoes I have paid $85. Colonel Ives drew my husband's pay for me. I sent Lawrence for it (Mr. Chesnut ordered him back to us; we needed a man servant here). Colonel Ives wrote that he was amazed I should be willing to trust a darky with that great bundle of money, but it came safely. Mr. Petigru says you take your money to market in the market basket, and bring home what you buy in your pocket–book.

· · ·

February 5th — When Lawrence handed me my husband's money (six hundred dollars it was) I said: "Now I am pretty sure you do not mean to go to the Yankees, for with that pile of money in your hands you must have known there was your chance." He grinned, but said nothing.

At the President's reception Hood had a perfect ovation. General Preston navigated him through the crowd, handling him as tenderly, on his crutches, as if he were the Princess of Wales's new–born baby that I read of to–day. It is bad for the head of an army to be so helpless. But old Blücher went to Waterloo in a carriage, wearing a bonnet on his head to shade his inflamed eyes — a heroic figure, truly; an old, red–eyed, bonneted woman, apparently, back in a landau. And yet, "Blücher to the rescue!"

Afterward at the Prestons', for we left the President's at an early hour. Major von Borcke was trying to teach them his way of pronouncing his own name, and reciting numerous travesties of it in this country, when Charles threw open the door, saying, "A gentleman has called for Major Bandbox." The Prussian major acknowledged this to be the worst he had heard yet.

Off to the Ives's theatricals. I walked with General Breckinridge. Mrs. Clay's Mrs. Malaprop was beyond our wildest hopes. And she was in such bitter earnest when she pinched Conny Cary's (Lydia Languish's) shoulder and called her "an antricate little huzzy," that Lydia showed she felt it, and the next day the shoulder was black and blue. It was not that the actress had a grudge against Conny, but that she was intense.

Even the back of Mrs. Clay's head was eloquent as she walked away. "But," said General Breckinridge, "watch Hood; he has not seen the play before and Bob Acres amazes him." When he caught my eye, General Hood nodded to me and said, "I believe that fellow Acres is a coward." "That's better than the play," whispered Breckinridge, "but it is all good from Sir Anthony down to Fag."

Between the acts Mrs. Clay sent us word to applaud. She wanted encouragement; the audience was too cold. General Breckinridge responded like a man. After that she was fired by thunders of applause, following his lead. Those mighty Kentuckians turned claqueurs, were a host in themselves. Constance Cary not only acted well, but looked perfectly beautiful.

During the farce Mrs. Clay came in with all her feathers, diamonds, and fallals, and took her seat by me. Said General Breckinridge, "What a splendid head of hair you have." "And all my own," said she. Afterward she said, they could not get false hair enough, so they put a pair of black satin books on top of her head and piled hair over them.

We adjourned from Mrs. Ives's to Mrs. Ould's where we had the usual excellent Richmond supper. We did not get home until three. It was a clear moonlight night — almost as light as day. As we walked along I said to General Breckinridge, "You have spent a jolly evening." "I do not know," he answered. "I have asked myself more than once to-night, 'Are you the same man who stood gazing down on the faces of the dead on that awful battle-field? The soldiers lying there stare at you with their eyes wide open. Is this the same world? Here and there?'"

We have laughed so at broken hearts — the broken hearts of the foolish love stories. But Buck, now, is breaking her heart for her brother Willie. Hearts do break in silence, without a word or a sigh. Mrs. Means and Mary Barnwell made no moan — simply turned their faces to the wall and died. How many more that we know nothing of!

When I remember all the true-hearted, the light-hearted, the gay and gallant boys who have come laughing, singing, and dancing in my way in the three years now past; how I have looked into their brave young eyes and helped them as I could in every way and then saw them no more forever; how they lie stark and cold, dead upon the battle-field, or moldering away in hospitals or prisons, which is worse — I think if I consider the long array of those bright youths and loyal men who have gone to their deaths almost before my very eyes, my heart might break, too. Is anything worth it — this fearful sacrifice, this awful penalty we pay for war?

A Meeting at Sea

BELLE BOYD

ABOARD THE *GREYHOUND*, MAY 1864

In the following passage, Belle Boyd, still doing cloak–and–dagger work for the Confederacy in 1864, was on her way to England with secret dispatches for Confederate agents abroad.

On the 8th of May, 1864 I bade farewell to many friends in Wilmington, North Carolina and stepped on board the *Greyhound*. It was, as may well be imagined an anxious moment. I knew that the venture was a desperate one; but I felt sustained by the greatness of my cause; for I had borne a part, however insignificant, in one of the greatest dramas ever yet enacted upon the stage of the world; moreover, I relied upon my own resources, and I looked to Fortune, who is so often the handmaid of a daring enterprise.

At the mouth of the river we dropped anchor, and decided to wait until the already waning moon should entirely disappear.

Outside the bar, and at the distance of about six miles, lay the Federal fleet, most of them at anchor; but some of their light vessels were cruising quietly in different directions. Not one, however, showed any disposition to tempt the guns of the fort over which the Confederate flag was flying.

There were on board the *Greyhound* two passengers, or rather adventurers, besides myself — Mr. Newell and Mr. Pollard, the latter the editor of the *Richmond Examiner*. We laughed and joked, as people will laugh and joke in the face of imminent danger, and even in the jaws of death.

Gentle reader, before you accuse us of levity, or of a reckless spirit of fatalism, reflect how, in the prison of La Force, when the reign of terror was at its height, the doomed victims of the guillotine acted charades, played games of forfeits, and circulated their *bon–mots* and *jeux d'esprit* within a few hours of a violent death. Remember also that the lovely Queen of Scots and the unfortunate Anne Boleyn met their fate with a smile, and greeted the scaffold with a jest.

About ten o'clock orders were given to get under way. The next minute every light was extinguished, the anchor was weighed, steam was got up rapidly and silently, and we glided off just as "the trailing garments of the night" spread their last folds over the ocean.

The decks were piled with bales of cotton, upon which our look–out men were stationed, straining their eyes to pierce the darkness and give timely notice of the approach of an enemy.

I freely confess that our jocose temperament had now yielded to a far more serious state of feeling. No more pleasantries were exchanged, but many earnest prayers were breathed. No one thought of sleep. Few words were spoken. It was a night never to be forgotten — a night of silent, almost breathless anxiety. It seemed to us as if day would never break; but it came at last, and, to our unspeakable joy, not a sail was in sight. We were moving unmolested and alone upon a tranquil sea, and we indulged in the fond hope that we had eluded our eager foes.

Steaming on, we ran close by the wreck of the Confederate iron–clad *Raleigh*, which had so lately driven the Federal blockading squadron out to sea, but which now lay on a shoal, an utter wreck, parted amidships, destroyed, not by the Federals, but by a visitation of Providence.

It was just noon, when a thick haze which had lain upon the water lifted, and at that moment we heard a startled cry of "Sail ho!" from the look–out man at the mast–head. These ominous words were the signal for a general rush aft. Extra steam was got up in an incredibly short space of time, and sail was set with the view both of increasing our speed and steadying our vessel as she dashed through the water.

Alas! it was soon evident that our exertions were useless, for every minute visibly lessened the distance between us and our pursuer; her masts rose higher and higher, her hull loomed larger and larger, and I was told plainly that, unless some unforeseen accident should favor us, such as a temporary derangement of the Federal steamer's steering apparatus, or a breaking of some important portion of her machinery, we might look to New York instead of Bermuda as our destination.

My feelings at this intelligence must be imagined: I can describe them but inadequately. "Unless," I thought, "Providence interposes directly in our behalf, we shall be overhauled and captured; and then what follows? I shall suffer a third rigorous imprisonment." Moreover, I was the bearer of dispatches from my Government to authorities in Europe; and I knew that this service, honorable and necessary at it was, the Federals regarded in the light of a heinous crime, and that, in all probability, I should be subjected to every kind of indignity.

The chase continued, and the cruiser still gained upon us. For minutes, which to me seemed hours, did I strain my eyes towards our pursuer and watch anxiously for the flash of the gun that would soon send a shot or shell after us, or, for all I could tell, into us. How long I remained watching I know not, but the iron messenger of death came at last. A thin, white curl of smoke rose high in the air as the enemy luffed up and presented her formidable broadside. Almost simultaneously with the hissing sound of the shell, as it buried itself in the sea within a few yards of us, came the smothered report of its explosion under water.

The enemy's shots now followed each other in rapid succession: some fell very close, while others, less skillfully aimed, were wide of the mark, and burst high in the air over our heads. During this time bale after bale of cotton had been rolled overboard by our crew, the epitaph of each, as it disappeared beneath the waves, being "By ———— ! there's another they shall not get."

Our captain paced nervously to and fro, now watching the compass, now gazing fixedly at the approaching enemy, now shouting, "More steam! more steam! give her more steam!" At last he turned suddenly round to me, and exclaimed in passionate accents —

"Miss Belle, I declare to you that, but for your presence on board, I would burn her to the water's edge rather than those infernal scoundrels should reap the benefits of a single bale of our cargo."

To this I replied, "Captain H., act without reference to me — do what you think your duty. For my part, sir, I concur with you; burn her by all means — I am not afraid. I have made up my mind, and am indifferent to my fate, if only the Federals do not get the vessel."

To this Captain H. made no reply but turned abruptly away and walked aft, where his officers were standing in a group. With them he held a hurried consultation, and then, coming to where I was seated, exclaimed —

"It is too late to burn her now. The Yankee is almost on board of us. We must surrender!"

During this time the enemy's fire never ceased. Round shot and shell were ploughing up the water about us. They flew before, behind, and above — everywhere but into us; and, although I knew that the first of those heavy missiles which should strike must be fatal to many, perhaps to all, yet so angry did I feel that I could have forfeited my own life if, by so doing, I could have balked the Federals of their prey.

At this moment we were not more than a half a mile from our tormentor; for we had luffed up in the wind, and stopped our engine. Suddenly, with a deep humming sound, came a hundred–pound bolt. This shot was fired from their long gun amidships, and passed just over my head, between myself and the captain, who was standing on the bridge a little above me.

"By Jove! don't they intend to give us quarter, or show us some mercy at any rate?" cried Captain H. "I have surrendered."

And now from the Yankee came a stentorian hail: "Steamer ahoy! haul down that flag, or we will pour a broadside into you!"

Captain H. then ordered the man at the wheel to lower the colors; but he replied, with true British pluck, that "he had sailed many times under that flag, but had never yet seen it hauled down; and," added he, "I cannot do it now." We were sailing under British colors, and the man at the helm was an Englishman.

All this time repeated hails of "Haul down that flag, or we will sink you!" greeted us, until, at last, some one I know not who, seeing how hopeless it must be to brave them longer, took it upon himself to execute Captain H.'s order, and lowered the English ensign.

Before the acknowledgment of our surrender had been made, a keg containing some twenty or thirty thousand dollars, equivalent in value to about six thousand pounds sterling, had been brought up on deck and consigned to the deep; whilst all my dispatches and letters of introduction, of which latter I had many, were consumed in the furnaces very shortly afterwards.

We were boarded by a boat's crew from our captor, under the command of the executive officer, Mr. Kempf. Mounting the side, he walked up to Captain H. and said —

"Good day to you Captain; I am glad to see you. This is a very fine vessel, and a valuable one. Will you be good enough to let me see your papers?"

To this Captain H. replied, "Good day to yourself, sir; but as to my being happy to see you, I cannot really say that I am. I have no papers."

The Federal lieutenant then said, "Well, Captain, your presence is required on board the United States steamer *Connecticut*, Captain Almy commanding; and, if you can prove yourself all right, you will, no doubt, be permitted to go."

To this Captain H. made no response, but, stepping into the cabin, donned his coat, and, returning on deck, said, "Now, sir, I am ready; shall we go?" Without further parley the two stepped together into the boat which was lying alongside, and immediately pulled for the *Connecticut*.

One Mr. Swasey was left in charge of our luckless *Greyhound* — an officer as unfit for authority as any who has ever trodden the deck of a man–of–war. His subordinates were, I imagine, well acquainted with his character and abilities; at all events, they treated his orders not with respect, but ridicule.

"Now, sergeant," said he, addressing the sergeant of marines, "look out for your men, and I will look out for mine. By–the–way, though, station one man here to guard the spirit–room, and don't let any one go below; the first man I catch doing so I will blow his brain out, I will; I would not let my own father have a drink."

He might possibly have resisted the solicitations of a thirsty parent, but he proved quite unable to withstand those of the men. He had hardly finished speaking, when a seaman, whom, by his *illigant* brogue, I recognized at once for a true son of Erin, approached and addressed Mr. Swasey with all the native eloquence and pathos of his country —

"Ah, Mr. Swasey, will yees be afther lettin' me have a small bottle of whiskey to kape out the could?"

The colloquy that ensued was ludicrous in the extreme, terminating in a victory of the Irish sailor over the federal officer. This example of successful insubordination once set, was soon followed; and in every instance Mr. Swasey yielded to the remonstrances, or rather to the mutinous appeals, of his men.

"Here," suddenly exclaimed he, catching a glimpse of myself, "sergeant of the guard! sergeant of the guard! put a man in front of this door, and give him orders to stab this woman if she dares to attempt to come out."

This order was given in a menacing voice and in the very words I have used.

Mr. Swasey then came to the cabin–door and introduced himself in these brief but delicate words — "Now, ain't ye skeared?"

My blood was roused, and I replied, "No, I am not; I was never frightened at a Yankee in my life!"

This retort of mine seemed to surprise him, as he walked away without another word. The effects of his displeasure, however, soon made themselves felt. To my ineffable disgust, the officers, and even the men, were permitted to walk at pleasure into my cabin, which I had hoped would have been respected as the sanctuary of a modest girl. In this hope, as in so many others, I calculated far too much upon the forbearance and humanity of Yankees; and these qualities were seldom exhibited when their enemies were defenseless, and, consequently, at their mercy.

Officers and men now proceeded to help themselves to the private wines of the captain, in spite of the protest of the sentry who had been placed in front of my door, and of whom it is but just to say that nature had qualified him to command when his superiors would have done well to obey.

While these scenes were being enacted, my maid, and a colored woman whom Captain H. was conveying to a lady in Bermuda, were subjected to the rude familiarities of the prize crew.

At this moment one of the *Connecticut's* officers, a Mr. Reveille, walked up to me and said, "Do you know that it was I who fired the shot that passed close over your head?"

"Was it?" replied I. "Should you like to know what I said of the gunner?"

"I should like to know."

"That man, whoever he may be, is an arrant coward to fire on a defenseless ship after her surrender."

To this rejoinder of mine, more sincere, perhaps, than prudent, he made no reply, but left the cabin with an embarrassed laugh.

Scarcely had the discomfited Yankee betaken himself, to my intense satisfaction, to the deck, when I noticed a young officer who had just come over the side.

He crossed the deck by the wheel, and approached the cabin. I saw at a glance he was made of other stuff than his comrades who preceded him; and I confess my attention was riveted by the presence of a gentleman — the first, I think my readers will allow, whom I had met in the hour of my distress.

His dark–brown hair hung down on his shoulders; his eyes were large and bright. Those who judge of beauty by regularity of feature only, could not have pronounced him strictly handsome. Neither Phidias nor Praxiteles would have chosen the subject for a model of Grecian grace; but the fascination of his manner was such, his every movement was so much that of a refined gentleman, that my "Southern proclivities," strong as they were, yielded for a moment to the impulses of my heart, and I said to myself, "Oh, what a good fellow that must be!"

To my secret disappointment, he passed by the cabin, without entering or making any inquiries about me. I asked one of the *Connecticut's* officers, who was close to me, the name of the new arrival in the party of pleasure. "Lieutenant Hardinge," was his reply.

Soon afterwards I heard the following conversation which I perfectly well remember, and which I transcribe *verbatim*, between Mr. Swasey and Mr. Hardinge: —

Mr. Swasey. — "Hallo Hardinge, any thing up? What is it?"

Mr. Hardinge. — "Yes, sir; by order of Captain Almy, I have come to relieve you of the command of this vessel. It is his order that you proceed forthwith on board the *Connecticut*: you will be pleased to hand over to me the papers you have in relation to this vessel."

Mr. Swasey. — "It is a lie! it is a lie! it ain't no such thing! I won't believe it. You have been lately juggling with the captain. confound it! That is the way you always do!"

Mr. Hardinge. — "Mr. Swasey, I am but obeying my orders; you must not insult me. If you continue to do so, I shall report you."

Mr. Swasey cooled at once, I suppose, as I heard nothing further on his side. He promptly handed over his orders, as desired by Mr. Hardinge, jumped into the boat alongside, and I caught the last sound of his charming voice as he uttered the word of command, "Give way there!" to the boat's crew.

Within a few minutes of the departure of our sometime prize–master, Mr. Hardinge, now in command, issued his orders to the sergeant of marines as to how the men were to be posted; and I overheard, not without an emotion of pleasure, the sergeant telling one of our officers that, although Mr. Hardinge might be a strict disciplinarian on duty, there was not a finer young fellow in the navy, and that his men would follow him anywhere.

Before long, Mr. Hardinge came aft, and bowing to me, asked permission to enter my cabin for a moment.

"Certainly," I replied; "I know that I am a prisoner."

"I am now in command of this vessel," said he; "and I beg you will consider yourself a passenger, not a prisoner."

With the commencement of Mr. Hardinge's command — I may safely say, from the very moment he came on board — the conduct of the prize crew underwent a complete change; and one of the Yankee officers remarked, in my hearing, that although Hardinge was young, he knew how to command other men, and had learned, early in life, the secret and the value of discipline.

Half an hour, or thereabouts, elapsed, and I was reconciling myself to my captivity, when the return on board of Captain "Henry" was the occasion of a ludicrous incident. Captain "Henry," coming on board, caught sight of a Federal sailor strutting about on the cottonbales in a pair of his (Captain H.'s) very best boots — boots which the captain most particularly cherished.

"Here, you fellow, what are you doing in my boots? Take them off at once, or I shall report you to the officer in command for stealing."

"But, sir," said the sailor, loth to part with his contraband goods, "I bought them from a messmate of mine, and chucked my own into the sea."

This subterfuge, however, did not impose upon Mr. Hardinge's sense of honor and discipline. The ancient mariner had to remove the stolen boots, and return barefooted to his ship.

The officers and crew of the *Greyhound* together with my fellow–passengers, Mr. Pollard and Mr. Newell, were taken on board the *Connecticut*. The captain, steward, cook, and cabin boy, myself and my maid, remained prisoners on board the prize.

Before we were taken — indeed, when we sailed from Wilmington — it had been agreed that "Belle Boyd" should be for the time ignored, and that "Mrs. Lewis" should take her place. It was obvious that, in the event of capture, I should run less risk, suffer fewer privations, and be exposed to less indignity, under an assumed name. Conceive then, my surprise and indignation when I found that my secret had been revealed through the treachery of an unworthy countryman!

Captain H. told me that the *Minnie*, a blockade–runner like the *Greyhound*, which had been captured the day before by the *Connecticut*, had been the means of our own mishap. There can be no doubt that one of her officers was a traitor to the cause of his country, and had, through fear, or actuated by some other unworthy motive, sacrificed those he should have defended with his life.

It is with reluctance that I record this instance of dishonor on the part of a southerner; but I am resolved to be an impartial historian, and although often severe to the Yankees, by dint of telling plainly their short–comings, I will not shrink from the truth when it is unfavorable to my countrymen.

A Cap for Mrs. Worthey

CÉLINE FRÉMAUX

JACKSON, LOUISIANA, MAY 1864

Céline Frémaux, the youngest of our diarists, was fourteen in 1864. Like Sarah Morgan, the Frémauxs were from Baton Rouge and had left there hoping to escape the fighting. Jackson, Louisiana, was not occupied, but was frequently raided by the Federals. Céline's father was serving in the Confederate army.

In 1864, the May party was held at Cool Springs near Thompson Creek. Emma Miller was Queen and a number of younger girls were flower girls. Everyone of them were bare footed, but their dresses were of the finest swiss muslin. Even the sashes of fine ribbon were fresh looking. People cared well for these fineries and they were worn very seldom. The underclothing was coarse, or really all patches, and shoes had disappeared so long ago as to be hardly remembered. I can see Sister yet, as she was that day, her long thick hair plaited in two braids, a fine white swiss dress, a scotch plaid sash and ribbon to match, a gold chain with coral pendants on her neck, and a long garland of flowers over her arms — barefoot, of course, like the others. Sister was pretty even then.

The party broke up suddenly. Some vedette announced that a regiment of Yankees was approaching from the cross roads. In great hurry we picked up our diverse belongings and scattered. I took off the little jewelry I had on and put it in the ticking bag each and every one of us wore under our skirts for the purpose of hiding things from the Yankee raiders. I tried to take off Sister's things, but she would have none of my advice. She fought and struggled and ran off. When we reached home just pell–mell with the vanguard of Yankees, her chain and pendants had disappeared. The whole regiment passed at full gallop. If the chain was in the dust, it must have been ground to pieces by the horses' hooves.

Even to the youngest of us, we wore a strap with a well made ticking bag under our clothes. In any moment of danger the silver spoons and forks and jewelry were thus distributed so as to be a burden to none. It did not clink and Yankees were not apt to search little children. Our house was searched several times and we hung around looking on but were never suspected. Ladies wore hoopskirts in those days and could hide much beneath them, and they were personally searched. Ma was little and thin and wore no "hoop"; she was never searched.

Once a ludicrous scene was enacted on one of the streets. Miss Jane Pond had her silverware and valuables attached in some way to her hoopskirt. The Yankees came suddenly; she ran for her home. In some way her things began to drop and tinkle on the hard earth of the sidewalks. Three Yankee officers dismounted and helped her pick them up. They were laughing but she was crying with vexation. They were gentlemen and kept nothing. Poor Miss Jane never heard the last of the affair.

Once, I do not remember the date, the Yankees came into the town quite unexpectedly. Several Confederate scouts were about. They tried to get away but with their underfed horses soon saw they would be captured, so two of them, Bob McLelland and another, whipped up their horses, caught the low limbs of a pine tree, and gained the topmost branches, which concealed them from view from below. We, from our school room, saw them very plainly, but we had seen them start up. The horses continued to gallop through the woods. They were pursued a moment and we saw the Yankees come back, tether their horses under that very pine and begin preparations for a meal. This was a sort of post on that side of town. It was getting dark. We were so interested that we stayed on and on in the school house, maybe fifty yards from the pine trees. Presently the Yankees lay back with their hats over their faces and presumably went to sleep. There were five of them. Indistinctly in the gathering darkness we saw our boys lower themselves, take each one a horse and gallop away. The Yankees shot at them, of course, but did not attempt to pursue them. Miss Mollie filed us out of the school room and we went home.

Once the Yankees went in at Mr. Worthey's to look for soldiers, they said, but they opened the most tiny chests and workboxes and took everything that struck their fancy. Old Mrs. Worthey was sick in bed. A Yankee approached her and said, "Old woman, you must get out of that. This bed must be searched."

Another, a young Irish looking man said, "She need not move, I'll do that." So saying, he took the top mattress by one edge and turned it quite over leaving the old lady half smothered between the two. Sallie was so enraged that she caught her bedstick and fell to beating the man. The others did not help him, and in a moment, he was routed and ran out the gate, got up on his horse and did not come in any more.

There was at that time a wounded C.S. in the house. As soon as the tramp of cavalry was heard, Mr. Vincent, the soldier, was made to get into a hogshead, in a garret. A dusty piece of sacking was put over him and a lot of old hand–irons, pokers, tongs, etc., were put atop of him. The Yankees went into the garret and one even took a poker from the heap, but he soon let it go, remarking that it took a War to shake the dust from Southern people's overplus. All day and all night Mr. Vincent remained in his cramped prison. I was present when he was helped out. His wound, not dressed for so long was very painful. He was half starved and he was dirty, oh, so dirty. Sallie gave him food then proceeded to dress his wound. "Come Frenchie," she said, "you must help me. I have no one else." She put a lot of bandages in order over one of my arms and as she took the soiled ones off put them over my other arm. All went well for awhile till she came down to the bloody ones. I began to feel weak in the knees. Then the head was bared. The hole was the size of a silver dollar and diminished to the size of a twenty–five cent piece where the brain showed; moving or pulsing it seemed to me. Then I opened my eyes. I was lying on the floor. Sallie was pinning on the last bandages. She turned to me. "Well," she said, "for a soldier's daughter you do not do well." I felt very mortified. She washed my face in cold water, made me a drink, and told me to lie on the bench a moment. Mr. Vincent was on the lounge. He seemed to be in great pain.

That evening Sallie called me again to help her. When she came to the blood, I closed my eyes but stayed erect. Afterward I often helped her with that, and other wounds. We had to learn many things.

In one of the Yankee raids on Mr. Worthey's place they wiped all the crockery from the pantry shelves with their swords and threw the spoons, forks and knives broadcast in the neighboring fields. They remained in the vicinity five days, then it rained two days. When we went in search of the things, we found three knives, four spoons more or less disfigured by the horses' feet, and also four forks, one whole, one with two prongs and two with only one prong a piece. With these few table utensils the family had to be content from the spring of 1864 to the end of the war. The day we searched for the things, Sallie sent word for Sister and I to come and spend the day, also for each of us to fetch along our own plate, knife and fork. We wondered why, and when we got there were informed of their loss. We insisted that some of the family use our silver forks and nice knives but they refused. The old lady, however, finished her dinner with my fork. There were around the table nine persons and there was not a whole dish or plate. Mr. Worthey had a large piece of a turkey dish, his wife had a portion of a deep dish, others had nicked or half plates. It seemed perfectly ridiculous and we all laughed very much during that meal, but it was not a laughing matter.

In a few days friends had divided their own and they were a little better off but no one had many to spare. Breakage went on during those four years and nothing could be replaced. Ma had barrels of crockery all packed up, but somehow, to my great chagrin, she did not send any. Afterward, when I went there I fetched nothing but ate as they did with a wooden paddle, a sharp stick or a roughly carved fork. As drinking vessels we used gourds. The pail stood on a chair near the table and whoever sat nearest it handed the water around.

No one seemed to mind in the least excepting old Mrs. Worthey. Month by month she seemed to sadden after her youngest son received the fearful wound in picking up the scattered remains of his friend. The old lady seemed to give up. Her distress was visible at all times and in every act. Such a dear old lady that she was, tall and erect with her white muslin caps, the ties of which she no longer tied under chin because it wore them out quicker than to let them hang. I loved her dearly. Mother had a number of caps, each more beautiful than the other, which had been Grandma's. Once after seeing Mrs. Worthey trying to darn an already very darned–up cap, I asked Ma if she would send Mrs. Worthey some of the beautiful caps. She gave me three. Timid as I was, it was an awful task to offer them. I showed them to Sallie first. She approved of them. Then I made my offer. Mrs. Worthey refused them. I insisted and she finally took one saying she would only wear it when the war was over, if she had a son left to welcome home, or if she died, she might be buried in it. The fact is, they did look out of place with the rest of the old lady's attire. Alas, when the war ended, the way of its ending was so sad that no one dressed up or made any show of joy, for next to the few that came home, hovered the shadow of those who would never return, and through the tears that veiled all those sad mothers' eyes, the forms of the dear departed seemed to be more distinct than the wretched living, sobbing men, who silently crept to their ruined fireside.

With the need of clothing, food, lights, medicines, etc., the patriotism of several women succumbed in a degree. The law required all cotton not used to be burned rather than let the enemy get possession of it. Yet some reconciled their conscience by driving to some point occupied by the Yankees and selling cotton then buying goods of all kinds with the proceeds. In order to *leave* the Yankee lines those persons were required to take "the Oath." It was an oath of allegiance to the U.S., then represented by those who were our enemies. Many times Ma was approached on the subject of selling cotton for one or the other. To Ma this appeared treason. Treason to her duty, treason to the law, treason to her heart — treason ever and always. How could she, with husband and son in the C.S. Army, take that oath? She always indignantly refused. She was a refugee among them. They could withdraw their friendship and their help, but they never would have to withdraw their respect. If her children starved or froze till they died, she would, with her diminished band, meet her equals as an equal when this awful time was passed.

Once Mr. Cerf made very generous offers to Ma, if she would go with a load of cotton to Baton Rouge. She would not have to take the oath, he said, as his wife had taken it and Ma would have the certificate with her. Ma, of course, refused. Several days later he offered Ma some provisions as a mark of esteem, he said. Ma would not take them. The next day we found in the hall ten yards of calico and a small bag of salt. Ma kept them and sent thanks to Mr. Cerf. He denied any knowledge of the gift. After the war we found they came from a most treasonable, conscience-less old reprobate of a deserter, who though unworthy, admired Ma's conception of duty.

And the months passed, as the years passed. I was well advanced in school. We had passed most of the algebra. The older girls would have taken up geometry, but only two books could be found in the parish. The boys, one after the other, had gone into the army. The oldest one left was fifteen years old. One was older but quite a cripple. Every day some one gave up another son. Mrs. Fluker was about to give up her seventh. The others were all dead, husband and six sons. His name was Joe. In two days he was to be seventeen years old. His mother was working on his kit and homespun uniform. He announced to Edith and me that he had enlisted. He was proud and gay and rode about telling everyone that he was a soldier now and would carry dispatches on the morrow as his uniform would be finished.

On the morrow he was in town again trying to get buttons to finish that dear uniform; but buttons were a luxury. The little band of new soldiers and a few officers to drill them were stopping across the gully on the south of town. Nightfall would see them on their way to camp. We met him on our way to school. An hour later we were dismissed as word came that the Yankees were at the cross road on their way to town. It was understood with Mrs. Jones that in an emergency Edith and Lola stopped with us, so home we three went. Joe Fluker was on a pony at our corner. Edith spoke to him and asked him what he was waiting for.

He said he was to notify "the boys" if the Yankees came across the branch. Being as yet without a uniform he ran little risk, he thought, of being shot. Someone had to act as vedette, why not he?

When the Yankees got on the top of the graveyard hill, it was plain they were not going to stop. They started their horses at full gallop. Joe started at a lope to warn his friends. The Yankees were firing as they came. Joe's horse began to limp. Joe shot over his shoulder at his nearest pursuer. Joe was gaining. We held our breath. We saw his arm drop and his pistol fall to the ground. He was going straight toward a bridge over a gully. We could no longer see him but we could see that the Yankees were crowding up. Something had happened. Edith was deathly pale.

"He is killed," she moaned, and so it proved. He went up the incline of the bridge, then discovered that only that portion was standing. He tried to leap the distance but it was very wide and the pony hurt, they fell into the debris, a fall of some twelve feet. The horse's neck was broken. Joe's head was slit wide on the very top. The Yankees crowded around. Some went down and pulled him upon the bluff. There they searched his pockets and his cap. Disappointed at finding nothing of dispatches or sign that he was a soldier, they struck him several blows over the head with the butt of their guns and threw him back in the gully. This time his face was in the water.

Some women, the Murdock girls who lived at the gully, saw the whole awful event. They ran down to the water, got Joe up, and carried him into their house. His eyes opened and shut many times but he did not speak. At this moment Ma, Edith, and I reached there. Edith was frantic and on her account we went. He opened his eyes and evidently recognized Edith. He sighed and that was all. Mrs. Fluker's seventh son was dead. A little boy was sent through the woods to tell her. He found her sewing. The uniform lay on her bed, finished all but for two buttons. In the stillness of the night he was put in a cart, drawn, they told me, by boys, and taken to his home seven miles. They took him to his last resting place in the uniform without the two buttons. I surmised a good deal from Edith's appearance, but she said nothing then and I asked nothing. Ventress came for her next morning. It was more than a week before I saw her again.

Barely an hour after Joe's death we heard loud talking right under the window. It was Dr. Barkdull, doctor and manager of the insane asylum. He had taken the oath, of necessity. He had to feed and keep the insane. He was telling as much to three or four Yankee soldiers and was in the act of pulling his papers from his pocket when a corporal came up and cursing, said, "What is up? Kill him and be done." So saying he leaned far into the buggy and shot twice. The horse started, Mr. Barkdull fell out, his papers still in his hand. Ma, Mrs. Fay, and another lady ran to him. They asked the Yankees to help lift him into a house. Ours was too high, Mrs. Fay's was low and next to ours. The men refused saying, "Many are buried in a trench, leave him in the gutter, and pile trash over him. He is dead all right." So the three ladies dragged him to Mrs. Fay's, up four or five steps and into the parlor on the floor. He was a large and fine man. All three of the ladies happened to be very diminutive women. It took them nearly one hour to get him to that parlor. Not before night could a doctor come. Mr. Barkdull was not dead. He lingered exactly one month, to the hour.

It happened that as they were burying him the Yankees again came. They came into the graveyard, and hearing of who was being buried, the murderer was called up by his superior officer and then, and there, congratulated on his zeal and patriotism. I was standing touching the officer, in the crowded enclosure, and Mrs. B and five children were immediately next to me. That day of horror ended with the town full of Yankees. Many slept in our yard that night. Edith pushed me and said, "Look." I looked and saw two Yankees in a mulberry tree just out of the window. They were looking toward our bed. I crept against the wall and let down the sash. With the window open they could have come in easily but with the sash down the ledge was too narrow and rotten to hold a man. We two, Edith and I, slept no more that night. I don't think she had slept any before. Joe's body being slowly taken home was too present and too painful to her. Ma was not sleeping either. Probably very few rested at all that night.

In the morning Ma had a sick headache and I had to go down into the kitchen with the children. Ma did not know the yard was full of Yankees and I did not want to tell for fear she would get up. I gathered up all I needed for the day and sent it up by the children and lastly having attended to baby Henry's necessities, I picked him up to get upstairs quickly. Two men emerged from a lumber room and one of them ordered, "Here, girl, draw me some water and be quick about it."

"Sir," I answered, "I never draw water. I am not strong enough." On that he began to curse me as a —— rebel, etc., etc. His companions dipped some water from a barrel near by and moved back a few steps. Number one still insisted that I draw him water from the well. The fact was that, alone, I could not draw it and I would not call on one of the others to help me draw water for a big man, and a Yankee at that. The Yankee got exasperated and said he would make me do it. All the while I was backing towards the steps. When I felt them at my heels, I stopped. I could not go up backward with the heavy child who was astride on my back. My arms were not strong enough.

Once more the man called out, "D——— you, are you going to come here?"

"No," I said, "Positively no."

So he put the barrel of his gun in the angle of the shed support and called out, "Well, then you are going to die, for I will kill you or get that water." I could see into the gun barrel. It seemed to be an inch wide and looked bright and smooth. I wondered if the ball would come straight or whirl in its flight. I told the baby to slip off my back and run up to Ma. I heard his little feet pattering down the hall, then the exploding of the gun. Before the smoke had cleared, I was up the five steps, flung the door shut, and then turned my back to the enemy and ran upstairs. The shot had startled Ma. She met me at the upper landing. We looked out the window. Mrs. Wiley's cow was dying some forty feet to the right of the steps, and the Yankees both together were drawing water.

The Yankee could not have meant to shoot me and missed that much, but when that gun went off it was pretty real to me. I had not noticed the deviation of the gun barrel in my anxiety to save the baby from my impending fate. All I cared for just then was not to be shot in the back, running.

A Funeral in the Rain

PHOEBE YATES PEMBER

RICHMOND, VIRGINIA, SUMMER 1864

In the summer of 1864 the Confederate Army was holding Petersburg, Virginia. The Yankees, who had besieged the city, dug a 500-foot tunnel under Confederate lines, and filled it with 8,000 pounds of gunpowder. When the charge was ignited, it made a crater 30 feet deep and 170 feet long. The explosion killed many Confederates, and the breach in their lines was exploited by black Federal troops. Some of the wounded from this engagement came to Phoebe Pember's hospital.

Now during the summer of 1864 began what is really meant by "war," for privations had to be endured which tried body and soul, and which temper and patience had to meet unflinchingly day and night. A growing want of confidence was forced upon the mind; and with doubts which though unexpressed were felt as to the ultimate success of our cause, there came into play the antagonistic qualities of human nature.

The money worthless, and a weak Congress and weaker financier failing to make it much more valuable than the paper it was printed on; the former refusing to the last to raise the hospital fund to meet the depreciation. Everything furnished through government contracts of the very poorest description, perhaps necessarily so from the difficulty of finding any supply.

The railroads were cut so constantly that what had been carefully collected in the country in the form of poultry and vegetables by hospital agents would be rendered unfit for use by the time the connection would be restored. The inducements for theft were great in this season of scarcity of food and clothing. The pathetic appeals made for the coarsest meal by starving men, all wore upon the health and strength of those exposed to the strain, and made life weary and hopeless.

The rations became so small about this time that every ounce of flour was valuable, and there were days when it was necessary to refuse with aching heart and brimming eyes the request of decent, manly–looking fellows for a piece of dry corn–bread. If given it would have robbed the rightful owner of part of his scanty rations. After the flour or meal had been made into bread, it was almost ludicrous to see with what painful solicitude Miss G. and myself would count the rolls, or hold a council over the pans of corn–bread, measuring with a string how large we could afford to cut the squares, to be apportioned to a certain number.

Sometimes when from the causes above stated, the supplies were not issued as usual, invention had to be taxed to an extreme, and every available article in our pantry brought into requisition. We had constantly to fall back upon dried apples and rice for convalescing appetites, and herb–tea and arrowroot for the very ill. There was only one way of making the last at all palatable, and that was by drenching it with whiskey.

Long abstinence in the field from everything that could be considered, even then, a delicacy, had exaggerated the fancy of sick men for any particular article of food they wanted into a passion; and they begged for such peculiar dishes that surgeons and nurses might well be puzzled. The greatest difficulty in granting these desires was that tastes became contagious, and whatever one patient asked for, his neighbor and the one next to him, and so on throughout the wards, craved also, and it was impossible to decide upon whom to draw a check.

No one unacquainted with our domestic relations can appreciate the difficulties under which we labored. Stoves in any degree of newness or usefulness we did not have; they were rare and expensive luxuries. As may be supposed, they were not the most convenient articles in the world to pack away in blockade–running vessels; and the trouble and expense of land transportation also seriously affected the quality of the wood for fuel, furnished us. Timber which had been condemned heretofore as unfit for use, light, soggy and decayed, became the only quality available. The bacon, too, cured the first two years of the war, when salt commanded an enormous price, in most cases was spoilt, from the economy used in preparing that article; and bacon was one of the sinews of war.

We kept up brave hearts, and said we could eat the simplest fare, and wear the coarsest clothing, but there was absolutely nothing to be bought that did not rank as a luxury. It was wasting time and brain to attempt to economize, so we bent to the full force of that wise precept, "Sufficient for the day is the evil thereof."

There really was a great deal of heroism displayed when looking back, at the calm courage with which I learned to count the number of mouths to be fed daily, and then contemplating the food, calculate not how much but how little each man could be satisfied with. War may be glorious in all its panoply and pride, when in the field opposing armies meet and strive for victory; but battles fought by starving the sick and wounded — by crushing in by main force day by day all the necessities of human nature, make victories hardly worth the name.

Another of my local troubles were the rats, who felt the times, and waxed strong and cunning, defying all attempts to entrap them, and skillfully levying blackmail upon us day by day, and night after night. Hunger had educated their minds and sharpened their reasoning faculties. Other vermin, the change of seasons would rid us of, but the coldest day in winter, and the hottest in summer, made no apparent difference in their vivacious strategy.

They examined traps with the air of connoisseurs, sometimes springing them from a safe position, and kicked over the bread spread with butter and strychnine to show their contempt for such underhand warfare. The men related wonderful rat–stories not well enough authenticated to put on record, but their gourmands ate all the poultices applied during the night to the sick, and dragged away the pads stuffed with bran from under the arms and legs of the wounded.

They even performed a surgical operation which would have entitled any of them to pass the board. A Virginian had been wounded in the very center of the instep of his left foot. The hole made was large, and the wound sloughed fearfully around a great lump of proud flesh which had formed in the center like an island. The surgeons feared to remove this mass, as it might be connected with the nerves of the foot, and lock–jaw might ensue. Poor Patterson would sit on his bed all day gazing at his lame foot and bathing it with a rueful face, which had brightened amazingly one morning when I paid him a visit. He exhibited it with glee, the little island gone, and a deep hollow left, but the wound washed clean and looking healthy.

Some skillful rat surgeon had done him this good service while in the search for luxuries, and he only knew that on awaking in the morning he had found the operation performed. I never had but one personal interview with any of them. An ancient gray gentleman, who looked a hundred years old, both in years and depravity, would eat nothing but butter, when that article was twenty dollars a pound; so finding all means of getting rid of him fail through his superior intelligence, I caught him with a fish–hook, well baited with a lump of his favorite butter, dropped into his domicile under the kitchen floor.

Epicures sometimes managed to entrap them and secure a nice broil for supper, declaring that their flesh was superior to squirrel meat; but never having tasted it, I cannot add my testimony to its merits. They staid with us to the last, nor did I ever observe any signs of a desire to change their politics.

Perhaps some curious *gourmet* may wish a recipe for the best mode of cooking them. The rat must be skinned, cleaned, his head cut off and his body laid open upon a square board, the legs stretched to their full extent and secured upon it with small tacks, then baste with bacon fat and roast before a good fire quickly like canvas–back ducks.

One of the remarkable features of the war was the perfect good nature with which the rebels discussed their foes. In no instance up to a certain period did I hear of any remark that savored of personal hatred. They fought for a cause and against a power, and would speak in depreciation of a corps or brigade; but "they fit us, and we fit them," was the whole story generally, and till the blowing up of the mine at Petersburg there was a gay, insouciant style in their descriptions of the war scenes passing under their observation.

But after that time the sentiment changed from an innate feeling the Southern soldiers had that mining was "a mean trick," as they expressed it. They were not sufficiently versed in military tactics to recognize that stratagem is fair in war, and what added to their indignation was pouring in of *negro* soldiers when the breach was effected. Incensed at the surprise, they craved foes worthier of their steel, not caring to rust it in the black cloud that issued from the crater. The men had heretofore been calm and restrained, particularly before a woman, never using oaths or improper language, but the wounded that were brought in from that fight emulated the talents of Uncle Toby's army in Flanders, and eyes gleamed, and teeth clenched as they showed me the locks of their muskets to which the blood and hair still clung, when after firing, without waiting to re–load, they had clenched the barrels and fought hand to hand. If their accounts could be relied upon, it was a gallant strife and a desperate one, and ghastly wounds bore testimony of the truth of many a tale then told.

Once again the bitter blood showed itself, when, after a skirmish, the foe cut the rail track, so that the wounded could not be brought to the city. Of all the monstrous crimes that war sanctions, this is surely the most sinful. Wounded soldiers without the shelter of a roof, or the comfort of a bed of straw, left exposed to sun, dew, and rain, with hardly the prospect of a warm drink or decent food for days, knowing that comfortable quarters awaited them, all ready prepared, but rendered useless by what seems an unnecessarily cruel act. Was it any wonder that their habitual indifference to suffering gave way, and the soldiers cursed loud and deep at a causeless unhumanity, which, if practiced habitually, is worse than savage! When the sufferers at last reached the hospital, their wounds had not been attended to for three days, and the sight of them was shocking.

Busy in my kitchen, seeing that the supply of necessary food was in preparation, I was spared the sight of much of the suffering, but on passing among the ambulances going in and out of the wards I descried seated up in one of them a dilapidated figure, both hands holding his head which was tied up with rags of all descriptions. He appeared to be incapable of talking, but nodded and winked and made motions with head and feet. In the general confusion he had been forgotten, so I took him under my especial charge. He was taken into a ward, seated on a bed, while I stood on a bench to be able to unwind rag after rag from around his head. There was no sensitiveness on his part, for his eye was merry and bright, but when the last came off, what a sight!

Two balls had passed through his cheek and jaw within half an inch of each other, knocking out the teeth on both sides and cutting the tongue in half. The inflammation caused the swelling to be immense, and the absence of all previous attendance, in consequence of the detention of the wounded until the road could be mended, had aggravated the symptoms. There was nothing fatal to be apprehended, but fatal wounds are not always the most trying.

The sight of this was the most sickening my long experience had ever seen. The swollen lips turned out, and the mouth filled with blood, matter, fragments of teeth from amidst all of which the maggots in countless numbers swarmed and writhed, while the smell generated by this putridity was unbearable. Castile soap and soft sponges soon cleansed the offensive cavity, and he was able in an hour to swallow some nourishment he drew through a quill.

The following morning I found him reading the newspaper, and entertaining every one about him by his abortive attempts to make himself understood, and in a week he actually succeeded in doing so. The first request distinctly enunciated was that he wanted a looking–glass to see if his sweetheart would be willing to kiss him when she saw him. We all assured him that she would not be worthy of the name if she would not be delighted to do so.

An order came about this time to clear out the lower wards for, the reception of improperly–vaccinated patients, who soon after arrived in great numbers. They were dreadfully afflicted objects, many of them with sores so deep and thick upon arms and legs that amputation had to be resorted to, to preserve life. As fast as the eruption would be healed in one spot, it would break out in another, for the blood seemed entirely poisoned. The unfortunate victims bore the infliction as they had borne everything else painful — with calm patience and indifference to suffering. Sometimes a favorable comparison would be made between this and the greater loss of limbs.

No one who was a daily witness to their agonies from this cause, can help feeling indignant at charges made of inhumanity to Federal prisoners of war, who were vaccinated with the same virus; and while on this subject, though it may be outside of the recollections of hospital life, I cannot help stating that on no occasion was the question of rations and medicines to be issued for Federal prisoners discussed in my presence; and circumstances placed me where I had the best opportunity of hearing the truth (living with the wife of a cabinet officer); that good evidence was not given, that the Confederate commissary–general, by order of the government issued to them the same rations it gave its soldiers in the field, and only when reductions of food had to be made in our army, were they also made in the prisons. The question of supplies for them was an open and a vexed one among the people generally, and angry and cruel things were *said*; but every one cognizant of facts in Richmond *knows* that even when General Lee's army lived on corn–meal at times that the prisoners still received their usual rations.

At a cabinet meeting when the Commissary–General Northrop advocated putting the prisoners on the half rations which our soldiers had been obliged to content themselves with for some time, General Lee opposed him on the ground that men animated by companionship and active service could be satisfied with less than prisoners with no hope and leading an inactive life. Mr. Davis sided with him, and the question was settled that night, although in his anger Mr. Northrop accused General Lee of showing this consideration because his son was a prisoner in the enemy's lines.

The Spring Campaign of 1864 again opened with the usual "On to Richmond." Day after day and night after night would the sudden explosion of cannon boom upon the air. The enemy were always coming, and curiosity seemed to have usurped the place of fear among the women. In the silence of night the alarm bells would suddenly peal out, till the order to ring them at any sign of danger was modified to a command to sound them only in case of positive attack. The people became so accustomed to the report of firearms, that they scarcely interrupted their conversation at corners of the streets to ask in what direction the foe was advancing or if there was any foe at all.

There was such entire reliance upon the military vigilance that guarded the city, and former attacks had been so promptly repelled, that whatever was ultimately to be the result of the war, no one trembled then for Richmond. So the summer of 1864 passed, and early in September our hearts were gladdened by the tidings that the exchange of prisoners was to be renewed. The sick and wounded of our hospital (but few in number just then) were transferred to other quarters, and the wards put in order to receive our men from Northern prisons.

Can any pen or pencil do justice to those squalid pictures of famine and desolation? Those gaunt, lank skeletons with the dried yellow flesh clinging to bones enlarged by dampness and exposure? Those pale, bluish lips and feverish eyes, glittering and weird when contrasted with famine–stricken faces, — that flitting, piteous, scared smile which greeted their fellow creatures, all will live forever before the mental vision that then witnessed it.

Living and dead were taken from the flag–of–truce boat, not distinguishable save from the difference of care exercised in moving them. The Federal prisoners we had released were in many instances in a like state, but our ports had been blockaded, our harvests burned, our cattle stolen, our country wasted. Even had we felt the desire to succor, where could the wherewithal have been found? But the foe — the ports of the world were open to him. He could have fed his prisoners upon milk and honey, and not have missed either. When we review the past, it would seem that Christianity was but a name — that the Atonement had failed, and Christ had lived and died in vain.

But it was no time then for vague reflections. With beating heart, throbbing head and icy hands I went among this army of martyrs and spectres whom it was almost impossible to recognize as human beings; powerless to speak to them, choking with unavailing pity, but still striving to aid and comfort. There was but little variety of appearance. From bed to bed the same picture met the eye. Hardly a vestige of human appearance left.

The passion of sympathy could only impede my efforts if yielded to, for my hand shook too tremulously even to allow me to put the small morsels of bread soaked in wine into their mouths. It was all we dared to give at first. Some lay as if dead with limbs extended, but the greater part had drawn up their knees to an acute angle, a position they never changed until they died. Their more fortunate comrades said that the attitude was generally assumed, as it reduced the pangs of hunger and relieved the craving that gnawed them by day and by night. The Federal prisoners may have been starved at the South, we cannot deny the truth of the charge, in many instances; but we starved with them; we had only a little to share with any — but the subject had better be left to die in silence.

One among them lingered in patience the usual three days that appeared to be their allotted space of life on their return. He was a Marylander, Richard Hammond Key, grandson of Francis Barton Key, author of "Star Spangled Banner," and hence heir to a name renowned in the history of his country. Though reared in affluence, he presented the same bluish, bloodless appearance common to all returned prisoners. Hoping that there would be some chance of his rallying, I gave him judicious nursing and good brandy. Every precaution was taken, but the third day fever supervened and the little life left waned rapidly. He gave me the trinkets cut from gutta percha buttons that he had beguiled his captivity in making at Point Lookout, to send to his family, handing me one of them for a souvenir; begged that he might be buried apart from the crowd in some spot where those who knew and cared for him might find him some day, and quietly slept himself to death that night.

The next morning was the memorable 29th September, 1864, when the enemy made a desperate and successful attack, taking Fort Harrison, holding it and placing Richmond in jeopardy for four hours. The alarm bells summoned the citizens together, and the shops being closed to allow those who kept them to join the city guards, there were no means of buying a coffin, or getting a hearse. It was against the rules to keep a body beyond a certain time on the hospital grounds, so little time was to be lost if I intended keeping my promise to the dead.

I summoned a convalescent carpenter from one of the wards, made him knock together a rough coffin from some loose boards, and taking the seats out of my ambulance had it, with the body enclosed, put in. My driver was at his post with the guards, so taking the reins and kneeling in the little space at the side of the coffin I started for Hollywood cemetery, a distance of five miles.

The enemy were then in sight, and from every elevated point the masses of maneuvering soldiers and flash of the enemy's cannon could be distinguished. Only stopping as I passed through the city to buy a piece of ground from the old cemetery agent, I reached Hollywood by twelve o'clock. Near the burying ground I met the Reverend J. D. McCabe, requested his presence and assistance, and we stood side by side while the sexton dug his grave. The rain was pouring in torrents, while the clergyman repeated the Episcopal burial service from memory. Besides ourselves there were but two poor women, of the humblest class of life — Catholics, who passing casually, dropped upon their knees, undeterred by the rain, and paid their humble tribute of respect to the dead.

He had all the honors of a soldier's burial paid to him unconsciously, for the cannon roared and the musketry rattled, mingling with the thunder and lightning of Heaven's artillery. The sexton held his hat over the small piece of paper on which I inscribed his name and birthplace (to be put on his headboard) to protect it from the rain, and with a saddened heart for the solitary grave we left behind I drove back to the city. The reverend gentleman was left at his home, and, perhaps, to this day does not know who his companion was during that strange hour.

I found the city in the same state of excitement, for no authentic news was to be heard, or received, except perhaps at official quarters; and it was well known that we had no troops nearer than Petersburg, save the citizens who had enrolled themselves for defense; therefore too anxious to return directly to the hospital, I drove to the residence of one of the cabinet ministers, where I was engaged to attend a dinner, and found the mistress of the establishment surrounded by her servants and trunks preparing for a hasty retreat when necessary. Some persuasion induced her to desist, and the situation of the house commanding an extensive view of the surrounding country, we watched the advance of the enemy from the extreme northeast, for with the aid of opera–glasses we could even distinguish the colors of their uniforms. Slowly onward moved the bodies of dark blue, emerging from and disappearing into the woods, seeming to be skirting around them, but not to be diminishing the distance between, although each moment becoming more distinct, which proved their advance, while not one single Confederate jacket could be observed over the whole sweep of ground.

Half an anxious hour passed, and then, far away against the distant horizon, one single mounted horseman emerged from a thick wood, looked cautiously around, passed across the road and disappeared. He was in gray, and followed by another and another, winding around and cutting off the foe. Then a startling peal at the bell, and a courier brought the news that Wade Hampton and his cavalry were close upon the rear of the enemy. There was no occasion for fear after this, for General Hampton was the Montrose of the Southern army, he who could make any cause famous with his pen and glorious with his sword. The dinner continued in course of preparation, and was seasoned, when served, by spirits brightened by the strong reaction.

Searching for Cartridge Boxes

CÉLINE FRÉMAUX

JACKSON, LOUISIANA, AUGUST 1864

Black troops, most of them freed slaves, were also used against the Confederates in Jackson, Louisiana. Many of the Confederate forces they fought against were guerrillas who were even less likely to give quarter to black soldiers than regular Confederate troops would have been.

The third of August 1864 was sister's 11th birthday. It was rumored that there would be an attack made on the Yankees who had been in full possession of the town for several days. A little boy, David Openhimer, told mother of it. Ma thought that if everybody knew it, even children, there was little chance of its being a surprise to the Yankees. David was very full of his tale. He said he had been with the Confederate soldiers, that they had no cannons because of coming by way of the sandy creek bed. "But that makes no difference," he added. "We will jump on them all of a sudden, take their cannons, and shoot them down with their own guns." David was eight years old.

"You need not believe me, Mrs. Frémaux, but you will hear in a few minutes. We were all ready, most, when I left." It was then deep dusk: and even as he spoke we heard the Pop Pop of musketry, toward the college. Léon darted off before Ma thought of stopping him and we began to pray downstairs in the hall. Then we stepped out on the side walk. The booming of cannon mixed with the lighter shot and a sort of roar like many voices and trampling of feet and hoofs. The fighting came nearer and nearer. We could see the fire and the dim forms at the end of both streets. Ma had not yet missed Léon. I felt that he was in the midst of it all and was very disturbed. Presently the noise neared, balls struck here and there at the corners and at the end of the street. Soldiers were coming at full gallop, all pell mell, and from their midst came Léon leading a fine horse. Paul opened the bars (gate) and he went straight into the cellar with his horse.

Ma soon made us go in, as the fighting was all around our house. We all went in the cellar with our dog Fingal. There Léon explained he had gone toward the college and got there after the battle had passed that spot. He saw five Yankee officers dead on the campus. Then it occurred to him that he might secure a horse from the next man he saw fall. He rushed among the combatants. A soldier ordered him away. He took momentary refuge on the steps of the Campbellite Church. The steps came up on both sides of the porch and were protected by a brick wall. Leaning his head against that wall, he was thinking and watching. All at once something hurt him on the side of the head. It was a bullet that had nipped a piece out of the brick. He had only felt the counter knock. At the same moment he saw a Yankee Major fall from his horse in the midst of a bayonet charge. Léon made one rush, caught the bridle, and pell mell with the men reached the corner and safety.

The fighting passed toward the bed of the branch and the asylum road. Up on the Asylum Hill the Yankees formed a battery. The ground formed a natural breast works. It had become evident to our officers that the Yankees had mistaken the Asylum road for the Port Hudson road. Ours knew that the battery once taken, the fight would be over, as it would degenerate into a disbanded rout. The order was given to charge, and up hill they charged. All the cannons were taken and the fugitives were pursued through the woods, where they had to leave their caissons full of ammunition.

When the cannons stopped booming Ma let us out of the cellar. It was a very large cellar and we were all in there with a horse and a dog in pitchy darkness. We were glad to get out. We could see nothing even then, but could feel under our feet a layer of chopped leaves which had been shot from the trees in the yard. We also counted forty indentations of bullets in two sides of the house — these of course we saw only the next morning after sunrise.

Ma took us all upstairs and we prayed for the dead, the wounded and those who loved them. The Yankees lost 7 white men, 82 niggers. Some 25 or 30 were taken prisoners. On our side there were ten wounded, none of them died. Ma sent us to bed. Léon crept under his sheets without undressing. When all was still he came into our room and from our window–sill got into a tree, then to the street. He came back before day break and, not being able to come up as he went down, he sat on the kitchen steps. At 5 a.m. Ma got up and so did we, and to my immense surprise she walked out with us all to the bed of the branch where the longest fighting had been done.

The sand, so smooth and white usually, was trampled and dug into deep uneven ruts. A broken caisson with three horses dead and one dying seemed the center of the confusion. Here and there a dead horse, and great spots of wet dotted the field. I felt a little sick and backed toward a fallen log overgrown with brambles. Just then from the clump came feeble groans. I called Léon. He spoke a few words to Ma and she took us home. Some men were coming our way searching for the wounded. Léon stayed. Decidedly Léon was getting out of Ma's jurisdiction. He came home in the evening looking worn and sad. He told me not to ask him questions, as he would not, or could not answer me. This was the first little line of severance to our childhood's chumminess.

Léon looked up a number of unexploded shells, unscrewed the caps and emptied the powder into dozens of quart jars (preserving jars). A few days later he gave it all over to our soldiers. They told him to keep one pint for his own use. He had an old gun all patched up. The barrel was perforated in several places. I can not think how it was that the old thing did not kill him and Paul when they shot it off. It was never shot off more than twice without needing a fix–up or an extra wire consolidation. It had been a musket for years before and the barrel had been shortened for some child. Léon found it in a field.

We also had Pa's little model carbine Morse gun. I used that for bird hunting. I was very careful with it, as our caps were running low and no others could be gotten. Léon and I would reload the shells (they were metal). We learned to make shot of different sizes. Our implements were crude, but the shot were nice and round. We never passed by a bullet, we looked for and picked them up always and everywhere. In fact looking for things on the ground had become a habit of the time.

We had been out of shoes for a long while. The battle furnished us with nice leather for shoe soles. We found many cartridge boxes and belts. One top or flap made a pair of soles for any of us but Léon. We had small feet. With Pa's razor Ma shaped them and dented them. From a velvet hunting suit we made shoes till the war ended. We had a spool of fine copper wire that I used to sew my shoes to the soles. It lasted seven or eight wearings, our home spun thread only *one* wearing.

Of course we wore them only for church. Then for visiting or school I went bare footed and put on my shoes and stockings on reaching the steps; same thing to return. We always carried a cloth to cleanse our feet; the soil being sandy we could do that easily enough.

One of my hardships was studying in short days. We had no lights. Even little tallow lamps were not always procurable — that is, the tallow was missing. What few mules or horses died from exhaustion in our district had not a spoonful of tallow about them. Cows were all but extinct and never killed. Hog fat was used for food. All that remained in the way of lights were pine torches for out door use and a fire for indoor illumination. To study by a fire is a poor help. I have had the top of my head so hot that I would put on a hat to sit and work out problems at night. The flicker and heat were very bad for my eyes and inflamed them very much. Some nights after one or two hours of study, I would go to bed but not to sleep for the smart and pain in my eyes.

You who read this try some of these experiments just for a few minutes, then judge what we suffered during four dreadful years.

I had become quite brave as to danger and hurt, but the Dark was still a sore point for me. Once we were all at prayer, I was on the threshold of my room, my back to it. There was very little light even in the living room. All at once I felt a weight on my collar bone. I gave a low moan and crouched to the floor and turned. "Danny! Danny!" was all I could say, and there stood Danny, the idiot of the town, grinning and seemingly enjoying the scene before him. He was an immense man, more like an overgrown boy. Perfectly harmless, everyone said, but I was so startled that for years, and even now, I have a decided objection to sitting with my back to an open door. Danny was given a piece of bread and gently led to the street. The street door was locked. He must have been asleep somewhere about the rooms before we locked up.

During the winter of 63–64 Ma had taken a fleecy bed spread and dyed it grey, then made us coats and cloaks as far as it went. Léon had a good coat; sister, a sizeable talma; and the baby a little sacque. Those garments looked comfortable but were more heavy than warm, as are cotton goods of the canton flannel order. I was not at all cold blooded and well it was, for my cashmere winter dress was getting as thin as barige at the back and at the elbows, and under that I wore a high neck and long sleeved under waist, *that* too was getting very small and thin. I could not spin enough to supply myself with an under garment, my time was too limited or crowded too full.

The coat of Léon caused me another fright. I had occasion to go down to the kitchen with one of the children. We had a few splinters of burning pine to light our way. That hall must have at one time been divided, but only a portion of that division was up when we occupied the house. As we were returning the little sticks nearly burned out. I held them up for the little ones to reach the 1st step, then I put the light out. As I did so I was caught in great wooly feeling arms, and groans were about my ears. I was so frightened that I fainted. Then it was Léon's turn to be frightened, for he it was, with his great coat on. Ma heard the racket; Léon thought I was dead. There was no more pine so of course no more light. I got over it, of course, but that partition in the hall was an object of dread. I was brave in the face of a visible enemy, but darkness and surprise were a tax on all my energies, but I was soon to have overcome even that.

After the little battle in Jackson quite a number of niggers had become separated from their command. They knew the law: All slaves taken armed against the whites were hung or shot. So they wandered about the woods for some days. Some of them, no doubt, found their way back to Port Hudson. Others were caught by the soldiers and summarily executed. I knew this was done but of course I never saw an execution. I knew they took place in the woods. The vagueness of the spot made all the woods a place of dread after dark.

It happened that one of the children was quite sick, and Ma sent me with one of the little ones for Dr. Jones. It was not exactly night, but deep dusk, a November day. Léon was away from home. To cut short we went through the college campus to the pine thicket behind the main building. I saw something moving and nearly lost my strength! Just before me, a little to one side, two niggers were hung to a tree limb, their feet just clear of the ground. I hid the sight from Paul with my skirt, tried to run, then tried to speak, but my tongue was frozen and my legs like cotton. Only the fear of Paul seeing gave me strength to move on. The horror — to me — was having them at my back. Cold chills ran up and down my spine. I thought I heard them moan, then laugh, then shriek. When fairly in sight of the doctor's house I had to stop and collect myself. I had almost forgotten what I came to ask. When I became composed I went on, got the doctor's instructions and started off by way of the big road. Doctor called out to take the short cut but I told him no, I preferred the long way, as it was lighter. The next day he remarked to Ma that he was glad I had taken the long way, for he had come the short cut and, seeing the hung men, knew I could have been frightened. Ma told him I had seen them going, and he could not get over it, that I had not asked some one to see us home. Thus I got a reputation for bravery, very little deserved, but which kept me ever striving to retain it. I was frightened many times after that, but no one ever knew it. I thought I owed it to Father and Grandfather to be as brave as a soldier.

Léon had secured a very fine horse from the battle field, but we had not the space for a horse to graze. Feed, of course was out of the question. Mr. Worthey told him he could put the horse in his pasture, which he did. A few days later, several C.S. officers needing horses, Léon's horse and 2 or 3 of Mr. Worthey's less broken down horses were pressed into service. They left there an old black mare and colt, nearly starved, lame, and with a sore back. For some reason or other, these were given to Léon. We worked with that old mare for weeks. The colt died; we cured the mare's back and diminished her lameness. I never worked so hard for a beast, cutting grass and tender cane and fetching it for miles for her. One day Léon swapped her off for a small bay filly and a pair of medium size shoes. The shoes he gave to Paul. The filly did well enough, but did not do for a "War horse" and Léon was cherishing the idea of getting off to the army at the first opportunity. A while later he went to Liberty on an errand for Mr. Delle Pianne. While there he swapped the filly for a "calico" horse and several pounds of tobacco. The tobacco he gave to the soldiers. "Calico" was considered as fit for a war–horse so on the 1st of September, 1864, Ma let Léon start for the Army. He was nearly 17. The C.S. law took the boys at 17, and Ma was willing he should obey the law but would have reproached herself if any thing should happen before the law claimed him. She made him promise not to join scouts or guerrillas but to go on to Mobile, meet Father, and follow his advice as to which corps to join. He was to be 17 on the 14th of September.

It was quite a business to fit him out for the trip. He left with one suit of unbleached under–clothing on and one in his bundle, his pair of college blankets, the top shirt he had on (made of mattress ticking), pants of Pa's surveying suit, and a coat of cotton wool bed spread (grey). He was also in possession of: three pairs of home–spun and knit socks, some lint, some old linen bandages, 3 needles, 6 bone buttons, and about one third of a spool of good thread; an old but sharp pocket knife, an old flint–lock musket, some powder, and balls that he and I had molded from an old black tin syringe and a piece of lead pipe; and spent bullets that we found in tree bark, sides of houses, or on the ground. At every place where a fight had taken place, we had been gathering them since the first days of the War. He also had a little cracked skillet. Léon was considered well equipped for a volunteer of 1864.

With Léon's departure went the last ray of gladness left to my "cut off" childhood. My grief was awful, but no one saw me in my agony; the pines back of Mr. Tomb's old house were my only witnesses. Women were sending their sons and husbands off with a smile. I could be as brave, but my bravery left me the moment I was alone in the woods.

With Léon gone the work was harder. He was stronger (though very small) than any three of those left to struggle with the coming winter. The winters were so hard.

Alone on the Road with Yankee

MARY A. H. GAY

ON THE ROAD NEAR ATLANTA, GEORGIA, NOVEMBER 1864

For anyone, woman or man, to travel alone through the recently conquered territory east of Atlanta in 1864 required enormous courage. Yankee raiders were not Mary Gay's only concern. She was also in danger of being annoyed or molested by Confederate stragglers and newly freed slaves.

"What is it Ma? Has anything happened?"

"No, only Maggie Benedict has been here crying as if her heart would break, and saying that her children are begging for bread, and she has none to give them. Give me a little of the meal or hominy that you have, that we may not starve until we can get something else to eat, and then take the remainder to her that she may cook it as quickly as possible for her suffering children."

We had spent the preceding day in picking out grains of corn from cracks and crevices in bureau drawers, and other improvised troughs for Federal horses, as well as gathering up what was scattered upon the ground. In this way by diligent and persevering work, about a half bushel was obtained from the now deserted camping ground of Garrard's cavalry, and this corn was thoroughly washed and dried and carried by me and Telitha [a slave] to a poor little mill (which had escaped conflagration, because too humble to attract attention), and ground into coarse meal. Returning from this mill, and carrying, myself, a portion of the meal, I saw in the distance my mother coming to meet me. Apprehensive of evil, I ran to meet her and asked:

"What is it Ma? Has anything happened?"

With flushed face and tear–toned voice she replied as already stated. My heart was touched and a division was soon made. Before starting on this errand, I thought of the probable delay that inexperience and perhaps the want of cooking utensils and fuel might occasion, and suggested that it would hasten the relief to the children to cook some bread and mush and carry it to them already for use. A boiling pot left on the camping ground, was soon on the fire ready to receive the well–prepared batter, which was to be converted into nutritious mush or porridge. Nor was the bread forgotten. While the mush was cooking the hoe–cakes were baking in good old plantation style. These were arranged one upon another, and tied up in a snow–white cloth; and a tin bucket, also a trophy from the company, was filled with hot mush. I took the bread, and Telitha the bucket, and walked rapidly to Doctor Holmes' residence, where Maggie Benedict had rooms for herself and her children. The Rev. Doctor and his wife had refugeed, leaving this young mother and her children alone and unprotected.

The scene which I witnessed will never be obliterated from my memory. On the doorsteps sat the young mother, beautiful in desolation, with a baby in her arms, and on either side of her a little one, piteously crying for something to eat. "Oh, mama, I want something to eat so bad." "Oh, mama, I am so hungry — give me something to eat." Thus the children were begging for what the mother had not to give. She could only give them soothing words. But relief was at hand.

While this needful food was being eaten with a zest known only to the hungry, I was taking in the situation, and devising in my own mind means by which to render more enduring relief. The meal we had on hand would soon be exhausted, and, though more might be procured in the same way, it would be hazardous to depend upon that way only. To leave this young mother in a state of absolute helplessness, and her innocent little ones dependent upon the precarious support which might be gleaned from a devastated country would be cruel indeed; but how to obviate this state of affairs was a serious question.

The railroad having been torn up in every direction communicating with Decatur, there seemed to be but one alternative — to walk — and that was not practicable with several small children.

"Maggie, this state of affairs cannot be kept up; have you no friend to whom you can go?"

"Yes," she replied, "Mr. Benedict has a sister near Madison, who has wanted me and the children to go and stay with her ever since he has been in the army, but I was too independent to do it."

"Absurd! Well, the time has come that you must go. Get the children ready, and I will call for you soon," and without any positive or defined plan of procedure, I took leave of Maggie and her children. I was working by faith, and the Lord directed my footsteps. On my way home I hunted up "Uncle Mack," a faithful old negro man, who preferred freedom in the midst of privation with his own white people, to following the Federal army around on "Uncle Sam's" pay–roll, and got from him a promise that he would construct a wagon out of the odds and ends left upon the streets of Decatur. The next thing to be done was to provide a horse, and not being a magician this undertaking must have seemed chimerical to those who had not known how often and how singularly these scarcely formulated plans had developed into success.

Next morning, before the sun rose, accompanied by the Morton girls, I was on my way to "the canebrakes." I had seen many horses, whose places had been taken by others captured from farmers, abandoned and sent out to the cane–brake to recuperate or to die, the latter being the more probable. Without any definite knowledge of the locality, but guided by an over–ruling providence, I went direct to the cane–brake, and there soon made a selection of a horse, which, from the assortment at hand, could not have been improved upon. By a dexterous throw of a lasso, constructed and managed by the young friends already mentioned, he was soon captured and on his way to Decatur to enter "rebel" service. His most conspicuous feature was a pair of as fine eyes as ever illuminated a horse's head, large, brown and lustrous. There were other conspicuous things about him, too; for instance, branded upon each of his sides were the tell–tale letters, "U.S.," and on his back was an immense sore which also told tales. By twelve o'clock, noon, Uncle Mack appeared upon the scene, pulling something which he had improvised which baffled description, and which, for the sake of the faithful service I obtained from it, I will not attempt to describe, though it might provoke the risibilities of the readers. Suffice it to say that as it carried living freight in safety over many a bridge, in honor of this I will call it a wagon. Uncle Mack soon had the horse secured to this vehicle by ropes and pieces of crocus sack, for harness was as scarce a commodity as wagons and horses. I surveyed the equipage from center to circumference, with emotions pathetic and amusing. It was awfully suggestive. And as I viewed it in all its grotesqueness my imagination pictured a collapse. As I turned my head to take a sly glance at my mother, our eyes met, and all restraint was removed. With both of us laughter and sobs contended for the mastery, and merriment and tears literally blended. Thus equipped, and with a benediction from my mother, expressed more by looks and acts than by words, I gathered the ropes and started like Bayard Taylor to take "Views Afoot," and at the same time accomplish an errand of mercy which would lead me, as I led the horse, over a portion of country that in dreariness and utter desolation baffles description

— enough to know that Sherman's foraging trains had been over it. Leading the horse, which was already christened "Yankee," to Dr. Holmes' door, I called Maggie to come on with her children.

"I can't bring my things out, Miss Mary. Somebody must come to carry them and put them in the wagon."

"I can," I said, and suiting the action to the word, ran into the house, where to my amazement three large trunks confronted me. What was to be done? If they could be got into the wagon, what guarantee was there that poor Yankee could haul them in that tumblesome vehicle? However, I went for Uncle Mack to put the trunks in the wagon, and in front of them, in close proximity to the horse's heels was placed a chair in which Maggie seated herself and took her baby in her lap, the other children nestling on rugs at her feet.

Poor Yankee seemed to feel the importance of his mission, and jogged along at a pretty fair speed, and I, who walked by his side and held the ropes, found myself more than once obliged to strike a trot in order to maintain control of him. Paradoxical as it may seem, I enjoyed this new phase in my service to the Confederacy — none but a patriot could render it, and the whole thing seemed invested with the glamour of romance, the sequel of which would be redemption from all connection with a people who could thus afflict another people of equal rights. While Maggie hummed a sweet little lullaby to her children, I contemplated the devastation and ruin on every side. Not a vestige of anything remained to mark the sites of the pretty homes which had dotted this fair country before the destroyer came, except, perhaps, a standing chimney now and then.

Maggie and the children became restive in their pent–up limits, and the latter clamored for something to eat, but there was nothing to give them. Night was upon us, and we had come only about eight miles, and not an animate thing had we seen since we left Decatur, not even a bird, and the silence was unbroken save by the sound of the horse's feet as he trod upon the rocks, and the soft, sweet humming of the young mother to her dear little ones. Step by step we seemed to descend into the caverns of darkness and my heart began to falter. The children, awe–struck had ceased their appeal for bread, and nestled closer to their mother, and that they might all the more feel her protecting presence, she kept up a constant crooning sound, pathetic and sad. Step by step we penetrated the blackness of night — a night without a moon, starless and murky. The unerring instinct of an animal was all we had to guide us in the beaten road, which had ceased to be visible to human ken.

A faint glimmer of light, at apparently no very great distance, gave hope that our day's journey was almost ended. Yankee also caught the inspiration and walked a little faster. Though the time seemed long, the cabin, for such it proved to be, was finally reached, and I dropped the ropes, and, guided by the glimmer of light through the cracks, went to the door and knocked, at the same time announcing my name. The door was quickly opened. Imagine my surprise when recognized and cordially welcomed by a sweet friend, whose most humble plantation cabin was a pretty residence in comparison with the one she now occupied. Maggie, too, as the daughter of a well–known physician, received cordial welcome for herself and children. And thus a kind of Providence provided a safe lodging place for the night.

Nature again asserted itself, and the children asked for something to eat. The good lady of the house kissed them, and told them that supper would soon be ready. The larger one of her little sons drew from a bed of ashes, which had been covered by glowing coals, some large yam potatoes which he took to a table and peeled. He then went outside the cabin and drew from a keg an earthen–ware pitcher full of sparkling persimmon beer, which he dispensed to us in cups, and then handed around the potatoes. And how much this repast was enjoyed! Good sweet yams thoroughly cooked, and the zestful persimmon beer! And I thought of my lonely mother at a desolated home, whose only supper had been made of coarse meal, ground from corn which her own hands helped to pick from crevices and cracks in improvised troughs, where Garrard's cavalry had fed their horses. After awhile the sweet womanly spirit that presided over this little group, got a quilt and a shawl or two, and made a pallet for the children. The boys put more wood upon the fire, and some in the jambs of the fireplace to be used during the night; and then they went behind us and lay down upon the floor, with seed cotton for pillows, and the roof for covering. Our kind hostess placed additional wraps over the shoulders of Maggie and myself, and we three sat in our chairs and slept until the dawn.

Accustomed to looking after outdoor interests, I went to see how Yankee was coming on, and found him none the worse for the preceding day's toil. Everything indicated that he had fared as sumptuously as we had — a partly–eaten pumpkin, corn, whole ears yet in the trough, and fodder near by, plainly showed the generosity of the noble little family that took us in and gave us the best they had. After breakfast we bade adieu to the good mother and her children, and went on our way, if not rejoicing, at least feeling better for having seen and been with such good people. There was a strong tie between us all. The husband and father was off in the army, like our loved ones. The generous feeding given to our steed had so braced him up that he began to walk faster and was keenly appreciative of every kind word; and I and he formed a friendship for each other that continued to his dying day. The road was very rough and hilly, and more than once he showed signs of fatigue; but a word of encouragement seemed to renew his strength, and he walked bravely on. Maggie would perhaps, have lightened his load by walking, now and then, but the jolting of the wagon kept the trunks in perpetual motion, and the lives of the children would thereby have been jeopardized.

Nothing of special interest transpired this second day of our journey. The same fiend of destruction had laid his ruthless hand upon everything within his reach. The woods had been robbed of their beauty and the fields of their products; not even a bird was left to sing a requiem over the scene of desolation, or an animal to suggest where once had been a habitation. Once, crouching near a standing chimney, there was a solitary dog who kept at bay every attempt to approach — no kind word would conciliate or put him off his guard. Poor, lonely sentinel! Did he remember that around the once cheerful hearthstone he had been admitted to a place with the family group? Was he awaiting his master's return? Ah, who can know the emotions, or the dim reasonings of that faithful brute?

Night again came on and I discovered that we were approaching the hospitable mansion of Mr. Montgomery, an excellent, courtly country gentleman, who was at home under circumstances not now remembered. He and his interesting family gladly welcomed me and my little charge and entertained us most hospitably. The raiders had been here and helped themselves bountifully, but they had spared the house for another time, and that other time came soon, and nothing was left on the site of this beautiful home but ubiquitous chimneys.

An early start the next day enabled Yankee to carry Maggie and her children and the trunks to Social Circle in time to take the noon train for Madison. So far as Maggie and her children were concerned I now felt that I had done all that I could, and that I must hasten back to my lonely mother at Decatur; but Maggie's tearful entreaties not to be left among strangers prevailed with me, and I got aboard the train with her, and never left her until I had placed her and her children in the care of good Mr. Thrasher at Madison, to be conveyed by him to the home of Mrs. Reeves, her husband's sister.

In Madison, I too, had dear friends and relatives, with whom I spent the night, and the morning's train bore me back to Social Circle, then the terminus of the Georgia Railroad — the war fiend having destroyed every rail between there and Atlanta. Arriving there, imagine my surprise and indignation when I learned that Mr. R———, whom I had paid in advance to care for Yankee while I was gone to Madison, had sent him out to his sorghum mill and put him to grinding cane; and it was with much difficulty and delay that I got him in time to start on my homeward journey that afternoon. Instead of his being rested, he was literally broken down, and my pity for him constrained me to walk every step of the way back to Decatur. While waiting for the horse I purchased such articles of food as I could find. For instance, a sack of flour, for which I paid a hundred dollars; a bushel of potatoes; several gallons of sorghum; a few pounds of butter, and a few pounds of meat. Even this was a heavy load for the poor jaded horse. Starting so late I could only get to the hospitable home of Mr. Crew, distant only about three miles from "The Circle."

Before leaving Mr. Crew's, the next morning, I learned that an immense Yankee raid had come out from Atlanta, and had burned the bridge which I had crossed only two days ago. This information caused me to take another route to Decatur, and my heart lost much of its hope, and my step its alacrity. Yet the Lord sustained me in the discharge of duty. Those were praying days with me, and now I fervently invoked God's aid and protection in my perilous undertaking, and I believed that He would grant aid and protection.

That I might give much needed encouragement to Yankee, I walked by his side with my hand upon his shoulder much of the time, an act of endearment which he greatly appreciated, and proved that he did so by the expression of his large brown eyes. One of my idiosyncrasies through life has been that of counting everything, and as I journeyed homeward, I found myself counting my steps from one to a thousand and one. As there is luck in odd numbers, says Roy O'Moore, I always ended with the traditional odd number, and by telling Yankee how much nearer home we were. And I told him many things, among them, *sotto voce*, that I did not believe he was a Yankee, but a captured rebel. If a tuft of grass appeared on the road side, he was permitted to crop it; or if a muscadine vine with its tempting grapes was discovered, he cropped the leaves off the low shrubbery, while I gathered the grapes for my mother at home.

In the early part of the day, during this solitary drive, I came to a cottage by the wayside that was a perfect gem — an oasis, and everything that could thrill the heart by its loveliness. Flowers of every hue beauti-

fied the grounds and sweetened the air, and peace and plenty seemed to
hold undisputed sway. The Fiend of Destruction had not yet reached this
little Eden. Two gentlemen were in the yard conversing. I perceived at a
glance that they were of the clerical order, and would fain have spoken
to them; but not wishing to disturb them, or attract attention to myself, I
was passing by as unobtrusively as possible, when I was espied and recognized by one of them, who proved to be a saintly man, Rev. Walter
Branham. He introduced me to his friend, Professor Shaw of Oxford.
Their sympathy for me was plainly expressed, and they gave me much
needed instruction regarding the route, and suggested that I would about
get to Rev. Henry Clark's to put up for the night. With a hearty shake of
the hand, and "Good bless you, noble woman," I pursued my lonely
way and they went theirs. No other adventure enlivened the day, and
poor patient Yankee did the best he could and so did I. It was obvious
that he had done about all he could. Grinding sorghum under a hard
taskmaster, with an empty stomach, had told on him, and he could no
longer quicken his pace at the sound of a friendly voice.

At length we came in sight of "Uncle Henry Clark's" place. I stood
amazed, bewildered. Elegant rosewood and mahogany furniture, broken
into a thousand fragments, covered the face of the ground as far as I
could see; and china and glass looked as if it had been sown. And the
house, what of that? Alas! it too had been scattered to the four winds of
heaven in the form of smoke and ashes. Not even a chimney stood to
mark its site. Near by stood a row of negro cabins, intact, showing that
while conflagration was going on they had been sedulously guarded.
And these cabins were occupied by slaves of the plantation. Men,
women, and children stalked about in restless uncertainty, and in surly
indifference. They had been led to believe that the country would be
apportioned to them, but they had sense enough to know that such a
mighty revolution involved trouble and delay, and they were supinely
waiting developments. Neither man, woman nor child approached me.
There was mutual distrust and mutual avoidance.

It took less time to take in this situation than it has to describe it. The
sun was almost down. What was I to do? The next nearest place that I
could remember that would perhaps give protection for the night was
Mr. Fowler's, and this was my only hope. With one hand upon Yankee's
shoulder, and the ropes in the other, I moved on, and not until my expir-
ing breath will I forget the pleading look which that poor dumb animal
turned upon me when I started. Utterly helpless, and in my hands, he
wondered how I could thus exact more of him. I wondered myself. But

what was I to do but to move on? And with continuous supplication for the Lord to have mercy upon me, I moved on. More than once the poor horse turned that look, beseeching and pathetic, upon me. It frightened me. I did not understand it, and still moved on. At last the hope of making himself understood forsook him, and he deliberately laid himself down in the road. I knelt by his side and told him the true state of affairs, and implored him not to desert me in this terrible crisis. I told him how cruel it would be to do so, and used many arguments of like character, but they availed nothing. He did not move, and his large, lustrous brown eyes seemed to say for him: "I have done all I can, and can do no more."

What could I do but rise from my imploring attitude and face my perilous situation? "Lord, have mercy upon me," was my oft-repeated invocation. The first thing which greeted my vision when I rose to my feet was a very distant but evidently an advancing object. I watched it with bated breath, and soon had the satisfaction of seeing a man on mule-back. I ran to meet him, saying: "O, sir, I know the good Lord sent you here." And then I recounted my trouble, and received most cordial sympathy from one who had been a Confederate soldier, but who was now at home in consequence of wounds that incapacitated him for further service. When he heard all, he said:

"I would take you home with me, but I have to cross a swimming creek before getting there, and I am afraid to undertake to carry you. Wait here until I see these negroes. They are a good set, and whatever they promise, they will, I think, carry out faithfully."

The time seemed interminable before he came back, and night, black night, had set in; and yet a quiet resignation sustained me.

When my benefactor returned, two negro men came with him, one of whom brought a lantern, bright and cheery. "I have arranged for you to be cared for here," said he. "Several of the old house servants of Mrs. Clark know you, and they will prove themselves worthy of the trust we repose in them." I accepted the arrangement made by this good man, and entrusted myself to the care of the negroes for the night. This I did with great trepidation, but as soon as I entered the cabin an assurance of safety filled my mind with peace, and reconciled me to my surroundings. The "mammy" that presided over it, met me with a cordial welcome and assured me that no trouble would befall me under her roof. An easy chair was placed for me in one corner in comfortable proximity to a large plantation fire. In a few minutes the men came in bringing my flour, potatoes, syrup, bacon, etc. This sight gave me real satisfaction, as I thought of my poor patient mother at home and hoped that in some way I should yet be able to convey to her thus much needed freight. I soon espied a table on which was piled many books and magazines; "Uncle Henry Clark's" theological books were well represented. I proposed reading to the women, if they would like to hear me, and soon had their undivided attention, as well as that of several of the men, who sat on the doorsteps. In this way several hours passed, and then "mammy" said "You must be getting sleepy." "Oh, no," I replied, "I frequently sit up all night reading." But this did not satisfy her; she had devised in her own mind something most hospitable for her guest, and she wanted to see it carried out. Calling into requisition the assistance of the men, she had two large cedar chests placed side by side, and out of these chests were taken nice clean quilts, and snow–white counterpanes, and sheets, and pillows — Mrs. Clark's beautiful bed–clothing — and upon those chests was made a pallet upon which a queen might have reposed with comfort. It was so tempting in its cleanliness that I consented to lie down. The sole occupants of that room that night were myself and my hostess — the aforesaid black "mammy." Rest, not sleep, came to my relief. The tramping of feet, and now and then the muffled sound of human voices, kept me in a listening attitude, and it must be confessed in a state of painful apprehension. Thus the night passed.

With the dawn of day, I was up and ready to meet the day's requirements. "Mammy's" first greeting was, "What's your hurry?" "I am accustomed to early rising. May I open the door?" The first thing I saw was Yankee, and he was standing eating; but he was evidently too weak to attempt the task of getting that cumbersome vehicle and its freight to Decatur. So I arranged with one of the men to put a steer to the wagon and carry them home. This he was to do for the sum of one hundred dollars. After an appetizing breakfast, I started homeward, leading Yankee in the rear of this turnout. Be it remembered, I did not leave without making ample compensation for my night's entertainment.

No event of particular interest occurred on the way to Decatur. Yankee walked surprisingly well, and the little steer acquitted himself nobly. In due time Decatur appeared in sight, and then there ensued a scene which for pathos defies description. Matron and maiden, mother and child, each with a tin can picked up off the enemy's camping ground, ran after me and begged for just a little something to eat — just enough to keep them from starving. Not an applicant was refused, and by the time the poor, rickety, cumbersome wagon reached its destination, its contents had been greatly diminished. But there was yet enough left to last for some time the patient loving mother, the faithful Telitha, and myself.

A summary of the trip developed these facts: To the faithfulness of Uncle Mack was due the holding together of the most grotesque vehicle ever dignified by the name of wagon; over all that rough road it remained intact, and returned as good as when it started. And but for the sorghum grinding, poor Yankee would have acted his part unfalteringly. As for myself, I labored under the hallucination that I was a Confederate soldier, and there seemed no task too great for me to essay, if it but served either directly or indirectly those who were fighting my battles.

Thirty Thousand Dollars Poorer

DOLLY LUNT BURGE

NEAR SOCIAL CIRCLE, GEORGIA, NOVEMBER 1864

Dolly Burge's plantation was southwest of Atlanta in the line of Sherman's march to the sea. She was a widow who, like Kate Stone's mother, had been operating her plantation alone since the death of her husband. Social Circle, sometimes referred to simply as the Circle, is a town in Georgia near the Burge plantation.

November 8, 1864. Today will probably decide the fate of the Confederacy. If Lincoln is reelected I think our fate is a hard one, but we are in the hands of a merciful God, and if He sees that we are in the wrong, I trust that He will show it unto us. I have never felt that slavery was altogether right, for it is abused by men, and I have often heard Mr. Burge say that if he could see that it was sinful for him to own slaves, if he felt that it was wrong, he would take them where he could free them. He would not sin for his right hand. The purest and holiest men have owned them, and I can see nothing in the scriptures which forbids it. I have never bought or sold slaves and I have tried to make life easy and pleasant to those that have been bequeathed me by the dead. I have never ceased to work. Many a Northern housekeeper has a much easier time than a Southern matron with her hundred negroes.

November 17, 1864. Have been uneasy all day. At night some of the neighbors, who had been to town, called. They said it was a large force of Yankees moving very slowly. What shall I do? Where go?

November 18, 1864. Slept very little last night. Went out doors several times and could see large fires like burning buildings. Am I not in the hands of a merciful God who has promised to take care of the widow and orphan? Sent off two of my mules in the night. Mr. Ward and Frank [a slave] took them away and hid them. In the morning took a barrel of salt, which had cost me two hundred dollars, into one of the black women's gardens, put a paper over it, and then on the top of that leached ashes. Fixed it on a board as a leach tub, daubing it with ashes [the old–fashioned way of making lye for soap]. Had some few pieces of meat taken from my smokehouse carried to the Old Place [a distant part of the plantation] and hidden under some fodder. Bade them hide the wagon and gear and then go on plowing. Went to packing up mine and Sadai's [her daughter's] clothes. I fear that we shall be homeless.

The boys came back and wished to hide their mules. They say that the Yankees camped at Mr. Gibson's last night and are taking all the stock in the county. Seeing them so eager, I told them to do as they pleased. They took them off, and Elbert [the black coachman] took his forty fattening hogs to the Old Place Swamp and turned them in.

We have done nothing all day — that is, my people have not. I made a pair of pants for Jack [a slave]. Sent Nute [a slave] up to Mrs. Perry's on an errand. On his way back, he said, two Yankees met him and begged him to go with them. They asked if we had livestock, and came up the road as far as Mrs. Laura Perry's. I sat for an hour expecting them, but they must have gone back. Oh, how I trust I am safe! Mr. Ward is very much alarmed.

November 19, 1864. Slept in my clothes last night, as I heard that the Yankees went to neighbor Montgomery's on Thursday night at one o'clock, searched his house, drank his wine, and took his money and valuables. As we were not disturbed, I walked after breakfast, with Sadai, up to Mr. Joe Perry's, my nearest neighbor, where the Yankees were yesterday. Saw Mrs. Laura [Perry] in the road surrounded by her children, seeming to be looking for some one. She said she was looking for her husband, that old Mrs. Perry had just sent her word that the Yankees went to James Perry's the night before, plundered his house, and drove off all his stock, and that she must drive hers into the old fields. Before we were done talking, up came Joe and Jim Perry from their hiding place. Jim was very much excited. Happening to turn and look behind, as we stood there, I saw some bluecoats coming down the hill. Jim immediately raised his gun, swearing he would kill them anyhow.

"No, don't!" said I, and ran home as fast as I could, with Sadai.

I could hear them cry, "Halt! Halt!" and their guns went off in quick succession. Oh God, the time of trial has come!

A man passed on his way to Covington. I halloed to him, asking him if he did not know the Yankees were coming.

"No — are they?"

"Yes," said I; "they are not three hundred yards from here."

"Sure enough," said he. "Well, I'll not go. I don't want them to get my horse." And although within hearing of their guns, he would stop and look for them. Blissful ignorance! Not knowing, not hearing, he has not suffered the suspense, the fear, that I have for the past forty–eight hours. I walked to the gate. There they came filing up.

I hastened back to my frightened servants and told them that they had better hide, and then went back to the gate to claim protection and a guard. But like demons they rush in! My yards are full. To my smoke–house, my dairy, pantry, kitchen, and cellar, like famished wolves they come, breaking locks and whatever is in their way. The thousand pounds of meat in my smoke–house is gone in a twinkling, my flour, my meat, my lard, butter, eggs, pickles of various kinds — both in vinegar and brine — wine, jars and jugs are all gone. My eighteen fat turkeys, my hens, chickens, and fowls, my young pigs, are shot down in my yard and hunted as if they were rebels themselves. Utterly powerless I ran out and appealed to the guard.

"I cannot help you, Madam; it is orders."

As I stood there, from my lot I saw driven, first, old Dutch, my dear old buggy horse, who has carried my beloved husband so many miles, and who would so quietly wait at the block for him to mount and dis-mount, and who at last drew him to his grave; then came old Mary, my brood mare, who for years had been too old and stiff for work, with her two–year–old mule, and her last little baby colt. There they go! There go my mules, my sheep, and worse than all, my boys [slaves]!

Alas! little did I think while trying to save my house from plunder and fire that they were forcing my boys from home at the point of the bayo-net. One, Newton, jumped into bed in his cabin, and declared himself sick. Another crawled under the floor, — a lame boy he was, — but they pulled him out, placed him on a horse, and drove him off. Mid, poor Mid! The last I saw of him, a man had him going around the garden, looking, as I thought, for my sheep as he was my shepherd. Jack came crying to me, the big tears coursing down his cheeks, saying they were making him go. I said:

"Stay in my room."

But a man followed in, cursing him and threatening to shoot him if he did not go; so poor Jack had to yield. James Arnold, in trying to escape from a back window, was captured and marched off. Henry, too, was taken; I know not how or when, but probably when he and Bob went after the mules. I had not believed they would force from their homes the poor, doomed negroes, but such has been the fact here, cursing them and saying that "Jeff Davis wanted to put them in his army, but that they should not fight for him, but for the Union." No! Indeed no! They are not friends to the slave. We have never made the poor, cowardly negro fight, and it is strange, passing strange, that the all–powerful Yankee nation with the whole world to back them, their ports open, their armies filled with soldiers from all nations, should at last take the poor negro to help them out against this little Confederacy, which was to have been brought back into the Union in sixty days' time!

My poor boys! My poor boys! What unknown trials are before you! How you have clung to your mistress and assisted her in every way you knew.

Never have I corrected them; a word was sufficient. Never have they known want of any kind. Their parents are with me, and how sadly they lament the loss of their boys. Their cabins are rifled of every valuable, the soldiers swearing that their Sunday clothes were the white people's, and that they never had money to get such things as they had. Poor Frank's chest was broken open, his money and tobacco taken. He has always been a money–making and saving boy; not infrequently has his crop brought him five hundred dollars and more. All of his clothes and Rachel's clothes, which dear Lou gave her before her death and which she had packed away, were stolen from her. Ovens, skillets, coffee–mills, of which we had three, coffee–pots — not one have I left. Sifters all gone!

Seeing that the soldiers could not be restrained, the guard ordered me to have their [the negroes'] remaining possessions brought into my house, which I did, and they all, poor things, huddled together in my room, fearing every moment that the house would be burned.

A Captain Webber from Illinois came into my house. Of him I claimed protection from the vandals who were forcing themselves into my room. He said that he knew my brother Orrington [the late Orrington Lunt, a well known early settler of Chicago]. At that name I could not restrain my feelings, but, bursting into tears, implored him to see my brother and let him know my destitution. I saw nothing before me but starvation. He promised to do this, and comforted me with the assurance that my dwelling–house would not be burned, though my out–buildings might. Poor little Sadai went crying to him as to a friend and told him that they had taken her doll, Nancy. He begged her to come and see him, and he would give her a fine waxen one.

He felt for me, and I give him and several others the character of gentlemen. I don't believe they would have molested women and children had they had their own way. He seemed surprised that I had not laid away in my house, flour and other provisions. I did not suppose I could secure them there, more than where I usually kept them, for in last summer's raid houses were thoroughly searched. In parting with him, I parted as with a friend.

Sherman himself and a greater portion of his army passed my house that day. All day, as the sad moments rolled on, were they passing not only in front of my house, but from behind; they tore down my garden palings, made a road through my backyard and lot field, driving their stock and riding through, tearing down my fences and desolating my home — wantonly doing it when there was no necessity for it.

Such a day, if I live to the age of Methuselah, may God spare me from ever seeing again!

As night drew its sable curtains around us, the heavens from every point were lit up with flames from burning buildings. Dinnerless and supperless as we were, it was nothing in comparison with the fear of being driven out homeless to the dreary woods. Nothing to eat! I could give my guard no supper, so he left us. I appealed to another, asking him if he had wife, mother, or sister, and how he should feel were they in my situation. A colonel from Vermont left me two men, but they were Dutch, and I could not understand one word they said.

My Heavenly Father alone saved me from destructive fire. My carriage–house had in it eight bales of cotton, with my carriage, buggy, and harness. On top of the cotton were some carded cotton rolls, a hundred pounds or more. These were thrown out of the blanket in which they were and a large twist of the rolls taken and set on fire, and thrown into the boat of my carriage, which was close up to the cotton bales. Thanks to my God, the cotton only burned over, and then went out. Shall I ever forget the deliverance?

Tonight, when the greater part of the army had passed, it came up very windy and cold. My room was full, nearly, with the negroes and their bedding. They were afraid to go out, for my women could not step out of the door without an insult from the Yankee soldiers. They lay down on the floor; Sadai got down and under the same cover with Sally, while I sat up all night, watching every moment for the flames to burst out from some of my buildings. The two guards came into my room and laid themselves by my fire for the night. I could not close my eyes, but kept walking to and fro, watching the fires in the distance and dreading the approaching day, which I feared, as they had not all passed, would be but a continuation of horrors.

• • •

November 20, 1864. This is the blessed Sabbath, the day upon which He, who came to bring peace and good will upon earth, rose from His tomb and ascended to intercede for us poor fallen creatures. But how unlike this day to any that have preceded it in my once quiet home. I had watched all night, and the dawn found me watching for the moving of the soldiery that was encamped about us. Oh, how I dreaded those that were to pass, as I supposed they would straggle and complete the ruin that the others had commenced, for I had been repeatedly told that they would burn everything as they passed.

Some of my women had gathered up a chicken that the soldiers shot yesterday, and they cooked it with some yams for our breakfast, the guard complaining that we gave them no supper. They gave us some coffee, which I had to make in a tea–kettle, as every coffee–pot is taken off. The rear–guard was commanded by Colonel Carlow, who changed our guard, leaving us one soldier while they were passing. They marched directly on, scarcely breaking ranks. Once a bucket of water was called for, but they drank without coming in.

About ten o'clock they had all passed save one, who came in and wanted coffee made, which was done, and he, too, went on. A few minutes elapsed, and two couriers riding rapidly passed back. Then, presently more soldiers came by, and this ended the passing of Sherman's army by my place, leaving me poorer by thirty thousand dollars than I was yesterday morning. And a much stronger Rebel!

A Birth in the Ruins

MARY JONES AND MARY MALLARD

LIBERTY COUNTY, GEORGIA,
DECEMBER 1864–JANUARY 1865

Mary Jones, her daughter, Mary Mallard, her friend, Kate King, and five children were living at Montevideo, one of the Jones plantations in Liberty County, Georgia, not far west of Savannah. Mary Jones was a widow. Mary Mallard's husband was in the Confederate army, as was Kate King's. Sherman's troops, that had come through Dolly Burge's plantation in November, had now been on the road for a month, pillaging and destroying much of whatever they could not carry away.

MRS. MARY S. MALLARD IN HER JOURNAL

December 7th, 1864. About four in the afternoon we heard the clash of arms and noise of horsemen, and by the time Mother and I could get downstairs we saw forty or fifty men in the pantry, flying hither and thither, ripping open the safe with their swords and breaking open the crockery cupboards. Fearing we might not have a chance to cook, Mother had some chickens and ducks roasted and put in the safe for our family. These the men seized whole, tearing them to pieces with their teeth like ravenous beasts. They were clamorous for whiskey, and ordered us to get our keys. One came to Mother to know where her meal and flour were, insisted upon opening her locked pantry, and took every particle. They threw the sacks across their horses. Mother remonstrated and pointed to her helpless family; their only reply was: "We'll take it!"

They flew around the house, tearing open boxes and everything that was closed. They broke open Mother's little worktable with an andiron, hoping to find money or jewelry; it contained principally little mementos that were valuable only to herself. Failing to find treasure, they took the sweet little locks of golden hair that her mother had cut from the heads of her angel children near a half century ago, and scattering them upon the floor trampled them under their feet. A number of them rifled the sideboard, taking away knives, spoons, forks, tin cups, coffeepots, and everything they wished. They broke open Grandfather's old liquor case and carried off two of the large square gallon bottles, and drank up all the blackberry wine and vinegar which was in the case. It was vain to utter a word, for we were completely paralyzed by the fury of these ruffians.

A number of them went into the attic into a little storeroom and carried off twelve bushels of meal Mother had stored there for our necessities. She told them they were taking all she had to support herself and daughter, a friend and five little children. Scarcely one regarded even the sound of her voice; those who did laughed and said they would leave one sack to keep us from starving. But they only left some rice which they did not want, and poured out a quart or so of meal upon the floor. At other times they said they meant to starve us to death. They searched trunks and bureaus and wardrobes, calling for shirts and men's clothes.

We asked for their officer, hoping to make some appeal to him; they said they were all officers and would do as they pleased. We finally found one man who seemed to make a little show of authority, which was indicated by a whip which he carried. Mother appealed to him, and he came up and ordered the men out. They instantly commenced cursing him, and we thought they would fight one another. They brought a wagon and took another from the place to carry off their plunder.

It is impossible to imagine the horrible uproar and stampede through the house, every room of which was occupied by them, all yelling, cursing, quarreling, and running from one room to another in wild confusion. Such was their blasphemous language, their horrible countenances and appearance, that we realized what must be the association of the lost in the world of eternal woe. Their throats were open sepulchres, their mouths filled with cursing and bitterness and lies. These men belonged to Kilpatrick's cavalry. We look back upon their conduct in the house as a horrible nightmare, too terrible to be true.

When leaving they ordered all the oxen to be gotten up early next morning.

MRS. MARY JONES IN HER JOURNAL

Montevideo, Saturday, December 17th, 1864. About four o'clock this morning, we were roused by the sound of horses; and Sue, our faithful woman, came upstairs breathless with dismay and told us they had come upon the most dreadful intent, and had sent her in to tell me what it was, and had inquired if there were any young women in my family. Oh, the agony — the agony of that awful hour no language can describe! No heart can conceive it. We were alone, friendless, and knew not what might befall us. Feeling our utter weakness and peril, we all knelt down around the bed and went to prayer; and we continued in silent prayer a long time. Kate prayed, Daughter prayed, and I prayed; and the dear little children, too, hearing our voices, got up and knelt down beside us. And there we were, alone and unprotected, imploring protection from a fate worse than death, and that our Almighty God and Saviour would not permit our cruel and wicked enemies to come nigh our persons or our dwelling. We rose from our knees and sat in darkness, waiting for the light of the morning to reveal their purposes, but trusting in God for our deliverance.

New squads were arriving. In the gray twilight of morning we looked out of the window and saw one man pacing before the courtyard gate between the house and the kitchen; and we afterwards found he had voluntarily undertaken to guard the house. In this we felt that our prayers had been signally answered.

MRS. MARY S. MALLARD IN HER JOURNAL

Montevideo, Saturday, December 17th, 1864. As soon as it was light Kate discovered an officer near the house, which was a great relief to our feelings. Mother and I went down immediately, when she said to him: "Sir, I see that you are an officer; and I come to entreat your protection for my family, and that you will not allow your soldiers to enter my dwelling, as it has been already three times searched and every particle of food and whatever they wanted taken." He replied it was contrary to orders for the men to be found in houses, and the penalty was death; and so far as his authority extended with his own men, none of them should enter the house. He said he and his squad (there were many others present) had come on a foraging expedition, and intended to take only provisions.

Upon Mother's inviting him to see some of the work of the previous evening he came in and sat awhile in the parlor. Before leaving he discovered a portable desk on a table and walked up and opened it. She said: "That is my private property; it is here for my own use, and has only a little paper in it." He closed it immediately. (It had previously escaped observation and removal.)

The Yankees made the Negroes bring up the oxen carts, and took off all the chickens and turkeys they could find. They carried off all the syrup from the smokehouse. We had one small pig, which was all the meat we had left; they took the whole of it. Mother saw everything like food stripped from her premises, without the power of uttering one word. Finally they rolled out the carriage and took that to carry off a load of chickens. They took everything they possibly could.

The soldier who acted as our volunteer guard was from Ohio, and older than anyone we had seen; for generally they were young men and so active that Mother called them "fiery flying serpents." As he was going Mother went out of the house and said to him: "I cannot allow you to leave without thanking you for your kindness to myself and family; and if I had anything to offer I would gladly make you some return."

He replied: "I could not receive anything, and only wish I was here to guard you always."

It was not enough that they should insult us by converting our carriage into a chicken–cart and take it away drawn by our own carriage horses; but they sent in to tell Mother if she wanted her carriage to send for it, and when they were done with it she might have it. We afterwards learned it was broken to pieces and left beyond Midway Church.

They took off today June, Martin, George, Ebenezer, Little Pulaski, our house servant Jack, and Carpenter Pulaski. Seeing the two last–named going away, Mother called to the soldier who had them in charge: "Why are you taking my young men away?"

He said: "They need not go if they do not want to."

She then asked: "Boys, do you wish to go or stay?"

They immediately replied: "We wish to stay."

She then said: "Do you hear that? Now, by what right do you force them away?"

They had Pulaski laden down with our turkeys, and wanted Jack to drive one of the carts. So they were all carried off — carriages, wagons, carts, horses and mules and servants, with food and provisions of every kind — and, so far as they were concerned, leaving us to starvation.

A little while after this party started, Mother walked to the smoke-house and found an officer taking sugar that had been put to drip. He was filling a bag with all that was dry. He seemed a little ashamed of being caught in the act, but did not return the sugar, but carried it off on his horse. He was mounted on Mr. Audley King's pet horse, a splendid animal which he had just stolen, and as he rode off said: "How the man who *owns* this horse will curse the Yankee who took him when he goes home and finds him gone!" He had Mr. King's servant mounted on another of his horses, and no doubt knew Mrs. King was with us and would hear the remark.

Immediately we went to work moving some salt and the little remaining sugar into the house; and while we were doing it a Missourian came up and advised us to get everything into the house as quickly as possible, and he would protect us while doing so. He offered to show Mother how to hide her things. She said: "We need instruction from Yankees, for we have never been accustomed to any such mean business." He said he had enlisted to fight for the *Constitution*; but since then the war had been turned into another thing, and he did not approve this abolitionism, for his wife's people all owned slaves. He told us what afterwards proved false — that ten thousand infantry would soon pass through Riceboro on their way to Thomasville.

Soon after this some twenty rode up and caught me having a barrel rolled toward the house. They were gentlemanly. A few only dismounted; said they were from various of our Confederate States. They said the war would soon be over, for they would have Savannah in a few days.

I replied: "Savannah is not the Confederacy."

They spoke of the number of places they had taken.

I said: "Yes, and do you hold them?"

One of them replied: "Well, I do admire your spunk."

They inquired for all the large plantations.

Squads came all day until near dark. We had no time to eat a mouthful. The remaining ox–wagons were taken to the cornhouse and filled with corn.

Sabbath, December 18th. We passed this day with many fears, but no Yankees came to the lot; though many went to Carlawter and were engaged carrying off corn, the key of the cornhouse having been taken from Cato the day before and the door ordered to be left open. A day comparatively free from interruptions was very grateful to us, though the constant state of apprehension in which we were was distressing.

In the afternoon, while we were engaged in religious services, reading and seeking protection of our Heavenly Father, Captain Winn's Isaiah came bringing a note from Mr. Mallard to me and one from Mr. John Stevens to Mother, sending my watch. This was our first intelligence from Mr. Mallard, and oh, how welcome to us all; though the note brought no hope of his release, as the charge against him was taking up arms against the U.S. Captain Winn had been captured but released. We were all in such distress that Mother wrote begging Mr. Stevens to come to us. We felt so utterly alone that it would be a comfort to have him with us.

• • •

Monday, December 19th. Squads of Yankees came all day, so that the servants scarcely had a moment to do anything for us out of the house. The women, finding it entirely unsafe for them to be out of the house at all, would run in and conceal themselves in our dwelling. The few remaining chickens and some sheep were killed. These men were so outrageous at the Negro houses that the Negro men were obliged to stay at their houses for the protection of their wives; and in some instances they rescued them from the hands of these infamous creatures.

Tuesday, December 20th. A squad of Yankees came soon after breakfast. Hearing there was one yoke of oxen left, they rode into the pasture and drove them up, and went into the woods and brought out the horse–wagon, to which they attached the oxen. Needing a chain for the purpose, they went to the well and took it from the well bucket. Mother went out and entreated them not to take it from the well, as it was our means of getting water. They replied: "You have no right to have even wood or water," and immediately took it away.

Wednesday, December 21st. 10 A.M. Six of Kilpatrick's cavalry rode up, one of them mounted on Mr. Mallard's valuable gray named Jim. They looked into the dairy and empty smokehouse, every lock having been broken and doors wide open day and night. They searched the servants' houses; then they thundered at the door of the dwelling. Mother opened it, when one of them presented a pistol to her breast and demanded why she dared to keep her house closed, and that "he be damned if he would not come into it."

She replied: "I prefer to keep my house closed because we are a helpless and defenseless family of women and children. And one of your officers informed me that the men were not to enter private dwellings. And it is also contrary to the published orders of your general."

He replied: "I'll be damned if I don't come in and take just what I want. Some of the men got wine here, and we must have some."

She told them her house had been four times searched in every part, and everything taken from it. And recognizing one who had been of the party that had robbed us, she said: "You know my meal and everything has been taken."

He said: "We left you a sack of meal and that rice."

Mother said: "You left us some rice; but out of twelve bushels of meal you poured out a quart or so upon the floor — as you said, to keep us from starving."

She then entreated them, on account of the health of her daughter, not to enter the house. With horrible oaths they rode off, shooting two ducks in the yard.

About half an hour after, three came. One knocked in the piazza and asked if Mother always kept her doors locked. She said she had recently done so by the advice of an officer; and Kate King said: "We have been compelled to do so since the house has been so repeatedly ransacked."

He said: "Well, I never do that and did not come for that." Asked if we knew Mrs. S —— of Dorchester, for he had turned some men out of her house who were ransacking it. He demeaned himself with respect, and did not insist upon coming in.

Upon one occasion one of the men as he sat on the bench in the piazza had his coat buttoned top and bottom, and inside we could plainly see a long row of stolen breast pins and jewelry — gallant trophies, won from defenseless women and children at the South to adorn the persons of their mothers, wives, sisters, and friends in Yankeeland!

One hour after, five came. Mother and Kate trembled from head to feet. It appeared as if this day's trials were more than they could bear. They knelt and asked strength from God; went down and found that three had already entered the pantry with false keys brought for the purpose. They immediately proceeded to cut open the wires of the safe and took all they wanted, amongst other things a tin kettle of eggs we had managed to get.

Mother said to them: "Why, you have entered my house with false keys!"

With demoniacal leer they said: "We want none of your keys," and tried to put in one of those they brought into the pantry door.

She told them: "Your soldiers have already broken the key in that lock, and it cannot be opened; but everything has already been taken." When they insultingly insisted the door should be opened, Mother told them: "Very well, break it open just as soon as you please."

She remonstrated against their coming over to the house, and told them of the order of the officers. They replied none of their officers prohibited them from coming in, and they would be damned if they would mind any such orders, would be damned if they did not go where they pleased, and would be damned if they did not take what they pleased. Mother remonstrated, and in her earnest entreaty placed her hand upon the shoulder of one of them, saying: "You must not go over to my house." Strange to say, they did not go beyond the pantry, and appeared restrained, as we afterwards believed, by the hand of God. They said they wanted pots and buckets, for they were in camp and had nothing to cook in. One asked for whiskey. To our amusement the man who stole the eggs stumbled and fell as he went down the steps and broke them all — but carried off the bucket. (Psalm 27:2 — "When the wicked, even mine enemies and my foes, came upon me to eat up my flesh, they stumbled and fell.")

At dinner time twelve more came — six or seven to the door asking for flour and meal. Mother told them she was a defenseless widow with an only daughter on the eve of becoming a mother, a young friend, and five little children dependent on her for food and protection. They laughed and said: "Oh, we have heard just such tales before!" They wanted to know why the house was kept locked; said it would make it worse for us. (This had proven false, for when the doors were open it was impossible to keep them out.) Kate observed a large cravat upon the neck of one made of a black silk dress of hers which had been taken by one of them a few days before. Every species of men's clothing in our trunks and bureaus and portmanteaus was taken, but none of our personal apparel, for we generally stood by when they were searching our wardrobes. They took every piece of jewelry they could find. Twelve sheep were found shot and left in the pasture — an act of wanton wickedness.

Late in the afternoon more came and carried off the few remaining ducks. Going to the Negro houses, they called Cato, the driver, and told him they knew he was feeding "that damned old heifer in the house," and they would "blow out his damned brains" if he gave her another morsel to eat, for they meant to starve her to death. Pointing to the chapel, they asked what house that was. Cato answered: "A church which my master had built for the colored people on the place to hold prayers in the week and preach in on Sunday." They said: "Yes, there he told all his damned lies and called it preaching." And with dreadful oaths they cursed him. To Patience, when they were taking good and valuable books from his library (as they said, to send to their old fathers at home), they said, when she spoke with honor of her master and his labors for the good of the colored people: "He was a damned infernal villain, and we only wish he was now alive; we would blow his brains out." To Sue they said, when she spoke of his goodness to the people: "We wish he was now here; we would cut his throat." They stole two blankets from July, and attempted to steal his hat. They took a piggin of boiled potatoes from Sue, and threw the piggin in the marsh when they had eaten them.

After all the day's trials, late at night came Kate's servant Prophet bringing her some clothing and chickens. We were rejoiced to see anyone. He reported South Hampton had been visited by a hundred and fifty men, who had taken all the corn given to the Negroes (three months' allowance), killed forty or fifty hogs and taken seven beef cattle, stolen all the syrup and sugar from the Negroes, and taken their clothing, crawling under their houses and beds searching for buried articles.

MRS. MARY JONES IN HER JOURNAL

Montevideo, Thursday, December 22nd, 1864. Several squads of Yankees came today, but none insisted upon coming into the house. Most of the remaining geese were killed by them. One attempted forcibly to drag Sue by the collar of her dress into her room. Another soldier coming up told him to "let that old woman alone"; and while they were speaking together she made her escape to the dwelling, dreadfully frightened and thoroughly enraged. The horrible creature then went to old Mom Rosetta; and she told him he had "no manners," and after a while got him away. Sue's running into the house sent a thrill of terror into Kate and myself, for we were momentarily expecting them to enter the house. My heart palpitates with such violence against my side that with pain I bear the pressure of my dress.

If it was not for the supporting hand of God, we must give up and die. His precious Word and prayer sustains our fainting souls. Besides our morning and evening devotions Kate, Daughter, and I observe a special season every afternoon to implore protection for our beloved ones and ourselves and deliverance for our suffering country. I have often said to the enemy: "I pray not for revenge upon you, but I pray daily for deliverance from you"; and always felt amid my deepest distresses: "Oh, if my country was but free and independent, I could take joyfully the spoiling of my goods!"

MRS. MARY S. MALLARD IN HER JOURNAL

Montevideo, Thursday, December 22nd, 1864. About midday the two little boys Mac and Pulaski made their appearance, having escaped from the Yankees at Midway. One of the officers told Pulaski Mr. Mallard was at the Ogeechee bridge, and had been preaching for them and walking at large. They had put no handcuffs on him, and he was walking at large, and they gave him plenty to eat. We are all thankful to hear from him.

Pulaski says he asked for the well chain. They cursed him and said his mistress should do without it.

One squad who came to the house asked Mother when she had seen any rebels, and if there were any around here. She told them her son–in–law had been captured more than a week before, and he was the only gentleman belonging to our household.

Looking fiercely at her, he said: "If you lie to me I will — " The rest of the sentence Mother did not quite understand; it was either "I'll kill you" or "I'll blow your brains out."

She immediately stepped out upon the little porch, near which he was sitting on his horse as he spoke to her, and said to him: "In the beginning of this war one passage of Scripture was impressed upon my mind; and it now abides with me: 'Fear not them which kill the body and after that have no more that they can do. But fear Him, who, after he hath killed, hath power to cast into hell.' I have spoken the truth, and do you remember that you will stand with me at the Judgment Bar of God."

There were quite a number around. One man said: "Madam, if that is your faith, it is a good one."

She replied: "It is my faith, and I feel that it has power to sustain me."

One of these men threatened Cato with a pistol at his breast that if he did feed his mistress they would kill him; called her an old devil, and applied other dreadful epithets such as are used by the lowest and most profane.

Early in the afternoon the same officer called who had previously been in the house. He immediately inquired if the men had done any injury since he was here last. Whilst he conversed with Kate and Mother his men were firing and killing the geese in the lot and loading their horses with them.

Before leaving he asked for a glass of water. Mother handed him a glass, saying: "I regret that I cannot offer a glass of fresh water, for you have taken even the chain from my well bucket."

He replied very quickly: "I did not do it. Neither did my men do it."

Having heard nothing from Mr. Stevens, Mother sent Charles to Captain Winn's (where he was staying) to ask him to come to us, as we were all in much distress. Charles returned saying Mr. Stevens would come, but was waiting for Uncle William, who had left Springfield the day before and walked to Dorchester; and they expected him the next day at Captain Winn's.

Friday, December 23rd. A day of perfect freedom from the enemy at our dwelling. Five or six rode through the pasture, but none came to the house or Negro houses.

MRS. MARY JONES IN HER JOURNAL

Montevideo, Saturday, December 24th, 1864. As we were finishing our breakfast, which we always had to take in the most hurried manner with every window tightly closed upstairs in my chamber, five Yankees made their appearance from different approaches to the house. Kate and I went down, as usual, with beating hearts and knees that smote together, yet trusting our God for protection.

One knocked at the door next to the river. I requested him to go around to the front door, and — most amazing — he answered "Yes, ma'am" and went around. When the door was unlocked he said: "We have come to search for arms."

I told him the house had again and again under that plea been thoroughly searched; not the minutest drawer or trunk but had been searched.

He replied: "I would not like to do anything unpleasant to you."

A Dutchman said: "I have come to search your house, mistress, and I mean to do it. If you have two or three thousand dollars I would not touch it; but I am coming into your house to search it from top to bottom."

I told him the officers had said the soldiers must not enter private dwellings.

He replied: "There is no officer; we are independent scouts and do as we please." He looked up at the windows, and went around the front of the house, remarking in the most cruel manner: "This house will make a beautiful fire and a great smoke."

I said: "Surely you would not burn a house that was occupied!"

He replied: "Your soldiers would do it. I came here to fight, and I mean to do it." Then he insisted upon coming in.

I told him of my daughter's situation and entreated him not to come in for she was daily expecting to be confined.

"Tell her to go to her room; we will not disturb her. We have not come to insult ladies."

I said: "If you are determined to search, begin your work at once." For they were pushing into the rooms, and with them an insolent little mulatto, who commenced running around the parlor. I called to the Dutchman and said: "Order that boy out of my house!"

He immediately stamped his foot and said: "Get out of this house and stay by the horses."

They searched from the attic down. One of the party wanted to take a comforter, but the Dutchman said: "Let it alone." Another of them emptied out all my spools for weaving and took the bag.

They insisted two rebels had been here the night before, for a man had

an instant's warning. My poor delicate, suffering, heart–weary child I have forced to lie down, and persuaded Kate to do so also.

Kept watch alone until two o'clock, and then called Kate, who took my place, and I threw myself on the bed for an hour.

May God keep us safe this night! To Him alone do we look for protection from our cruel enemies.

MRS. MARY S. MALLARD IN HER JOURNAL

Montevideo, Sunday, December 25th, 1864. With great gratitude we hailed the light this morning, having passed the night. And no enemy has come nigh our persons or our dwelling; although there are appearances of horse tracks, which we have observed before, and believe they are often around at night to try and detect any gentlemen ("rebel," as they call them) coming here.

We were much alarmed towards morning by Sue's calling to have the house opened; Prophet had come to bring Kate some beef and meal.

At breakfast two Yankees rode around the lot, but seeing nothing to take went away; and we were not further interrupted.

George and June came back, saying the ox–wagon had been cut to pieces and the oxen killed. They were carried to the Ogeechee, where George saw Mr. Mallard and says he preached to the Yankees.

Monday, December 26th. Saw no one all day. Towards evening we ventured out with the poor little children, and as we were returning saw one at a distance.

Tuesday, December 27th. No enemy today. Bless the Lord for this mercy!

Wednesday, December 28th. Another day without the appearance of the Yankees. Could we but know we should be spared one day we would breathe freely, but we are in constant apprehension and terror. Everyone that comes has some plea for insult or robbery. Was there ever any civilized land given up for such a length of time to lawless pillage and brutal inhumanities?

Thursday, December 29th. Free from intrusion until afternoon, when three Yankees and one Negro came up. Lucy ran into the house and locked the door after her, which seemed to provoke them. Three came to the door, and after knocking violently several times one broke open the door. Mother and Kate went down as soon as they could, and when he saw them he cursed awfully. They insisted upon coming in, and asked for that "damned wench" that had locked the door, threatening to "shoot her damned brains out," using the Savior's name in awful blasphemy.

Nothing seemed to keep them from going over the house but Mother's telling them the officers had advised the locking the doors, and the men had no right to enter the house, under General Sherman's orders. She told them the situation of her family and her daughter. One went into the parlor and pantry and one into one or two other rooms; and one went into the room we are compelled to cook in, and crouched like a beast over the fire. He was black and filthy as a chimney sweep. Indeed, such is the horrible odor they leave in the house we can scarcely endure it.

The cook, seeing the party, locked herself into the cooking room; but they thundered at the door in such a manner I had to call to her to open it, which when she did I could scarce keep from smiling at the metamorphosis. From being a young girl she had assumed the attitude and appearance of a sick old woman, with a blanket thrown over her head and shoulders, and scarcely able to move. Their devices are various and amusing. Gilbert keeps a sling under his coat and slips his arm into it as soon as they appear; Charles walked with a stick and limps dreadfully; Niger a few days since kept them from stealing everything they wanted in his house by covering up in bed and saying he had "yellow fever"; Mary Ann kept them from taking the wardrobe of her deceased daughter by calling out "Them dead people clothes!"

Friday, Saturday, Sabbath, and Monday. No enemy came to the dwelling. They sometimes are at the cornhouse and do not come over. We view them from our upper windows taking provisions and see them killing the sheep and hogs and cattle. We regard it as a great mercy when we are delivered from their presence within the house.

Mrs. Mary Jones in her Journal

Montevideo, Tuesday, January 3rd, 1865. Soon after breakfast three Yankees rode up and wanted to search for rebels and arms. They dismounted and sat upon the front porch. With much entreaty, and reminding them of the orders of their commander and the feeble condition of my daughter, they refrained from coming in.

One said to Kate and myself: "I guess you are too great rebels to go North, but if you will take good advice you will do so," and offered to get us a pass to Savannah if we would go.

I replied: "We prefer to remain in our own home and country."

Four others rode up and proceeded to search the outhouses. In the loft to the washroom they found some ear corn that we had concealed there to sustain our lives. They immediately commenced knocking off the shingles, and soon broke a large hole in the roof, those within hallooing and screaming and cursing to those without to come and see what they had found.

The one who had been speaking to us assured us they would do us personally no harm. I asked him to prevent their breaking down the house.

He called out: "Stop, boys!"

They replied: "We have found a lot of corn!"

"Well, you must let it alone." (I had told him we put it there to keep ourselves and the servants from starving.)

After this they ceased knocking off the shingles.

Seeing there was some trace of humanity in him, I related Mr. Mallard's capture, and that he was a minister of gospel.

He asked: "What denomination?"

I replied: "Presbyterian," and asked if they had any professors of religion in their army.

He said: "Yes — many when they left their homes; but I do not know where you will find them now."

He was a Methodist, but had many friends who were Presbyterians; his parents Baptist. I asked him to stay and protect us while this lawless squad remained; but he said they must go, and rode off, while the others proceeded to gather all they wanted from the people's houses, making the Negroes fill the bags and take them out.

Sue in her kindness had hid away a few potatoes for the little children. She entreated for them, but they took every one, and tore a breadth from her new woolen dress which she was making and had sewing in her hands to make strings to tie up their bags of plunder. They have stolen even the drawers and petticoats of the women for that purpose; and sometimes they have taken their nether garments and put them on, leaving in their stead their filthy crawling shirts.

Having one ham, I have given it to Sue to keep for me. They found it; and being an old one they chopped it up and flung it to the dogs, Sue exclaiming: "Massa! Yo do poor Niggers so?" This was the only morsel of meat we had left.

They stayed a long while and finally rode off.

Wednesday, January 4th. At daylight my daughter informed me she was sick. She has been in daily expectation of her confinement for two weeks. I went immediately for the servants and ordered my little riding pony, Lady Franklin, which the Yankees had taken and dragged several miles by the neck (because she would not lead) and finally let go, when she returned. And we have tried to keep her out of sight for this very purpose, saddled with my sidesaddle. Prepared a yellow flag for Charles (in case he met the Yankees) and wrote to Dr. Raymond Harris, three miles off and the only physician I know of in the county: "I entreat you to come to the help of my suffering child." Charles started before sunrise, going through the woods.

My heart was filled with intense anxiety and distress, especially as my child had an impression something was wrong with her unborn infant — the consequence of injuries received from a severe fall from a wagon, breaking her collarbone and bruising her severely, as they were making their retreat from Atlanta on the approach of General Sherman.

Dr. Harris, with a kindness and courage never to be forgotten, came without delay and in the face of danger; for the enemy was everywhere over the county. He looked very feeble, having been recently ill with pneumonia. Soon after being in her room he requested a private interview, informing me that my child was in a most critical condition, and I must be prepared for the worst. For if he did not succeed in relieving the difficulty, her infant at least must die.

I replied: "Doctor, the mother first."

"Certainly," was his answer.

He returned to her room and with great difficulty and skill succeeded in effecting what he desired. God, our compassionate Savior, heard the voice of faith and prayer; and she was saved in childbearing, and at eleven o'clock gave birth to a well–formed infant — a daughter.

During these hours of agony the yard was filled with Yankees. It is supposed one hundred visited the place during the day. They were all around the house; my poor child, calm and collected amid her agony of body, could hear their conversation and wild halloos and cursing beneath her windows. Our dear friend Kate King had to meet them alone. She entreated that they would not come in or make a noise, for there was sickness in the house.

She stepped upon the porch and implored if there was one spark of humanity or honor about them that they would not come in, saying: "You compel me to speak plainly. There is a child being born this very instant in this house, and if there is an officer or a gentleman amongst you I entreat you to protect the house from intrusion."

After a while they left, screaming and yelling in the most fiendish way as they rode from the house.

Dr. Harris returned with Charles as a guide and reached his home safely, having met only one of the enemy.

In the afternoon a very large party rode up; said they wanted to know the meaning of the yellow flag which was placed over the front porch. Had we sick soldiers, or was this a hospital? I told them it indicated sickness in my family: my daughter was ill. One asked for matches; I had none to give. And taking Carpenter Pulaski, they rode to the neighboring plantations. They searched all the Negro houses, within and without and under, taking whatever they wanted. They have taken Gilbert's knife and watch and chain, July's pants and blankets, George and Porter's blankets and clothes, the women's pails, piggins, spoons, buckets, pots, kettles, etc., etc.

Thursday, January 5th. Three Yankees rode up in the forenoon and asked for me. I met them at the front porch. They wished to know if there were sick soldiers in the house.

"No, my daughter is sick."

They propounded the usual questions. I told them of the capture of my daughter's husband, and as they were Kilpatrick's men, asked if they would take a letter to him. They said they would, and I wrote telling him of the birth of the baby; and Daughter sent him her Greek Testament, Kate sent a letter North, and Mrs. King one to Clarence.

This man told me he was from Indiana; was a Virginian by birth. Said there was great dissatisfaction in the army on account of the present object of the war, which now was to free the Negroes.

Looking at me, he said: "Have you sons in the army?"

I replied: "Could you suppose I would have sons who would not defend their country and their mother?"

He said: "If your sons are now in the house I would not take them."

Understanding his trickery, I bowed and said: "I am happy to say you will not have the opportunity. If my sons are alive, they are far away and I hope at the post of duty."

We gave him the letters, which he put in one pocket, and the Greek Testament in the other, and rode off; but lingered a great while on the plantation, making the Negroes shell and grind corn for them, shooting down the sheep in the fields, some of which they skinned and carried away.

This man said his name was James Y. Clark, and was the only one of all we saw whose name we heard. A mere youth with him said he had a brother who had been a prisoner in Georgia, and when sick had been taken into a family and nursed; and whenever he met a Georgian he would treat him as well as his own men. They spoke more kindly than any we have conversed with.

Before going to bed about twelve o'clock — Driver John came to say a letter sent to my brother in Southwest Georgia and letters sent by Kate to Mrs. King and a letter to my sister Mrs. Cumming had all been found on the person of Lewis, a most faithful man, who had come late the previous night to receive them. Flora had ripped up his sleeve and sewed them in. On account of his fidelity some of his own color informed the Yankees that he carried letters for rebels. They put him in custody, and while in their hands he managed to send the old man John to us to say they had taken our letters, and he wanted us to know it and be prepared for them if they came to trouble us. My letter contained only a truthful account of our present condition. These very men that spoke so fair to us this morning had our letters then in their possession and read them aloud at the Negro houses. Where will all this perfidy, insult, and injury to the helpless, the fatherless, and the widow end?

As night closes in upon us I place my darling little Ruthie in bed. Kate sees her little ones at rest; and Daughter with the baby is sleeping, and so are little Mary and Charlie. I often walk alone up and down the front piazza to mark the light against the sky of the low lingering flame of the last burnt dwelling or outhouse. I can locate them all around on the neighboring plantations. I look with fear and trembling in the direction of our venerable old church at Midway. We hear the Baptist church in Sunbury has been consumed — burnt as a signal fire to indicate by the troops on this side the safe arrival of this portion of the army to that on the opposite shore in Bryan County.

Bless the Lord for the great mercy of nights free from the presence of the enemy! We would certainly go deranged or die if they were here day and night.

Friday, January 6th. No enemy appeared here today, but we have firing around on different places.

The people are all idle on the plantations, most of them seeking their own pleasure. Many servants have proven faithful, others false and rebellious against all authority or restraint. Susan, a Virginia Negro and nurse to my little Mary Ruth, went off with Mac, her husband, to Arcadia the night after the first day the Yankees appeared, with whom she took every opportunity of conversing, informing them that the baby's father was Colonel Jones. She has acted a faithless part as soon as she could. Porter left three weeks since, and has never returned to give any report of Patience or himself or anyone at Arcadia. Little Andrew went to Flemington and returned. I sent him back to wait on our dear sister and family and to be with his own. I hope he will prove faithful. Gilbert, Flora, Lucy, Tenah, Sue Rosetta, Fanny, Little Gilbert, Charles, Milton and Elsie and Kate have been faithful to us. Milton has been a model of fidelity. He will not even converse with the Yankees, and in their face drives up and milks the cow, without the milk of which little Julia would fare badly, for she is just weaned. His brother Little Pulaski, refused even to bring a pail of water, and took himself off a week since.

Saturday, January 7th. Forenoon. No enemy thus far. God be praised for His goodness and mercy! Our nights have been free from intrusion.

A keen northwester is sweeping over the lawn and whistling among the trees, from the branches of which the long gray moss is waving. The pall of death is suddenly thrown over our once cheerful and happy home. Not a living creature stirs in garden or yard, on the plain or in the grove. Nature wears a funereal aspect, and the blast, as it sweeps through the branches, is sighing a requiem to departed days.

As I stand and look at the desolating changes wrought by the hand of an inhuman foe in a few days, I can enter into the feelings of Job when he exclaimed: "Naked came I out of my mother's womb, and naked shall I return thither; the Lord gave, and the Lord hath taken away; blessed be the name of the Lord." All our pleasant things are laid low. Lover and friend is put far from us, and our acquaintance into darkness. We are prisoners in our own home; we dare not open windows or doors. Sometimes our little children are allowed under a strict watch and guard to run a little in the sunshine, but it is always under constant apprehension. The poor little creatures at a moment's warning — just let them hear "Yankee coming!" — rush in and remain almost breathless, huddled together in one of the upper rooms like a bevy of frightened partridges. To obtain a mouthful of food we have been obliged to cook in what was formerly our drawing room; and I have to rise every morning by candlelight, before the dawn of day, that we may have it before the enemy arrives to take it from us. And then sometimes we and the dear little ones have not a chance to eat again before dark. The poor servants are harassed to death, going rapidly for wood or water and hurrying in to lock the doors, fearing insults and abuse at every turn. Do the annals of civilized — and I may add savage — warfare afford any record of brutality equaled in extent and duration to that which we have suffered, and which has been inflicted on us by the Yankees? For one month our homes and all we possess on earth have been given up to lawless pillage. Officers and men have alike engaged in this work of degradation. I scarcely know how we have stood up under it. God alone has enabled us to "speak with the enemy in the gates," and calmly, without a tear, to see my house broken open, entered with false keys, threatened to be burned to ashes, refused food and ordered to be starved to death, told that I had no right even to wood or water, that I should be "humbled in the very dust I walked upon," a pistol and carbine presented to my breast, cursed and reviled as a rebel, a hypocrite, a devil. Every servant, on pain of having their brains blown out, is forbidden to wait upon us or furnish us food. Every trunk, bureau, box, room, closet has been opened or broken open and searched, and whatever was wanted of provisions, clothing, jewelry, knives, forks, spoons, cups, kettles, cooking utensils, towels, bags, etc., etc. from this house taken, and the whole house turned topsy–turvy.

In all my intercourse with the enemy I have avoided conversation or any aggravating remarks, even when I felt a sword pierced through my soul. For instance, when they reviled the memory of my beloved and honored husband, or taunted me with the want of courage on the part of my countrymen (charges which I knew to be as base and false as the lips that uttered them), they always addressed me as an uncompromising rebel, and I never failed to let them know that before High Heaven I believed our cause was just and right. The isolated and utterly defenseless condition of my poor family compelled me often to use entreaties; but after the day was over I frequently inquired of Kate and Daughter: "Tell me, girls, did I act like a coward?"

PART V
Last Things
1 8 6 5

April 28. *We have no mail communication, and can hear nothing from General Johnston. We go on as usual, but are almost despairing. Dear M., in her sadness, has put some Confederate money and postage stamps into a Confederate envelope, sealed it up, and endorsed it, "In memory of our beloved Confederacy." I feel like doing the same, and treasuring up the buttons, and the stars, and the dear gray coats, faded and worn as they are, with the soiled and tattered banner, which has no dishonouring blot, the untarnished sword, and other arms, though defeated, still crowned with glory. But not yet — I cannot feel that all is over yet.*

May 4. *General Johnston surrendered on the 26th of April. "My native land good–night."*

— Judith McGuire, 1865

Lucifer in Starlight

EMMA LECONTE

COLUMBIA, SOUTH CAROLINA, FEBRUARY 1865

When they reached Savannah, Sherman's troops turned north and entered South Carolina which, with some justice, the Federals regarded as the birthplace of secession. Sherman had further reason to dislike Columbia: it was the home of General Wade Hampton, Phoebe Pember's "Montrose of the South." Emma's house escaped the conflagration because it was on the college campus where the library was being used as a Federal hospital.

February 18. Saturday Afternoon. At about seven o'clock I was standing on the back piazza in the third story. Before me the whole southern horizon was lit up by camp fires which dotted the woods. On one side the sky was illuminated by the burning of Gen. Hampton's residence a few miles off in the country, on the other side by some blazing buildings near the river. I had scarcely gone downstairs again when Henry told me there was a fire on Main Street. Sumter Street was brightly lighted by a burning house so near our piazza that we could feel the heat. By the red glare we could watch the wretches walking — generally staggering — back and forth from the camp to the town — shouting — hurrahing — cursing South Carolina — swearing — blaspheming — singing ribald songs and using such obscene language that we were forced to go indoors.

The fire on Main Street was now raging, and we anxiously watched its progress from the upper front windows. In a little while, however, the flames broke forth in every direction. The drunken devils roamed about, setting fire to every house the flames seemed likely to spare. They were fully equipped for the noble work they had in hand. Each soldier was furnished with combustibles compactly put up. They would enter houses and in the presence of helpless women and children, pour turpentine on the beds and set them on fire. Guards were rarely of any assistance — most generally they assisted in the pillaging and firing.

The wretched people rushing from their burning homes were not allowed to keep even the few necessaries they gathered up in their flight — even blankets and food were taken from them and destroyed. The firemen attempted to use their engines, but the hose was cut to pieces and their lives threatened. The wind blew a fearful gale, wafting the flames from house to house with frightful rapidity. By midnight the whole town (except the outskirts) was wrapped in one huge blaze. Still the flames had not approached sufficiently near us to threaten our immediate safety, and for some reason not a single Yankee soldier had entered our house. And now the fire instead of approaching us seemed to recede. Henry said the danger was over and, sick of the dreadful scene, worn out with fatigue and excitement, we went downstairs to our room and tried to rest. I fell into a heavy kind of stupor from which I was presently roused by the bustle about me. Our neighbor, Mrs. Caldwell, and her two sisters stood before the fire wrapped in blankets and weeping. Their home was on fire, and the great sea of flame had again swept down our way to the very Campus walls.

I felt a kind of sickening despair and did not even stir to go and look out. After awhile Jane came in to say that Aunt Josie's house was in flames — then we all went to the front door. My God! What a scene! It was about four o'clock and the State House was one grand conflagration. Imagine night turned into noonday, only with a blazing, scorching glare that was horrible — a copper colored sky across which swept columns of black, rolling smoke glittered with sparks and flying embers, while all around us were falling thickly showers of burning flakes. Everywhere the palpitating blaze walling the streets with solid masses of flames as far as the eye could reach, filling the air with its horrible roar. On every side the crackling and devouring fire, while every instant came the crashing of timbers and the thunder of falling buildings.

A quivering molten ocean seemed to fill the air and sky. The library building opposite us seemed framed by the gushing flames and smoke, while through the windows gleamed the liquid fire. This, we thought, must be Aunt Josie's house. It was the next one, for although hers caught frequently, it was saved. The College buildings caught all along that side, and had the incendiary work continued one half hour longer than it did, they must have gone. All the physicians and nurses were on the roof trying to save the buildings, and the poor wounded inmates, left to themselves, such as could crawled out while those who could not move waited to be burned to death.

The Common opposite the gate was crowded with homeless women and children, a few wrapped in blankets and many shivering in the night air. Such a scene as this with the drunken, fiendish soldiery in their dark uniforms, infuriated, cursing, screaming, exulting in their work, came nearer realizing the material ideal of hell than anything I ever expect to see again. They call themselves 'Sherman's Hellhounds.'

Mother collected together some bedding, clothing and food which Henry carried to the back of the garden and covered them with a hastily ripped–up carpet to protect them from the sparks and flakes of fire. He worked so hard, so faithfully, and tried to comfort Mother as best he could while she was sobbing and crying at the thought of being left shelterless with a delicate baby. While this was going on, I stood with Mary Ann at the kitchen door. She tried to speak hopefully — I could not cry — it was too horrible. Yet I felt the house must burn. By what miracle it was saved I cannot think. No effort could be made — no one was on the roof, which was old and dry, and all the while the sparks and burning timbers were flying over it like rain. When the few things she tried to save were moved, Mother took up little Carrie, who was sleeping unconsciously, and wrapping ourselves in shawls and blankets, we went to the front door and waited for the house to catch.

There we stood watching and listening to the roaring and crashing. It seemed inevitable — they said they would not leave a house, and what would become of us! I suppose we owe our final escape to the presence of the Yankee wounded in the hospital. When all seemed in vain, Dr. Thomson went to an officer and asked if he would see his own soldiers burnt alive. He said he would save the hospital, and he and his men came to Dr. T's assistance. Then, too, about this time, even the Yankees seemed to have grown weary of their horrible work — the signal for the cessation of the fire — a blast on the bugle — was given, and in fifteen minutes the flames ceased to spread. By seven o'clock the last flame had expired.

About six o'clock a crowd of drunken soldiers assaulted the campus gate and threatened to overpower the guard, swearing the buildings should not be spared. By great exertions Dr. Thomson found Sherman, and secured a strong guard in time to rescue the hospital. Mrs. C., who had been to see after her house, now returned, and sitting down, sobbed convulsively as she told us of the insults she had received from the soldiery engaged in pillaging her home. An officer riding by ordered the men to stop. So broken down and humbled by the terrible experience of the night was she that she cried out, 'Oh, sir, please make them stop! You don't know what I suffered this night.' 'I don't give a damn for your suffering,' he replied, 'but my men have no right to pillage against orders.'

The sun arose at last, dim and red through the thick, murky atmosphere. It set last night on a beautiful town full of women and children — it shone dully down this morning on smoking ruins and abject misery.

During the forenoon Aunt Josie and Aunt Jane came over to see how we had fared. We met as after a long separation, and for some seconds no one could speak. Then we exchanged experiences. They were nearer the flames than we, but they had Dr. Carter with them — someone to look to and to help them. Aunt Josie says the northern side of their house became so heated that no one could remain on that side of the house, and it caught fire three times. Being outside the hospital buildings they were more exposed than we.

Once a number of Yankees rushed in, saying the roof was on fire. Andrew, the negro boy, followed them up, saw them tear up the tin roofing and place lighted combustibles, and after they went down he succeeded in extinguishing the flames. A tolerably faithful guard was some protection to them. The view from their attic windows commands the whole town, and Aunt Josie said it was like one surging ocean of flame. She thought with us that it was more like the medieval pictures of hell than anything she had ever imagined. We do not know the extent of the destruction, but we are told that the greater portion of the town is in ashes — perhaps the loveliest town in all our southern country. This is civilized warfare. This is the way in which the 'cultured' Yankee nation wars upon women and children! Failing with our men in the field, *this* is the way they must conquer! I suppose there was scarcely an able bodied man, except the hospital physicians, in the whole twenty thousand people. It is so easy to burn the homes over the heads of helpless women and children, and turn them with insults and sneers into the streets. One expects these people to lie and steal, but it does seem such an outrage even upon degraded humanity that those who practise such wanton and useless cruelty should call themselves men. It seems to us even a contamination to look at these devils. Think of the degradation of being conquered and ruled by such a people! It seems to me now as if we would choose extermination. I have only had to speak once to one of the blue–coated fiends. I went to the front door to bid Francena and Nellie C. goodbye early this morning, when a soldier came up the steps and asked me who was the Mayor. 'Dr. Goodwyn,' I answered and turned away. 'Do you know his initials?' 'No,' and I shut the door quickly behind me.

The State House, of course, is burned, and they talk of blowing up the new uncompleted granite one, but I do not know if it can be done in its unfinished unroofed condition. We dread tonight. Mother asked Dr. Thomson (who has been very kind about coming in and keeping us posted) for a guard, but he says it is unnecessary as double guards will be placed throughout the city. Dr. T. says some of the officers feel very much ashamed of last night's work. Their compunctions must have visited them since daylight. The men openly acknowledged that they received orders to burn and plunder before they crossed the river. The drunken scoundrels who tried to force their way into the Campus this morning have been under guard at the gate — several hundred of them — fighting and quarrelling among themselves for sever[al] hours. Poor Father! What will be his state of mind when he hears of all this? The first reports that reach him will be even exaggerated. It is some comfort to us in our uncertainty and anxiety to hope that he may be safe. The explosion last night was [the] accidental blowing up of the Charleston freight depot. There had been powder stored there and it was scattered thickly over the floor. The poor people and negroes went in with torches to search for provisions.

When will these Yankees go that we may breathe freely again! The past three days are more like three weeks. And yet when they are gone we may be worse off with the whole country laid waste and the railroads cut in every direction. Starvation seems to stare us in the face. Our two families have between them a few bushels of corn and a little musty flour. We have no meat, but the negroes give us a little bacon every day.

8 p.m. There has been no firing as yet. All is comparatively quiet. These buildings are surrounded by a heavy guard, and we are told they are distributed throughout the city. All day the devils have been completing their work of plunder, but in the hospital here we have been exempt from this. When I remember how blest we have been, I cannot be too thankful. We have the promise of a quiet night but I dare not trust our hopes — there is no telling what diabolical intentions they may have. Oh, if they were only gone — even to the last straggler! What a load would be lifted from our hearts. We are anxious to learn the fate of our friends, but the little we can gather (except from Aunt Josie and Mrs. Green) is through the negroes, and ours scarcely dare venture uptown. The Yankees plunder the negroes as well as the whites, and I think they are becoming somewhat disgusted with their *friends*. Although the servants seem quite willing, it is difficult to get any work out of them on account of the wild excitement.

Ah, the dreadful excitement — I seem to stand it very well, but it seems to me we must all be ill when it is over. Anxiety, distress, want of rest and food must tell upon us. Mrs. Wilson (Mr. Shand's daughter) with a babe one week old was moved last night from her father's burning house. The Burroughs escaped with only the clothing they wore. Many, many fared similarly. Some tried to save a little food — even this was torn from their hands. I have heard a number of distressing incidents but have not time to write them down. Oh, the sorrow and misery of this unhappy town!

From what I can hear, their chief aim, while taunting helpless women, has been to 'humble their pride' — 'Southern pride.' 'Where now,' they would say, 'is all your pride — see what we have brought you to! This is what you get for setting yourselves up as better than other folks.' The women acted with quiet dignity and refused to lower themselves by any retort. Someone told me the following: Some soldiers were pillaging the house of a lady. One asked her if they had not humbled her pride *now*. 'No, indeed,' she said, 'nor can you ever.' 'You *fear* us anyway.' 'No,' she said. 'By G——, but you *shall* fear me,' and he cocked his pistol and put it to her head. 'Are you afraid now?' She folded her arms and, looking him steadily in the eye, said contemptuously, 'No.' He dropped his pistol, and with an exclamation of admiration, left her.

February 21st. Tuesday. The destruction and desolation around us which we could not feel while under such excitement and fear now exerts its full sway. Sad? The very air is fraught with sadness and silence. The few noises that break the stillness seem melancholy and the sun does not seem to shine as brightly, seeming to be dimmed by the sight of so much misery. I was at Aunt Josie's this morning and there learned for the first time the extent of suffering. Oh, God! When we think of what we have escaped and how almost miraculously we have been saved we should never rise from our knees. There is not a house, I believe, in Columbia that has not been pillaged — those that the flames spared were entered by brutal soldiery and everything wantonly destroyed. The streets were filled with terrified women and children who were offered every insult and indignity short of personal outrage — they were allowed to save nothing but what clothes they wore, and there is now great suffering for food. It would be impossible to describe or even conceive the pandemonium and horror. There is no shadow of doubt that the town was burned by Sherman's order. All through Georgia, it is said, he promised his men full license in South Carolina. The signals both for firing and ceasing were given — the soldiers were provided with the materials for the work — and yet I hear that he already denies it and tries to put the responsibility on Gen. Hampton. At one time Friday night, when Aunt Josie's house and other buildings were taking fire, the College buildings were given up and the poor wounded soldiers who could not be moved resigned themselves to death.

February 22nd. Wednesday. I meant last night to write down some description of what I had seen, but was too wretchedly depressed and miserable to even think of it. This morning we have heard that he [Father] is safe and I can take up my journal again. Yesterday afternoon we walked all over the town in company with Miss Ellen LaBorde. The entire heart of the city is in ashes — only the outer edges remain. On the whole length of Sumter Street not one house beyond the first block after the Campus is standing, except the brick house of Mr. Mordecai. Standing in the center of the town, as far as the eye can reach, nothing is to be seen but heaps of rubbish, tall dreary chimneys and shattered brick walls, while 'in the hollow windows, dreary horror's sitting.'

Blanding Street, crossing Main and Sumter at right angles, the finest street in town, is also a sad picture. The Preston house, with its whole square of beautiful gardens, escaped. It was Gen. Logan's headquarters. The Crawford house, the Bryce's, the Howe's and one or two others also escaped. All nearer Main Street were burned. The Clarkson house is a heap of brick with most of its tall columns standing, blackened by the smoke. Bedell's lovely little house is in ruins while, as if in mockery, the shrubbery is not even scorched. But I cannot particularize — with *very* few exceptions all our friends are homeless. We enter Main Street — since the war in crowd and bustle it has rivalled a city thoroughfare — what desolation! Everything has vanished as by enchantment — stores, merchants, customers, all the eager faces gone — only three or four dismal–looking people to be seen picking their way over heaps of rubbish, brick and timbers. The wind moans among the bleak chimneys and whistles through the gaping windows of some hotel or warehouse. The market [is] a ruined shell supported by crumbling arches, its spire fallen in and with it the old town clock whose familiar stroke we miss so much.

The South lies prostrate — their foot is on us — there is no help. During this short time we breathe, but — oh, who could have believed who has watched this four years' struggle that it could have ended like this! They say *right* always triumphs, but what cause could have been more just than ours? Have we suffered all — have our brave men fought so desperately and died so nobly for *this*? For four years there has been throughout this broad land little else than the anguish of anxiety — the misery of sorrow over dear ones sacrificed — for *nothing*! Is all this blood spilled in vain — will it not cry from the ground on the day we yield to these Yankees! *We* give up to the *Yankees*! How *can* it be? How can they talk about it? Why does not the President call out the women if there are not enough men? We would go and *fight*, too — we would better all die together. Let us suffer still more, give up yet more — anything, anything that will help the cause, anything that will give us freedom and not force us to live with such people — to be ruled by such horrible and contemptible creatures — to submit to them when we hate them so bitterly.

I used to dream about peace, to pray for it, but this is worse than war. What is such peace to us? What horrible fate has been pursuing us the last six months? Not much farther back than that we had every reason to hope for success. What is the cause of this sudden crushing collapse? I *cannot* understand it. I never loved my country as I do now. I feel I could sacrifice *everything* to it, and when I think of the future — oh God! It is too horrible. What I most fear is a conciliatory policy from the North, that they will offer to let us come back as before. Oh, no, no! I would rather we were held as a conquered province, rather sullenly submit and bide our time. Let them oppress and tyrannize, but let us take no favors of them. Let them send us away out of the country — anywhere away from them and their hateful presence.

Hetty Cary's Wedding

CONSTANCE CARY HARRISON

RICHMOND, VIRGINIA, JANUARY TO APRIL 1865

Constance Cary Harrison's cousin, Hetty Cary, was generally acknowledged to be the most beautiful woman in the Confederacy, an opinion shared by Mary Chesnut.

The engagement of my cousin Hetty Cary to Brigadier–General John Pegram having been announced, their decision to be married on January 19, 1865 was a subject of active interest. My aunt, Mrs. Wilson Miles Cary, of Baltimore, had before Christmas obtained from Mr. Lincoln, through General Barnard (chief of the United States Engineer Corps, married to her adopted daughter), a pass to go to Richmond to visit her children. The presence of Mrs. Cary gave General Pegram opportunity to urge that his marriage should not be longer delayed, and such preparations as were possible were hurried on. My aunt was stopping at the house of her niece, Mrs. Peyton, whence the ceremony took place. On the evening of January 19 all our little world flocked to St. Paul's Church to see the nuptials of one called by many the most beautiful woman in the South, with a son of Richmond universally honored and beloved. Two days before, I being confined to my room with a cold, Hetty had come, bringing her bridal veil that I, with our mothers, might be the first to see it tried on her lovely crown of auburn hair. As she turned from the mirror to salute us with a charming blush and smile, the mirror fell and was broken to small fragments, an accident afterward spoken of by the superstitious as one of a strange series of ominous happenings.

While a congregation that crowded floor and galleries of the church waited an unusually long time for the arrival of bride and groom, my aunt and the other members of our family being already in their seats, I stood in the vestibule outside with Burton Harrison and Colonel L.Q.C. Lamar, speculating rather uneasily upon the cause of the delay. Mr. Harrison told us that Mrs. Davis (who tenderly loved and admired the bride) had begged to be allowed to send the President's carriage to drive her to the church, and he was sure it had been in prompt attendance at Colonel Peyton's door. Directly after, a shabby old Richmond hack drove up, halting before the church, and from it issued the bride and groom, looking a little perturbed, explaining that at the moment of setting out the President's horses had reared violently, refusing to go forward, and could not be controlled, so that they had been forced to get out of the carriage and send for another vehicle, at that date almost impossible to secure in Richmond.

When the noble–looking young couple crossed the threshold of the church, my cousin dropped her lace handkerchief and, nobody perceiving it, stooped forward to pick it up, tearing the tulle veil over her face to almost its full length, then, regaining herself, walked with a slow and stately step toward the altar. As she passed there was a murmur of delight at her beauty, never more striking. Her complexion of pearly white, the vivid roses on her cheeks and lips, the sheen of her radiant hair, and the happy gleam of her beautiful brown eyes seemed to defy all sorrow, change, or fear. John Pegram, handsome and erect, looked as he felt, triumphant, the prize–winner — so the men called him — of the invincible beauty of her day. Miss Cary's brother, Captain Wilson Miles Cary, representing her absent father, gave away the bride. After the ceremony we, her nearest, crowded around the couple, wishing them the best happiness our loving hearts could picture. General Pegram's mother, brothers, and sisters did the same; then, as they passed out, all eyes followed them with real kindness and unalloyed good feeling. There was but a small reception afterward, but one felt in the atmosphere a sense of sincere gladness in happy love, very rare on such occasions.

Three weeks later, to the day, General Pegram's coffin, crossed with a victor's palms beside his soldier's accoutrements, occupied the spot in the chancel where he had stood to be married. Beside it knelt his widow swathed in crape. Again Dr. Minnegerode conducted the ceremony, again the church was full. Behind the hearse, waiting outside, stood his war charger, with boots in stirrups. The wailing of the band that went with us on the slow pilgrimage to Hollywood will never die out of memory. Burton Harrison drove in the carriage with me and my mother, my poor cousin with her mother, brother, and General Custis Lee, her husband's intimate friend, who stood beside her, as, leaning on her brother's arm, she remained during the service close to the grave. General Pegram's family clustered beyond her. Snow lay white on the hill–sides, the bare trees stretched their arms above us, the river kept up its ceaseless rush and tumble, so much a part of daily life in our four years of ordeal that we had grown accustomed to interpret its voice according to our joy or grief.

The newly married couple had gone directly to General Pegram's

head–quarters, near Petersburg, where he was at the head of Early's division. Their new home was in a pleasant farm–house nine miles out of
Petersburg, close to the line of General Pegram's command, near
Hatcher's Run. Here, within constant sound of shot and shell, her taste
and skill busied itself in fitting up rooms that seemed to her soldier the
perfection of beauty and comfort, and in preparing for him little dishes
that transformed their ordinary fare. When she rode beside him during
their short honey–moon, the men thronged to look at her with pride in
their leader's lovely wife. On February 5 a demonstration was made by
the enemy against General Lee's extreme right, in which General
Pegram's forces were engaged. He returned to their lodgings and, before
daylight on the 6th, was aroused by the information that the enemy was
about to renew attack. His wife made coffee and prepared breakfast for
him in the gray of dawn; then, after seeing him ride off, spent the day
with her mother, who had fortunately arrived upon a visit to her son,
Captain Cary. As the short winter's day closed in, a messenger arrived
from General Pegram to say he had come safely through the fight.

The ladies were at this time sitting in an ambulance at some distance
away carding lint. At sunset a new charge was formed against the enemy,
General Pegram leading it, sword in hand, when a minie–ball (claimed to
have been fired by a sharp–shooter a great way off) entered his heart,
killing him instantly, after striking the sword from his hand and filling its
scabbard with his blood. Of his comrades, none was found who would
volunteer to break the news to my cousin.

Captain Gordon McCabe, of Richmond, a close friend of General
Pegram, has thus written to me:

"I can tell you of the tragic time after he was killed, when our guns
pulled past the ambulance where she was carding lint and I heard her
laughing merrily within. I knew he was dead, shot at the head of his division, while she sat there waiting for him to come to her. After his body
had been tenderly placed in the room used as the adjutant–general's
office at head–quarters, word was sent to her that 'she might safely
return to their quarters and go to bed, for it *would be late* before he
could get back.' So she slept peacefully that night, in the room above his
body — a bride of three weeks.

"In the morning an old gentleman, a civilian, volunteered to go up
and call her down to where Pegram lay. Kneeling beside the body, she
put her hand into the breast of his coat, drawing out first his watch, still
ticking, that she had wound for him just before they parted; next a
miniature of herself, both stained with life blood. My aunt and her son

accompanied the widow to Richmond in a freight car, she sitting beside the coffin. No one of us is likely to forget the sad days that followed. She was like a flower broken in the stalk."

On the morning of April 2, a perfect Sunday of the Southern spring, a large congregation assembled as usual at St. Paul's. I happened to sit in the rear of the President's pew, so near that I plainly saw the sort of gray pallor that came upon his face as he read a scrap of paper thrust into his hand by a messenger hurrying up the middle aisle. With stern set lips and his usual quick military tread, he left the church, a number of other people rising in their seats and hastening after him, those who were left swept by a universal tremor of alarm. The rector, accustomed as he was to these frequent scenes in church, came down to the altar rail and tenderly begged his people to remain and finish the service, which was done.

Before dismissing his congregation the rector announced to them that General Ewell had summoned the local forces to meet for defence of the city at three in the afternoon. We knew then that Longstreet's regulars must have been suddenly called away, and a sick apprehension filled all hearts.

On the sidewalk outside the church we plunged at once into the great stir of evacuation, precluding the beginning of a new era. As if by a flash of electricity, Richmond knew that on the morrow her streets would be crowded with her captors, her rulers fled, her government dispersed into thin air, her high hopes crashed to earth. There was little discussion of events. People meeting each other would exchange silent hand grasps and pass on. I saw many pale faces, some trembling lips, but in all that day I heard no expression of a weakling fear. Movement was everywhere, nowhere panic. Begarlanded Franklin Street, sending up perfume from her many gardens, was the general rendezvous of people who wanted to see the last of their friends. All over town citizens were aiding the departure of the male members of their family who could in any way serve the dispossessed government. In the houses we knew, there was everywhere somebody to be helped to go; somebody for whose sake tears were squeezed back, scant food prepared, words of love and cheer spoken. Those good, dear women of Richmond, who had been long tried as by fire, might bend but would not break.

Between two and three in the afternoon formal announcement was made to the public that the government would vacate Richmond that evening. By nightfall all the flitting shadows of a Lost Cause had passed away under a heaven studded by bright stars. The doomed city lay face to face with what it knew not.

Food for the Wounded

PHOEBE YATES PEMBER

RICHMOND, VIRGINIA, APRIL 1865

After the surrender of the city Phoebe Pember remained with her patients until she was no longer needed.

The Federal authorities had as yet posted no guards around, and as our own had been withdrawn, or rather had left, being under no control or direction, not a sound broke the stillness of the sad night. Exhausted with all the exciting events of the day, it was not to be wondered at that I soon fell asleep heavily and dreamlessly, to be awakened in an hour by the crash of an adjoining door, and passing into my pantry from whence the sound proceeded I came upon a group of men, who had burst the entrance opening upon the back premises.

As my eye traveled from face to face, I recognized them as a set of "hospital rats" whom I had never been able to get rid of, for if sent to the field one week, they would be sure to be back the next, on some trifling pretext of sickness or disability. The ringleader was an old enemy, who had stored up many a grievance against me, but my acts of kindness to his sickly wife naturally made me suppose his wrath had been disarmed. He acted on this occasion as spokesman, and the trouble was the old one. Thirty gallons of whiskey had been sent to me the day before the evacuation, and they wanted it.

"We have come for the whiskey!"

"You cannot, and shall not have it."

"It does not belong to you."

"It is in my charge, and I intend to keep it. Go out of my pantry; you are all drunk."

"Boys!" he said, "pick up that barrel and carry it down the hill. I will attend to *her!*"

But the habit of obedience of four years still had its effect on the boys, for all the movement they made was in a retrograde direction.

"Wilson," I said, "you have been in this hospital a long time. Do you think from what you know of me that the whiskey can be taken without my consent?"

He became very insolent.

"Stop that talk; your great friends have all gone, and we won't stand that now. Move out of the way!"

He advanced towards the barrel, and so did I, only being in the inside, I interposed between him and the object of contention. The fierce temper blazed up in his face, and catching me roughly by the shoulder, he called me a name that a decent woman seldom hears and even a wicked one resents.

But I had a little friend, which usually reposed quietly on the shelf, but had been removed to my pocket in the last twenty-four hours, more from a sense of protection than from any idea that it would be called into active service; so before he had time to push me one inch from my position, or to see what kind of an ally was in my hand, that sharp click, a sound so significant and so different from any other, struck upon his ear, and sent him back amidst his friends, pale and shaken.

"You had better leave," I said, composedly (for I felt in my feminine soul that although I was near enough to pinch his nose, that I had missed him), "for if *one* bullet is lost, there are five more ready, and the room is too small for even a woman to miss six times."

There was a conference held at the shattered door, resulting in an agreement to leave, but he shook his fist wrathfully at my small pop-gun.

"You think yourself very brave now, but wait an hour; perhaps others may have pistols too, and you won't have it entirely your way after all."

My first act was to take the head of one of the flour barrels and nail it across the door as tightly as I could, with a two-pound weight for a hammer, and then, warm with triumph and victory gained, I sat down by my whiskey barrel and felt the affection we all bestow on what we have cherished, fought for, and defended successfully; then putting a candle, a box of matches, and a pistol within reach of my hand, I went to sleep, never waking until late in the morning, having heard nothing more of my visitors.

The next day the steward informed me that our stores had been taken possession of by the Federal authorities, so we could not draw the necessary rations. The surgeons had all left; therefore I prepared for a visit to headquarters, by donning my full-dress toilette: boots of untanned leather, tied with thongs; a Georgia woven homespun dress in black and white blocks — the white, cotton yarn, the black, an old silk, washed, scraped with broken glass into pulp, and then carded and spun (it was an elegant thing); white cuffs and collar of bleached homespun, and a hat plaited of the rye straw picked from the field back of us, dyed black with walnut juice, a shoe–string for ribbon to encircle it; and knitted worsted gloves of three shades of green — the darkest bottle shade being around the wrist, while the color tapered to the loveliest blossom of the pea at the finger–tips. The style of the make was Confederate.

Thus splendidly equipped I walked to Dr. M.'s office, now Federal headquarters, and making my way through a crowd of blue coats, accosted the principal figure seated there, with a stern and warlike demand for food, and a curt inquiry whether it was their intention to starve their captured sick. He was very polite, laid the blame on the obstructions in the river, which prevented their transports getting up.

I requested that as such was the case I might be allowed to reclaim my ambulance, now under their lock and key, in order to take some coffee then in my possession to the city and exchange it for animal food. It had been saved from rations formerly drawn, and donations given. He wished to know why it had not been turned over to the U.S. government, but did not press the point as I was not communicative, and gave me the necessary order for the vehicle. Then polite conversation commenced.

"Was I a native of Virginia?"

"No; I was a South Carolinian, who had gone to Virginia at the commencement of the war to try and aid in alleviating the sufferings and privations of the hospitals."

"He had lost a brother in South Carolina."

"It was the fate of war. Self–preservation was the first law of nature. As a soldier he must recognize defense of one's native soil."

"He regretted the present state of scarcity, for he could see in the pale faces and pinched features of the Richmond women, how much they had suffered during the war."

I retorted quickly this wound to both patriotism and vanity.

He meant to be polite, but that he was unlucky was shown by my answer.

"If my features were pinched, and my face pale, it was not caused by privations under the Confederacy, but the anguish consequent upon our failure."

But his kindness had once again put my ambulance under my control, and placing a bag of coffee and a demijohn of whiskey in it, I assumed the reins, having no driver, and went to market. The expedition was successful, as I returned shortly with a live calf, for which I had exchanged them, and which summoned every one within hearing by its bellowing. I had quite won the heart of the Vermonter who had been sentry at my door, and though patriotic souls may not believe me, he paid me many compliments at the expense of the granite ladies of his state. The compliments were sincere, as he refused the drink of whiskey my gratitude offered him.

My next visit was to the commissary department of my hospital in search of sugar. Two Federal guards were in charge, but they simply stared with astonishment as I put aside their bayonets and unlocked the door of the place with my pass–key, filled my basket, with an explanation to them that I could be arrested whenever wanted at my quarters.

After this no one opposed my erratic movements, the newcomers ignoring me. No explanation was ever given to me, why I was allowed to come and go, nurse my men and feed them with all I could take or steal. All I ever gathered was from one of our errand–boys, who had fraternized with a Yankee sutler, who told him confidentially that the Federal surgeon in charge thought that woman in black had better go home, and added on his own responsibility, "He's awful afraid of her."

Away I was compelled to go at last, for my sick were removed to another hospital, where I still attended to them. There congregated the ladies of the neighborhood, bringing what delicacies they could gather, and nursing indiscriminately any patient who needed care. This continued till all the sick were either convalescent or dead, and at last my vocation was gone, and not one invalid left to give me a pretext for daily occupation.

And now when the absorbing duties of the last years no longer demanded my whole thoughts and attention, the difficulties of my own position forced themselves upon my mind. Whatever food had been provided for the sick since the Federal occupation had served for my small needs, but when my duties ceased I found myself with a box full of Confederate money and a silver ten–cent piece; perhaps a Confederate *gage d'amitie*; which puzzled me how to expend. It was all I had for a support, so I bought a box of matches and five cocoa–nut cakes. The wisdom of the purchase there is no need of defending. Should any one ever be in a strange country where the currency of which he is possessed is valueless, and ten cents be his only available funds, perhaps he may be able to judge of the difficulty of expending it with judgment.

But of what importance was the fact that I was houseless, homeless, moneyless, in Richmond, the heart of Virginia? Who ever wanted for aught that kind hearts, generous hands or noble hospitality could supply, that it was not there offered without even the shadow of a patronage that could have made it distasteful? What women were ever so refined in feeling and so unaffected in manner; so willing to share all that wealth gives, and so little infected with the pride of purse that bestows that power? It was difficult to hide one's needs from them; they found them out and ministered to them with their quiet simplicity and the innate nobility which gave to their generosity the coloring of a favor received; not conferred.

I laughed carelessly and openly at the disregard shown by myself for the future, when every one who had remained in Richmond, apparently had laid aside stores for daily food, but they detected with quick sympathy the hollowness of the mirth, and each day at every hour of breakfast, dinner and supper, would come to me a waiter, borne by the neat little Virginia maid (in her white apron), filled with ten times the quantity of food I could consume, packed carefully on. Sometimes boxes would be left at my door, with packages of tea, coffee, sugar and ham, or chicken, and no clue given to the thoughtful and kind donor.

Would that I could do more than thank the dear friends who made my life for four years so happy and contented; who never made me feel by word or act, that my self–imposed occupation was otherwise than one which would ennoble any woman. If ever any aid was given through my own exertions, or any labor rendered effective by me for the good of the South — if any sick soldier ever benefited by my happy face or pleasant smiles at his bedside, or death was ever soothed by gentle words of hope and tender care, such results were only owing to the cheering encouragement I received from them. They were gentlewomen in every sense of the word, and though they might not have remembered that "*noblesse oblige*" they felt and acted up to the motto in every act of their lives. My only wish was to live and die among them, growing each day better from contact with their gentle, kindly sympathies and heroic hearts.

It may never be in my power to do more than offer my heartfelt thanks, which may reach their once happy homes; and in closing these simple reminiscences of hospital experience, let me beg them to believe that whatever kindness my limited powers have conferred on the noble soldiers of their state, has been repaid tenfold, leaving with me an eternal, but grateful obligation.

There is one subject connected with hospitals on which a few words should be said — the distasteful one that a woman must lose a certain amount of delicacy and reticence in filling any office in them. How can this be? There is no unpleasant exposure under proper arrangements, and if even there be, the circumstances which surround a wounded man, far from friends and home, suffering in a holy cause and dependent upon a woman for help, care and sympathy, hallow and clear the atmosphere in which she labors. That woman must indeed be hard and gross, who lets one material thought lessen her efficiency. In the midst of suffering and death, hoping with those almost beyond hope in this world; praying by the bedside of the lonely and heart–stricken; closing the eyes of boys hardly old enough to realize man's sorrows, much less suffer by man's fierce hate, a woman *must* soar beyond the conventional modesty considered correct under different circumstances.

If the ordeal does not chasten and purify her nature, if the contemplation of suffering and endurance does not make her wiser and better, and if the daily fire through which she passes does not draw from her nature the sweet fragrance of benevolence, charity, and love, — then, indeed a hospital has been no fit place for her!

A Garland for Mrs. Stuart

MRS. ALEXANDER H. MAJOR

NORTH GEORGIA, APRIL 15, 1865

Mrs. Alexander H. Major is mistaken in saying that Sherman's march to the sea began at Chattanooga. The town she called "R———" is probably Rome, Georgia, which was occupied by the Federals soon after the Battle of Chickamauga.

I had been going about with my husband, who was in the commissary department of Sherman's division, ever since that famous "march to the sea" was begun from Chattanooga, May 6, 1864. It was a rather rough life for a woman, but as I had lived for a number of years in Eastern Kansas during the time she was enduring her exciting border warfare, I found this march rather to my liking. Besides, as we had no children, my husband liked to have his family, as he called me, with him for company.

Many a Union man, homesick for wife or mother, would come to our wagon and talk to me, just because I was a woman. Many a letter from home was read to me just for the comfort the boys got in hearing my comments upon the simple events which it related. And when some poor fellow became sick unto death he liked to be taken to our camp, to have me do for him as he imagined his own women folks would do if they had been there; so that the months that we spent upon the march were on the whole very satisfying ones to me. I did all I could to soften the rigors of war to all with whom I came in contact. Nevertheless, it was with feelings of gladness that we entered the town of R——— with a detachment of Union troops nearly a year from the time that we had left Chattanooga. All the Confederate families who could have left the town at our approach, but there was one Southern woman, a Mrs. Stuart, who declared she would never leave her house until they carried her out feet foremost.

We, that is, my husband and I, were boarding at her house, and whether it was because I was sympathetic or because my father had been a Southern man, I know not, but she became very confidential to me. She told me how her husband had fallen at Antietam, and how her son, only a lad of 15, had gone with Stonewall Jackson as drummer boy and had likewise died upon the field of battle. "I hate the Yanks," she exclaimed fiercely. "I hate them, and I never will forgive Abraham Lincoln for having brought on this terrible war that has not only beggared us financially, but has taken away our loved ones and left us bankrupt in affections. I wear black for my dead and I weep, but if anything happened to him I think I should shout for joy and be tempted to flaunt the gaudiest colors I could find." I quieted her as best I could, for I feared that some of the Union boys might overhear her, for we were seated at the time on the front veranda, and make it unpleasant for her.

R——— was intensely excited, as was every city, town, and hamlet in the whole country, when, on the 15th of April, the word came that Lincoln had been shot the evening before. "Thank God," cried Mrs. Stuart, "the wretch has gotten his just deserts." "Take care, madam," cried a stalwart boy in blue who had brought the message to my husband; "were you a man you would never live to repeat that remark. As it is, I advise you to keep a civil tongue in your head before the rest of the boys, who may not regard your sex as a protection as I have done."

Little was done that day but talk over the dreadful happening. Loud threats of vengeance on one hand and muttered rejoicings on the other filled the air. And when later on another message flashed over the wires that the President had died from the effects of the shot of the night before, the excitement knew no bounds. The stores were ransacked for black material to hang forth as symbols of mourning. Every house was ordered to be draped in black, and where the rebel inmates refused, it was done for them by the Union boys. A squad of Northern boys organized themselves into an inspection committee and went from street to street to see that no house was left undraped. When I suggested to Mrs. Stuart that she had better hang out something black and save trouble, she turned upon me and exclaimed passionately: "I'd rather die first." We had nothing of black whatever in our possession except my husband's coat, and as he had to wear that, I asked him to go down the street to buy a few yards of some black goods, which I intended to hang out from our bedroom window as a token that we grieved at the terrible calamity that had befallen a great and good man. It was while my husband was gone that the committee that I spoke of a few moments before came down the street upon which Mrs. Stuart lived, and seeing the house undraped, halted before it. There was a dead silence for a few moments that was more ominous than curses would have been. Then hoarse cries of "rebel sympathizer" broke from the crowd. The ringleader, who was the very boy who had brought the message to the house the day before, and who had unfortunately heard Mrs. Stuart's passionate outburst, stalked forward and pushed open the door without ceremony and demanded to know why the house was not draped. I sprang forward and stood between him and Mrs. Stuart and tried to explain to him that my husband had gone down street to get us some black, and that as soon as it came I would hang it out. "Yes; but she must hang it up," he cried, pointing threateningly at Mrs. Stuart, "Every d——d rebel must this day kiss the dust for this dastardly act. She must do it herself" — and he added as an afterthought, "It must be something of her own, too."

"What, I show a sign of mourning for Abraham Lincoln — I, who but for him would not be husbandless and childless today!" came from Mrs. Stuart's lips.

"Well, now, we'll see about that," he replied. "Come, boys," he called to the squad without, "some of you hold this she–devil while the rest of us search her house for something black." The front room, dining hall and kitchen downstairs and my bedroom upstairs yielded nothing, but when they entered Mrs. Stuart's private room, just back of mine, I knew from the shouts of triumph that they had found something; but I was hardly prepared for the sight when a few minutes later they came rushing down the stairs waving with frantic gesticulations Mrs. Stuart's long crepe veil; the veil that she had worn as a widow for her husband who had given his life for a cause that to him was holy and just; the veil that she had worn in double bereavement when her son had shed his young blood for his beloved South. Alas, the irony of fate!

"Here, madam, we have found just the thing," cried the leader, "and you yourself must hang it up right in front, too, where all may see it, or, by George, your life won't be worth a candle!" My heart ached for the proud southern woman, but I dared not say anything for fear of precipitating matters and making it worse for her than it already was. She stared at them for a few seconds with eyes in which hate, horror, and revenge strove for mastery. Then, with a mighty effort, she shook herself free from her captors and in a strangely calm voice said: "Give it to me, I will hang it up where you wish. Only leave the room, leave the premises; go across the street; you can see me from there; and you, madam," she said, turning to me, "you go with them."

"Come, young men," said I, turning to them and leading the way out of the room, "let us spare her pride as much as possible. Her life has been keenly embittered and her heart sorely bruised by this war." We all crossed the street and looked anxiously at Mrs. Stuart's front door. Some of the boys even expressed regret that they had carried the matter so far, and would, I believe, have gone on so as not to be witnesses of the humbling of the poor woman's pride, when just then she came out on the veranda. I noticed she had changed her dress since we had come away. She was all in black — her best black; her mourning weeds. She carried a chair in one hand, while the crepe veil was thrown over her shoulder and wound once around her neck. We all watched her intently. Her movements were slow and deliberate. She mounted the chair and began tenderly pushing aside the trailing jasmine from the center fretwork above her head. Then she took the veil, the badge of her stricken life, and threw it through the opening, while at the same time she put something else through. What it was we could not tell at that distance, and then, O horrors! she gave her chair a vigorous push with her foot and her body hung suspended in midair. Several seconds elapsed, in which we all stood as if frozen to the spot, staring at that dangling body across the street. Then, with a cry of horror from each apprehensive heart, we rushed over. A dozen hands reached to get her down, and a dozen eyes filled with tears as we realized it was too late. Under the crepe veil floating out upon the April–kissed breezes, with a strong cord firmly knotted about her neck, hung all that was mortal of that once proud southern woman.

The End of All We Cherished

JUDITH BROKENBROUGH MCGUIRE

RICHMOND, VIRGINIA, APRIL AND MAY 1865

Richmond fell six days before Lee surrendered to Grant at Appomattox.

April 3. Agitated and nervous, I turn to my diary to–night as the means of soothing my feelings. We have passed through a fatal thirty–six hours. Yesterday morning (it seems a week ago) we went, as usual, to St. James's Church, hoping for a day of peace and quietness, as well as of religious improvement and enjoyment. How short–sighted we are, and how little do we know of what is coming, either of judgment or mercy! The sermon being over, as it was the first Sunday in the month, the sacrament of the Lord's Supper was administered. The day was bright, beautiful, and peaceful, and a general quietness and repose seemed to rest upon the congregation, undisturbed by rumours and apprehensions. While the sacred elements were being administered, the sexton came in with a note to General Cooper, which was handed him as he walked from the chancel, and he immediately left the church. It made me anxious; but such things are not uncommon, and caused no excitement in the congregation. The services being over, we left the church, and as the congregations from the various churches were being mingled on Grace Street, our children, who had been at St. Paul's, joined us, on their way to the usual family gathering in our room on Sunday. After the salutations of the morning J. remarked, in an agitated voice, to his father, that he had just returned from the War Department, and that there was sad news — General Lee's lines had been broken, and the city would probably be evacuated within twenty–four hours. Not until then did I observe that every countenance was wild with excitement. The inquiry, "What is the matter?" ran from lip to lip. Nobody seemed to hear or to answer. An old friend ran across the street, pale with excitement, repeating what J. had just told us, that unless we heard better news from General Lee the city would be evacuated. We could do nothing; no one suggested any thing to be done. We reached home with a strange, unrealizing feeling. In an hour J. received orders to accompany Captain Parker to the South with the Corps of Midshipmen. Then we began to understand that the Government was moving, and that the evacuation was indeed going on. The office–holders were now making arrangements to get off. Every car was ordered to be ready to take them south. Baggage–wagons, carts, drays, and ambulances were driving about the streets; every one was going off that could go, and now there were all the indications of alarm and excitement of every kind which could attend such an awful scene. The people were rushing up and down the streets, vehicles of all kinds were flying along, bearing goods of all sorts and people of all ages and classes who could go beyond the corporation lines. We tried to keep ourselves quiet. We could not go south, nor could we leave the city at all in this hurried way. J. and his wife had gone. The "Colonel," with B., intended going in the northern train this morning — he to his home in Hanover County, and she to her father's house in Clarke County, as soon as she could get there. Last night, when we went out to hire a servant to go to Camp Jackson for our sister, we for the first time realized that our money was worthless here, and that we are in fact penniless. About midnight she walked in, escorted by two of the convalescent soldiers. Poor fellows! all the soldiers will go who can, but the sick and wounded must be captured. We collected in one room, and tried to comfort one another; we made large pockets and filled them with as many of our valuables as we could suspend from our waists. The gentlemen walked down to the War Office in the night to see what was going on. Alas! every sight and sound was grievous and heavy.

A telegram just received from General Lee hastened the evacuation. The public offices were all forsaken. They said that by three o'clock in the morning the work must be completed, and the city ready for the enemy to take possession. Oh, who shall tell the horror of the past night! Hope seemed to fade; none but despairing words were heard, except from a few brave hearts. Union men began to show themselves; treason walked abroad. A gloomy pall seemed to hang over us; but I do not think that any of us felt keenly, or have yet realized our overwhelming calamity. The suddenness and extent of it is too great for us to feel its poignancy at once. About two o'clock in the morning we were startled by a loud sound like thunder; the house shook and the windows rattled; it seemed like an earthquake in our midst. We knew not what it was, nor did we care. It was soon understood to be the blowing up of a magazine below the city. In a few hours another exploded on the outskirts of the city, much louder than the first, and shivering innumerable plate–glass windows all over Shockoe Hill. It was then daylight, and we were standing out upon the pavement. The Colonel and B. had just gone. Shall we ever meet again? Many ladies were now upon the streets. The lower part of the city was burning. About seven o'clock I set off to go to the central depot to see if the cars would go out. As I went from Franklin to Broad Street, and on Broad, the pavements were covered with broken glass; women, both white and coloured, were walking in multitudes from the Commissary offices and burning stores with bags of flour, meal, coffee, sugar, rolls of cotton cloth, etc.; coloured men were rolling wheelbarrows filled in the same way. I went on and on towards the depot, and as I proceeded shouts and screams became louder. The rabble rushed by me in one stream. At last I exclaimed, "Who are those shouting? What is the matter?" I seemed to be answered by a hundred voices, "The Yankees have come." I turned to come home, but what was my horror, when I reached Ninth Street to see a regiment of Yankee cavalry come dashing up, yelling, shouting, hallooing, screaming! All Bedlam let loose could not have vied with them in diabolical roarings. I stood riveted to the spot; I could not move nor speak. Then I saw the iron gates of our time–honoured and beautiful Capitol Square, on the walks and greensward of which no hoof had been allowed to tread, thrown open and the cavalry dash in. I could see no more; I must go on with a mighty effort, or faint where I stood. I came home amid what I thought was the firing of cannon. I thought that they were thundering forth a salute that they had reached the goal of their ardent desires; but I afterwards found that the Armory was on fire, and that the flames having reached the shells deposited there for our army, they were exploding. These explosions were kept up until a late hour this evening; I am rejoiced they are gone; they, at least, can never be turned against us. I found the family collected around the breakfast–table, and was glad to see Captain M.'s family with them. The captain has gone, and the ladies have left their home on "Union Hill" to stay here among friends, Colonel P. having kindly given them rooms. An hour or two after breakfast we all retired to our rooms exhausted. No one had slept; no one had sought repose or thought of their own comfort. The Federal soldiers were roaming about the streets; either whiskey or the excess of joy had given some of them the appearance of being beside themselves. We had hoped that very little whiskey would be found in the city, as, by order of the Mayor, casks were emptied yesterday evening in the streets, and it flowed like water through the gutters; but the rabble had managed to find it secreted in the burning shops, and bore it away in pitchers and buckets. It soon became evident that protection would be necessary for the residences, and at the request of Colonel P. I went to the Provost Marshal's office to ask for it. Mrs. P. was unfortunately in the country, and only ladies were allowed to apply for guards. Of course this was a very unpleasant duty, but I must undertake it. Mrs. D. agreed to accompany me, and we proceeded to the City Hall — the City Hall, which from my childhood I had regarded with respect and reverence, as the place where my father had for years held his courts, and in which our lawyers, whose names stand among the highest in the Temple of Fame, for fifty years expounded the Constitution and the laws, which must now be trodden under foot. We reached it. After passing through crowds of negro soldiers there, we found on the steps some of the elderly gentlemen of the city seeking admittance, which was denied them. I stopped to speak to Mr. ———, in whose commission house I was two days ago, and saw him surrounded by all the stores which usually make up the establishment of such a merchant; it was now a mass of blackened ruins. He had come to ask protection for his residence, but was not allowed to enter. We passed the sentinel, and an officer escorted us to the room in which we were to ask our country's foe to allow us to remain undisturbed in our own houses. Mrs. D. leant on me tremblingly; she shrank from the humiliating duty. For my own part, though my heart beat loudly and my blood boiled, I never felt more high-spirited or lofty than at that moment. A large table was surrounded by officials, writing or talking to the ladies, who came on the same mission that brought us. I approached the officer who sat at the head of the table, and asked him politely if he was the Provost Marshal. "I am the Commandant, madam," was the respectful reply. "Then to whom am I to apply for protection for our residence?" "You need none, madam; our troops are perfectly disciplined, and dare not enter your premises." "I am sorry to be obliged to undeceive you, sir, but when I left home seven of your soldiers were in the yard of the residence opposite to us, and one has already been into our kitchen." He looked surprised, and said, "Then, madam, you are entitled to a guard. Captain, write a protection for the residence on the corner of First and Franklin Streets, and give these ladies a guard." This was quickly done, and as I turned to go out, I saw standing near me our old friend, Mrs.———. Oh! how my heart sank when I looked into her calm, sad face, and remembered that she and her venerable and highly esteemed husband must ask leave to remain in peace in their home of many years. The next person who attracted my attention was that sweet young girl, S.W. Having no mother, she of course must go and ask that her father's beautiful mansion may be allowed to stand uninjured. Tears rolled down her cheeks as she pressed my hand in passing. Other friends were there; we did not speak, we could not; we sadly looked at each other and passed on. Mrs. D. and myself came out, accompanied by our guard. The fire was progressing rapidly, and the crashing sound of falling timbers was distinctly heard. Dr. Read's church was blazing. Yankees, citizens, and negroes were attempting to arrest the flames. The War Department was falling in; burning papers were being wafted about the streets. The Commissary Department, with our desks and papers, was consumed already. Warwick & Barksdale's mill was sending its flames to the sky. Cary and Main Streets seemed doomed throughout; Bank Street was beginning to burn, and now it had reached Franklin. At any other moment it would have distracted me, but I had ceased to feel any thing. We brought our guard to Colonel P., who posted him; about three o'clock he came to tell me that the guard was drunk, and threatening to shoot the servants in the yard. Again I went to the City Hall to procure another. I approached the Commandant and told him why I came. He immediately ordered another guard, and a corporal to be sent for the arrest of the drunken man. The flames had decreased, but the business part of the city was in ruins. The second guard was soon posted, and the first carried off by the collar. Almost every house is guarded; and the streets are now (ten o'clock) perfectly quiet. The moon is shining brightly on our captivity. God guide and watch over us!

April 12. I try to dwell as little as possible on public events. I only feel that we have no country, no government, no future. I cannot, like some others, look with hope on Johnston's army. He will do what he can; but ah, what can he do? Our anxiety now is that our President and other public men may get off in safety. O God! have mercy upon them and help them! For ourselves, like the rest of the refugees, we are striving to get from the city. The stereotyped question when we meet is, "When and where are you going?" Our country relatives have been very kind. My brother offers us an asylum in his devastated home at W. While there we must look around for some other place, in which to build up a home for our declining years. Property we have none — all gone. Thank God, we have our faculties; the girls and myself, at least have health. Mr. McGuire bears up under our difficulties with the same hopeful spirit which he has ever manifested. "The Lord will provide," is still his answer to any doubt on our part. The Northern officials offer free tickets to persons returning to their homes — alas! to their homes! How few of us have homes! Some are confiscated; others destroyed. The families of the army and navy officers are here. The husbands and sons are absent, and they remain with nothing to anticipate and nothing to enjoy. To–day I met a friend, the wife of a high official, whose hospitality I have often enjoyed in one of the most elegant residences in Virginia, which has been confiscated and used as a hospital for "contrabands." Our conversation naturally turned on our prospects. Hearing where we were going, she replied, "I have no brother, but when I hear from my husband and son, I shall accept the whole–souled invitation of a relative in the country, who has invited me to make his house my home; but," she added, as her beautiful eyes filled with tears, "when are our visits to end? We can't live with our ruined relatives, and when our visits are over, what then? And how long must our visits of charity last?" The question was too sad; neither of us could command our voices, and we parted in silence and tears.

Remembering God's Promises

CORNELIA PEAKE MCDONALD

LEXINGTON, VIRGINIA, APRIL TO OCTOBER 1865

Cornelia McDonald had brought her family from Winchester to Lexington, where she was living when the war ended. Mrs. Pendleton who befriended her was the wife of General William N. Pendleton, Lee's chief of artillery, and the mother of Colonel Alexander S. (Sandie) Pendleton who died at the Battle of Fisher's Hill, November 1864.

The eventful 9th of April came, and the day after we heard of Lee's surrender. I can never forget the effect the intelligence had on me and on my family. I felt as if the end of all things had come, at least for the Southern people.

Grief and despair took possession of my heart, with a sense of humiliation that till then I did not know I could feel. The distress of the children was as great as mine; their poor little faces showed all the grief and shame that was in their hearts, and each went about sad and dejected as if it was a personal matter. I remember once glancing out at the window and seeing Donald who was too proud to show his concern to the family, walking up and down under the window with his fat little face streaming with tears, and wringing his hands in utter despair. By and by the dismal train of returning refugees began to pass by. Mr. Sherrard and Mr. James Marshall came, and called to me as they passed by. Their white hair was whiter than ever and their faces hopeless and sad. They were on their way to their ruined homes, which they had not seen for three years, to try and gather up the remains of their scattered fortunes, or to find some place of rest where they could be with their families. Every day came by returning soldiers and refugees and some among them were glad to have the privilege of going back to reunite their broken households. Though it came in so dreadful a shape, it is certainly true that the return of peace brought joy to many; to them at least, it was a "white winged angel," and they were glad to bury pride, patriotism, all, if they could see an end to destruction and bloodshed. And so, of the crowds that lined the roads, though some were gloomily going up, not knowing if they should find any house remaining, others were happy at the thought of being released from danger, hunger and weariness, and of seeing their homes again, even if they were robbed of so much that had made them happy, and though death had left its shadow there.

By far the greatest number, however, seemed to regard peace as a dire misfortune, and many had resolved, and were on their way to leave the country. Among those who were returning came old Dr. Foote of Romney, one who in earlier and happier days I had cordially disliked, and who, though he was a Presbyterian minister, was very bitter and inimical to my husband on account of some difference about the management of a public institution. This difference and bitterness extended itself to the two families, and had arrived at such a pitch that the different members of each ceased all intercourse. My surprise was great then, when the door opened and Dr. Foote entered. A feeling of sympathy prompted me to offer my hand; he did not speak, but burst into a flood of tears.

For some time nothing was said. At last he sobbed out, "I could not believe it, I would not believe it, when they came to tell me Lee had surrendered. I told them I could not hear it, that it was false. I laid on my bed and covered my face and would not see or speak to any one for fear they would tell me that false and harrowing story. I prayed that God would take me then." "Yes," he said, "I laid for days. I would not look out to see the sun shine if it looked on our wretched country and ruined people." I wept, too, with the old man, and loved him then as much as I had once hated him. What was remarkable was that he was a Connecticut man. He had come to Virginia in his youth to teach, and had been living there for fifty years. He told me the coat he had on was made by his daughter of the skirt of her riding habit. He told me of privations that were great for any one, but for an old man dreadful. "And all for nothing," he said. "I would have borne ten times more if I could only have seen our country free from her enemies."

My house was full day after day, of passers by; friends, on their way, some to go home, others to leave the country. Many young men came, members of the different regiments that had been disbanded. The Maryland Line, my old friends and neighbors, was represented by Mr. Thomas, young Sully, the son of the great painter, and a few others. I inquired about the rest of them. Only a few were left of the groups that used to gather about my fire on the cold winter evenings at Winchester. Mr. Iglehart who, on marching away had given me his Bible to keep, was killed in the trenches.

Those of them who lived could be counted on the fingers. One day a commotion among the children announced Harry's arrival. He looked worn and weary, and before he spoke, on coming in, he covered his face with his hands and wept. "To think it is all over and I did not strike a blow," were his first words.

He had reached Lee's army as they were on their retreat, and was set to guarding wagons. He worked on with the dispirited and starving throng till the end came. An officer offered him his horse as he did not care to surrender it, and taking it gladly he made his way home.

When the news of Gen. Lee's surrender was made known at Lexington, the quartermaster there divided among those persons who had been connected with the army the stores and provisions that were left there. Some fell to my share, some bacon and beans, and so I had something to give to the hungry men who daily came to ask a meal. Mr. Sherrard told me that his whole fortune being in bank stock, was gone when the currency became so depreciated, and that only a few months before he had received from California, $7,000, left him by his son, Robert, who had died there; that to show his confidence in the cause, and inspire others with the same, he had invested it all in Confederate bonds. "Now," said he, "I have not a dollar." I could fully realize what that meant when I looked at his aged, withered face and snow white hair, and thought of the old wife, and daughters who had for months been wanderers, driven from home by the enemy. After some days I learned that Edward had been dreadfully wounded on the last day of the struggle. Retreating with his command, he fought as he went, turning to fire on his pursuers.

Once as he turned, he received a ball in his face which passed through his jaw, splintering and tearing it fearfully. Finding himself severely wounded he made his way off from the scene of the fight, and determined to get to a place where he could receive attention, he rode on, weak and bleeding as he was, for sixty miles, in all that time not able to take a mouthful to nourish or revive him.

He reached Charlottesville, and there lay for many weeks with scarcely a hope of recovery.

I sent Harry as soon as I heard he was there to take care of him, but finding his brother Angus already there, he returned home.

All the Northern papers I saw were full of joy and exultation over the great victory; and there was much less bitterness expressed than I supposed would be; indeed, they seemed ready to welcome the poor Southern rebels as friends, now that they could fight no longer, and compel them to waste their money on the sinews of war. Now they could return to their money–getting, thanks to the poor rebels who had been whipped.

Some papers even ventured to suggest that Gen. Lee should go to the North and show himself, saying that if he would do so, he would receive an ovation such as no Hero ever had, not even Grant.

They admired his high character, and appreciated his soldierly qualities, as well as his military greatness, and I believe that if his proud humility would have suffered him to make himself a spectacle to be gazed at, they would have showered honours on him. They were accustomed to such coarse–minded heroes as Grant, and such vain–glorious boasters as McClellan, and Pope, and they could not understand such a man as our Hero was.

In a very short time the kind and forbearing feelings our late enemies seemed to entertain for us were displaced by bitter hatred and furious rage, for when the bullet of Booth took away the life of Lincoln, I thought it was just what he deserved; he that had urged on and promoted a savage war that had cost so many lives; but a little reflection made me see that it was worse for us than if he had been suffered to live, for his satisfaction had been great when we were disarmed, and he was disposed to be merciful. Now no mercy was to be expected from a nation of infuriated fanatics whose idol of clay had been cast down.

We expected nothing but that the Southern people would be accused of planning the murder and procuring its execution; we knew that vengeance would be taken and that the crime would be visited upon our leaders, and prominent men who would be the most assailable objects for their vengeance; but were not prepared for the extent of diabolical rage which they manifested in their treatment of President Davis when he fell into their hands, or that their pitiless fury should demand that a helpless and innocent woman, innocent, as their own failure to prosecute her son proved, should perish at the hand of the hang man.

July 1865. In those dreary days I used to go and see Mrs. Dailey, the one person left to whom I could speak of my situation. Hers was little better, for her husband had gone back to his old home to see if a living could be made, and to try to establish his family. While he was gone they were in a great state of distress, being even for a time without bread. One morning when I went there I found her eyes red with weeping, and she told me she had just sent her mother's silver bowl to the mill to exchange for a barrel of flour; it was a great trial to her to part with it and she was of course very sad. I had been obliged to do the very same thing, only it was a ladle that we bought bread with. Her messenger soon returned with the bowl and the flour also; he brought also a message from Dr. Leyburn, owner of the mill, that she must keep the bowl and send for flour whenever she wanted it.

It seemed to me at this time that matters were so bad that they could not possibly be worse, but I found that they could be much worse; and I found also that God was so good, that with the trial he provided the needful help. One morning when the servant was engaged in another part of the house, I had taken her place in the kitchen.

There was a large fireplace but no stove, and it was very difficult for my inexperienced hands to take the kettle from it without setting fire to my clothes. With great effort I succeeded in taking it off full of boiling water, and having poured it into the tea pan took the pan by the handles and attempted to carry it upstairs to the dining room for the purpose of washing the breakfast things. It fell from my hands, I know not how or why, but all the boiling water poured over my right foot.

Of course I shrieked out with pain and fright, and in a moment many persons had gathered around the house to see what the trouble was. I ran by them all up stairs, and on taking off the stocking all the skin came with it.

For many weeks I was confined to the bed and suffered greatly. My boys had to remain at home to take care of the younger children and attend to me. I could not turn in the bed, and could not endure a footstep that would occasion the slightest jar. A door shut too suddenly, would occasion a nervous shock and intense pain. All this time my good boys, Harry and Allan, lifted me, and did all they could to keep the house quiet and me undisturbed.

How they fared, poor things, I did not know. I could not even think of them. I was remembered by my friends in the village, who sent every day nice breakfasts and dinners, so that I suffered for nothing in the way of food.

All my friends came to see me and were very kind. The Pendletons especially were more like relatives than strangers. Little Madge Paxton came every morning, and with her neat ways and pretty gentle face made me feel happy and cheerful as she moved about the room setting things in order and arranging all as nicely as possible.

She also superintended the washing and dressing of Nelly and Hunter, and when Nell had diphtheria during my sickness, Madge attended to her and washed her throat out every morning with the utmost care. Whenever she came in the morning she brought a bunch of grapes or an orange or something else nice for Nell and me. Dear little Madge, good and sweet she is, and I hope she may be as happy in this world as she deserves to be, and meet with her reward in the next one. Dr. Graham attended my injuries with constant care and skill, and in two months I was able to move about the room on crutches.

In the mean time, Dr. Dailey returned and prepared to take his family away to Romney. Mrs. Dailey spent the day before she left with me in my room, and I felt that I was losing my only real intimate friend; one who knew all my circumstances, and to whom I was not ashamed to confess my destitution. I wished to go when they went, to go anywhere that some change might be effected in our sad, hard lot. When they were gone I felt doubly forlorn and undone, and when I could go about the house, the sight of the destitution, the want of every thing was more than I could bear. Then came the darkest and saddest of all those sad times. I had no one now to whom I could confide any part of my misery.

Mrs. Powell had been long gone, and now Mrs. Dailey and the Doctor, who had been my friends for long years, ever since I was married, and to whom I had no hesitation in speaking of my trouble, were also gone, and I felt forsaken. It is true I had many friends, but though they were kind, and would have helped if they had known the conditions of things, yet they were friends of a very recent date, and how could I, when they came to pay a visit, make them uncomfortable by telling them we had nothing to eat! No, I would sit and talk to them, and be as cheerful as I could, but not the less did I when they were gone, go up stairs and throw myself on my knees and cry to God for food.

Aug. 1865. One day, I can never forget. I had been sitting at the table eating nothing. How could I eat bean soup and bread? I loathed it and could not taste it. The children did not ever complain, though it was easy to see they disliked it. But I was starving; I felt so weak and helpless and every thing seemed so dark, that for a time I was seized with utter despair. I felt that God had forsaken us, and I wished, oh! I wished that He would at one blow sweep me and mine from the earth. There seemed no place on it for us, no room for us to live.

I laid on a sofa through all those dreadful hours of unbelief and hopelessness; I had lost the feeling that God cared for us, that He even knew of our want. The whole dreadful situation was shown to my doubting heart; the empty pantry, for even the beans and bread were exhausted, and I should have to send the servant away. The house rent to be paid, and no money for it, although it had been due and demanded some time before. The coming cold weather and the want of everything that could make life bearable, made me wish it would end. I did not think; nor did I care to pray the impious prayer that God would destroy us, but I wished it; I desired at that moment to be done with life, for no one seemed to care for us, whether we lived or died. How long I lay there I do not know, but after a while came the remembrance of the goodness my God had shown me in the former dark hours I had passed through; how he had been near, my Heavenly Father, and how I had leaned on and trusted Him; with that remembrance came the resolve, "Though He slay me, yet will I trust in Him." I got up, saying, or trying to say:

> "Although the vine its fruit deny,
> The budding fig tree droop and die,
>   No oil the olive yield.
> Yet will I trust me in my God,
> Yea bend rejoicing to his rod,
> And by His stripes be healed."

For days the remembrance of that dreadful hour clung to me, and made me afraid to dwell in thought for a moment on my own miseries. I feared the attacks of the Tempter, and so tried to busy myself about something. But what was there to do, what had I to do anything with? My drawing class had melted away as the summer advanced, and when my foot was scalded, of course it had all to be given up.

One day a package was sent me from Winchester by some friends who had not forgotten me. Some frocks and shoes for Nelly, and underclothing for myself. I was thankful for it, but how many more wants were there for which there was no supply. I determined at last to try to get the class together again, and with the assistance of Miss Baxter succeeded in getting back two or three of my scholars. But how small a sum it brought, not enough to do more than buy bread. The struggle went on seeming more and more hopeless every day as the cold days and nights drew near and no provision for them. When October came and brought its mellow sunshine, and the soft veil lay over the mountains and river, I used to walk, to take long walks, and try to enjoy the delight of breathing the pure air, and to get back a little of the pleasure I used to have in the woods and fields at that sweetest of all seasons. But I could scarcely lift my heavy eyes to the blue hills, or endure the light of the lovely sunsets.

The sight of the smooth, peaceful river gave me no joy of heart, or the songs of the birds, the incense–laden air, nothing, for always the thought of the desolation of our penniless home was before me, and my heart ached continually.

Oct. The misery of those weeks in October, I must remember always, for with the pressure of present want and the knowledge that though I was there close to a college where the sons of my neighbors would go and be educated, that mine could not have the benefit of an education, as they could not pay the fees, or procure clothes to wear. I had written to Missouri to a lawyer to employ him in collecting my dower in land my husband owned there, but as yet had received nothing.

One evening I went out to walk, as much to get away from the gloomy house as for any thing else, and as I passed up the street saw into the pleasant houses the bright fires, looking so cheerful, and the people that sat by them looking so contented, that it made me feel all the more desolate.

I felt too wretched and forlorn to go where people were, but turned and went into the cemetery. I sat there by Sandy [Sandie] Pendleton's grave for some time, trying to regain courage and hope. The evening was cold and clear, and the shadows were darkening over the lovely mountains opposite where I sat. The deep purple became deeper, till at last their huge outlines began to grow dim, and I could not stay longer, but turned and came out.

Near the gate I met Mrs. Pendleton going to visit her only son's grave. She met me and as she looked in my face she exclaimed: "What can be the matter, you look so dreadfully? Come home with me now, I will go back."

I only burst out crying, for her words of kindness upset all my composure. She held my hands and begged me to tell her. I smothered pride and said, "We are starving, I and my children." "Comfort yourself," she said. "I meant to have come and told you that help is coming for you. You are to receive a sum of money in a few days. William has given in your name to those who have charge of it, and you and Kate will each receive one hundred dollars. You must not ask where it comes from."

I went to bed that night with a happy heart and a thankful one.

I learned long after that the money was a part of a sum that had been sent to Canada for secret service; that after the surrender those in whose hands it was, determined to devote it to the relief of the destitute widows and orphans of Confederate soldiers. Gen. Edmund Lee was there, and gave my name and Kate Pendleton's, Sandy's widow, to them. General Pendleton having suggested it in writing to him.

The next morning I felt cheerful enough to go and see Mrs. McElwee, intending to spend the day, not to get something to eat, but to enjoy her kind and friendly talk. After staying a while she told me she had just had a quarter of beef sent, and insisted on giving me a roast. I accepted it gladly, and immediately decided on returning home to have it cooked for the children's dinner. This I did, wrapping it in paper I put it under my shawl and carried it home.

Mrs. McElwee had received a sum of money from the estate of her brother who had been killed at Chickamauga, and a few days after she came and offered to lend me three hundred dollars. I accepted it, and with a light and happy heart set about making provision for the winter. Some time after Edward came and brought me money to pay my rent. He had found and collected a bond of his father's, and brought me part of the money. He and William had rented a farm in Clarke County, and he farmed while William taught school. Susan and Flora kept house for them. Edward wanted one of the boys sent to them, so I decided on sending Allan, as Harry was old enough to go to college, and I had determined to send him.

And here ends my account of my trials; and though they were not at an end entirely, I was able in various ways to take care of my family till they were fitted to be of use themselves; and when they were able to bear the burden they took it up manfully, and acquitted themselves well.

The Last March Home

ELIZA ANDREWS

WASHINGTON, GEORGIA, SUMMER 1865

Jefferson Davis passed through Washington, Georgia, about seventy–five miles east of Atlanta, after the collapse of the Confederacy, as did many ex–Confederate soldiers who were going home.

May 1, Monday — Crowds of callers all day. The Irvin Artillery are back, and it was almost like a reception, so many of them kept coming in. Capt. Thomas called again with Capt. Garnett. They staid a long time, and we enjoyed their visit, except for a stupid blunder. Capt. Thomas informed us that he was a widower, with one child, but he looked so boyish that we thought he was joking and treated the matter with such levity that we were horribly mortified later, when Capt. Garnett told us it was true. I told Metta [Eliza's sister] neither of us could ever hope to be stepmother to that little boy.

Men were coming in all day, with busy faces, to see Mr. Harrison, and one of them brought news of Johnston's surrender, but Mr. Harrison didn't tell anybody about it except father, and the rest of us were left in ignorance till afternoon when Fred came back with the news from Augusta. While we were at dinner, a brother of Mrs. Davis came in and called for Mr. Harrison, and after a hurried interview with him, Mr. Harrison came back into the dining–room and said it had been decided that Mrs. Davis would leave town to–morrow. Delicacy forbade our asking any questions, but I suppose they were alarmed by some of the numerous reports that are always flying about the approach of Yankees. Mother called on Mrs. Davis this afternoon, and she really believes they are on their way here and may arrive at any moment. She seemed delighted with her reception here, and, to the honor of our town, it can be truly said that she has received more attention than would have been shown her even in the palmiest days of her prosperity.

The conduct of a Texas regiment in the streets this afternoon gave us a sample of the chaos and general demoralization that may be expected to follow the breaking up of our government. They raised a riot about their rations, in which they were joined by all the disorderly elements among both soldiers and citizens. First they plundered the Commissary Department, and then turned loose on the quartermaster's stores. Paper, pens, buttons, tape, cloth — everything in the building — was seized and strewn about on the ground. Negroes and children joined the mob and grabbed what they could of the plunder. Col. Weems' provost guard refused to interfere, saying they were too good soldiers to fire on their comrades, and so the plundering went on unopposed. Nobody seemed to care much, as we all know the Yankees will get it in the end, any way, if our men don't. I was at Miss Maria Randolph's when the disturbance began, but by keeping to the back streets I avoided the worst of the row, though I encountered a number of stragglers, running away with their booty. The soldiers were very generous with their "confiscated" goods, giving away paper, pens, tape, &c., to anybody they happened to meet. One of them poked a handful of pen staves at me; another, staggering under an armful of stationery, threw me a ream of paper, saying "There, take that and write to your sweetheart on it." I took no notice of any of them, but hurried on home as fast as I could, all the way meeting negroes, children, and men loaded with plunder. When I reached home I found some of our own servants with their arms full of thread, paper, and pens, which they offered to sell me, and one of them gave me several reams of paper. I carried them to father, and he collected all the other booty he could find, intending to return it to headquarters, but he was told that there is no one to receive it, no place to send it to — in fact, there seemed to be no longer any headquarters nor any other semblance of authority. Father saved one box of bacon for Col. Weems by hauling it away in his wagon and concealing it in his smokehouse. All of Johnston's army and the greater portion of Lee's are still to pass through, and since the rioters have destroyed so much of the forage and provisions intended for their use, there will be great difficulty in feeding them. They did not stop at food, but helped themselves to all the horses and mules they needed. A band of them made a raid on Gen. Elzey's camp and took nine of his mules. They excused themselves by saying that all government stores will be seized by the Yankees in a few days, any way, if left alone, and our own soldiers might as well get the good of them while they can. This would be true, if there were not so many others yet to come who ought to have their share.

Our back yard and kitchen have been filled all day, as usual, with soldiers waiting to have their rations cooked. One of them, who had a wounded arm, came into the house to have it dressed, and said that he was at Salisbury when Garnett [Eliza's brother] was shot and saw him fall. He told some miraculous stories about the valorous deed of "the colonel," and although they were so exaggerated that I set them down as apocryphal, I gave him a piece of cake, notwithstanding, to pay him for telling them.

May 2, Tuesday — Mr. Harrison left this morning, with a God–speed from all the family and prayers for the safety of the honored fugitives committed to his charge.

The disorders begun by the Texans yesterday were continued to–day, every fresh band that arrived from the front falling into the way of their predecessors. They have been pillaging the ordnance stores at the dépot, in which they were followed by negroes, boys, and mean white men. I don't see what people are thinking about to let ammunition fall into the hands of the negroes, but everybody is demoralized and reckless and nobody seems to care about anything any more. A number of paroled men came into our grove where they sat under the trees to empty the cartridges they had seized. Confederate money is of no more use now than so much waste paper, but by filling their canteens with powder they can trade it off along the road for provisions. They scattered lead and cartridges all over the ground. Marshall went out after they left and picked up enough to last him for years. The balls do not fit his gun, but he can remold them and draw the powder out of the cartridges to shoot with. I am uneasy at having so much explosive material in the house, especially when I consider the careless manner in which we have to live. There is so much company and so much to do that even the servants hardly have time to eat. I never lived in such excitement and confusion in my life. Thousands of people pass through Washington every day, and our house is like a free hotel; father welcomes everybody as long as there is a square foot of vacant space under his roof. Meeting all these pleasant people is the one compensation of this dismal time, and I don't know how I shall exist when they have all gone their ways, and we settle down in the mournful quiet of subjugation. Besides the old friends that are turning up every day, there is a continual stream of new faces crossing my path, and I make some pleasant acquaintance or form some new friendship every day. The sad part of it is that the most of them I will probably never meet again, and if I should, where, and how? What will they be? What will I be? These are portentous questions in such a time as this.

We had a larger company to dinner to-day than usual, but no one that specially interested me. In the afternoon came a poor soldier from Abbeville, with a message from Garnett that he was there, waiting for father to send the carriage to bring him home. He sat on the soft grass before the door, and we fed him on sorghum cake and milk, the only things we had to offer. I am glad the cows have not been emancipated, for the soldiers always beg for milk; I never saw one that was not eager for it at any time. After the soldier, Ed Napier came in, who was a captain in Garnett's battalion and was taken prisoner with him. He says that Garnett covered himself with glory; even the Yankees spoke of his gallantry and admired him.

It seems as if all the people I ever heard of, or never heard of, either, for that matter, are passing through Washington. Some of our friends pass on without stopping to see us because they say they are too ragged and dirty to show themselves. Poor fellows! if they only knew how honorable rags and dirt are now, in our eyes, when endured in the service of their country, they would not be ashamed of them. The son of the richest man in New Orleans trudged through the other day, with no coat to his back, no shoes on his feet. The town is full of celebrities, and many poor fugitives, whose necks are in danger, meet here to concert plans for escape, and I put it in my prayers every night that they may be successful. Gen. Wigfall started for the West some days ago, but his mules were stolen, and he had to return. He is frantic, they say, with rage and disappointment. Gen. Toombs left to-night, but old Governor Brown, it is said, has determined not to desert his post. I am glad he has done something to deserve respect, and hope he may get off yet, as soon as the Yankees appoint a military governor. Clement Clay is believed to be well on his way to the Trans-Mississippi, the Land of Promise now, or rather the City of Refuge from which it is hoped a door of escape may be found to Mexico or Cuba. The most terrible part of the war is now to come, the "Bloody Assizes." "Kirke's Lambs," in the shape of Yankee troopers, are closing in upon us; our own disbanded armies, ragged, starving, hopeless, reckless, are roaming about without order or leaders, making their way to their far-off homes as best they can. The props that held society up are broken. Everything is in a state of disorganization and tumult. We have no currency, no law save the primitive code that might makes right. We are in a transition state from war to subjugation, and it is far worse than was the transition from peace to war. The suspense and anxiety in which we live are terrible.

• • •

May 3, Wednesday — Fred started for Abbeville in the carriage to bring Garnett home. We hear now that the Yankees are in Abbeville, and, if so, I am afraid they will take the horses away and then I don't know how Garnett will get home. They are father's carriage horses, and we would be in a sad plight with no way to ride. Our cavalry are playing havoc with stock all through the country. The Texans are especially noted in this respect. They have so far to go that the temptation is greater in their case. There is hardly a planter in Wilkes County who has not lost one or more of his working animals since they began to pass through. They seize horses, even when they are already well–mounted, and trade them off. They broke into Mr. Ben Bowdre's stable and took possession of his carriage horses, and helped themselves to two from the buggies of quiet citizens on the square. Almost everybody I know has had horses stolen or violently taken from him. I was walking with Dr. Sale in the street yesterday evening, and a soldier passed us leading a mule, while the rightful owner followed after, wasting breath in useless remonstrances. As they passed us, the soldier called out: "A man that's going to Texas must have a mule to ride, don't you think so, lady?" I made no answer, Dr. Sale gave a doubtful assent. It is astonishing what a demoralizing influence association with horses seems to exercise over the human race. Put a man on horseback and his next idea is to play the bully or to steal something. We had an instance of ill behavior at our house last night — the first and only one that has occurred among the hundreds — thousands, I might almost say, that have stopped at our door. Our back yard and kitchen were filled all day with parties of soldiers coming to get their rations cooked, or to ask for something to eat. Mother kept two servants hard at work, cooking for them. While we were at supper, a squad of a dozen or more cavalry men rode up and asked for a meal. Every seat at the table was filled, and some of the family waiting because there was no room for us, so mother told mammy to set a table for them on the front piazza, and serve them with such as we had ourselves — which was nothing to brag on, I must own. They were so incensed at not being invited into the house that mammy says they cursed her and said Judge Andrews was a d—d old aristocrat, and deserved to have his house burned down. I suppose they were drunk, or stragglers from some of the conscript regiments enrolled after the flower of our armies had been decimated in the great battles.

We had a good laugh on Capt. Irwin this morning. He is counting on the sale of his horse for money to carry him home, and seems to imagine that every man in a cavalry uniform is a horse thief bent on capturing his little nag. A Capt. Morton, of the cavalry, called here after breakfast, with a letter of introduction from friends, and our dear little captain immediately ran out bare–headed, to stand guard over his charger. I don't know which laughed most when the situation was explained. Capt. Palfrey and Capt. Swett, of Gen. Elzey's staff, called later to bid us good–by. They have no money, but each was provided with a card of buttons with which they count on buying a meal or two on the way. Cousin Liza added to their store a paper of pins and Cora another card of buttons. We laughed very much at this new kind of currency.

About noon the town was thrown into the wildest excitement by the arrival of President Davis. He is traveling with a large escort of cavalry, a very imprudent thing for a man in his position to do, especially now that Johnston has surrendered, and the fact that they are all going in the same direction to their homes is the only thing that keeps them together. He rode into town ahead of his escort, and as he was passing by the bank, where the Elzeys board, the general and several other gentlemen were sitting on the front porch, and the instant they recognized him they took off their hats and received him with every mark of respect due the president of a brave people. When he reined in his horse, all the staff who were present advanced to hold the reins and assist him to dismount, while Dr. and Mrs. Robertson hastened to offer the hospitality of their home. About forty of his immediate personal friends and attendants were with him, and they were all half–starved, having tasted nothing for twenty–four hours. Capt. Irwin came running home in great haste to ask mother to send them something to eat, as it was reported the Yankees were approaching the town from two directions closing in upon the President, and it was necessary to hurry him off at once. There was not so much as a crust of bread in our house, everything available having been given to soldiers. There was some bread in the kitchen that had just been baked for a party of soldiers, but they were willing to wait, and I begged some milk from Aunt Sallie, and by adding to these our own dinner as soon as Emily could finish cooking it, we contrived to get together a very respectable lunch. We had just sent it off when the president's escort came in, followed by couriers who brought the comforting assurance that it was a false alarm about the enemy being so near. By this time the president's arrival had become generally known, and people began flocking to see him; but he went to bed almost as soon as he got into the house, and Mrs. Elzey would not let him be waked. One of his friends, Col. Thorburne, came to our house and went right to bed and slept fourteen hours on a stretch. The party are all worn out and half–dead for sleep. They travel mostly at night, and have been in the saddle for three nights in succession. Mrs. Elzey says that Mr. Davis does not seem to have been aware of the real danger of his situation until he came to Washington, where some of his friends gave him a serious talk, and advised him to travel with more secrecy and dispatch than he has been using.

Mr. Reagan and Mr. Mallory are also in town, and Gen. Toombs has returned, having encountered danger ahead, I fear. Judge Crump is back too, with his Confederate treasury, containing, it is said, three hundred thousand dollars in specie. He is staying at our house, but the treasure is thought to be stored in the vault at the bank. It will hardly be necessary for him to leave the country, but his friends advise him to keep in the shade for a time. If the Yankees once get scent of money, they will be sure to ferret it out. They have already begun their reign of terror in Richmond, by arresting many of the prominent citizens. Judge Crump is in a state of distraction about his poor little wandering exchequer, which seems to stand an even chance between the Scylla of our own hungry cavalry and the Charybdis of Yankee cupidity. I wish it could all be divided among the men whose necks are in danger, to assist them in getting out of the country, but I don't suppose one of them would touch it. Anything would be preferable to letting the Yankees get it.

Among the stream of travelers pouring through Washington, my old friend, Dr. Cromwell, has turned up, and is going to spend several days with us. Capt. Napier, Col. Walter Weems, Capt. Shaler Smith, and Mr. Hallam ate supper with us, but we had no sleeping room to offer them except the grass under the trees in the grove. Capt. Smith and Mr. Hallam are Kentuckians, and bound for that illusive land of hope, the Trans–Mississippi. They still believe the battle of Southern independence will be fought out there and won. If faith as a grain of mustard seed can move mountains, what ought not faith like this to accomplish! Mr. Hallam is a high–spirited young fellow, and reminds me of the way we all used to talk and feel at the beginning of the war. I believe he thinks he could fight the whole Yankee nation now, single–handed, and whip them, too. He is hardly more than a boy, and only a second lieutenant, yet as he gravely informed me, is now the chief ordnance officer of the Confederate army. He was taken prisoner and made his escape without being paroled, and since the surrender of Lee's and Johnston's armies, he really is, it seems, the ranking ordnance officer in the poor little remnant that is still fixing its hope on the Trans–Mississippi. They spent the night in the grove, where they could watch their horses. It was dreadful that we had not even stable room to offer them, but every place in this establishment that can accommodate man or beast was already occupied.

May 4, Thursday — I am in such a state of excitement that I can do nothing but spend my time, like the Athenians of old, in either hearing or telling some new thing. I sat under the cedar trees by the street gate nearly all the morning, with Metta and Cousin Liza, watching the stream of human life flow by, and keeping guard over the horses of some soldier friends that had left them grazing on the lawn. Father and Cora went to call on the President, and in spite of his prejudice against everybody and everything connected with secession, father says his manner was so calm and dignified that he could not help admiring the man. Crowds of people flocked to see him, and nearly all were melted to tears. Gen. Elzey pretended to have dust in his eyes and Mrs. Elzey blubbered outright, exclaiming all the while, in her impulsive way: "Oh, I am such a fool to be crying, but I can't help it!" When she was telling me about it afterwards, she said she could not stay in the room with him yesterday evening, because she couldn't help crying, and she was ashamed for the people who called to see her looking so ugly, with her eyes and nose red. She says that at night, after the crowd left, there was private meeting in his room, where Reagan and Mallory and other high officials were present, and again early in the morning there were other confabulations before they all scattered and went their ways — and this, I suppose, is the end of the Confederacy. Then she made me laugh by telling some ludicrous things that happened while the crowd was calling. . . . It is strange how closely interwoven tragedy and comedy are in life.

The people of the village sent so many good things for the President to eat, that an ogre couldn't have devoured them all, and he left many little delicacies, besides giving away a number of his personal effects, to people who had been kind to him. He requested that one package be sent to mother, which, if it ever comes, must be kept as an heirloom in the family. I don't suppose he knows what strong Unionists father and mother have always been, but for all that I am sure they would be as ready to help him now, if they could, as the hottest rebel among us. I was not ashamed of father's being a Union man when his was the down–trodden, persecuted party; but now, when our country is down–trodden, the Union means something very different from what it did four years ago. It is a great grief and mortification to me that he sticks to that wicked old tyranny still, but he is a Southerner and a gentleman, in spite of his politics, and at any rate nobody can accuse him of self-interest, for he has sacrificed as much in the war as any other private citizen I know, except those whose children have been killed. His sons, all but little Marshall, have been in the army since the very first gun — in fact, Garnett was the first man to volunteer from the county, and it is through the mercy of God and not of his beloved Union that they have come back alive. Then, he has lost not only his negroes, like everybody else, but his land, too.

The President left town about ten o'clock, with a single companion, his unruly cavalry escort having gone on before. He travels sometimes with them, sometimes before, sometimes behind, never permitting his precise location to be known. Generals Bragg and Breckinridge are in the village, with a host of minor celebrities. Gen. Breckinridge is called the handsomest man in the Confederate army, and Bragg might well be called the ugliest. I saw him at Mrs. Vickers's, where he is staying, and he looks like an old porcupine. I never was a special admirer of his, though it would be a good thing if some of his stringent views about discipline could be put into effect just now — if discipline were possible among men without a leader, without a country, without a hope. The army is practically disbanded, and citizens, as well as soldiers, thoroughly demoralized. It has gotten to be pretty much a game of grab with us all; every man for himself and the Devil (or the Yankees, which amounts to the same thing) take the hindmost. Nearly all government teams have been seized and driven out of town by irresponsible parties — indeed, there seems to be nobody responsible for anything any longer. Gen. Elzey's two ambulances were taken last night, so that Capt. Palfrey and Capt. Swett are left in the lurch, and will have to make their way home by boat and rail, or afoot, as best they can.

Large numbers of cavalry passed through town during the day. A solid, unbroken stream of them poured past our street gate for two hours, many of them leading extra horses. They raised such clouds of dust that it looked as if a yellow fog had settled over our grove. Duke's division threatened to plunder the treasury, so that Gen. Breckinridge had to open it and pay them a small part of their stipend in specie. Others put in a claim too, and some deserving men got a few dollars. Capt. Smith and Mr. Hallam called in the afternoon, and the latter showed me ninety dollars in gold, which is all that he has received for four years of service. I don't see what better could be done with the money than to pay it all out to the soldiers of the Confederacy before the Yankees gobble it up.

While we were in the parlor with these and other visitors, the carriage drove up with Fred and Garnett and Garnett's "galvanized" attendant, Gobin. As soon as I heard the sound of wheels coming up the avenue, I ran to one of the front windows, and when I recognized our carriage, Metta, Cora, and I tore helter–skelter out of the house to meet them. Garnett looks very thin and pale. The saber cuts on his head are nearly healed, but the wound in his shoulder is still very painful. His fingers are partially paralyzed from it, but I hope not permanently. Gobin seems attached to him and dresses his wounds carefully. He is an Irish Yankee, deserted, and came across the lines to keep from fighting, but was thrown into prison and only got out by enlisting in a "galvanized" regiment. I wonder how many of the patriots in the Union army have the same unsavory record! He is an inconvenient person to have about the house, anyway, for he is no better than a servant, and yet we can't put him with the negroes. Garnett says the report about his galvanized troops having behaved badly in the battle was a slander. They fought splendidly, he says, and were devoted to their officers. If the war had lasted longer, he thinks he could have made a fine regiment out of them, but somehow I can't feel anything but contempt for that sort of men, nor put any faith in them.

Aunt Sallie invited Mr. Habersham Adams, her pastor, and his wife, to dinner, and Cousin Liza, Mary Day, Cora, Metta, and me, to help them eat it. She had such a dinner as good old Methodist ladies know how to get up for their preachers, though where all the good things came from, Heaven only knows. She must have been hoarding them for months. We ate as only hungry Rebs can, that have been half–starved for weeks, and expect to starve the rest of our days. We have no kind of meat in our house but ham and bacon, and have to eat hominy instead of rice, at dinner. Sometimes we get a few vegetables out of the garden, but everything has been so stripped to feed the soldiers, that we have never enough to spread a respectable meal before the large number of guests, expected and unexpected, who sit down to our table every day. In spite of all we can do, there is a look of scantiness about the table that makes people afraid to eat as much as they want — and the dreadful things we have to give them, at that! Cornfield peas have been our staple diet for the last ten days. Mother has them cooked in every variety of style she ever heard of, but they are cornfield peas still. All this would have been horribly mortifying a year or two ago, but everybody knows how it is now, and I am glad to have even cornfield peas to share with the soldiers. Three cavalry officers ate dinner at the house while we were at Aunt Sallie's. Mother says they were evidently gentlemen, but they were so ragged and dirty that she thought the poor fellows did not like to give their names. They didn't introduce themselves, and she didn't ask who they were. Poor Henry is in the same plight, somewhere, I reckon. The cavalry are not popular about here just now; everybody is crying out against them, even their own officers. On their way from Abbeville, Fred and Garnett met a messenger with a flag of truce, which had been sent out by some (pretended) cavalrymen who had plundered a government specie wagon at the Savannah River and professed to be hunting for Yankees to whom they might surrender. Garnett says he does not think there are any Yanks within forty miles of Abbeville, though as the "grape vine" is our only telegraph, we know nothing with certainty. Boys and negroes and sportsmen are taking advantage of the ammunition scattered broadcast by the pillaging of the ordnance stores, to indulge in fireworks of every description, and there is so much shooting going on all around town that we wouldn't know it if a battle were being fought. Capt. Irwin came near being killed this afternoon by a stray minié ball shot by some careless person. The R.R. dépot is in danger of being blown up by the quantities of gunpowder scattered about there, mixed up with percussion caps. Fred says that when he came up from Augusta the other day, the railroad between here and Barnett was strewn with loose cartridges and empty canteens that the soldiers had thrown out of the car windows.

I have so little time for writing that I make a dreadful mess of these pages. I can hardly ever write fifteen minutes at a time without interruption. Sometimes I break off in the middle of a sentence and do not return to it for hours, and so I am apt to get everything into a jumble. And the worst of it is, we are living in such a state of hurry and excitement that half the time I don't know whether I am telling the truth or not. Mother says that she will have to turn the library into a bedroom if we continue to have so much company, and then I shall have no quiet place to go to, and still less time to myself. It seems that the more I have to say, the less time I have to say it in. From breakfast till midnight I am engaged nearly all the time with company, so that the history of each day has to be written mostly in the spare moments I can steal before breakfast on the next, and sometimes I can only scratch down a few lines to be written out at length whenever I can find the time. I have been keeping this diary so long and through so many difficulties and interruptions that it would be like losing an old friend if I were to discontinue it. I can tell it what I can say to no one else, not even to Metta. . . . But after all, I enjoy the rush and excitement famously. Mett says that she don't enjoy a man's society, no matter how nice he is, till she knows him well, but I confess that I like change and variety. A man that I know nothing about — provided, of course, he is a gentleman — is a great deal more interesting to me than the people I see every day, just because there is something to find out; people get to be commonplace when you know them too well.

May 5, Friday — It has come at last — what we have been dreading and expecting so long — what has caused so many panics and false alarms — but it is no false alarm this time; the Yankees are actually in Washington. Before we were out of bed a courier came in with the news that Kirke — name of ill omen — was only seven miles from town, plundering and devastating the country. Father hid the silver and what little coin he had in the house, but no other precautions were taken. They have cried "wolf" so often that we didn't pay much attention to it, and besides, what could we do, anyway? After dinner we all went to our rooms as usual, and I sat down to write. Presently some one knocked at my door and said: "The Yankees have come, and are camped in Will Pope's grove." I paid no attention and went on quietly with my writing. Later, I dressed and went down to the library, where Dr. Cromwell was waiting for me, and asked me to go with him to call on Annie Pope. We found the streets deserted; not a soldier, not a straggler did we see. The silence of death reigned where a few hours ago all was stir and bustle — and it is the death of our liberty. After the excitement of the last few days, the stillness was painful, oppressive. I thought of Chateaubriand's famous passage: "Lorsque dans le silence de l'abjection" &c. News of the odious arrival seems to have spread like a secret pestilence through the country, and travelers avoid the tainted spot. I suppose the returning soldiers flank us, for I have seen none on the streets to–day, and none have called at our house. The troops that are here came from Athens. There are about sixty–five white men, and fifteen negroes, under the command of a Major Wilcox. They say that they come for peace, to protect us from our own lawless cavalry — to *protect* us, indeed! with their negro troops, runaways from our own plantations! I would rather be skinned and eaten by wild beasts than beholden to *them* for such protection. As they were marching through town, a big buck negro leading a raw–boned jade is said to have made a conspicuous figure in the procession. Respectable people were shut up in their houses, but the little street urchins immediately began to sing, when they saw the big black Sancho and his Rosinante:

> *"Yankee Doodle went to town and stole a little pony;*
> *He stuck a feather in his crown and called him Macaroni."*

They followed the Yanks nearly to their camping grounds at the Mineral Spring, singing and jeering at the negroes, and strange to say, the Yankees did not offer to molest them. I have not laid eyes on one of the creatures myself, and they say they do not intend to come into the town unless to put down disturbances — the sweet, peaceful lambs! They never sacked Columbia; they never burnt Atlanta; they never left a black trail of ruin and desolation through the whole length of our dear old Georgia! No, not they! I wonder how long this sugar and honey policy is to continue. They deceive no one with their Puritanical hypocrisy, bringing our own runaway negroes here to protect us. Next thing they will have a negro garrison in the town for our benefit. Their odious old flag has not yet been raised in the village, and I pray God they will have the grace to spare us that insult, at least until Johnston's army has all passed through. The soldiers will soon return to their old route of travel, and there is no telling what our boys might be tempted to do at the sight of that emblem of tyranny on the old courthouse steeple, where once floated the "lone star banner" that Cora and I made with our own hands — the first rebel flag that was ever raised in Washington. Henry brought us the cloth, and we made it on the sly in Cora's room at night, hustling it under the bed, if a footstep came near, for fear father or mother might catch us and put a stop to our work. It would break my heart to see the emblem of our slavery floating in its place. Our old liberty pole is gone. Some of the Irvin Artillery went one night before the Yankees came, and cut it down and carried it off. It was a sad night's work, but there was no other way to save it from desecration.

Gen. Elzey, Col. Weems, and several other leading citizens went to the Yankee camp soon after they arrived to see about making arrangements for feeding the paroled men who are still to pass through, and to settle other matters of public interest. It was reported that father went with them to surrender the town, but it was a slander; he has not been near them. Garnett's galvanized Yank immediately fraternized with them, and Garnett is going to send him away to–morrow. Gen. Elzey looks wretched, and we all feel miserable enough.

When Capt. Irwin came home to supper, he told me that he had been trying to draw forage from the Confederate stores for his horse, but could not get any because it was all to be turned over to the new masters. He was so angry that he forgot himself and let out a "cuss word" before he thought, right in my presence. And I wouldn't let him apologize. I told him I was glad he did it, because I couldn't swear myself and it was a relief to my feelings to hear somebody else do it. While we were talking, old Toby's bark announced a visitor, who turned out to be Capt. Hudson. Metta brought out her guitar, and she and Garnett tried to sing a little, but most of the evening was spent in quiet conversation. It seemed hard to realize as we sat there talking peacefully in the soft moonlight, surrounded by the dear old Confederate uniforms, that the enemy is actually in our midst. But I realized it only too fully when I heard the wearers of the uniforms talk. They do not whine over their altered fortunes and ruined prospects, but our poor ruined country, the slavery and degradation to which it is reduced — they grow pathetic over that. We have a charming circle of friends round us now. Judge Crump, especially, is one of the most entertaining men I ever knew. He has traveled a great deal and I was very much interested in his account of Dickens's wife, whom he knows well. He says that she is altogether the most unattractive woman he ever met. She has a yellowish, cat–like eye, a muddy complexion, dull, coarse hair of an undecided color, and a very awkward person. On top of it all she is, he says, one of the most intolerably stupid women he ever met. He has had to entertain her for hours at a time and could never get an idea out of her nor one into her. Think of such a wife for Dickens!

Porter Alexander has got home and brings discouraging reports of the state of feeling at the North. After he was paroled he went to see the Brazilian minister at Washington to learn what the chances were of getting into the Brazilian army. He says he met with very little encouragement and had to hurry away from Washington because, since Lincoln's assassination the feeling against Southerners has grown so bitter that he didn't think it safe to stay there. He says the generality of the people at the North were disposed to receive the Confederate officers kindly, but since the assassination the whole country is embittered against us — very unjustly, too, for they have no right to lay upon innocent people the crazy deed of a madman.

The Yankee papers are now accusing Mr. Davis and his party of appropriating all the money in the Confederate Treasury to their own use, but thank Heaven, everybody in Washington can refute that slander. The treasury was plundered here, in our midst, and I saw some of the gold, with my own eyes, in the hands of Confederate soldiers — right where it ought to be.

The talk now is, judging from the ease with which Breckinridge was allowed to slip through this morning, that the military authorities are conniving at the escape of Mr. Davis. Breckinridge, when he found that the Philistines were about to be upon him, used a carefully planned stratagem of war to deceive Wilcoxson, by which he imagined that he gained time to destroy his papers and give him the slip, while in reality, they say, the Yanks were making no effort to detain him, and he might have gone openly with his papers unmolested. The general belief is that Grant and the military men, even Sherman, are not anxious for the ugly job of hanging such a man as our president, and are quite willing to let him give them the slip, and get out of the country if he can. The military men, who do the hard and cruel things in war, seem to be more merciful in peace than the politicians who stay at home and do the talking.

Epilogue

We have no record of what happened to some of the women whose work appears here. We don't know how long Judith Brokenbrough McGuire lived or whether she ever returned to Alexandria. After the war she published two books: *The Diary of a Southern Refugee during the War* (1867) and *General Robert E. Lee, the Christian Soldier* (1873). When the latter was published, she would have been sixty.

Julia Morgan was still alive in the 1892 when her book was published. We have part of a letter that she wrote sometime during the 1890's on stationery of the Morgan Pickle Works in Nashville of which her husband was secretary and treasurer. Mary Ann Gay was still alive and unmarried when her diary appeared in 1894. Dolly Lunt Burge died in 1891. Of Lucy Nickolson Lindsay, Mrs. Alexander Major and of Catherine Hopley we know almost nothing. Mrs. Major's husband, who was a quartermaster, probably survived the fighting. I cannot determine what happened to the Confederate officer Lucy Nickolson married.

Loréta Velazquez, who went west after the war, was courted successively by two men in Austin, Texas, the second of whom she married. She went to California, then to Colorado, then to Utah with her husband who was chasing gold, had a baby in Salt Lake City — the dates of these events are unclear in her narrative; but she does not mention her husband as she and the baby make a slow, and, to Loréta, an interesting, progress east. When her book was published in 1876, she was still alive.

The first of these women to die was Rose Greenhow. A year after her release from prison in 1862, she went abroad as an agent of the Confederacy. The story of her imprisonment was well known in England, and the publication of her memoir there increased her fame. She was presented to both the English and the French Courts — she had a private audience with Napoleon III — and was said to be engaged to the second Lord Granville. In 1864 the ship on which she was returning to the Confederacy ran aground off the coast of North Carolina. Fearing capture by the Federal navy, she attempted to reach shore in a small boat which capsized, and Rose, then forty–nine years old, was drowned. Her remains lie in Oakdale Cemetery in Wilmington.

After the war Mary Jones attempted briefly to continue to operate the three plantations she had managed since the death of her husband in 1863. Early in 1868, at the urging of her children, she went to New Orleans to live with Mary Mallard, her daughter whose child had been born during Sherman's march to the sea. She died, aged sixty–one, in 1869 and was buried in Lafayette Cemetery. Mary Mallard survived another twenty years, died while on a visit to Marietta, Georgia, and was buried near her mother in New Orleans. She was fifty–four.

At the end of the war Mary Chesnut returned with her husband to Camden, where he reentered state politics and attempted to restore his damaged plantations. For a while Mary Chesnut made and sold butter through a factor in Charleston. She organized a book club, wrote stories and articles, and edited and rewrote the manuscript of her diary. The Chesnuts, before the war one of the richest families in the South, were never able to recoup their personal fortune. They could afford occasionally to visit friends in Virginia and to vacation at Saratoga, but they were forced to sell some of the family heirlooms, including a portrait of George Washington by Gilbert Stuart. She died in 1886, a little over a year after the death of her husband. She was sixty–three.

After her capture at sea in 1864, Belle Boyd was allowed to proceed to England where, later that year, she married Lt. Sam Hardinge, who had been one of her captors. Hardinge died soon thereafter, leaving Belle with a daughter, but by now the publication of her memoirs had made Belle famous, and she began a career on the English stage. She returned to America in 1866, continued acting, married John Hammond, an Englishman who had fought for the North in the war, lived with him sixteen years, bore him three children, then divorced Hammond to marry Nathaniel High, a fellow actor seventeen years her junior. Though their fortunes as actors declined, her marriage to High was apparently happy. Belle was fifty–six when she died in 1900 in Kilbourn (since renamed Wisconsin Dells) Wisconsin. The Kilbourn women's auxiliary of the G.A.R. paid for her funeral.

In 1865 Kate Stone returned with her family to Brokenburn, where after a disastrous first year, they were able to support themselves by raising cotton. In 1868 Kate married Henry Bry Holmes whom she had met when he was a lieutenant in the Confederate army. She and her husband settled in Talullah, Louisiana, where two of their four children lived to maturity. Kate Stone founded the Madison Infantry Chapter of the United Daughters of the Confederacy, helped organize the Madison Parish Book Club, and helped plan and execute the construction of a

Confederate memorial on the town square. She was sixty–six when she died in 1907.

Sarah Morgan and her mother went to live with her brother, Jimmy, in Charleston, after the death of his wife in childbirth in 1872. A year later, Sarah began to write for the Charleston *News and Courier,* and a year after that she married Frank Dawson who was editor and part owner of the newspaper. She was embittered by the murder of her husband in 1889, and ten years later she followed Warrington Dawson, one of her two surviving children to Paris. She found new friends, continued to write, and died in Paris in 1909, at the age of sixty–six. She was buried beside her husband in Charleston.

At the end of the war, Kate Cumming, who never married, returned to Mobile, then moved with her father to Birmingham in 1874, where she taught school and music and did volunteer work for the Episcopal Church of the Advent, the United Daughters of the Confederacy, and the United Confederate Veterans. She was seventy–four when she died in 1909. She was buried in Mobile.

After Cornelia McDonald's rescue from starvation in the autumn of 1865, her life and her fortunes improved. She received sufficient money from several sources to support and educate her children, and she began once more to teach classes in the arts. She remained in Lexington until 1873, then moved to Louisville where most of her children were living. There she continued to teach and to do charitable work until her death in 1909, three months before her eighty–seventh birthday.

Sarah Pryor remained with her children in Petersburg while her husband, nearly penniless and without prospects, sought a new beginning as a lawyer in New York in 1865. Sarah joined him in 1867, and she gave music lessons to augment the family income. Soon Roger Pryor's practice prospered, and in 1890 he became a judge. Sarah helped found the Daughters of the American Revolution, and was active in other antiquarian, historical, and charitable societies. She became a contributor to several magazines and published four books: *The Mother of Washington and Her Times, Reminiscences of Peace and War, The Birth of a Nation,* and *My Day: Reminiscences of a Long Life.* The first of these appeared when she was seventy–three. She died in 1912, three days before her eighty–second birthday.

Phoebe Yates Pember never remarried. When she had finished her work at Chimborazo Hospital, she returned to her family in Georgia and then spent a good deal of her time traveling both in this country and abroad. *A Southern Woman's Story,* her only publication, was released in 1879. Phoebe Pember died in Pittsburgh in 1913, at the age of eighty–nine, and was buried beside her husband in Savannah.

Constance Cary lived with her mother in Europe from October 1866 until November 1867, when she returned to this country to marry Burton Harrison, who, like Roger Pryor, practiced law in New York. In the mid–1870s she began to write short stories. Beginning in 1890, she published a series of popular novels, sometimes as often as once a year. After the death of her husband in 1904, she lived abroad, then settled in Washington where she wrote *Recollections Grave and Gay*. She died in 1920, at seventy–seven, and was buried in Washington.

Eliza Andrews began her teaching career in Washington, Georgia, after the death of her father in 1873. She served as principal of girls' schools, first in Mississippi, then in Georgia. She taught French and literature at Wesleyan Female College in Macon, and then returned to Washington to teach botany in the public high school. Her career as a writer began in 1876 with the publication of *A Family Secret*, the first of three novels, all of which sold well. Besides her *Wartime Journal*, her other publications include two textbooks on botany. She was ninety when she died in Rome, Georgia, in 1931.

Emma LeConte, who married Farish Furman, a lawyer and planter, was left a widow with two daughters in 1883. She successfully managed her plantation, raised and educated her daughters, and was living with one of them in Macon in 1917 when she began once more knitting socks for soldiers. She was active in the Red Cross, worked with the women's societies of two churches, promoted women's suffrage, and fostered the education of black children. She was eighty–five when she died in 1932.

In 1865 the Frémaux family moved to Mobile, then to New Orleans, and for a while Céline returned as a boarding student to the Judson Institute in Alabama. In 1872 she married Joe Garcia of New Orleans, bore four children, and managed the family's financial affairs while Joe's printing business prospered. The Garcias were active in New Orleans civic and social life until Céline's death in 1935, fifteen years after the demise of her husband. She was eighty–five. The youngest of the diarists included here, she was the last survivor.

Bibliography

Andrews, Eliza Frances. *The War-Time Journal of a Georgia Girl 1864–1865.* New York: D. Appleton & Company, 1908.

Boyd, Belle. *Belle Boyd: In Camp and Prison.* London: Saunders, Otley & Company, 1865.

Burge, Dolly Sumner Lunt. *A Woman's Wartime Journal.* Macon: J. W. Burke Company, 1927.

Chesnut, Mary Boykin. *A Diary From Dixie,* edited by Isabella D. Martin and Myrta Lockett Avary. New York: D. Appleton & Company, 1905.

Cumming, Kate. *A Journal of Hospital Life in the Confederate Army of Tennessee from the Battle of Shiloh to the End of the War.* Louisville: John P. Marton & Company, 1866.

Garcia, Céline Frémaux. *Céline: Remembering Louisiana, 1850–1871,* edited by Patrick J. Geary. Athens: University of Georgia Press, 1987.

Gay, Mary Ann Harris. *Life in Dixie During the War.* Atlanta: Charles P. Byrd, 1897.

Greenhow, Rose O'Neal. *My Imprisonment and the First Year of Abolition Rule at Washington.* London: Richard Bentley, 1863.

Harrison, Mrs. Burton (Constance Cary). *Recollections Grave and Gay.* New York: Charles Scribner's Sons, 1912.

Hopley, Catherine Cooper. *Life in the South From the Commencement of the War.* London: Chapman and Hall, 1863.

LeConte, Emma. *When the World Ended: The Diary of Emma LeConte,* edited by Earl Schenck Miers. New York: Oxford University Press, 1957.

McDonald, Cornelia Peake. *A Diary with Reminiscences of the War and Refugee Life in the Shenandoah Valley, 1860–1865,* edited by Hunter McDonald. Nashville: Cullum and Gehrtner, 1934.

McGuire, Judith Brokenbrough. *Diary of a Southern Refugee during the War, by a Lady of Virginia.* New York: E. J. Hale & Son, 1867.

Meyers, Robert Manson, editor. *The Children of Pride.* New Haven: Yale University Press, 1972.

Morgan, Mrs. Irby (Julia). *How it Was: Four Years Among the Rebels.* Nashville: Publishing House Methodist Episcopal Church, South, 1892.

Morgan, Sarah. *The Civil War Diary of Sarah Morgan,* edited by Charles East. Athens: University of Georgia Press, 1991.

Pember, Phoebe Yates. *A Southern Woman's Story.* New York: G. W. Carlton & Company, 1879.

Pryor, Sarah Rice. *Reminiscences of Peace and War.* New York: Macmillan Company, 1904.

Stone, Sarah Katherine. *Brokenburn: The Journal of Kate Stone 1861 – 1868,* edited by John Q. Anderson. Baton Rouge: Louisiana State University Press, 1955.

Velazquez, Loréta Janéta. *The Woman in Battle: A Narrative of the Exploits, Adventures and Travels of Madame Loréta Janéta Velazquez, Otherwise Known as Lieutenant Harry T. Buford, Confederate States Army.* Hartford, Connecticut: T. Belknap, 1879.

Woodson, Mrs. Blake L., et al. *Reminiscences of the Women of Missouri During the Sixties.* St. Louis: Missouri Division, United Daughters of the Confederacy, 1920.

Index